Exploring
Coastal
Massachusetts

Exploring Coastal Massachusetts

New Bedford to Salem

by BARBARA CLAYTON
and
KATHLEEN WHITLEY

Illustrated with photographs
Maps by Wendy Walden

DODD, MEAD & COMPANY / NEW YORK

1 2 3 4 5 6 7 8 9 10

Library of Congress Cataloging in Publication Data

Clayton, Barbara, 1931-
  Exploring coastal Massachusetts.

  Includes index.
  1. Massachusetts—Description and travel—
1981-   —Guidebooks. 2. Coasts—Massachusetts—
Guide-books. I. Whitley, Kathleen. II. Title.
F62.3.C53   1983   917.44′0443′09146   83-1791
ISBN 0-396-08131-2 (pbk.)

Acknowledgments

We wish to express our deep appreciation to historians with local expertise who helped us in our research and reviewed our manuscript—New Bedford: John Bullard, Richard Kugler, Richard A. Pline, Antone G. Souza, Jr., Philip F. Purrington; Fairhaven: Rita Steele; Mattapoisett: Priscilla Hathaway; Marion: Marion L. Channing, H. Edmund Tripp; Wareham: Raymond Rider; Cape Cod: Michael J. Frucci; Martha's Vineyard: Jo-Ann Walker; Plymouth: James Baker, Rose Briggs, Judith M. Ingram, Laurence R. Pizer, Allen Russell; Kingston: Doris Johnson; Duxbury: Dorothy Wentworth; Marshfield: Cynthia H. Krusell; Scituate: Kathleen Laidlaw; Cohasset: Constance Parker, Burtram J. Pratt; Hull: Anne Kinnear; Hingham: G. Harris Danzberger, the Reverend Donald F. Robinson; Weymouth: Chester B. Kevitt; Quincy: H. Hobart Holly; Boston: Edie Shean-Hammond, Larry Meehan; Lynn: Faith Magoun; Nahant: Mrs. Winthrop Sears; Swampscott: Margaret C. Tatro; Marblehead: Marian Gosling; Salem: Dean Lahikainen, Irene Norton, Genevieve R. K. Riley; Beverly: Jack MacLean.

Further thanks to those who graciously shared their knowledge with us— New Bedford: George C. Avila, Joli Gonsalves, Peter Jacobsen, Herbert R. Waters, Jr., Shelley Wheeler-Carreiro; Mattapoisett: Winfield Jenney, Mildred Jones Keefe, Frank F. Sylvia; Wareham: Robert F. Packard; Cape Cod: Ranger Michael E. Whatley; Plymouth: Anne Borden Harding, Mrs. Gordon Howland, Jeanne Mills; Duxbury: Ruth and Norman Martin, Daniel N. Pearce; Marshfield: Janet Peterson; Cohasset: Mrs. B. J. Broe, Stella Collins; Hingham: Harriet Allen, Mrs. E. S. Beveridge; Weymouth: Mrs. Paul Quinton; Quincy: Mrs. David J. Bohl, Wilhelmina Harris, the Reverend Steele Martin, Robert Parlow, Pat Shaheen, Nina Valante; Boston: Lt. Shan Delmar, Leon B. White; Lynn: Roberta Bedrosian, Eleanore S. Jorgenson, Joseph Shanahan; Swampscott: Louis Gallo, Barbara Hall, Sister Josette; Marblehead: Dorothy Miles, Mrs. Gregory Smith; Salem: Joyce Duffie, Anne Farnum, Dorothy Freeman, Byron Getchell, Mrs. John Pickering, Phyllis Shutzer, Edward Stevenson, the Reverend John R. B. Szala, Professor William Thompson, Bryant F. Tolles, Jr.

We are especially grateful to our husbands, Lee Whitley and Ray Clayton and our families, Mark and Matthew Clayton, Nancy and Scott Whitley, for their constant support, encouragement, and patience. And to our parents Howard and Laura Lee White, Frederic Whitley, Marion Clayton; and in memorial Pauline Langdon Perrin and Arthur Langdon, J. Raymond Clayton, and Dorothy Burt Whitley, we add special appreciation.

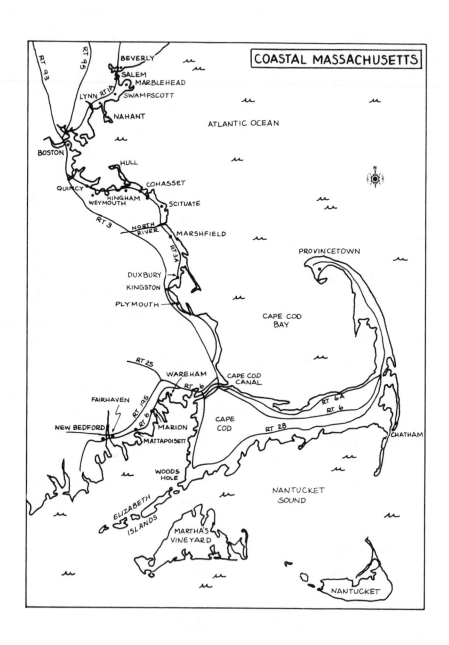

CONTENTS

*Starred items throughout indicate there is more information
elsewhere in text; see index.
HABS—Historic American Building Survey
SPNEA—Society for the Preservation of New England Antiquities
NHM—National Historic Monument
NRHP—National Register of Historic Places
NHL—National Historic Landmark
NHS—National Historic Site

SETTING THE STAGE

This is the land of Pilgrims and Puritans, home of the leading whaling ports of the world, tinderbox of the American Revolution, and birthplace of three United States Presidents. As you tour these coastal towns, be aware of the trials, tribulations, hopes, and dreams of the many generations between the first inhabitants and today's busy citizens. Browse through their homes, museums, and historic buildings, for it is through these physical reminders that you picture a way of life which has preceded you. Walk her beaches all seasons of the year, whether in summer, when they are calm and inviting, or during winter, when exciting storms turn the ocean into a reckless giant assaulting beaches, harbors, and inlets with an untamed fury.

The prelude to the settlement of Massachusetts began in England in the 1500s, when many members of the Anglican Church became dissatisfied with the authority of the clergy and the ceremonialism of services. Those wishing to "purify" the church became known as Puritans, and those who wished to separate and worship in their own way became known as Separatists. By the late 1500s, one Separatist group, led by William Brewster,* tired of religious persecution, left England and settled in Leyden, Holland. Finding growing problems in Holland, these pilgrims from England sailed for the New World, where they believed they could live in peace with themselves and their God. There they founded the Plymouth Colony in 1620.

In England nine years later, approximately 1,000 Puritans, led by John Winthrop,* obtained and carried to the New World a charter for a Massachusetts Bay Colony. They landed in what is now Salem,* but soon moved to the Massachusetts Bay area and founded Boston.* With John Winthrop as governor a strong and powerful Puritan Colony developed.

Religion, government, and private lives were all controlled by strict religious beliefs. It was undoubtedly this uncompromising faith which gave these English settlers the fortitude and endurance to leave behind all that was safe and familiar and journey across a treacherous ocean to an unknown world. The Pilgrim Plymouth Colony paved the

1

way and proved that settlers could survive, succeed, and prosper in the
New World. Yet they never attained the wealth, population, and power
of the better-organized Puritan Massachusetts Bay Colony, which
absorbed them by 1691.

Coastal settlers, realizing the countryside was too difficult to tame
for a profitable agricultural economy, turned to the sea. They reaped
its bountiful resources of fish, whales, and seafood as well as using it as
a prosperous avenue of trade with the world. Cod fishing became so
successful that even today a replica of the "sacred cod" can be seen in
the Massachusetts House of Representatives in Boston. Ships were
built for domestic use and for profitable sale in England and France.
New England was indeed nourished by the sea.

Through the years of the Indian Wars (1675–1763), England supported her colonial troops. But when the hardships and threats ended,
colonists quickly forgot England's help and returned to their independent ways. In order to replenish a depleted treasury and regain

Mayflower II under sail

Massachusetts Department of Commerce and Development, Division of Tourism

authority over the colonies, England passed a series of Acts in the mid-1700s. The seeds of separation sprouted quickly as colonists defied the Acts of Assistance, the Sugar Act, the Stamp Act, and the Townshend Acts, and sponsored the Boston Tea Party. As a result England closed the Port of Boston. Positive retaliation quickly followed with the First Continental Congress; the Battles of Concord, Lexington, and Breed's Hill; the Second Continental Congress; and the forced British evacuation of Boston. All helped lead to the Declaration of Independence on July 4, 1776. Once again the colonists took up arms to preserve lands they had only recently wrested from the wilderness and defended against the French and Indians. However, this time when they lay down their muskets, they were no longer colonists but Americans proud of their new country.

During the Revolution shipbuilding, offshore fishing, and foreign trade were critically depressed. Following the war, resourceful, independent Yankees set out for brighter horizons and established new and ultimately more lucrative trade routes with the East Indies, Russia, China, and India. This new trade resulted in a more opulent and worldwise society. Homes were soon furnished with the luxuries and delicacies of the Far East, thus enriching and enlivening the earlier Puritan way of life.

The War of 1812 temporarily halted American trade, depressing coastal economy, which rebounded afterward in a boom far surpassing any that had been known. The superior American fleet dominated the Seven Seas amassing fortunes for their owners in whaling, trade, and passenger service. Few things surpassed the beauty and speed of the American clipper ship; for with billowing sails and sleek hull, she captured the spirit and pride of the maritime economy during the mid-1800s.

The advent of steam power in the same century had a profound effect on coastal towns. The beauty and excitement of sail lost out to the efficiency of steam, and shipyards turning out sailing vessels grew strangely quiet. Yet even as this industry declined, New England's resourceful craftsmen joined in the industrial revolution. First water-powered and later steam-powered factories sprung up along coastal rivers, turning home crafts into big business. In the late 1800s and early 1900s, New England became famous for its textile, shoe, clock, and furniture industries, to name only a few.

An additional bonus from steam was the emergence of railroads, which took over coastal trade, broadened domestic markets, and ushered in a new and prosperous industry—tourism. In the mid-1800s railroads provided quick and comfortable access to the seashore areas. What had been quiet farming, fishing, and shipbuilding towns blossomed into coveted summer resorts.

Just as the early settlers turned to the sea for their livelihood and prosperity, so once again these coastal towns are benefiting from the ever-changing natural beauty, allure, and wonder of the seemingly endless ocean and seashore. The coastal towns from New Bedford to Salem and Beverly are still nurtured and strengthened by the sea.

LIVING ARCHITECTURE

Studying New England's architecture reveals the fascinating lives of her people. You can see how they thought, what they valued, and how they survived, adapting Old World ideas and applying "Yankee Ingenuity."

New England is fortunate in retaining many buildings from each architectural period. Using the following chart as a bird watcher uses his guidebook, you can distinguish these periods and better understand the people whose living created them.

A Field Guide to Architectural Styles

FIRST PERIOD—to 1715

New England's first settlers, concerned with immediate survival, built shelters with designs probably influenced by a combination of remembered English huts, Indian wigwams, and available materials. Even while struggling with this strange climate, Indians, disease, and each other, these pioneers began the evolution of the First or Colonial Period of American architecture. A primitive one-room home expanded to two rooms by raising the roof. The plan was repeated on the chimney's other side to create the four room, central chimney Colonial. Often rooms were added by a lean-to across the back, with this addition sometimes modified by raising the roof to add more rooms.

Characteristics:
Steeply pitched gable roof; massive central chimney; windows small, many paned, randomly placed, close to eaves; entry not emphasized, door small, not centered; walls nearly touch ground, shingled or clapboarded; feeling: defensive, isolated, like sealed box

First Period, Alden House

GEORGIAN PERIOD—c.1715–1785

By about 1715, New England's prosperity set the stage for change in her architecture. Improved communication brought books of building designs and new ideas; the influx of skilled immigrant craftsmen provided the ability; and American industrial advancement provided the tools to launch the Georgian Period of classical architecture. Named for the first three Kings George of England, the period's designs were based mainly on the rediscovered work of Andrea Palladio.

Life was changing, with time now for more than mere practical survival. Great areas were provided for purely social functions— spacious central halls, dining rooms, formal drawing rooms—and the addition of closets revealed expanded wardrobes.

Characteristics:

Georgian, Derby House

Massive, symmetrical, intricate, harmonious, square; more windows, larger, fewer panes, balanced; door centered, arched or rectangular lights above; focus on decorative front entry, headed windows, pedimented portico; quoined corners, some ashlar effect, water table and string course, horizontal focus; Palladian central window; roof hip or gambrel, low pitch, ornamental eaves; more chimneys, symmetrical; fencing and balustraded captain's walk at roof; often two stories plus dormered third story, four rooms per floor; interior spacious, grand central hall and stairway; heavy elaborate molding and paneling, higher ceilings; feeling: inviting, social, established, affluent

Massachusetts Department of Commerce and Development, Division of Tourism

FEDERAL PERIOD—c.1785–1820

After the Revolution, Charles Bulfinch* in Boston and Samuel McIntire* in Salem ushered in the Federal style. Less massive than the earlier Georgian, it was based on the work of the English Adams brothers. New England was reaping her rewards from the sea— through whaling, shipbuilding, and world trade—and found the Federal style the most appropriate expression of this opulence.

Characteristics:
Vertical focus, symmetrical, immense, yet delicate, lighter than Georgian; usually forty feet square; three stories tall; roof low-pitched, hip, balustraded, pierced by tall, slender chimneys; windows more and larger, smaller on top floor, often Palladian above portico; columned portico emphasized with semielliptical lights over door extending over side lights; elaborate fences, posts, finials; quoined corners; interior, ornate yet delicate woodwork, broad, sweeping stairs; feeling: commanding, simple elegance, economic and social success, reflects confident new Independence

Massachusetts Department of Commerce and Development, Division of Tourism

Federal, Gardner-Pingree House

GREEK REVIVAL—c.1820–1850

As rewards from the sea produced the opulent Federal Period, so the receding economic tides caused by Jefferson's Embargoes and the War of 1812 brought that period to a close. With focus no longer on the sea, national interest broadened. Interestingly, Jefferson, blamed for New England's wounded economy which closed the Federal Period, led American interest directly to the cultures and architecture of ancient Rome and Greece. In New England, Greek became the language of democracy and this intellectual awakening was expressed in her architecture.

Characteristics:
Greek temple features; stone or wood cut and painted to resemble stone; usually on high granite foundation; gable end facing street; entrance not centered, transom and side lights around door rectangular; six over six windows, heavy lintels; Greek portico small or extended across whole front; columns, pilasters at portico and corners; large, flat frieze tops wall, under eaves; ornamentation heavy; feeling: powerful, grand display, intellectual freedom

City of Bedford

Greek Revival, William R. Rodman House

VICTORIAN ERA—c.1840s–1890s

The Industrial Revolution sparked intense changes in architecture. The theme was Revivalism. Revivalism was the outgrowth of advances in communications, education, and the corresponding cultural emphasis, plus the technology of the Industrial Revolution. It was the expression of Victorian character—enthusiastic optimism and restless individuality. Fascinating and confusing, the nineteenth century's styles are selections and combinations from two thousand years of the world's finest architecture. The features were often varied and styles combined.

The following Victorian styles are the most frequently found examples along the Massachusetts coast.

GOTHIC STYLE—1830s–1870s

Characteristics:
Often asymmetrical; pointed arch; steep roof, pointed gables, tall finials; tower or turret; pinnacles, battlements; gingerbread bargeboards; window tracery; veranda

Gothic, William J. Rotch House

ITALIANATE—c.1840s–1890s

Characteristics:
Asymmetrical; rectangular; slightly pitched gabled and/or hip roof; projecting eaves with brackets; tower or cupola, off-centered; round headed windows, often grouped, veranda, balcony, quoins

Italianate, 330 Union Street

FRENCH SECOND EMPIRE—c.1850s–1890s

Characteristics:
Combines colors, materials, heavy detail; tall mansard roof, enveloping entire floor, with curb at top; dormer windows; brackets featured; tall, bold

French Second Empire, 91 State Street

QUEEN ANNE—c.1870s–1890s

Characteristics:
Irregular plan and mass; variety of color, texture, windows; projections, gables, turrets; roofs high and multiple; chimneys emphasized, often incorporated into dormer window

Queen Anne, J. A. Beauvais

RICHARDSONIAN ROMANESQUE—c.1870s–1890s

Characteristics:
Varying facade; round arch style; rock-faced masonry with different stone in trim; squat, clustered columns; heavy, bulging mass

Richardsonian Romanesque

HISTORY OF NEW BEDFORD

New Bedford is authentic. It is not a reconstructed town built with outside money to recreate the past. Rather it is the past, intermingled with the present, still living, still active, and still working. When you enter a ship's chandlery you know that ships' captains and seamen have entered these same doors for as long as anyone can remember. This is how it has been and will continue to be in New Bedford, for this is the normal everyday life of a working, active, throbbing New England seaport.

In the mid-1600s Baptists and Quakers, who were severely persecuted by the Pilgrims, as well as other dissatisfied settlers from the Plymouth area settled in this wilderness frontier. Their descendants, remembering early persecutions, would offer these same sacred freedoms to other ethnic groups.

During the mid-1700s two Josephs, Russell* and Rotch,* led the village from infancy through adolescence. New Bedford founder Joseph Russell III laid out streets and house lots, introduced whaling, set up the first whale oil factory and candle-house, and developed foreign trade. By 1765 the foundation was well laid for the arrival of Joseph Rotch from Nantucket Island. His outstanding knowledge of whaling, enthusiasm, and strong financial reserves gave whaling the final impetus it needed. Whaling and merchant ships were launched, and the village, named for the Duke of Bedford, entered its greatest era—that of whaling.

The American Revolution temporarily curtailed whaling and foreign trade as British men-of-war harassed and captured colonial ships. Bedford Harbor became a haven for colonial privateers, who in turn preyed on and caused great loss to British shipping. However, few privateersmen were Bedfordites, for most were Quakers, whose faith kept them from participating in such aggressive actions. Nevertheless, the British in retaliation invaded and burned Bedford Village Septem-

Information in this chapter is derived and condensed from the book *Guide to New Bedford*, by Barbara Clayton and Kathleen Whitley, published by the Globe Pequot Press, Old Chester Road, Chester, Connecticut 06412.

ber 5, 1778, destroying ships, wharves, and buildings on the waterfront. Undaunted Bedford arose from her ashes and rebuilt. Peace, prosperity, and growth followed, and in 1787 Bedford Village became the independent town of "New" Bedford. Whaling and merchant ships sailed in and out of her harbor, and barrels of whale oil covered her wharves. By 1830, in the Midas world of whaling, New Bedford had surpassed Nantucket as the leading whaling port.

This growth and prosperity was due in great part to the indomitable character and devotion of the early Quakers, who were leading shipowners and merchants in the late 1700s and early 1800s. As a group they believed in harmonious, unpretentious family living, hard work, strict self-discipline, and equality and freedom of thought for all. In most towns the three "R's" stood for the rudiments of education, but to New Bedford they represented three Quaker families: Russells, Rotches, and Rodmans.* Beside these three "R's" stood other important families—Hathaways, Howlands,* Tabers, Grinnells,* Morgans,* and Crapos.* These were the personalities who launched and guided the town through the exciting days of whaling, its incorporation as a city in 1847, and into the economic boom of the textile industry in the last half of the 1800s.

Events took place in the mid-1800s which eventually ended the proud whaling industry. Sperm whales became scarce, gold was discovered in California, competitive oil was discovered in Pennsylvania, whalers were captured or sunk during the Civil War, and the crushing Arctic ice and other natural disasters took their toll of ships and men. Seeing the writing on the wall, New Bedfordites wisely shifted their economy from sea-related to land-related industries. Mills and factories soon commanded the skyline, allowing the economic blood of New Bedford to flow unimpeded. Wamsutta,* the largest and first of the successful cotton mills, was chartered in 1846. By the 1880s New Bedford was a leading textile manufacturing center in New England.

The textile industrial boom rode confidently into the 1900s only to meet disaster in the 1920s from overproduction following World War I, poor management, southern competition, local strikes, and finally the national depression of 1929. Factories closed; skilled laborers were attracted elsewhere; buildings became vacant and began to deteriorate; and proud historic homes faced neglect and vandalism. New Bedford entered an economic crisis.

New Bedford realistically faced her problems. First, her citizens developed an Industrial Park in 1956. Second, with much of their economy dependent on their harvest from the sea, they built a multi-million-dollar hurricane barrier* in 1965. This gave New Bedford the unique advantage of a harbor area completely safe from storm and flood damage. Third, during the late 1960s and 1970s North and South Terminals were built along the Acushnet River. At South Terminal a new bulkhead opened nineteen acres of waterfront land, which in turn gave birth to modern fish processing plants. This furthered an industry that started in the 1750s, and now finds New Bedford the scallop capital of the United States and leading port on the east coast in dollar value of catch. Fourth, New Bedford's present and past reunited through tourism and historic preservation—adding their twin values to the rising economy.

Even though New Bedford's industries have been the mainstay of her economy, it has been her people who have carried her through her successes and trials. Since her inception in 1652, New Bedford has always valued the individual, regardless of religion, color, or ethnic background. While others turned away so called "different" people, New Bedford welcomed Quakers, Baptists, American Indians, Blacks, West Indians, Cape Verdeans, Azoreans, Madeirans, and Europeans. Today these varied bloods, pulsating through the veins of New Bedfordites, provide the strength and character of the city. It is a city where all, though still loyal to their own ancestry, have shared that ancestry and their special talents and aptitudes. Just as many different colors create the beautiful rainbow with its pot of gold, so the different ethnic groups have created New Bedford—a city all its citizens are proud to call home.

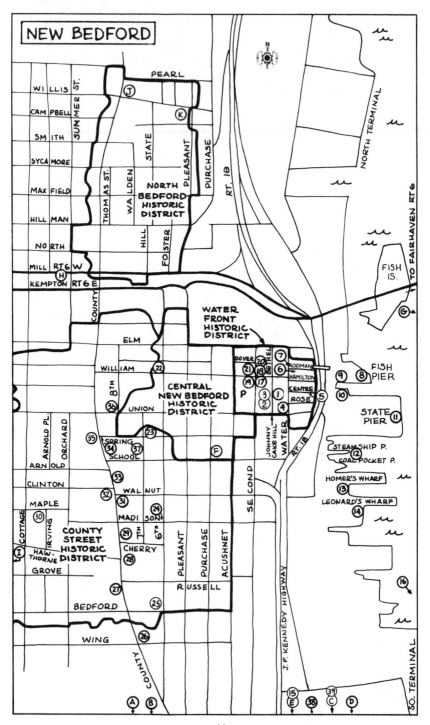

NEW BEDFORD

NEW BEDFORD

DIRECTIONS:
New Bedford is easily reached from Route 195, Route 140, or Route 6. From 195 take Exit 15, following the "Downtown" signs. As you near the city from all routes, signs for "Downtown" and the "Moby Dick Trail" will guide you to the Whaling Museum and the heart of the city where the tour begins. There are two centrally located parking areas, one on William Street at Second Street and the other at the foot of Second Street on Elm Street.

WATERFRONT HISTORIC DISTRICT
NRHP, National Landmark District

New Bedford's Waterfront District has been the vital center since her early days. Derelict after the decline of whaling, this historic district was rescued from sunken oblivion through the combined efforts of interested citizens, responsible and far-thinking government, and WHALE* (Waterfront Historic Area LeaguE) in the 1960s and 1970s. The narrow, cut-stone streets, brick and cobblestone walks, lighted by replicas from the past, invite you to discover the old whaling port as well as experience the life of today's active, successful seaport.

#1
The Whaling Museum
Old Dartmouth Historical
Society
Johnny Cake Hill
1904
Open all year, fee charged

To reach the Whaling Museum from either parking lot, return to Second and William Streets; walk one block toward the water; turn right on Johnny Cake Hill; and the Museum is on the left.

The saga of the whale and the men dedicated to hunting it comes alive at the Whaling Museum which contains treasures collected throughout the world—the whalers' vast fishing grounds. Paintings, photographs, figureheads, stern boards, ship models, and fascinating logbooks tell the story of whaling.

Whaling Museum, half-scale model of Whaling Bark Logoda

The long voyage of a whale ship, often three or four years, produced a life of its own. This life is reflected in the collections of the true American folk art of scrimshaw and paintings depicting whaling adventures and life in remote parts of the world. Portions of the quarter-mile-long Purrington and Russell panorama of a worldwide whaling voyage are highlighted. Supporting industries of whaling are presented in a series of separate room displays—of a chandlery, tin and copper shop, blockmaker, cooperage, and countinghouse.

The *Lagoda*, a half-scale replica of a square-rigged whaler, is the main feature of the central Bourne Building. The exact detail of the model adds to the fun of climbing aboard and exploring. It provides a perfect background in which to relive the days of whaling. The suspended skeleton of a small humpback whale fits the scale of the *Lagoda*. Nearby, a meticulously rigged whaleboat looks as if it had just been lowered from the davits of a whale ship, ready to row or sail closer to the sighted whale.

The Museum has grown since 1904 to its present harmonious many-building complex, which is unified by beautiful landscaping, formal gardens, and iron emblematical harpoon fence. The central Bourne Building honors Jonathan Bourne,* successful whaling merchant and owner of more whaling ships than anyone else in New England, including the original *Lagoda*.

The Museum offers informative daily walking tours in season, a movie, concerts, and many other educational experiences. This Museum of New Bedford history is actually a view into world history. For, as you lose yourself in its interesting, well-displayed exhibits, following the paths of early whalers, you circumnavigate the globe.

#2   *Across the street from the Whaling Mu-*
Seamen's Bethel   *seum stands the Seamen's Bethel.*
15 Johnny Cake Hill
1832
Open every weekend, daily
in season, no fee

Sit where captains and sailors have been sitting for decades. Consider the bowsprit-shaped pulpit, a familiar sight to seamen easily translated into a symbolic ship of faith. The Bethel has served seamen from all over the world, each in his own way seeking an inner strength and faith. Through these doors has gone a lasting influence that has touched people in every port and on every ocean.

The spirit of the sea is evident everywhere, from the three-masted whaler high atop the Bethel down to the very pew cushions covered with sailcloth. One such pew was occasionally occupied by Herman Melville. The cenotaphs on the walls are each in memory of crewmen who lost their lives at sea. Directly below the chapel is the "Old Salt Box." It was named for the hold of a ship where fish were preserved in salt, possibly symbolic of the preserving of men's souls.

In the early 1800s all levels of society existed in New Bedford—from the social elite, through many levels of a working society, down to derelicts, harlots, thieves, and murderers. Annually 5,000 sailors came through this port. In an attempt to counteract the ills of society, local businessmen headed by Samuel Rodman* founded the New Bedford Port Society in 1830 and built the Bethel which opened on May 2, 1832. Over the years this nondenominational Christian service has counseled and supported seamen and their families and placed thousands of Bibles aboard ships. During the whaling era the Society served as an invaluable source of contact by listing the crews of every ship sailing from New Bedford.

The Bethel has had its humorous side. Prior to an 1866 fire the pulpit was on the street side. To facilitate late arrivals, when the church was

Seamen's Bethel

renovated the seating arrangement was reversed, putting the pulpit where it is today. The congregation, being victims of habit, when they stood for hymns and scripture readings still turned to face the street side, backs to the pulpit. This was effectively remedied when a visiting preacher, feeling the congregation was being impolite, stood and gave his entire sermon with his back to the congregation. Needless to say, he got his point across.

This simple, gray clapboard building, without fanfare or fancy ecclesiastical trapping, has inspired a world.

#3   *The Mariners' Home is next to the Bethel.*
Mariners' Home
Johnny Cake Hill
c.1790
Not open to public

Since the Mariners' Home opened in 1857 it has been a haven to any seaman who has been at sea within the last six months. For a nominal fee he receives a clean bed, good food, a friendly ear, and reliable information concerning ships in port.

This restored three-story, gray clapboard Federal mansion built for William Rotch, Jr.* is one of the few to remain from the Revolutionary Period. It was originally built c.1790 at the corner of William and North Water Streets on the foundation of the home of William's grandfather, Joseph Rotch,* New Bedford's early leader of its whaling industry. In 1850 William Rotch's daughter, Sarah, deeded the mansion to the Port Society as a home for sailors. Her husband, James Arnold,* financed the move to its present location.

#4
Sundial Building
Union and Water Streets
c.1820
HABS

Continue down Johnny Cake Hill to Union Street and turn left. Go one block to the Sundial Building at the corner of Union and Water Streets. The Sundial Building is now owned by the Whaling Museum.

The Sundial Building was named for the interesting sundial above its entrance. Referred to as "New Bedford time" by seamen, the dial's time was trusted to set nautical instruments used by New Bedford sailors throughout the world.

The late Federal building was constructed c.1820 by Charles and Seth Russell, Jr., to house their dry goods store. The land, which had previously held a West India goods store, had been sold to their father by his uncle, New Bedford founder, Joseph Russell III.*

In 1977 a sudden explosion and fire partially destroyed the Sundial Building, which was rescued and restored by WHALE.* Fortunately, the Whaling Museum suffered slight damage, though the impact filled the sails of the *Lagoda*, making the whaler appear to be leaving the scene under full sail. The garden next to the Sundial Building incorporated fieldstone and brick, from buildings lost to the explosion, and made them into an attractive background for the plantings.

#5
William Tallman
Warehouse, North
corner Front and Centre
Streets,
c.1790, open as business,
HABS

Walk down Union Street one block. Turn left on cobblestoned Front Street, which parallels the main highway, Route 18. Walk one block to Centre Street.

**WHALE, Waterfront
Historic Area
LeaguE, office in Tallman
Warehouse**

**Caleb Spooner House,
22 Centre Street,
1806, shop open**

**Henry Beetle House, 24
Centre Street, 1804, private**

Historically important and presently significant, Centre Street is directly across from the working waterfront. Once it was lined with commercial buildings on both sides and whaling try-pots at the foot of the street.

The *William Tallman Warehouse*, one of New Bedford's oldest buildings, was constructed in the Federal commercial style about 1790 by William Tallman, whaling pioneer and partner of New Bedford founder Joseph Russell III. During the revolution, Tallman, a patriotic Quaker, was a commissary of subsistence. The 1778 British raid destroyed his goods in Bedford Village, took him prisoner, and confiscated his knee buckles, shoe buckles, and favorite horse. His liberty, horse, and buckles were returned at the order of the British general. Tallman continued his leading role in New Bedford as first selectman from 1787 until his death in 1802.

WHALE, the nonprofit Waterfront Historic Area LeaguE, has its offices in the historic Tallman Warehouse. WHALE was responsible for the Warehouse's preservation and adaptive reuse, as it has been for much of the Waterfront District. WHALE is dedicated to saving historically important structures and using them in modern, productive ways.

Across Centre Street, the *Caleb Spooner House* is typical of early 1800 New Bedford. This tidy Cape, built in 1806 by bricklayer Caleb Spooner for his bride, remained in the Spooner family for nearly a century. WHALE was instrumental in moving it from its West End demolition site and partially restoring it.

Next door, the Federal Period *Henry Beetle House* has been home to three generations of sparmakers in the Beetle family and to Thomas Thompson, the "man in overalls" mayor of New Bedford. Tom Thompson came up through the Wamsutta Mills where he began working at the age of eleven. A self-educated man and accomplished marble

cutter, his marble shop became a drawing center for a variety of
people. Thompson, always leader of this forum, was a lively, quick-
thinking speaker, who published his own paper with his forum's views.

#6   *Walk away from the water up Centre*
Double Bank Building   *Street and turn right on Water Street. Go*
Water Street   *one block. On the right between Hamilton*
1831–1835   *and Rodman Streets is the Double Bank*
Private offices   *Building.*
HABS

This Greek temple of early finance was constructed on Water Street
when whaling was king and Water Street was known as the Wall Street
of New Bedford. Located in the center of banking, insurance, and legal
offices, this Double Bank Building housed both the Merchants Bank
and the Mechanics Bank. Now the Fishermen's Union and other fishing
related interests occupy the historic building.

Architect Russell Warren* designed the Greek Revival structure
with its massive Ionic portico and polished granite steps and facade. It
was built by two different builders who disagreed on the slope of the
huge full-height pillars. Purportedly only the four pillars on the south
are the correct interpretation of Warren's plan.

#7   *Next on Water Street, across Rodman*
Rodman Candleworks   *Street, is the Rodman Candleworks.*
Water and Rodman Streets
1810
Open as businesses
NRHP

Samuel Rodman, Sr.,* who became a leading entrepreneur in New
Bedford with his many whaling-related ventures, built this candleworks in 1810. It was one of the first to produce the superior spermaceti candles. The light given off by one spermaceti candle set the
standard for one candle power.

After Samuel, Sr.'s death, the Candleworks remained in the family
until 1890 under the leadership of son-in-law Andrew Robeson.* He
was aided by another son-in-law, Charles W. Morgan,* owner of the
famous whaling ship now at Mystic Seaport, Connecticut, and Rodman's sons, Benjamin* and Samuel, Jr.*

The Candleworks building served a variety of business ventures until finally, damaged by fire and time, it was abandoned in the 1960s. Its successful rescue and rehabilitation are the result of cooperating efforts by the city, with Community Development grants; WHALE; and ACT, Architectural Conservation Trust for Massachusetts.

The strong, Federal-style structure has two-foot-thick, native granite rubble walls with stucco facing scored to resemble granite blocks. The windows and arched doors are detailed with rough-cut granite quoins repeated at the building's corners. The unusual color is believed to be authentic. Adaptive reuse includes a ground-floor restaurant, the New Bedford Five Cents Savings Bank, and offices.

#8
Fish Pier and Waterfront Park
On the waterfront by the Rodman Overpass
Open all year,
no fee

To be part of this historic seaport, it is necessary to walk her waterfront and be caught up in the workaday world of the fishermen, with its excitement, drudgery, dangers, and rewards. Access to the working waterfront and Waterfront Park is available via the Pedestrian Overpass. The overpass, with its observation deck, can be reached from Rodman Street east of the Candleworks to see #8-16. Fish Pier is on the water side of the overpass and the park continues along the waterfront.

Two separate piers are now combined into one large open pier to provide better service for New Bedford's fishing fleet and the daily auctions at Wharfinger's,* the brick building adjacent to the pier. Of New Bedford's fishing fleet, roughly one-third can be found in port at any given time. You will see the ships tied up two, three, and four abreast here and at the many wharves on both sides of the river. The vessels vary from $300,000 draggers to million-dollar scallopers, from rusty hulls with peeling paint to new steel hulled ships with polished wood.

#9
Wharfinger's Building
Fish Pier
1934
Admission by permission of Fishermen's Union

Wharfinger's is found on Fish Pier to the right of the overpass. Cuttyhunk Ferry leaves from Fish Pier.

Wharfinger's, an unassuming brick building on Fish Pier, built in 1934 for the harbor master, is undoubtedly the most important building on the waterfront today. For here is decided the economic fate of every ship's catch. The world prices for scallops and yellow-tail flounder are set here in New Bedford every morning. The scallop auction is at 7:00 A.M. and the fish auction at 8:00 A.M. By their appointed time, fishing captains crowd into Wharfinger's, where they list their catch on a board. A bell rings, and in less than a minute representatives from the processing plants have registered their bids. The captains then have fifteen minutes to decide if they will accept the bid price. Another bell rings, and the auction is finalized. Seven to ten days hard work at sea is decided in a few hectic minutes. The boats then move to the processing plants at South Terminal, where the catch is unloaded, processed, and shipped out by truck, thus completing the vital cycle in the life of the fisherman.

#10
Coast Guard
Commemorative Exhibition
Lightship *New Bedford*
Foot of Union Street, north
side of State Pier
1976
Open seasonally, Lightship,
fee charged; Dome Exhibit,
no fee

The Coast Guard Memorial is just south of Wharfinger's on State Pier.

Moored next to the working vessels she once protected is the now retired Lightship *New Bedford*. Visitors are invited aboard to explore the ship. Here you picture life in the days when a lightship was anchored as a vital aid to navigation in a strategic location too difficult for a lighthouse. Her powerful beacons, thunderous foghorns, and essential radio beacon kept a constant lonely vigil in all weather and seasons.

New Bedford was the first winter home of the Coast Guard Academy. The idea was established in 1876 to have a two-year training of cadets from which to draw officers. The first school of instruction, an old schooner, was soon replaced by the new bark *Salmon P. Chase*. When the *Salmon P. Chase* wintered in New Bedford, the school continued in a sail loft. The training school evolved into the well-known Coast Guard Academy in New London, for which this exhibition is a centennial commemorative.

The geodesic dome of the exhibit could easily symbolize a Fresnel lens, used in lighthouses to concentrate and intensify light. Under this symbolic dome are housed special exhibits of the Coast Guard including a thirty-six foot, self-righting rescue boat.

#11
State Pier
Open all year, no fee

State Pier is adjacent to the Coast Guard memorial; access by traffic light.

All foreign imports and exports for New Bedford pass through State Pier, operated by the Commonwealth of Massachusetts. In addition to being a busy freight terminal for international ships, it is also home port to United States Coast Guard cutters which serve vessels in distress as well as represent Uncle Sam while patrolling the two-hundred-miles offshore fishing areas from Canada to Florida.

Along with large freighters, it is interesting to watch local fishing boats tying up just long enough to sell their shack fish (additional seafood brought up with the main catch) to truck buyers. This is also an excellent vantage point from which to enjoy the architecturally varied skyline of New Bedford, the beautiful protected harbor lined with its familiar fishing boats, and the steepled skyline of Fairhaven across the river.

#12
Steamship and Coal Pocket
Piers
Open all year, no fee

South of State Pier are Steamship and Coal Pocket Piers. Brick path leads to grass and bench area overlooking piers.

Steamship Pier is aptly named, for between 1891 and 1933 it served as docking terminal for picturesque white side-wheelers, *Monnohansett* and *Martha's Vineyard*. These proud ferries running from New Bedford to Nantucket and Martha's Vineyard brought their own special kind of glamor to New Bedford. Following World War Two, they were replaced by modern car ferries. The excitement of the side-wheelers gone, people soon drove directly to Woods Hole, thus ending the Nantucket run by 1961.

Directly south is *Coal Pocket Pier* which during the whaling era received and stored thousands of barrels of whale oil. By the late 1800s whale oil had been replaced by coal which was stored in high containers or pockets while waiting to be shipped out by wagon for local use—thus the name Coal Pocket Pier.

Today these piers have been converted to receive small commercial boats and to serve as a municipal pier, where pleasure, charter, and sight-seeing boats tie up while visiting New Bedford, creating a recreational window on a working waterfront. Future plans call for the berthing of historically significant ships, which would be open to the public.

#13
Bourne Counting House
Durant Sail Loft
Merrill's Wharf
1847–1848
Open as businesses
NRHP

The next wharf south is Merrill's (also called Homer's) Wharf, on which the Bourne Counting House is located.

In this indomitable building were Jonathan Bourne's* counting rooms for over forty years. From this vantage he noted the arrival and departure of whaling vessels. He was said to own more whaling tonnage than anyone else in the country. This most successful whaling merchant began his career in New Bedford at age seventeen by clerking in a grocery. He came from an industrious, self-reliant farming family in Bourne, a town which was later named for him.

Whaling king Jonathan Bourne became a major adviser of the textile industry, which rapidly filled the gap left by whaling's decline. He was president and/or director of many banks, mills, utilities, and railroads here and in Fall River. An interested and powerful politician, he was a long-time alderman, state representative, and member of the Governor's Council.

The building remained an integral part of New Bedford's sea-oriented life when it became the Durant Sail Loft in the first part of this century. In 1934 the sail loft made the sails for the *Charles W. Morgan,** probably the only sails made for a whaler in half a century.

The Bourne Counting House is located on Captain Edward Merrill's Wharf, where more whale oil was landed than anywhere else in New Bedford.

Restoration began with the city's Community Development funds when this magnificent waterfront granite block structure was a neglected, fire-gutted, boarded-up derelict. Now quality shops, an inn, and top floor restaurant offer spectacular panoramic views of the harbor and city and a chance to appreciate this historic treasure.

#14
Leonard's Wharf
Open all year, no fee

Adajcent to and south of Merrill's Wharf and the Bourne Counting House is Leonard's Wharf, which is beyond parking lot and restaurant.

Walk along Leonard's Wharf and step into the world of the fisherman. Observe the fishing boats with their radar and sonar gear, trawling nets, scallop draggers, and dinghies perched in some cases atop cabin roofs. Be aware that everything has a purpose; there are few frills.

Leonard's Wharf was named for Samuel Leonard, who originally owned a wharf down river where a prosperous and extensive lumber business ran from 1830 until the mid-1900s. The present Leonard's Wharf illustrates an affable combination of work and pleasure. Along with the commercial fishing boats are harbor tour boats and ferries to Cuttyhunk and Martha's Vineyard.

#15
Hurricane Barrier
1965–1966
Barrier open all year, building by appointment, no fee

From here you can see the Hurricane Barrier. For directions to access see #38.

Battered ships, broken bulkheads, twisted wharves, and flooded waterfront factories are a thing of the past in New Bedford. For today's harbor is protected by a 9,100-foot long and twenty-foot high hurricane barrier running from Fort Phoenix in Fairhaven to Clark's Point in New Bedford. The disastrous effects of the 1938 and 1954 hurricanes and the knowledge that New Bedford is in a flood plain brought about the building of this multi-million-dollar stone barrier in 1965-1966 through the combined efforts of local, state, and federal agencies.

The actual barrier opening, manned twenty-four hours a day, is controlled by two 400-ton gates, each operated by its own twenty-five horsepower engine. When the gates are open a strobe light flashes. But let the direction and force of the wind, tide height, and weather conditions combine to threaten the inner harbor, and the men at the barrier spring into action. The strobe light increases to constant flashing, an alarm goes off, radio announcements are made, and the gate closes. Within twelve minutes New Bedford and her harbor, like the walled city of Jericho, are sealed off from the raging sea. Once inside the gate, the sailors know they are safe from wind, tide, and storm, a truly sheltered port—one of the few on the New England coast.

On calm days the top of the barrier, looking like the Appian Way in Rome, provides an ideal setting for harbor viewing, walking, or fishing. From here you can see Sconticut Neck in Fairhaven, Cape Cod, and the Elizabeth Islands, with Martha's Vineyard on the horizon.

#16   *Palmer Island is just inside the Hurri-*
Palmer Island   *cane Barrier.*
Palmer Island Lighthouse
1849
Not accessible

This six-acre island was named for early pioneer William Palmer, who was scalped by Indians. During the King Philip's War the island served as a detention camp for Indians and later as a garrison which offered protection to local colonists.

It is especially hard to believe, looking at today's deserted island, that at different times during the 1800s the island supported a summer home, hotel, dance hall, bowling alley, and amusement park. Following successive failures of these enterprises the island was sold to different companies and is now owned by the city.

In 1849, in an effort to protect local seamen, the government built the present light and a light-keeper's house. The light, though charred and derelict, speaks of a proud history. During New Bedford's golden era as a whaling port and through her prominence as a fishing port, this familiar light welcomed mariners for over one hundred years.

Until 1938 a keeper and his family were always on duty. The last keeper, Arthur A. Small, and his wife, Mabel, served Palmer Island from 1922 until the tragic hurricane of 1938. During the storm, Keeper Small lost his footing and was swept off the island. His wife, in a heroic effort to save him, tried to launch the dory only to be hit by a huge wave which washed her, along with the boathouse and keeper's house, into the raging river. Small, even after seeing his wife drown, managed to retain consciousness and swim to the island. In spite of injuries and fatigue, he kept the light burning, true to the traditions of the light service. By 1941 the light was automated, ending a special era and tradition on Palmer Island. In 1965 it was replaced by the Hurricane Barrier* light.

#17
Andrew Robeson House
William and Second Streets
1821
Future use uncertain

Return via the overpass from Fish Pier to Rodman Street. Walk up Rodman Street to Water Street. Turn left and make an immediate right on William Street. Continue to William two blocks to the Andrew Robeson House on the SE corner of William and Second Streets.

This dominating Federal house is truly symbolic of New Bedford. It was built by a prominent whaling and manufacturing entrepreneur and rescued and rehabilitated by the cooperative, mountain-moving efforts of the city and WHALE.*

Mountain-moving is an appropriate description, as this 700-ton edifice was painstakingly moved here from its original site behind the Pairpoint Glassworks, shredding nine green-oak "shoes" along the way. Neither insurance snags, doubting experts, Christmas-shopping traffic, nor the wild winter of 1978 kept this mansion from its appointed new site. The move was necessitated by the long-sought return to New Bedford of the Pairpoint Glassworks.*

Owner Andrew Robeson was a prominent Quaker who had interest in whaleships, built a whale-oil refinery, headed several banks, managed the Rodman Candleworks,* and founded a pioneering calico print works in Fall River.

His appropriately magnificent house was surrounded by gardens covering two city blocks. Large, flat pieces of chlorite rock formed the rubblestone walls, faced with brick brought individually wrapped from Robeson's native Philadelphia. Simply ornamented with unusual semi-eliptical fanlight and brick arches surmounting the entrance and lower windows, the mansion has a Dutch cap roof and European glass remaining in some windows.

#18
New Bedford Institution for
Savings; Third District
Court of Bristol
33 William Street
1853
Open as business, Museum
MHB, HABS, NHL

The New Beford Institution for Savings is across the street, on the NE corner of William and Second Streets.

The pioneering New Bedford Institution for Savings has recently repurchased and revived its former home, which had served many uses since its first construction as a bank here in 1853. Now revitalized, the building contains a limited teller operation in an 1800s setting amid handcrafted reproduction mahogany counters and cages.

When the New Beford Institution for Savings was created in 1825, its aim was to provide for the saver of moderate means at a time when commercial banks were for the wealthy. Deposits were invested in local commerce, mainly related to whaling. Home mortgages were offered, allowing more to own homes and New Bedford to grow. The bank moved to their fine new building in 1854 and remained here for nearly half a century. Later this building housed the Third District Court of Bristol from 1899 until 1914.

The brick and brownstone structure combines Greek and Italian Renaissance Revival styles. The shape of the pediment over the front entry is repeated in the larger pediment crowning the front facade. The dentil course in the upper pediment is similar to that of the Pantheon in Rome.

#19
U.S. Custom House
Second and William Streets
1834–1836
Open all year, no fee
NRHP, HABS

The U.S. Custom House is on the SW corner of William and Second Streets.

The impressive Greek Revival style Custom House is appropriate for this sea-oriented city. Here sea captains of old called to enter and clear their ships and cargos, and seamen from the world over came to register for their papers. This largest and most elaborate of the four New England customhouses is the oldest customhouse to continue in the United States. Here duties and tariffs are logged and collected, and offices deal with Coast Guard documentation, the National Fisheries Service, and foreign travel.

This New Bedford structure was designed by Washington Monument architect Robert Mills, and possibly Russell Warren, at a total cost of $32,000. The front facade is carefully hewn white granite and varied stone texture. The dominating classic-style portico is supported by four massive Doric columns of tooled granite. The interior features an unsurpassed cantilevered stairway—its solid stone worn by visitors from all over the world.

#20
New Bedford Glass
Museum, 1978
Benjamin Rodman House,
1820
50 Second Street
Open all year, fee charged

*Walk north on Second Street. On the right
side is the New Bedford Glass Museum.
Parking is available in rear.*

In 1976 when the New Bedford Glass Society, with the help of
community support, restored the Benjamin Rodman House, a new star
rose on the horizon of historic preservation. In this history-laden house
developed a museum of silver and fine glasswork illustrating unique
beauty in varying hues, designs, textures, cuts, and engravings. Here
is displayed the famous glass majesty of Pairpoint, Mount Washington,
and Gundersen Glass Works, as well as tools used in making the
masterpieces.

In 1974, the New Bedford Glass Society, under the direction of
George Avila, needed a building in which to display the artistic history
of glassmaking in New Bedford. At the same time the Federal-style
Benjamin Rodman House, the only waterfront mansion still standing
on its own foundation, was in need of restoration.

The simple, dignified Quaker mansion, originally built in 1820 with
an impressive portico and graciously landscaped, had by 1890 been
completely enclosed by storefronts, and its interior walls removed for
use as a warehouse. In 1965 Catherine Crapo Bullard freed the building
from its foreign attachments and had the exterior restored. The Glass
Society purchased it in 1976 and spent nearly two years reproducing
the interior walls and woodwork and returning the Rodman house to
its past glory. On May 21, 1978, the museum within a museum opened.
Two historic dreams had successfully united to preserve New
Bedford's unique glassmaking heritage along with one of her historic
mansions.

#21
Pairpoint Glass Works,
1894, 1977
Bourne Warehouse, 1885
Second Street
Open: visitors welcome to
observe craftsmen at work,
no fee

*Across the street is the Pairpoint Glass
Works.*

The history of Pairpoint Glass and the development of superior glass art are synonymous. Watching the artisans at work you appreciate the long hours and intricate steps involved in making a single piece of Pairpoint glass. After a twenty-one year absence, the company returned to New Bedford when it leased and refurbished the old Bourne Warehouse in 1977. Over the years this building served as a warehouse, bank, and motor repair shop before becoming the home of Pairpoint Glass.

The story of Pairpoint Glass began in 1866 when local businessmen founded the New Bedford Glass Company. Three years later this was purchased by the Mount Washington Glass Works, which moved to New Bedford, where it represented outstanding craftsmanship and quality. Ten years later a Pairpoint Manufacturing Company opened, becoming one of the largest manufacturers of silver plate in the country. In 1894 these two companies joined silver and glass artistry to form Pairpoint Corporation. At the height of their prosperity, they employed 2,000 people and encompassed twenty buildings. The 1929 depression followed by other economic problems led to its final closing in 1956. Later, Robert Bryden bought the name and formulas and opened a factory in Sagamore, Massachusetts, where success returned. Glass was made for such well-known names as Tiffany's and the Metropolitan Museum of Art in New York. It is this company that has brought the famous Pairpoint trademark back to New Bedford.

#22
First Baptist Church
149 William Street
1829
Open for services all year
NRHP

On Second Street return to William Street, turn right, and walk up past the City Hall *and* Library *to the First Baptist Church on the right.*

This white-steepled, Federal and Greek Revival church stands as a monument to religious freedom, for the early settlers in the Dartmouth-New Bedford area were mainly Baptists and Quakers seeking freedom from the Puritan-minded Plymouth settlement. The church traces its history back to the Reverend John Cooke,* who came to the New World as a boy aboard the *Mayflower* and in 1685 founded the Baptist Church in Tiverton. More than a century passed before eighteen members from the Tiverton Church organized their own church in New Bedford in 1813, meeting in Kempton Hall on Second

Street. After eight months their pastor, the Reverend George Hough, became a missionary to Burma, where he was the first to print the Bible in Burmese. Through his early missionary actions, the Baptist Foreign Missionary Society was founded.

From Kempton Hall the congregation moved to the old Town Hall on Second and School Streets and was incorporated in 1828. A year later ground was broken for the present building. The imposing, sky-reaching steeple has long served as a guide to mariners, thus its prominence on the seal of New Bedford. As the steeple has reached out to mariners, so the church has reached out to the community and during the 1890s established mission churches for Portuguese-, French-, and Swedish-speaking members.

Massachusetts Department of Commerce and Development, Division of Tourism

Whaleman's Statue in front of Public Library

A noteworthy member from 1862 to 1865 was Captain Henry Martyn Robert (see #39). One evening, while conducting a church meeting, he had so much trouble maintaining order that he was later inspired, in 1876, to write *Robert's Rules of Order*.

Just beyond the church, the 1856 neoclassical *City Hall* bears a notably artistic frieze in the pediment crowning the front entrance. The important industries of New Bedford are illustrated: fishing, whaling, textiles, shipping, railroads. The motto on the New Bedford seal, "Lucem Diffundo" or "We light the world," is a living reminder of New Bedford's greatness as a whaling center, whose whale oil provided light for the world.

Across the street from the City Hall is the *New Bedford Free Public Library* with an impressive whaling statue near the entrance. The Greek Revival building, designed by Russell Warren,* was originally the Town Hall and market place. Damaged by fire and remodeled, the interior is now Egyptian Revival.

#23
Friends Meeting House
Spring Street
Society 1785, building
c.1822

From the waterfront parking areas, exit onto William Street going east toward the river. At bottom of hill turn right on Water Street and go to Union Street. Turn right on Union and continue west to Sixth Street. Turn left, and park on Sixth Street near the corner of Spring Street. The Friends Meeting House is to the right on Spring Street.

Quakers first came to the New Bedford/Dartmouth area in 1664 seeking freedom from persecution. By the mid-1700s they were joined by Quakers from Nantucket, who brought with them an invaluable expertise in whale fishery. This expertise, combined with the ethical, spiritual, and economic strengths of the Quakers, formed the foundation for New Bedford's greatness as the whaling capital of the world and later as a leading textile center.

In 1785 they built their meetinghouse on Spring Street on land given by Joseph Russell III. As the Society of Friends grew to seven hundred strong, including such familiar names as Howland, Russell, Rotch, and Rodman, it became necessary to build a larger meetinghouse. The old one was moved to 17 Seventh Street (see #37).

The present austere brick building, completed about 1822, has two sets of hand-chiseled stone steps leading to separate entrances, for men and women. The simple severity is broken only by the slight curve in the stair railing. The inside is equally Spartan with hand-planed, cushioned benches, simple glass fixtures, unadorned walls, and plain molding around curtainless windows.

Quakers, who believe God's spirit is present in every person, showed an early concern for the welfare of others. They strongly opposed slavery, freeing all their slaves by 1785—seventy-eight years before the Emancipation Proclamation. They established one of the early anti-slavery societies in 1834, and through the underground railroad helped hundreds of slaves to freedom.

#24
George Howland, Jr.,
House
37 Sixth Street
1834
Private apartments

Continue on Sixth Street to Madison. On the NW corner of Madison and Sixth is the George Howland, Jr., House.

George Howland, Jr., expanded the strong heritage of his family's economic prowess to become a leading force in New Bedford in the mid-1800s. At fourteen he joined the business of his father, George Howland, Sr., a leading whaleship owner and merchant and one of New Bedford's first millionaires. George Howland, Jr., held long-standing positions in several banks and railroads, was a selectman and later mayor for five terms.

George, Jr., and his half-brother, Matthew, still supported whaling investments after the 1840s prime. As late as 1867 they had the beautiful whaler *Concordia* built. It was a gallant gesture of faith, a Howland tribute to their nearly full century of successful whaling.

#25
New Bedford Fire Museum
Bedford and Sixth Streets
1867
Open seasonally and by
appointment, fee charged
NRHP

Continue south on Sixth Street to Bedford Street. The Fire Museum is on the right, the NW corner.

The museum spans years of fire protection, service, and bravery, showing the development of city fire-fighting techniques. The visitor is guided by wall murals in three languages made at the Swain School of Design.* The proudly gleaming ancient engines are the huge 1855 hand pump, the 1866 steam pump, and fire engines of 1884, 1928, and 1934, all of which served long years in New Bedford. Fire buckets, tools, models, trumpets, awards, logbooks, clothing, and photographs tell the history of fire fighting and the pride, dedication, and courage of the fire fighter. Working exhibits include clothing to try on, a pole to slide down, and bells to ring.

The Fire Museum shares the building of Fire Station # 4 established in 1867, oldest active station in Massachusetts until decommissioned in 1979.

#26
St. John the Baptist Church
County and Wing Streets
Parish 1871, building 1913
Open for services

Continue south on Sixth Street to County Street, and turn right. Drive one block north, and the church is on the right on the corner of County and Wing Streets.

This beautiful granite Romanesque church, completed in 1913, speaks eloquently of a parish that is the first Portuguese Catholic parish in the United States. In the mid-1800s Portuguese seamen, from islands barely able to supply them with the basic needs of life, began coming to New Bedford aboard the many whaling ships that sailed the seven seas.

At first they worshipped at St. Mary's Catholic Church but soon sought a church home where they could have their own language and customs. Their prayers were answered in 1871 when the parish of St. John the Baptist was established under the devoted leadership of Father Joao Ignacio de Azevedo.

The present stone church was erected in 1913. The domelike altar area is highlighted by beautiful paintings depicting special events in the life of Christ. Stations of the Cross, meaningfully done in relief, and bold brilliant colors of stained glass windows all add to a feeling of beauty, solemnity, and spiritual strength. This church and the other twenty-some Catholic churches in the city have all had a strong positive influence on New Bedford since the 1800s.

#27
Joseph Grinnell Mansion
379 County Street
1832
Future uncertain
HABS

Continue north on County Street. Just past Bedford Street, on the left, is the Joseph Grinnell Mansion next to the Joseph Kennedy Youth Center.

Joseph Grinnell, whose life spanned nearly a century, was an astute businessman, a successful manufacturer, and able politician. He began as a clerk and proceeded to found many companies. He was president of a bank, a railroad, and Wamsutta Mills,* which he was instrumental in founding. A member of the Governor's Council, he also served four terms in the United States House of Representatives.

Grinnell's austere yet imposing mansion of Quaker precision and simplicity was designed by Russell Warren.* That noted architect contributed many fine buildings to New Bedford, primarily as a result of Joseph Grinnell's patronage. Originally Greek Revival in style, the solid massive, granite ashlar square is dominated by the giant Doric portico. The supporting fluted Doric columns were destroyed by fire, and the square shaft replacements are not replicas of the originals. The wooden third floor was added in 1893 when the gable was removed. The rough-cut granite, hauled by oxen, came from the Quincy quarry which supplied the granite for Boston's Bunker Hill monument.* Some of the earlier elegance remains in tall rounded mahogany doors and in intricate oak leaf moldings.

Here Grinnells hosted John Q. Adams, Daniel Webster, and Abraham Lincoln among others. The mansion remained in the family until 1940, when it was given to St. John the Baptist Church.* It is a fine example of New Bedford's interest in classical architecture and the ability of her citizens to afford it, though it presently needs restoration.

#28
William R. Rodman
Mansion
Swain School of Design
388 County Street
1833
Open during school hours

In the next block on County Street, at the head of Hawthorn Street is the William R. Rodman Mansion. Across the street at 19 Hawthorn is the William Crapo Art Gallery, open all year, no fee.

This imposing Greek Revival mansion, with its six impressive fluted columns topped by Corinthian capitals, its granite facade, and its setting amidst gracious grounds, cost as much to build as any other in the United States during the 1830s.

The house was built at a cost of $75,000 for William Rotch Rodman, director and president of the Mechanics' National Bank, a successful whaling merchant, and one of the wealthiest men in town by the time he died in 1855. Unlike his more conservative Quaker ancestors, he hosted many a lavish party here.

The Honorable Abraham H. Howland bought the mansion in 1856 at auction for $25,000. Howland brought his own prestige to the mansion, having served as New Bedford's first mayor from 1847 to 1852. Also a prosperous whaling merchant, he was involved in the early distillation of kerosine and coal oil and obtained the first charter for the Wamsutta Mills. Abraham H. Howland, Jr., whose career paralleled his father's, served as mayor and lived for several years in this distinguished residence.

Following the Rodmans and Howlands, who were basically whaling merchants, came Joseph F. Knowles, Thomas S. Hathaway, and Frederick Grinnell, who were all textile merchants from old New Bedford families. Later the house was owned by Walter H. Langshaw, an English immigrant who worked his way up to be president of Dartmouth Manufacturing Co. Much of today's interior decor dates to his ownership.

The present day Swain School of Design owes its existence to the generous spirit of William W. Swain and his wife, Lydia Russell. Having financial success, loving children, and having tragically lost their only sons, they set up a Free School through his will in 1858. It was to be operated for those of high character, regardless of religious or political affiliation, who could not afford to continue their education beyond public school.

Following Mrs. Swain's death, the school opened in 1882 in the Swain home, fulfilling their dream of children learning and growing up in their home. The school, a memorial to a man and woman who lost two children but educated thousands, is now housed in the beautiful Rodman Mansion and has progressed from a faculty of three to a four-year accredited school of art.

#29
William Rotch, Jr., Estate
396 County Street
1834
Open all year and by
appointment, fee charged

The William Rotch, Jr., Estate is the next on the right, between Cherry and Madison Streets. Check with WHALE for hours open or appointment.

The William Rotch, Jr., Estate is important today not only for its beautifully preserved Greek Revival house but because it is the only one to retain the formal gardens, greenhouse, coachman's house, and well-maintained spacious grounds of a prominent mid-nineteenth century whaling merchant of New Bedford. Praised by John Q. Adams as one of the finest frame mansions in New Bedford, its only alteration over the years has been the addition of dormers on the third floor.

William Rotch, Jr., born on Nantucket in 1759, came to New Bedford after the Revolution and contributed his outstanding mercantile talents to the Rotch enterprises and economic growth of New Bedford. He was a founder and first president of the New Bedford Institution for Savings. He contributed nearly half the money raised for the building of the Friends Academy in 1811, and served as an officer until his death in 1850.

He owned two significant homes, the first on the corner of William and Water Streets, where he lived with his first wife, Elizabeth Rodman. (see #3) The second he built here for his second wife, Lydia Scott. In William's day, his homes were ones of open hospitality to all, whether rich or poor, slave or freeman, newcomer or old-timer.

Following Rotch's death in 1850 the home was sold to Edward Coffin Jones, who, as whaling merchant and incorporator of the Marine Bank, was one of the richest men in New Bedford. In 1935 the house passed to its third owner, the highly successful Mark Duff who was connected with the New Bedford Hotel, Union Street Railroad Company, and the Merchants National Bank. Recently this historic home was purchased by WHALE to preserve its personal history as well as its significant architectural and horticultural values.

#30
William J. Rotch Gothic
Cottage
19 Irving Street
1846
Private

Turn left on Madison Street and drive to end. Turn right on Orchard Street and immediately left on Maple Street. The Gothic Cottage is on the left at the corner of Irving and Maple Streets.

The lines of this early Gothic Revival Cottage create an atmosphere of strength, high purpose, and gracious living. Notice the elaborate, carved fretwork under the steeply angled eaves, the pinnacle dramatically piercing the gable over the front entrance, and the tall narrow double windows with triangular glass panes. Designed by Alexander Jackson Davis,* it was listed in A. J. Downing's *The Architecture of Country Houses*, 1850.

Born in 1819, William James Rotch* married Emily Morgan, daughter of Charles W. Morgan.* The honeymooning couple became fascinated with Gothic style cottages along the Hudson River. Upon returning they surprised tradition-minded New Bedford with their own Gothic cottage, built here in 1846 on land deeded to William by his grandfather, William Rotch, Jr.* The cottage was surrounded by well-maintained rolling lawns, circular drive, and stables, and originally faced Orchard Street. To accommodate his growing family, Rotch built a large Gothic Revival addition.

During William J. Rotch's unusually varied and productive lifetime, he was mayor of the city, on Governor Clifford's military staff, served two terms in the Massachusetts Legislature, was a founder of the local Republican Party, served on the board of directors of almost every corporation in town, and for forty-two years was president and/or treasurer of the Friends Academy.

Five years after the death of his first wife, Emily, he married her sister, Clara, in 1866. In 1872 they moved their large family into the mansion on County Street left to William by his uncle, James Arnold. (see #35)

The Gothic Cottage was rented to William Wallace Crapo, a man who faithfully served the business and political interests of his city, state, and country. In 1879 William Rotch's son Morgan married and asked the Crapos to move, so that he could return to his childhood home. He extended Irving and Maple Streets, moved the addition to 112 Cottage Street, where it now stands, and sold some of the property for house lots.

In 1928 Morgan's widow sold the house to Henry H. Crapo, who had lived here as a boy. In 1945 Henry's niece, Catherine, and her husband, John M. Bullard, nephew of Morgan Rotch, moved into this home of common ancestral bonds. Today the home is owned by their grandson, John K. Bullard. In the tradition of the Rotch family he also is concerned with the welfare of New Bedford, having been the driving force behind the historic preservation and economic revival of the waterfront.

#31
Joseph Arthur Beauvais
House
404 County Street
1883
Private

Return via Maple, Orchard, and Madison Streets to County Street and turn left. The Joseph Arthur Beauvais House will be on the right at the corner of Walnut and County Streets. 398 through 405 County Street interestingly display a contrasting variety of architecture.

Joseph Beauvais, whaleship owner and merchant, became a leader in other business fields. He was an officer of several manufacturing companies, a banker, church leader, and active in insurance and real estate.

His interesting house is a fine example of Queen Anne Style, which was one of the most popular in New Bedford. Main features are the projecting gables and bays, ornate chimneys—one with incorporated dormer—variety of wall textures, windows with differing pane sizes and emphasis, and decoratively carved pediment.

#32
Gilbert Russell House
405 County Street
c.1805, 1868
Private

Across County Street, at the head of Walnut Street, on the SW corner of County and Clinton Streets is the Gilbert Russell House.

In 1805 Gilbert Russell lived here in his fine Federal home, second of three he had built in New Bedford. Russell, a successful merchant, was the son of New Bedford founder Joseph Russell III.*

In 1868 later owner Dr. Edward P. Abbe completely remodeled the house to its present mostly French Second Empire Style. Its Moorish feeling is a well-unified combination of massive Federal core with decorative wooden quoins, Italianate brackets, and a dramatic French mansard roof with unusual Oriental upsweep. The octagonal cupola is a fitting crown for this elegant example of New Bedford's individualistic style.

#33
Samuel W. Rodman House
412 County Street
c.1842
Open as offices

Diagonally across County Street is the Samuel W. Rodman House, on the east side of County Street.

Samuel W. Rodman, of the prominent New Bedford Quaker family, built this solid house. The fortresslike, rough cut, massive, granite block construction seems like a Quaker adaptation of the usually lighter Gothic Cottage style. The sharply peaked slate roof has decorative pinnacles at the gables.

#34
Samuel Rodman, Jr., House
106 Spring Street
1827–1828
Open as Social Agencies
HABS

Continue on County Street to Spring Street. The Samuel Rodman, Jr., House is on the SE corner of Spring and County Streets.

Samuel Rodman, Jr., inherited a fine tradition of Quaker determination, morality, and business acumen, which he nurtured and expanded. His father, Samuel, Sr.,* began work in a Newport countinghouse at thirteen to support his widowed mother and six younger sisters. He developed into a leading Nantucket and later New Bedford whaling merchant and textile pioneer.

Samuel Rodman, Jr., continued the family's business successes, was a dedicated abolitionist and a concerned public benefactor. A diarist, his detailed and thoughtful entries, spanning 1821–1859, make the interested reader feel a part of his life and times. He recorded temperature and weather observations which his son Thomas continued. Those ninety-three years of meteorological records, which showed New Bedford uniquely adaptable for weaving and spinning fibers, have been given to the federal government.

Like an upright Quaker the Federal style house stands tall and unadorned, with simple porticoes and hip roof. Cement covers the random granite walls, originally "light Quaker brown." The Rodman family gave the house to Grace Episcopal Church.

#35
James Arnold Mansion
Wamsutta Club
421 County Street
1821
Private club

Across County Street from the Samuel Rodman, Jr., House is the James Arnold Mansion.

Here in earlier days lived two of New Bedford's well-known personalities, James Arnold* and William James Rotch.* The main brick Federal section of the mansion was built by James Arnold in 1821 on eight beautiful acres of what was originally the Abraham Russell farm. Amateur botanist Arnold made the formal gardens a showplace with special varieties of shrubs, flowers, and trees brought from European trips. The Arnold estate originally included a greenhouse, bowling alley, and stables.

James Arnold, like his home, was an outstanding figure on the New Bedford landscape during the 1800s. Born in Providence, Rhode Island, he came to New Bedford to work in William Rotch, Jr.'s* countinghouse. He soon became a full partner, married William's daughter, Sarah,* and ultimately became one of New Bedford's merchant princes.

Arnold felt a deep concern for the less fortunate. He gave freely to the needy and was an early abolitionist, actively supporting the underground railroad. Through his will he left financial support to the New Bedford Port Society, of which he had been president. He also left $100,000 to Harvard for the advancement of horticulture, the beginning of famous Arnold Arboretum.*

The house was left to his nephew, William James Rotch,* who moved into the mansion with his wife, Clara Morgan, and their seven children in 1872. (see #30) William added the third floor and Second Empire period mansard roof. He died here in 1893 and Clara in 1919, after which the lovely mansion became the Wamsutta Club.

#36
First Unitarian Church
Union and Eighth Streets
1838
Open for services, office
open daily

From County Street turn right on Union Street, and go one block. The Unitarian Church is on the left, the NW corner of Union and Eighth Streets.

Its ecumenical three-aisle Gothic Hall displays banners representing many religions of the world. Its spiritual atmosphere is enhanced by a beautiful mosaic Tiffany window. Its fortresslike exterior, designed by Alexander Jackson Davis* and Russell Warren,* looks as if it would be at home among castles of medieval England. This unusual rough-cut stone early Gothic Revival church traces its history back to the First Congregational Society of Acushnet in 1708.

That first Congregational church was built under the auspices of the Puritan-minded General Court of Massachusetts, which believed in taxing all colonists for church support. However, New Bedford's selectmen refused to tax local Baptists and Quakers for support of a church foreign to their beliefs. Consequently, these conscientious selectmen were soon imprisoned. Help was sought in England. As a result, in 1729 the General Court ruled that Baptists and Quakers were exempt from taxes levied to support town churches. A giant step toward true freedom of religion had been taken.

In 1796 New Bedford built its own church on land given by Quaker William Rotch. A division occurred in 1810. The orthodox group left to form the North Congregational Church. The more liberal group retained the building and called Dr. Orville Dewey, a leader in the Unitarian movement, to be their minister. A group of influencial Quakers, who had recently been alienated from the Society of Friends, also found a spiritual home in this intellectually open atmosphere. Old prejudices had indeed been overcome. This church originally Puritan and Congregational became the First Unitarian Church in 1956.

Pause for a moment to explore events in New England which caused many Congregational churches to become Unitarian. As a reaction to the years of strict Puritan discipline and control and strong Calvinistic convictions, a liberal wing developed in Congregational churches during the late 1700s. The first split was recognized in 1805 when liberal thinker Dr. Henry Ware was appointed to the Hollis professorship of Theology at Harvard College. Then in 1819 William Ellery Channing preached a sermon in which he set forth what would become the Unitarian views. With Harvard turning out liberal-minded ministers and Channing Unitarians taking hold, many Congregational churches split. Liberals formed Unitarian churches, and conservatives held to Congregational doctrines. Consequently, many of the first churches in Massachusetts coastal towns are now Unitarian, though Congregationalism is considered the traditional church of early New England.

Today as you drive through Massachusetts, steepled churches in every town still emphasize the continuing importance of religion regardless of denomination. Catholics, Baptists, Methodists, Episcopalians, Quakers, Presbyterians, and many others have all added their strengths and beliefs to the New England spirit.

#37
Nathan and Polly Johnson
Properties
17–23 Seventh Street
1785
Private

Go one block east on Union Street, and turn right on Seventh Street. After crossing Spring Street, you can see the Johnson Properties on the right side, starting at the corner from 17 through 23.

Nathan and Polly Johnson lived at number 17-19 and ran a confectionary store on the site of number 21, which was a front for an active underground railroad during the 1800s. A close friend was Frederick Douglass—speaker, writer, and nationally known Black antislavery leader—who lived for a time with the Johnsons. In fact it was Nathan who gave Frederick Douglass his name.

The Johnsons' home was originally the Quakers' first meetinghouse,* built on Spring Street in 1785 and moved here in 1821. Later this austere, Federal building, served as Mrs. Waite's School, a private residence and dentist office, was severely damaged by fire, and is now apartments.

The Friends Society organized a branch of the Anti-Slavery Society as early as 1834 and were active in the underground railroad. It seems fitting that their old meetinghouse should have been sold to Nathan Johnson, himself a black and strong supporter of the abolitionist movement.

#38
Butler's Flats Light
Off East Beach
1898
City owned, privately maintained

Return to Union Street and turn right. Follow Union to the end and turn right on J. F. Kennedy Highway, Route 18. After entering highway keep left at fork. Drive to end of highway, turn left and go one block to Front Street. Turn right and go one block to Gifford Street. Turn left and park at end of Gifford to walk out on Hurricane Barrier.* Return on Gifford and take first left on Morton Court. Go one block to Cove Street and turn left. At the Hurricane Barrier wall Cove Street bears right and becomes East Rodney French Boulevard. A 1¹/₂-mile scenic drive leads by Butler's Flats Light.

Butler's Flats Light still glows its welcome to men coming home from the Grand Banks. The Coast Guard had planned to destroy the light when a superior beacon was placed on the new Hurricane Barrier,* but the immediate flood of protests was heeded by them. The preserved light was deactivated in 1978 and is now owned by the city and privately maintained and lighted by those who saved it.

The light was constructed in 1898 for $34,000. Construction was a challenge, as the light has no natural rock foundation. A thirty-five-foot-diameter cylinder was filled with stone and concrete, and the light built fifty-three feet above mean low-level tide. Living quarters eighteen feet in diameter housed the lightkeepers, with the wide balcony providing the only walking exercise space.

Three generations of Captains Baker devotedly tended Butler's Flats Light. Captain Amos Baker, a retired whaler and keeper of the old light on Clark's Point, became the first keeper of Butler's Flats. He was succeeded by his son, Captain Amos Baker, Jr., and his son, Captain Charlie Baker. In 1942 the Coast Guard manned the light, ending the eighty-two years of service by the Bakers.

#39
Fort Taber
Clark's Point
1860
Open seasonally, donations
NRHP

Follow East Rodney French Boulevard to the tip of Clark's Point. Enter Fort Rodney. Drive straight ahead, staying next to the shoreline. Follow the road around to Fort Taber.

This well-preserved and partially restored Civil War fort beckons you through its sally port entrance. Once inside, explore the officers' and enlisted men's quarters and the gun emplacements; climb circular granite stairs to the earth-covered summit; and sense the paradoxical feeling of standing atop a military fortification while enjoying the beauty and peacefulness of Buzzards Bay.

Clark's Point, where Fort Taber now stands, has long served as guardian to the harbor and New Bedford. Earthworks were here during the Revolutionary War. A coastal defense plan including the fortification of Clark's Point was devised by the United States Board of Engineers in 1818, the first such plan done entirely by American engineers. In 1846 Major Richard Delafield, known as the father of American coastal defense, and ironically Captain Robert E. Lee, who would soon lead the Confederacy against the Union, collaborated on a design for Fort Taber.

The building of Fort Taber, named for the Honorable Isaac C. Taber, mayor of New Bedford during the Civil War, began in 1860. Part of the construction was directed by Captain Henry M. Robert.* (see #22) By 1869 the mode of warfare had so changed that this type of fortification was no longer adequate and work was stopped.

In 1892 the fort was turned over the the city for a park, to be reclaimed six years later during the Spanish-American War. The observation tower was built, the east bastions were converted to mining casemates for control of mines in the habor, and a searchlight unit was installed. The fort was reactivated for the last time during World War One.

Clark's Point first became important as a navigational aid for mariners at the time of the American Revolution. In 1797 town merchants financed the first lighthouse and turned it over to the government in 1800. The light, replaced several times due to fire, served for years as a friendly guide to ocean-weary sailors. In 1869 the light was moved to the fort's northeast corner. Again fire struck, destroying the light in 1965. The copper cupola atop the present light, now inoperative, is all that remains. A climb to the top of the light rewards you with a magnificent view of the harbor, bay, and Elizabeth Islands with Martha's Vineyard on the horizon.

This ends the guided tour section of New Bedford. To continue the tour exit from fort complex and turn left on Rodney French Boulevard. Follow it around west side of Clark's Point, staying on Rodney French Boulevard West straight through Brighton Square. Take second left on Cove Street. At end of Cove Street turn right on County Street and follow it back through city to Route 6, Kingston Street, and turn right. Follow Route 6 over bridge to Fairhaven.

New Bedford Beaches and Parks and Additional Points of Interest

(A) West Beach
W. Rodney French Boulevard near Valentine Street

Across from Hazelwood Park; southern beach is rocky, sandy nearer city; view of Clark's Cove and out to sea; facilities: (in season) bathhouse, boat launching, concessions, lifeguards, pavilion, rest rooms; limited parking; open all year, no fee

(B) Hazelwood Park
W. Rodney French Boulevard

Panoramic vista of West Beach, South Dartmouth, Clark's Cove; bowling on the green; facilities: basketball courts, fields, picnicking, rest rooms, tennis, tot playground; parking; open all year, no fee

(C) Fort Taber*
(See #39)
Clark's Point

Historic, scenic vantage point of early defense; climb fort and lighthouse tower for fantastic view of harbor and bay; parking; fort open seasonally, donations

(D) East Beach
E. Rodney French Boulevard

New Bedford's longest sandy beach, view of outer harbor, Butler's Flats Light,* Fort Taber,* open sea; facilities: (in season) concession stand, lifeguards, playground, rest rooms, showers; parking; open all year, no fee

(E) Hurricane Barrier Access*
(See #15, 38)
Gifford Street

Walk the huge blocks across the harbor for great views of river and waterfronts and open bay beyond; facilities: fishing, picnicking, walking; parking; open all year, no fee

(F) **State Theatre**
Purchase Street between
Spring and School Streets

Another WHALE* rescued landmark; future plans to restore to former elegance of original 1923 appearance and maintain as performing arts center

(G) **Marine Park**
Popes Island
Route 6
Fairhaven Bridge

Extensive harbor view; fishing party boat rental; facilities: fishing, picnicking; parking; open all year, no fee

(H) **Sergeant William H.**
Carney House
128 Mill Street

Home of Sergeant Carney, first Black awarded Congressional Medal of Honor; Black Heritage Trail designed by Mrs. Jane C. Waters includes sites throughout city; inquire at visitors' center

(I) **Buttonwood Park**
Rockdale Avenue and
Hawthorn Street

Zoo, natural setting for thirty-five different kinds of animals, special exhibits, petting zoo; greenhouse; tree-lined paths; open air stage; facilities: ball fields, fishing, ice skating, paddleboats, picnicking, playground, refreshments, rest rooms, tennis, train rides; parking; open all year, no fee

(J) **John Avery Parker Wing**
53 Willis Street
1834
private

Once small part of huge estate built for Parker who arrived as pauper, belongings in wheelbarrow; became one of first millionaires; was shipbuilder; owner, manager of cotton and iron mills, bank president, director, railroad incorporator, state representative, senator, church worker; palace was designed by Russell Warren,* outstanding granite architecture, solid mahogany woodwork, silver doorknobs, quality so great doors closed with solid authority of bank vault, rest of mansion destroyed

(K) **Charles Russell House**
Hetty Green Residence
1061 Pleasant Street
1830
private convent

Impressive Greek Revival-Federal built by Charles Russell; became home of Hetty Green, "Witch of Wall Street," bizarre upbringing, read and understood financial pages at age six, lived here with grandfather in overstated frugality; as adult craftily parlayed large inheritance into fortune, yet lived in cheap flat where son lost leg from mother's penuriousness

Harbor tours, cruises, ferries	Whaling City Ferry, Inc., Leonard's Wharf* (997-1653) Fishing boat rental: Popes Island* Steamship and Coal Pocket Piers*
Battleship Cove and Marine Museum **Fall River** **Exit 5 Route 195**	Battleship *USS Massachusetts*, Destroyer *USS J. P. Kennedy, Jr.*, Submarine *Lionfish*, Gunboat *Asheville*, *PT 796*—climb aboard these fighting ships, explore their maindecks and topsides, relive their heroic past; visit the museum of great sailships and steamships; parking; open all year, fee

HISTORY OF FAIRHAVEN

Fairhaven was made famous by the adventurous and independent spirit of a Baptist minister, the compassion of a whaling captain, and the generosity of a capitalist.

The Reverend John Cooke,* rejected in the Plymouth Colony for his Baptist views, was one of the thirty-six original colonists to purchase the area that included today's Fairhaven. (see #16) A man of great spiritual strength and leadership, he sparked this infant community and helped kindle it into a permanent settlement, guiding moral, economic, and political values until his death in 1695.

As the settlers entered the 1700s, they began to turn their thoughts from the harvest of the land to the potential harvest of the sea with its bounty of fish and whales. Small ships for fishing and local whaling were built and the colonists moved forward with one hand on the plow and one hand on the tiller.

1760 saw the town of Fairhaven begin to take shape. The section between what is now North and Cherry Streets and the river became the Village of Oxford and prospered as an early shipbuilding, fishing, and whaling center. At the same time twenty acres of land, which today is roughly bordered by Main and Washington Streets and the river, was deeded to such families as Delano, Hathaway, Nye, Taber, and Church and became the center of the future Fairhaven.

The American Revolution had a lasting effect on the people of Fairhaven, causing the first real crack in the unity between Fairhaven and New Bedford. The two communities reacted very differently to British harassment of their ships at sea and their loss of offshore fishing and foreign trade. The general sentiment of Quaker-dominated New Bedford was one of nonaggression, while Fairhaven was a hotbed of zealous patriots and active privateersmen. Fairhaven seamen went forth to do battle, curtail British shipping, and benefit from the spoils of privateering. They were so successful that on September 5, 1778, the British, tired of their many losses at the hands of the Fairhaven ships, attacked the harbor, landing first on the New Bedford side and burning Bedford Village, then crossing over and destroying and burning much of Fairhaven. (see #11)

Following the war, limited prosperity returned to the town. With the building of a bridge c.1796 between Fairhaven and New Bedford the main waterfront activities shifted from Oxford Village to "the center" wharves. Then at the outbreak of the War of 1812 political differences were so strong between the two towns (Fairhaven for the Jefferson Embargoes and New Bedford against) that Fairhaven was set off as a separate town February 22, 1812.

Between 1815 and 1876 five hundred whalers sailed from Fairhaven in search of the elusive yet profitable whale. Prosperity came to the town, streets were laid out, banks opened, and a railroad was built between Fairhaven and Tremont.

Whaling Captain William H. Whitfield,* through a compassionate act, brought fame to Fairhaven and a lasting friendship between his hometown and Japan. In 1841 he rescued Manjiro Nakahama,* a Japanese boy of fifteen, from an island in the China Sea. He befriended the boy and brought him back to Fairhaven where he educated him and treated him like a son. In later years Nakahama returned to Japan. During Commodore Perry's visit in 1853 Nakahama acted as interpreter and helped to bring about the successful opening of Japanese trade with the world. Because a Fairhaven captain cared, two nations met, ideas were exchanged, cultures were enriched, and an enduring friendship was formed.

The drilling of the first successful oil well in 1859 along with the Civil War and other factors brought to an end the prosperous whaling industry. For Fairhaven this discovery was to prove a special blessing. The finding of oil awakened the intellectual and business curiosity of young Henry Huttleston Rogers.* In 1861 Rogers went to Pennsylvania to learn the oil business. Following a series of partnerships and mergers, Rogers joined the Standard Oil organization becoming a vice-president and director. He soon sat on the board of directors of many of the major corporations of his time becoming a multimillionaire. Yet with all his success, he never forgot his hometown and returned here regularly for peace and renewal. (see #9)

Today Fairhaven is a warm friendly place to live. Town industries provide employment; the waterfront is busy servicing, repairing, and unloading fishing vessels; and her people, rich in Yankee, Portuguese, Scandinavian, Polish, Canadian, and English background and tradition, work together in common unity for this historic seafaring town they are proud to call home.

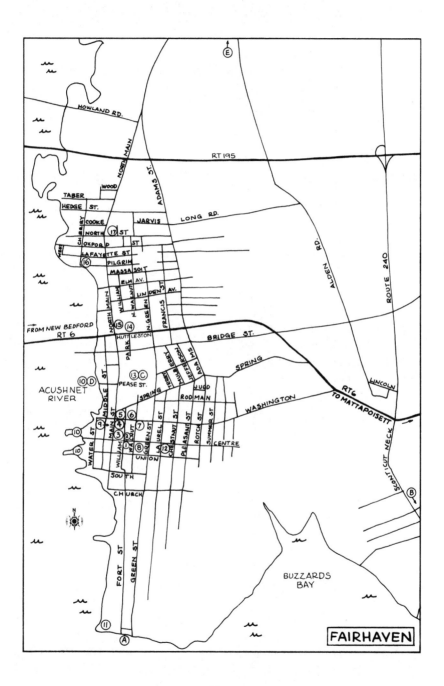

FAIRHAVEN

51

FAIRHAVEN

DIRECTIONS:
Enter Fairhaven by way of Route 6 over the bridge from New Bedford.

#1
Millicent Library
Centre and William Streets
1893
Open all year, no fee

After crossing the bridge on Route 6 into Fairhaven, take second right on Main Street; follow Main Street to Centre Street. Turn left on Centre and go one block to the Millicent Library on the corner of Centre and William Streets. Park your car in this area. Points of interest #1-8 can best be seen on foot.

The Millicent Library is best described by its well-known admirer, Mark Twain: "Books are the liberated spirits of men, and should be bestowed in a heaven of light and grace and harmonious color and sumptuous comfort, like this . . ."[1] So spoke Twain to the trustees of the library in a letter which is part of the extensive collection of Mark Twain letters and manuscripts housed here.

The Millicent Library, designed by noted Boston architect Charles Brigham, was built by Henry Huttleston Rogers and given to the town of Fairhaven by his children in memory of their sister, Millicent. (see #9) It is a masterpiece of Italian Renaissance architecture, rough-cut granite shaping the asymmetrical mass, with projecting yet incorporated towers and conical forms. The strength is refined by decorative bas-relief symbols and swags.

The interior is lavish and warmly inviting. Marble statuary, paintings, and etchings are among the museum-quality treasures found here. An example is Albert Bierstadt's "Martha Simon," the portrait of the last Wampanoag Indian; a deep and moving study in facial expression telling a life story.

Signatures of every United States president are in the priceless collection of letters, state papers, and signed photographs begun by Fairhaven's Delano* family, ancestors of President Franklin Delano Roosevelt. The Mark Twain Collection of manuscripts and letters is

52

Millicent Library

augmented by a memorial tablet with his famous epigram: "Always do right. You will gratify some people and astonish the rest."[2] A unique display of Japanese gifts is doubly valued as symbolic of the often-renewed and still strong ties with Japan, which began with the rescue in 1841 of a Japanese fisherman. (see history) Papers, portraits, and other treasures of the generous Rogers family are evident.

#2
Fairhaven Town Hall
Centre Street
1894
Open all year, no fee

The Town Hall is across Centre Street from the Millicent Library.

The Town Hall, another generous Rogers gift, is one of Fairhaven's imposing public buildings which form the ordered, stately town center. The breathtaking French-Gothic structure was designed by architect Charles Brigham and given to the town in 1894 by Abbie Palmer Gifford Rogers, wife of Henry Huttleston Rogers.* A friend of the Rogers, Mark Twain,* gave the dedication speech, and this master of words concluded that this building best speaks for itself.

The exterior, with fascinating irregular outline, is composed of turrets and towers, hips and ridges, pillars and balustrades, with windows grouped and individual, rectangular and arched, stained and plain. This remarkable effect is created with ashlar granite, Red Beach granite, Delmonico Brick, terra-cotta ornamentation, tile, red slate, and copper.

The surprisingly symmetrical interior features polished, carved quartered oak, a great double staircase, gleaming stained and leaded glass, and much brass and bronze. The active business of the town is carried out against this magnificent architectural backdrop.

#3
First Congregational
Church
Centre and William Streets
1794, 1844
Open for services

The First Congregational Church is across William Street from the Town Hall.

Here stands a mighty brick fortress to God, the fruits of Fairhaven's first congregation. This Gothic style church has a central tower entranceway flanked by windows composed of hundreds of diamond shaped panes which direct the eye heavenward. Inside, the elaborately carved mahogany pews and pulpit, the light-brown walls made to look like blocks of cut stone, and the interior buttresses which appear to streak across the ceiling, all combine to give the feeling of reverence and spiritual renewal.

Prior to 1794 the only church in the area was in Acushnet, then part of New Bedford. As more families moved into Fairhaven they sought a church nearer their own homes. Consequently on July 23, 1794, twenty-six members founded the Second Church of Christ in New Bedford here in Fairhaven. Symbolically, they built their first building, high on a ledge on Main and Centre Streets where its bell rang out over the community for all to hear. In 1809, causing great controversy, they showed their progressive spirit by allowing women to take part in the calling of a new minister. The year 1811 saw dissension when a group broke away to form the Third Church. But ties were strong, and by 1820 the two groups had reunited. They again survived a split in 1841 when members left to form the Centre Congregational Church.

1845 witnessed the dedication of the present brick edifice, which became the First Congregational Church in Fairhaven. This beautiful Gothic church was originally erected with its hundred-foot steeple dramatically pointing skyward. Its light served as a guide for mariners, until it was destroyed during a vicious southeast gale in 1869.

#4   *The Sawin-Howland-Grinnell Mansion is*
Sawin-Howland-Grinnell   *one block north on the corner of William*
Mansion   *and Washington Streets.*
44 William Street
1841–1844
Private
NRHP

This impressive, beautifully restored Greek Revival mansion was the first of Fairhaven's grand mansions, one of the few to survive. It was completed in 1844 for Ezekiel Sawin, ships' chandler, agent, and first president of the National Bank of Fairhaven. In 1867 it was purchased by Weston Howland, remaining in the Howland family for a century, until purchased by Mr. and Mrs. Peter Grinnell.

The magnificent mansion was possibly designed by Boston architect Isaiah Rogers. Three stories tall, with shiplap boarding, it is nearly surrounded by an impressive portico supported by twenty-two Ionic columns. Broad pilasters and Greek wreaths ornament the exterior. Each story is recessed, with the third-floor monitor roof capping the balustraded second-floor roof, a design which required over 650 feet of gutters! The mansion was featured in the classic 1921 movie, *Down to the Sea in Ships.*

#5   *Continue on William Street, crossing*
Sawin Hall   *Washington Street. The fourth building*
Advent Church   *on the left is Sawin Hall.*
52 William Street
c.1850s
Open as Grange Hall

This unassuming Greek Revival hall has been the setting for varied, unusual activities. Built in the 1850s, it hosted entertainments such as circus sideshows and magicians and, from 1859 to 1864, fiery town meetings. Circa 1866 the Adventists began seventy-five years of worship here.

A most forceful personality, sea captain Joseph Bates was raised in Fairhaven and is credited with being cofounder of Seventh Day Adventism and founder of Fairhaven's Temperance Society. He became part of William Miller's (see #6) Second Advent group believing that the second coming of Christ would occur between 1843 and 1844. After experiencing deep disappointment when the expected date passed, Elder Bates focused on keeping the commandments, particularly the sabbath, which led to his part in founding the Seventh Day Adventists.

This hardy sea captain–reformer demonstrated the courage of his convictions when he put to sea without the usual supply of rum considered essential. To a crew who were strangers to him, he announced his new rules of the voyage: no spirits, no leave on Sunday, no swearing, no nicknames, regular holy book readings and worship services. The peaceful voyage testifies to the strength of this man.

#6
Boys Club of Fairhaven
Washington Street
Christian Church
Walnut and Washington
Streets
1832
Open for club activities

Return on William Street to Washington Street. Turn left on Washington and go one block to the Boys Club on the corner of Walnut and Washington Streets.

This building, now serving as home to Fairhaven Boys Club, is the shell of a once beautiful church edifice built by the Washington Street Christian Church. In earlier days a series of six windows allowed light into a reverent sanctuary. The church originally supported a two-tier bell tower adding grace and continuity to the building.

The history of this church dates to 1819 when a group, opposed to the strong Calvinistic views of the day, met and formed their own Christian Church under Elder Moses Howe. Using the Bible as their authority, they followed Unitarian doctrine and Baptist practices. The following year the church was formally organized with Elder Charles Morgridge their first ordained minister. In 1832 members met at Captain Warren Delano's home to raise money to build this, their first church building, at a cost of $4800.

In 1841 Elder William Miller,* a strong supporter of the Second Advent doctrine, gave a series of sermons which resulted in a doctrinal split within the church. Following his sermons thirty-three members left to form the Second Advent Society. (see #5) Three years later the remaining members of the Washington Street Christian Church took a stand for Unitarianism.

In 1901 ground was broken for the new Unitarian Memorial Church built by Henry H. Rogers on Green and Centre Streets. (see #8) Mr. Rogers had the old church remodeled for use as an elementary school. It was recently further adapted, in its continuing cycle of serving people, for use as a boys club.

#7
Captain Warren Delano
Estate
39, 41-43 Walnut Street
Washington Street
1835
Private

Diagonally across the street from the Boys Club are the three houses which originally formed the Delano Estate. They face on Washington and Walnut Streets. Turn right on Walnut Street.

The Delano* family owned this estate for over 110 years. Their ancestry is traced to the first Delanos who bought lots in the initial subdivision of Fairhaven Center in 1760. From the beginning Delanos have had a strong positive influence on the town of Fairhaven.

The patriarch of the Delano estate was Captain Warren Delano, born in Fairhaven in 1779. He went to sea at nineteen, was twice captured by the British, and retired at thirty-six after captaining vessels that traveled the world. He became a successful merchant, trader, and local town leader and was instrumental in building the Washington Street Christian Church. (see #6)

In 1835 Captain Delano began building the Delano Estate, creating an impressive meandering Greek Revival home, which included three buildings. The house at 39 Walnut Street was the front section; the building now at 41-43 Walnut was the center section; and the building now facing Washington Street was the rear section. The sections were separated in 1942 and moved to their present locations where they serve today as separate homes. Note the matching Palladian windows in the different sections and the columned Greek Revival front portico capped by balustrades.

Captain Warren and his wife, Deborah Church, had eight children. Warren Jr. was the only one to marry. His daughter, Sara, became the mother of thirty-second president, Franklin Delano Roosevelt. Franklin spent many happy hours here in his mother's childhood home. Warren Jr. carried on the family name and business abilities, obtaining great wealth through the lucrative China trade.

Unitarian Memorial Church

#8
Unitarian Memorial
Church Complex
Walnut, Centre, Green, and
Union Streets
1904
Open for services

Continue south on Walnut Street to Centre Street. The entire block enclosed by Walnut, Centre, Green, and Union Streets encompasses the Unitarian Church Complex.

The Unitarian Church is a granite tower of love showing a man's dedication to his faith and his devotion to his mother. Henry Huttleston Rogers* gave this beautiful fifteenth-century English Gothic-style church complex as a memorial to his mother, Mary Eldredge Huttleston Rogers. His close friend, Mark Twain, was one of the speakers when the church was dedicated October 4, 1904.

This magnificent cathedral, equal to any in Europe, is done in the perpendicular style. The bell tower is 165 feet high, supporting eleven bells, weighing 14,000 pounds, which send their sweet "D" chimes out over the neighborhood, calling the faithful to worship. The exterior of the building is granite from Rogers's estate, with the decorative areas royal blue Indiana limestone. Elaborate carvings by Italian artisans symbolizing Scriptural people and events adorn the exterior, along with pinnacles and flying buttresses, which combine in perfect harmony.

The interior is equally beautiful, creating a sense of beauty and spiritual peace. The walls are of soft buff Indiana limestone, the floors of Italian marble, and the woodwork of bog oak from the Black Forest intricately carved by Bavarian craftsmen. Everywhere you look— woodwork, stonework, stained-glass windows—you see symbols of Biblical personages, scriptural teachings, and the life of Christ. The windows, by Robert Reid of New York, illustrate teachings of Christ both individually and collectively. Starting at the front of the church with the Nativity scene, the emphasis is on the light coming from the Christ child which lights up the deep blue of the night sky. The colors then move from the deeper blues through the nine Beatitude windows, gradually lightening until they burst forth in the glowing colors of day and the Sermon on the Mount window. Notice how Christ appears to be giving his benediction to the church's own congregation.

This beautiful cathedral was one of Rogers' last major donations to the hometown he loved so well. His generosity serves as his own perpetual memorial.

#9
Henry Huttleston Rogers's
Boyhood Home
39 Middle Street
c. 1840
Private

Return to your car. Drive west on Centre Street two blocks to Middle Street and turn right. Notice on the far corner at 28 Middle Street the plain Federal square, with its Georgian overtones, built c.1830 by Ezekiel Sawin who later built #4. Henry H. Rogers's home is near the end of the block on the right at 39 Middle Street.

Henry Huttleston Rogers* was born during the Whaling Era, when all energies worked together for the pursuit of the mighty whale, whose oil was the Midas-like source of Fairhaven's and New Bedford's prosperity. Ironically Henry Rogers would help bring the prosperous whaling era to an end and yet begin another era that would affect the economy of the world, the personal results of which would prove to be Fairhaven's greatest blessing.

Henry was born January 29, 1840, to Mary Huttleston and Rowland Rogers. He grew up in Fairhaven, instilled with Yankee values of thrift, practicality, and hard work. After graduating with the first graduating class of the high school, he worked in his father's store, delivered papers, and was a baggage master and brakeman for the Old Colony Railroad. This last job gave him an income of $1.16 per day—an unpretentious beginning for a future multimillionaire.

In 1859 the success of the first drilled oil well sparked Rogers's imagination. In 1861 he joined fellow Fairhavenite Charles H. Ellis in Titusville, Pennsylvania, near which they established an oil refining company. He encountered new and unfamiliar ways of life—ones of loose living, get-rich-quick schemes, crooked deals, and intense competition. In reaction, he developed practical, exacting, shrewd—sometimes secretive—business skills, which guided his business dealings the rest of his life.

In 1862 he married his childhood sweetheart, Abbie Palmer Gifford, and returned to Titusville, where they settled down to the exciting world of oil. He quickly moved from a partnership with Ellis to one with Charles H. Pratt (later founder of Pratt Institute, Brooklyn, New York), in which they made Pratt Refinery one of the most successful in the country in 1874.

During this time, John D. Rockefeller entered the oil business in Ohio. Rockefeller soon saw the advantages of a monopoly and began buying, or merging with, other oil refineries to form the powerful Standard Oil Company.

At first Rogers encouraged others to stand strong against Standard Oil, but by late 1874, seeing the writing on the wall, Pratt and Rogers merged with Standard Oil. Rogers emerged vice-president of their United Pipe Lines. By 1890 he was a vice-president and member of the board of directors of the mighty Standard Oil Trust.

Ever seeking additional financial horizons, he later joined William Rockefeller and James Stillman (President of National City Bank of New York) to become the financial powers behind Union Pacific, Santa Fe, and Lackawanna railroads, Anaconda Copper Company, and the United States Steel Corporation. Rogers also established the Consolidated Gas Company and Virginia Railroad, ultimately holding corporate positions in over twenty-one companies and corporations throughout the country. This was his business world.

His domestic world was best seen in Fairhaven, which held his happiest memories and served as his sanctuary from the world of business. At his eighty-five room mansion on Fort Street, he spent pleasant, relaxed hours with his wife and five children. To this beloved town he was a golden benefactor. He gave the Rogers grammar school in 1885, the Millicent Memorial Library* in 1893, and founded the Fairhaven Water Company with all stock assigned to the library to provide a continuous income. He gave the Town Hall* in 1894. He added to and improved the city's streets at his own cost while Superintendent of Streets in 1895. He created Cushman Park* in 1903. In 1904 he gave the high school and the Unitarian Church Complex.* He also donated the old Bank of Commerce building in New Bedford, which now serves as part of the Whaling Museum.* He built a business block in Fairhaven center which includes the George H. Taber Masonic Lodge, named for a lifelong friend. In addition his will provided trust funds to support many of these gifts.

People were also important to Rogers. He was benefactor and close friend to Mark Twain,* whom he guided from financial ruin to financial security. He contributed to Helen Keller's Radcliffe education and continued to help her throughout her life. He strongly supported Booker T. Washington.

Henry Huttleston Rogers faced life as if he were involved in a life-size game of Monopoly. The game itself—the financial wheeling-dealing and matching of power, shrewdness, and intellect—was as important to him as the final victory. He played with great intensity, practicality, and seriousness—yet once victorious, he became a man of enormous generosity.

#10
Waterfront–Fairhaven
Center
Water Street
Access: end of Pease,
Union, and Ferry Streets

Cross the next street, Washington Street, and drive one-half block to Pease Street to free public parking and launching area on the left, which gives public access to the river. Exit right from parking area, going south on Middle Street. Take first right on Water Street, then turn left for access to commercial wharves—Mullins (Old North), Kelly (Old South), Union, and Hathaway-Braley.

Visit the waterfront and let yourself be engulfed in the sea's aura and excitement that has existed here since the late 1700s. During the early whaling days, whale blubber was brought back to port, where the oil was extracted in tryworks on Old North Wharf (Mullins Wharf), then owned by Richard Delano. Soon larger ships were built with tryworks aboard, and Fairhaven men were sailing the seven seas for months and years at a time in search of the profitble whale. From 1830 to 1857

Fairhaven's economy was dependent on whaling from the building and servicing of ships to the selling of whale oil and whale bone and their many by-products.

The discovery of oil in Pennsylvania and the Civil War radically changed the waterfront scene from whalers lining docks piled with barrels of whale oil to wharves busy with fishing boats unloading their catch for processing. S. P. Dunn promoted Fairhaven's fledgling fishing industry in 1868 by setting out weirs, or pounds, which soon brought in more than a million pounds of fish annually. David Kelly bought the Old South Wharf where he introduced the complete fishing business from catch through curing and packaging. The waterfront successfully survived the transition from whaling to fishing.

Today along the waterfront scallopers, draggers, and quahogers laden with a fresh catch tie up to unload; the sound of machinery repairing and servicing ships is in the air; the smell of fish permeates your thoughts; and you are caught up in the age-old world of the fisherman.

#11
Fort Phoenix
Fort Street
1777
Open all year, no fee
NRHP

From Water Street turn left on Union Street; go one block to Middle Street. Near the corner of Middle and Union Streets is an old wooden structure—the remains of the Old Pump, *where whalesmen of old came to fill casks for their long sea adventures. Continue on Union Street one block to Main Street. Turn right, follow Main around a sharp left-hand curve (away from water) to Fort Street, the first right, and turn right. Drive along Fort Street .2 mile and you will see the* Candleworks Building *on the right, which is part of Fairhaven Marine at 50 Fort Street. Though it looks sad and neglected now, when built in the 1800s this rough, square stone building represented one of the first industries in town, that of candlemaking. Continue .4 mile south on Fort Street to Fort Phoenix. Notice the lovely old carefully restored homes on the way.*

Peaceful and serene now, Fort Phoenix still commands the harbor from its vantage atop natural granite ledges. With cannons still poised, ready to defend Fairhaven against unwanted invaders, the ancient fort

Fort Phoenix

stands in fascinating contrast with its massive twentieth-century neighbor, the Hurricane Barrier. (see New Bedford #15) The unobstructed panoramic view sweeps from Fairhaven wharves, the Acushnet River and inner harbor, Butler's Flats Light,* the New Bedford coastline, and Fort Taber, across Buzzards Bay to the Elizabeth Islands and Cape Cod, and east to Sconticut Neck, Fairhaven.

This commanding fort was built in the vicinity of an ancient fort which predated 1762. Fort Phoenix was completed in 1777 to protect the entrance to the important Acushnet River during the Revolution. Constructed of the granite on which it stands, it was manned by thirty-eight patriots. Eleven cannon were acquired, some from a supply surrendered during an engagement in which John Paul Jones took part. Thus Jones appropriately aided the defense of the harbor into which he occasionally brought his captured prize ships.

In September, 1778, the harbor was overwhelmingly assaulted by the British, under Major General Charles Grey, in retaliation for the heavy losses inflicted by local Colonial privateersmen. A frigate, a brig, and thirty-six troop transports carrying British and mercenary Hessian soldiers ruthlessly leveled much of New Bedford's waterfront and caused considerable damage in Fairhaven. Finally a daring rally led by Major Israel Fearing* prevented further havoc, and the British left the harbor, though not before severely damaging the fort.

In Buzzards Bay, during the unsettled times of the War of 1812, enemy ships were constantly sighted, especially the dreaded British *Nimrod*. Strategically placed Fort Phoenix remained a tower of strength protecting the harbor.

Though reactivated and modified during the Civil War, Fort Phoenix saw no enemy action and was finally deactivated in 1876. It was purchased by the town of Fairhaven in 1925 with funds provided by Henry Huttleston Rogers's daughter, Mrs. Urban H. Broughton of England, Lady Fairhaven.

#12
Our Lady's Haven
Tabitha Inn
71 Centre Street
1904–1905
Open as home for elderly

Exit from Fort parking area and turn right; go one block to Green Street and entrance to Phoenix Beach. Turn left and drive back on Green Street to Centre Street (Unitarian church on corner) and turn right. Go one block to Our Lady's Haven on the right.

Great architecture is supposed to adapt to change gracefully and this theory is beautifully proven here. In 1904 Henry Huttleston Rogers* began the Tabitha Inn, which was designed by Charles Brigham and named for Rogers's maternal great-grandmother. It flourished as a first-class resort hotel until 1942, when it housed Coast Guard trainees. Since 1944 it has been Our Lady's Haven, a healing, devoted home for elderly. Its early elegant opulence flourishes in its new use, with impressive parlor now a graceful chapel, and museum-quality original light fixtures, table lamps, and much of the early furnishings preserved.

The Elizabethan design is reminiscent of the hostelry of Shakespeare's England, when U-shaped buildings formed inn-yard stages for traveling actors. The massive brick structure, trimmed with limestone and timbered with cypress, is symmetrical and features many large gables, conical towers, and tall chimneys. The stained glass contains representations to demonstrate old hostelry hospitality.

#13
Cushman Park
Main, Bridge, Green,
Spring Streets
1903–1908
Open year round, no fee

Return on Centre Street to Green Street and turn right. Follow Green to Bridge Street and turn left; go one block to Cushman Park. Facilities: band shell, playgrounds, rest rooms, tennis.

Looking at the open park, you find it hard to visualize this land before the twentieth century and Henry Huttleston Rogers.* Fed by Herring River it was once a naturally formed, protected harbor of over ten acres, which could snugly lay up vessels of seventy tons. When the town built Main Street, in 1795, a bridge was built which cut off access by masted ships. Gradually the pond became choked with mud, eel-filled, marshy, and offensive.

This grim scene violently contrasted with the magnificent buildings given by Rogers. In 1903 he remedied the situation with the creation of Cushman Park. Rogers liked to tell the story of himself as a child being admonished by a passerby to refrain from throwing stones into the pond, "For thee will fill it up!"[3] So, many years later, for the further improvement of Fairhaven, he did indeed "fill it up!"

The nearly overwhelming project took almost six years, requiring an average of fifty men working each day. A street and twenty-five houses had to be elevated. So much fill was required that a small railroad about a mile long was constructed from the pond to the fill source. It carried thirteen trainloads of fill a day, every day, for two years!

#14
Fairhaven High School
Rogers Memorial
Huttleston Avenue, Route 6
1904
Open as high school

Leave car and walk up Park Street one block to Route 6 and look across at the high school.

Fairhaven High School is one of the boldly designed, solidly constructed, magnificent gifts of Henry Huttleston Rogers* to his beloved town of Fairhaven. Benefactor extraordinaire, Rogers was not content to merely supply the town with outstanding public buildings, he also sustained a deep interest in each project.

He was especially concerned with education. Rogers actively participated in the two years of educational and architectural planning for this high school, supplemented the incomes of several highly favored educators to obtain them for Fairhaven, and provided facilities, such as the extensive laboratory equipment, which are extravagent even by today's standards and still in use here. The study hall was made especially beautiful at Rogers' request to motivate juniors and seniors, whose homeroom it was, to remain to graduate. No detail escaped him. During the final days of construction, when he discovered the auditorium had not received the chairs designed for it, he acted immediately. Through several hours of phoning, he located the chairs on a railroad siding in the south, cleared the tracks for the special train he arranged to collect them, and had workers busy from Saturday through midnight Sunday installing them for Monday's dedication.

Architecturally, the structure is an Elizabethan masterpiece of granite-ashlar quarried from Fairhaven's Fort Phoenix ledge, surmounted by limestone and brick, and capped by a thirty-five-foot turret containing a four-faced clock. Porches, terraces, archways, marble pillars, red-tiled floors, quartered oak paneling, stained glass, and elaborate ceilings abound.

The *Henry Huttleston Rogers Monument* was erected by the citizens of Fairhaven in 1912. In 1965 it was moved here to the grounds of the Fairhaven High School. The appropriate Latin inscription translates: "If you would seek his monument—look around you."

#15
Fairhaven Academy
Building
Main Street
1798
Open, contact Millicent
Library for appointment
HABS

Turn right on Bridge Street, go ¹/₂ block to Main Street and turn right. Follow Main Street across Route 6 to the Academy Building on the right just past high school.

Fairhaven Academy, the town's first school of higher education, was a "Gentlemen's School," preparing pupils for Harvard and Yale. In 1907 the building was purchased and moved to this location by Henry H. Rogers.*

The eye-catching two-story shingle structure is graced by an interesting fanlight over the front entry, capped by a bell tower, and features an original schoolroom complete with old benches, desks, school bell, and teacher's elevated platform. Once the scene of social and political gatherings, the Academy Building now includes a collection of authentic Colonial Period spinning wheels, furniture, clocks, and trunks.

#16
John Cooke and Joshua
Slocum Memorials
Pilgrim Street
Open all year, no fee

Continue on Main Street; take third left on Pilgrim Street. At the bend in the road on the right are the two memorials.

Cooke Memorial: Fairhaven owes much to her founder and early leader, the Reverend John Cooke,* who came to the New World at age fifteen aboard the *Mayflower.* He grew up in Plymouth, where surprisingly he followed the Baptist faith. He was respected as an individual, serving as deputy to the General Court, but not as a Baptist minister. In 1652 he joined in purchasing land ultimately including Fairhaven. Acting as clerk he signed the deed along with John Winslow and Chief Wamsutta.*

In the 1660s, Cooke and his family left Plymouth and settled here along the Acushnet River. He served as agent and magistrate and representative to the General Court, and built a garrison to protect the settlers during King Philip's War. (plaque on Howland Road) The Reverend Cooke planted seeds of moral strength and integrity deep in this fertile land, and from them Fairhaven has grown.

Slocum Memorial: Here beside the calm waters of the Acushnet River, Captain Joshua Slocum rebuilt the thirty-seven-foot, nine-ton sloop *Spray,* given to him by Captain Eben Pierce of Fairhaven. When all was in readiness he sailed her to Boston. On April 24, 1895, leaving Boston Harbor, he headed out alone across the Atlantic Ocean and around the world on what would become a three-year historic voyage, making him the first person to circumnavigate the globe alone. The courage, excitement, and endurance of his trip can be experienced in reading his personal account, *Sailing Alone Around the World.*

Ironically, this ship which brought him fame would also carry him on his final voyage. At age sixty-five he again set sail alone aboard the *Spray,* heading for the Orinoco River in Venezuela. The voyage was never completed. The sea he loved so well became his final resting-place.

#17
Old Oxford Stone
Schoolhouse
North Street
1828
Open by appointment,
contact Millicent Library

Return to Main Street, turn left, go three blocks to North Street and turn right. The schoolhouse is at the end of the first block on the left.

This unusual stone schoolhouse was the first public school in Fairhaven. Now painted white, with plain rectangular windows and hip roof, the Old Oxford Stone Schoolhouse has been carefully restored by the Fairhaven Historical Society and is under the supervision of the Fairhaven Historical Commission.

This ends the guided tour section of Fairhaven. Follow Main Street back to Route 6 and turn left to continue tour to Mattapoisett.

Fairhaven Beaches and Parks and Additional Points of Interest

(A) **Fort Phoenix Beach State Reservation End of Green Street (south end)**

Open sandy beach, panoramic water vista; facilities: bathhouses, ice skating, lifeguards, picnicking, swimming, tennis; ample parking; open all year, no fee

(B) **West Island Beach End of Sconticut Neck and Island Causeway off Bass Creek Road**

Sandy beach, huge panoramic view of distant islands and Dartmouth, Mattapoisett, and Marion shores; watch parade of passing ships; parking; seasonally restricted to residents; open off season, no fee

(C) **Cushman Park (See #13) Access Park Avenue**

Open green space; facilities: band shell, playground, rest rooms, tennis; open all year, no fee

(D) **Pease Park Fairhaven Harbor off Middle Street**

View of New Bedford; boat launching ramp; parking; open all year, no fee

(E) **Fairhaven Doll Museum 384 Alden Road**

Heaven for doll fanciers, interesting museum home to over 450 dolls; doll hospital services provided; occasional duplications available for sale; all antique dolls; open all year, limited hours or by appointment; fee

HISTORY OF MATTAPOISETT, MARION, AND WAREHAM

Mattapoisett, Marion, and Wareham stand put as three polished diamonds in the crown of Buzzards Bay. Each adds its own particular luster and radiance, yet they share common ancestral bonds and filial ties. The ever-present aura of historic New England seems to speak to you as you wander the roads and byways of these history-laden towns.

Prior to the white man's coming, Sippican Indians of the Wampanoag Tribe freely roamed this area, and their main village was located where today is found the town of Marion. Between 1679 and 1682 a group of Proprietors purchased Sippican lands between Plymouth and the Fairhaven settlement, which today include Mattapoisett, Marion, and Wareham. In 1686 the area was set off as the town of Rochester, named for Rochester, England.

In Rochester, as in many other New England towns, life centered around God and meetinghouse. The initial preacher, Mr. Samuel Shiverick, held services outside, on what is now Minister's Rock* in Marion. Their first real meetinghouse was erected on Rochester Common, officially organizing under the Reverend Samuel Arnold in 1703. Over the years this mother church grew, was rebuilt, and divided, giving new spiritual life to four separate offsprings—Mattapoisett in 1736, Wareham in 1739, North Rochester in 1753, and Sippican (Marion) in 1798.

During the early 1700s, homesteads were scattered throughout the area, with small villages at Mattapoisett, Sippican, Rochester Common, and Wareham. The economy was based on farming, lumbering, local fishing, and grist and fulling mills. By the mid-1700s the annual herring run was adding variety to farmers' tables, and shipbuilding and coastal and foreign trade opened new horizons to these self-reliant pioneers. As the shadows of the American Revolution drew closer, the young colonists supported the cause of freedom. Local sea captains, whose economy depended on open ports and unencumbered trade, entered the patriotic, prosperous, and dangerous world of privateering. Every British ship captured aided the Revolutionary cause and reaped large financial rewards for the privateersmen.

Following the temporary decline brought on by the Revolutionary War and the War of 1812, the indomitable New England spirit of these villagers again emerged to create an even better economy during the first half of the 1800s. The whaling era, with all its supporting industries, was upon them. Their shipyards built brigs, sloops, schooners, and barks with some of the finest whalers in the world built at Mattapoisett. Salt marshes were alive with windmills pumping seawater to the many salt works, producing as much as 20,000 bushels of salt in one year. Wareham's natural bog ore formed the basis of her iron industry, and nail manufacturing produced a prosperous economy.

These were good times for seacoast towns whose docks were but stepping stones to every port-of-call throughout the world. Many a youth left these wharves to return a tried and tested mate or captain, molded and strengthened by the unbending laws of the sea. This independent, self-sufficient spirit began to be felt in the villages, inspiring individual autonomy. Wareham was incorporated in 1739. In 1852 Sippican became the town of Marion, named for their southern hero, Swamp Fox General Francis Marion. Mattapoisett became an independent town in 1857.

The removal of duty on foreign salt and the introduction of canning methods, gold fever, the advent of railroads, the Civil War, depletion of bog ore to make iron, and the decline of whaling in the mid-1800s all combined to undermine the economy. A new and different life-style awaited Marion, Mattapoisett, and Wareham. With improved transportation, these towns became havens for summer residents, and real estate values began to climb during the late 1800s. The roads became busy with summer visitors from all over the country coming to enjoy the peaceful atmosphere, beautiful beaches, and summer recreation. Pleasure craft and small fishing boats filled the harbors.

Along with beach lovers came people of the arts and literary world seeking an atmosphere of creative renewal and compatible hospitality. Each town had its special summer residents. Oliver Wendell Holmes and Edward Atkinson summered in Mattapoisett, Daniel Webster and Rufus Choate in Wareham, and Marion was twice blessed. In the 1870s Elizabeth Sprague Pitcher Taber* returned to her hometown. The unusual vitality of this eighty-year-old lady benefactor resulted in a new town library, Congregational chapel, town hall, Tabor Academy, and Music Hall, as well as the future beautification of the town. Also came four personages who set the social and intellectual climate for more than a decade: President and Mrs. Grover Cleveland* and Mr. and Mrs. Richard Watson Gilder,* he a poet and editor of *Century Magazine* and she an artist. Soon young talents such as Ethel Barrymore, Richard Harding Davis,* Charles Dana Gibson,* and Henry James were sharing their interests and enthusiasm with the people of Marion, creating a unique, inviting atmosphere.

These differing eras of the past still have a positive, continuing influence on Mattapoisett, Marion, and Wareham, which are now modern, peaceful, productive coastal towns. Here you still encounter the timelessness of salt air and balmy days and the ever-changing shoreline sometimes lost in the morning mist or magnificently outlined by brilliant sunlight or soft glow of moonlight.

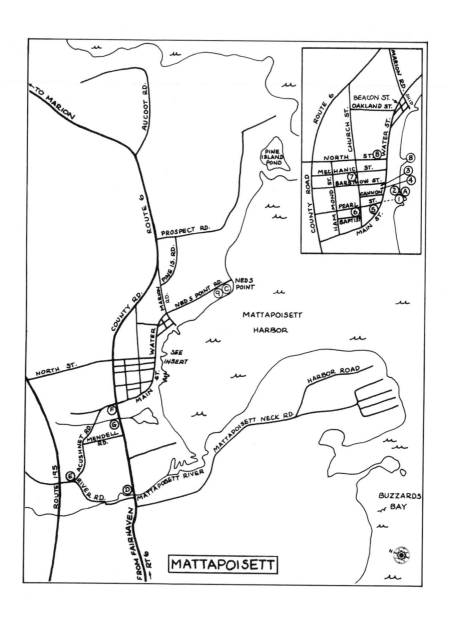

MATTAPOISETT

MATTAPOISETT

DIRECTIONS:
From Fairhaven follow Route 6 east into Mattaposiett. Continue on
Route 6 to Main Street.

#1
Town Wharf and Harbor
Water Street, at Cannon
Street
1700s
Open all year, seasonal
parking fee for
nonresidents

*Turn right on Main Street (traffic light).
Continue on Main which becomes Water
Street. Shortly after reaching the harbor
area, the entrance to Town Wharf is on the
right, opposite Cannon Street. Facilities:
boat berths and moorings, fishing, parking, rest rooms, square dancing in summer. Suggest parking here to see #1-8.*

The present Town Wharf is descended from Ebeneezer Cannon, Jr.'s
shipyard, built here in 1792. It was active until 1834, when the
Mattapoisett Wharf Company assumed ownership. Just west of this
site, during the late 1700s and early 1800s, the busy Barstow shipyards
launched some of the finest ships in all New England. Barstow and
Cannon were well respected along the New England coast as builders
of superior ships. It is believed over 150 vessels slid down the way at
Barstow yards, which was also home to the largest ship built in
Mattapoisett, the 650 ton *George Lee.*

Today the Town Wharf is still the center of marine activity. During
summer the wharf is a beehive of activity, servicing pleasure boats
from Florida to Canada, as well as Mattapoisett's fishing fleet. During
winter docks are almost silent, servicing only a few small fishing boats
covered with frozen salt spray and dusted with snow. The ice-covered
harbor is broken here and there by the trail of a determined fishing
boat.

On Saturday nights during the summer, the air is charged with the
toe-tapping sound of good country fiddling, and the dock is alive with
colorful square dancers. Every night an electric beacon shines over the
wharves, guiding late sailors into port.

#2
Shipyard Park
Water Street
1740–1878
Open all year, no fee

Walk from the wharves toward the lawn
area along the water with bandstand, flag-
pole, and large memorial rock. Facilities:
benches, summer concerts.

Mattapoisett may mean "place of rest," but during the 1800s it was home to some of the busiest and most talented of shipyards in New England. Along what is now Water Street dedicated craftsmen, using broadaxes, adzes, and whipsaws with the delicate touch of a surgeon, turned rough-cut lumber into the finest of whaling ships. While New Bedford was the leading whaling port, it was Mattapoisett's shipyards that supplied many of those ships which brought New Bedford her economic wealth and fame. In addition to whaling ships, Mattapoisett shipbuilders created superior barks, brigs, schooners, sloops, and merchant ships for almost every port on the New England coast and the European, Chinese, West Indies, and coastal trades.

It began here at the head of the harbor in 1752, when shipwright Charles Stetson from Scituate established the first shipyard. By the Revolutionary War, six shipbuilders had set up shipyards as far east as Ship Street. Here were three necessary ingredients for successful shipbuilding: a good harbor, a seemingly inexhaustible supply of virgin lumber, and nearby ports, such as Nantucket and New Bedford, eager to buy their products.

Shipyard Park marks the actual site of the Holmes Shipyard, established in 1812 by Josiah Holmes, Sr. In 1878 the bark *Wanderer* slid down the ways, marking the end of a vital era, for she was the last ship built in Mattapoisett.

In 1976 the Bicentennial Committee placed a plaque on a boulder in Shipyard Park to commemorate that earlier Mattapoisett. In those times, four hundred men worked in the shipyards; wagons loaded with lumber rumbled down the unpaved roads; the bowsprits of unfinished ships reached over the roadways; fifty whalers were launched between 1830 and 1840; and local business consisted of blacksmith shops, sail lofts, rope walks, and other supporting services. Sawdust was heavy in the air and days were counted by the launching of ships.

#3
Mattapoisett Inn
Water Street
c.1790s
Open as inn and restaurant

Across Water Street from Shipyard Park
is the inn.

This intriguing waterfront inn, with its warmly inviting tavern, dining rooms, and lodging, claims lineage back to the 1790s when Joseph Meigs built his home here. Meigs, a civic leader and shipyard master carpenter, operated the first tavern and general store on these premises.

At Joseph's death in 1846 the property descended to his son Loring Meigs, state representative, captain of Mattapoisett Guards, shipbuilder, and whaling vessel agent. It was his heavily laden whaleship, the *Joseph Meigs*, which spectacularly burned at anchor off Neds Point Light. That night, in 1846, exploding caskets of oil skyrocketed, flaming oil streamed in all directions, and the harbor glare was brighter than daylight.

The inn has been a home, tavern, general store, ship's chandlery, China-trade storehouse, and a speakeasy. One longtime occupant was Captain Charles Bryant, whaling captain and first governor of Alaska. It is said that here he worked long hours on memoirs that have yet to be found.

#4 **Francis Davis Millet** **Birthplace** **Water and Cannon Streets** **Private**	*As you leave the inn, turn right and walk along Water Street two houses to the Millet Birthplace on the near corner of Water and Cannon Streets.*

Here in this First Period style house, Francis Davis Millet was born in 1846. Millet was a drummer boy who became a noted war correspon-

Clamshell Alley

Authors

dent, author, artist, and illustrator. Tragically, he was lost when the *Titanic* went down on April 15, 1912. The house, which contained the first town library and later a post office, stands at the corner of Cannon Street. Picturesque Cannon Street was affectionately called Clamshell Alley, originally constructed of crushed clamshells thrown there by the inhabitants.

#5
Elijah Willis House
Corner Main and Pearl
Streets
1809
Private

Continue one more block on Water Street, which becomes Main Street, to the Willis House on the far corner of Main and Pearl Streets.

This large, quiet Federal, with crowning cupola, features an entranceway capped with elliptical light, and ells and carriage house extending in back.

A fascinating letter was found, written by Mrs. Elijah Willis, graphically describing the terror of the War of 1812 for those who lived near the sea. She recounted the *Nimrod** and other British ships kept all alert with shore guns of alarm frequently fired. Any man not already on duty raced to defend the harbor, while women alerted neighbors and gathered terrified children to seek safety.

#6
Mattapoisett Historical
Society Museum and
Carriage House
5 Church Street
1821
Open seasonally and by
appointment, fee charged

Turn right and walk up Pearl Street to Church Street and turn left for one block. The museum is on the near corner of Church and Baptist Streets.

The story of Mattapoisett is beautifully told here in two museums of this shipbuilding and farming town whose horizons extended to much of the world through whaling and trading. The Home and Whaling Museum is housed in the 1821 First Christian Meetinghouse, and the Farm and Country Museum is contained in the attached Carriage House. The restored white clapboard church is quietly Greek Revival, and the sturdy Carriage House is a replica of a 1700s barn, complete with huge white-pine timbers and broad haymows, serving as galleries.

The Historical Society's collections are extensive and varied. Deeds, commissions, ships' sailing papers, and vellum templates are signed by John Hancock, Justice Oliver Wendell Holmes, Henry Clay, John Q. Adams, James Monroe, and Andrew Jackson. The templates were actually proof that the United States had paid tribute to Barbary pirates. In those days pirates would halt a ship, board her, and capture or free her, depending upon the captain's producing one of these templates whose key matched the pirate's! Other interesting exhibits include treasures of the China trade, commemorative plates, half-models of ships built in Mattapoisett, marine prints, navigational instruments, scrimshaw, lacquer, silver, and sandwich glass.

The replica barn exhibit focuses on outdoor tools and activities as well as a 1700s cooking area complete with implements of all kinds, a spinning room with looms, carpenter's shop, and 1890 kitchen. A fascinating saltworks model demonstrates and explains the activity so common here when this area was a major salt producer.

#7
Fourth Meeting House
Barstow and Church
Streets
1703, 1736, 1842
Open for services and
church office hours

Continue on Church Street to the Meeting House on the corner of Barstow and Church Streets. Notice the school across the street. This was built for the town by millionaire Fairhaven-benefactor Henry Huttleston Rogers.*

Enter the sanctuary of Mattapoisett's fourth meetinghouse for a feeling of reverence. The light, open atmosphere inspires parishioners to be receptive to God's love and the needs of their fellow men.

To trace the congregation's history, you must go back to 1736 when settlers in Mattapoisett had grown tired of the long trek to the church on Rochester Common. To alleviate these arduous Sunday journeys, the Second Church of Rochester was established in Mattapoisett under the Reverend Elisha Tupper. In 1737 the first meetinghouse was built. It served until 1772 when twenty-four-year-old Reverend Lemuel LeBaron* was called as minister. He quickly won the enthusiastic support of his congregation. A new larger meetinghouse was begun, which served until destroyed by the 1815 hurricane. The Reverend LeBaron preached and lived the gospel of peace and love, strengthening and guiding his flock for sixty-four years.

During LeBaron's pastorate the congregation moved from the site of their first two meetinghouses to build in 1816 a third and even larger building on Route 6. (see F) The 1828 records of this third building give the first indication of any type of heating in Mattapoisett's meetinghouses. Fire and brimstone sermons must have kept the hardy congregation warm for the preceding 129 years.

By 1842 the congregation had again filled the meetinghouse to overflowing. Thus the Fourth Meeting House, designed by Solomon K. Eaton, was built. This large, white Greek Revival church, with cupola-styled bell tower and steeple, still serves Mattapoisett. At night the lighted steeple can be seen from the harbor and throughout the town. It seems to symbolize the constant protection and spiritual guidance that the church has given the area.

#8
R. L. Barstow House
North and Water Streets
c.1753
Private

Continue two blocks on Church Street to North Street, turn right, and walk one block to Water. The Barstow House is on the left corner of North and Water Streets.

Rogers L. Barstow, who built the present house, was considered a most important whaling agent in town, a business which he pursued from 1839 to 1860. Whalers regularly sailed from the wharf across the street. His fields overflowed with whaling-oriented necessities— masts, cordage, timber, anchors, chains, casks. Barstow's bakeshop and whaleboat shop provided for his fleet.

#9
Neds Point Lighthouse
Veterans Memorial Park
Neds Point Road
1837
Open all year, no fee

Return to your car, exit from wharf area. Turn right on Water Street and follow Water, which becomes Neds Point Road. Continue on Neds Point Road to the park at the end. Facilities: cook out and picnicking, fishing, open cabana, rest rooms, swimming; open all year, parking, no fee charged.

The whitewashed stone lighthouse, capped with black cupola and beacon light, stands on this open, rock-strewn shore, guarding Mattapoisett Harbor and welcoming home her sailors.

It was constructed in 1837 by versatile businessman Leonard Hammond, government lighthouse contractor, who ran a shipyard, the county house, a saltworks, and a coastwise trade. The story is told of his hasty preparations for a government inspector, including a

Neds Point Lighthouse

"friendly glass of rum" designed to take attention from unfinished areas. Unfortunately, the inspector fell through the improvised floor and had to be fished out! All survived, and the lighthouse was completed.

The light included a keeper's house until 1923 when the house was loaded onto a barge and floated across the bay to Wings Neck. Apparently the move included the keeper who even cooked his breakfast en route.

The picturesque expanse of land on which Neds Point Lighthouse stands overlooks a panoramic view of Mattapoisett, snugly nestled at the harbor base.

This ends the guided tour section of Mattapoisett. Take Neds Point Road back, taking the first right turn, and follow road to Route 6. Turn right on Route 6 to continue with Marion tour.

Mattapoisett Beaches and Parks and Additional Points of Interest

(A) Town Wharf* & Shipyard Park*
Water Street

Boat berths, benches, fishing, rest rooms, square dances, summer concerts, open all year, seasonal parking fee

(B) Mattapoisett Bathing Beach
Water Street at North Street

Bathhouse, cabana shelters, lifeguards, swimming, play ground, rest rooms, open all year, fee, seasonal parking fee

(C) Veterans Memorial Park
Neds Point Light*
Neds Point Road

Cookout and picnic facilities, fishing, open cabana, rest rooms, open all year, parking, no fee

(D) Herring Weir
Route 6 and River Road
Open all year, active
March and April no fee

Early spring scene of wild activity; thousands of herring fight way up river to spawning grounds twelve miles away; nets scoop one hundred bushels on good day; used since early settlers needed food, bait, fertilizer; once carefully allotted by family, added to town income, now sold

(E) The Reverend Lemuel LeBaron* House
88 Acushnet Road
c.1775
private

Home of beloved pastor, over sixty years service including chaplain of Revolution; grandson of Dr. Francis LeBaron* who mystified Plymouth, and great, great grandson of Governor Bradford*; old manse retains classical First Period lines in open farm setting

(F) The Grange
Third Meeting House
Route 6 and Main Street
1816, 1854
Open for special town activities
NRHP

Dignified Federal with Italianate adaptations; built as church, remodeled as Mattapoisett Academy, then Barstow School, later Grange

(G) Dexter Mill Site
Route 6 Between Main and Mendell Streets
c.1837
Open all year, no fee

Partially restored mill once produced shingles, boxes; old turbine found four feet under stream basin, restored to original platform; stonework of millpond and sluice gates rebuilt; illuminated at Christmas

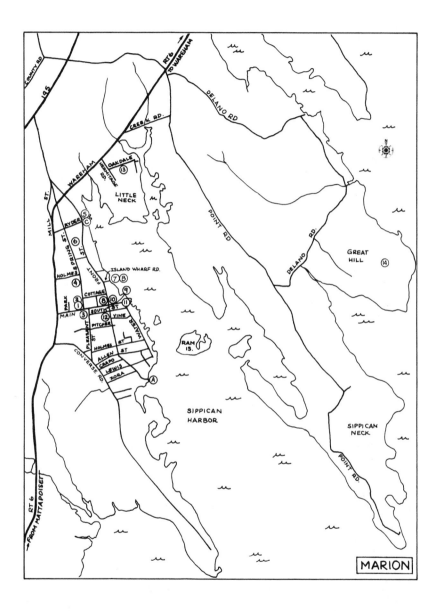

MARION

MARION

DIRECTIONS:
Drive north on Route 6 from Mattapoisett to Marion.

#1
Town House
Spring Street
1876
Open for town business

Follow Route 6 north from Mattapoisett. Turn right on Main Street and follow it two blocks toward Marion Center to Spring Street. Park here to see #1–3. The Town House is on the corner of Spring and Main Streets.

This dignified Town House was created by an eighty-four-year-old lady, who wanted to "put some snap" into Marion. Eighty-some years after her birth here in 1791, Elizabeth Taber* returned a wealthy widow. Her perceptive ideas and generous funds created a new library and natural history museum (see #2), a new educational institution

Town House

Authors

82

called Tabor Academy (see #6), Union Hall, Congregational Chapel (see #9), Music Hall, Evergreen Cemetery, Marion Lower Village improvement, and a new town hall.

The Town House was first built as Tabor Academy,* a farsighted institution of higher learning for both sexes. The sprightly Mrs. Taber searched for and purchased the land, planned the academy, and, though ancient and lame, travelled by cost-saving oxcart to supervise construction.

The imposing Italianate structure has an impressive bell tower, elaborate Greek-columned front portico, full-height corner pilasters, and ornamental brackets. The feather-pen weather vane symbolizes Marion's concern with school and knowledge. In 1937 this structure became the Town House in the "Tabor Swap," when the academy was relocated to the waterfront in keeping with its nautical orientation.

#2
Elizabeth Taber Library
and Natural History
Museum
Spring Street
1872
Open as library, all year, no fee;
Museum, limited hours and by appointment, no fee

The library is next to the Town House on Spring Street.

The first gift of Marion's ubiquitous benefactress, Mrs. Elizabeth Taber,* was this library and museum. She wanted to give village children the opportunity to know good books and value education.

At the same time Mrs. Taber provided the second-floor home of the Marion Museum of Natural History. Remaining virtually unchanged over the century, it is now highly valued as an example of a nineteenth-century museum. The fine displays include butterflies, birds, minerals, Indian artifacts, shells, phrenology, and an American eagle brought down by a pitchfork at Great Hill.*

The grand late Federal structure complements its neighbor, the Italianate Town House. Elaborate Corinthian pillars support the portico; corners combine quoins and pilasters; and brackets and dentils are featured at roof and pediment lines.

#3
Marion Art Center, former
Universalist Church
80 Pleasant Street
1833
Open all year, fee charged
for some events
HABS

Walk back Spring Street to Main Street.
The Marion Art Center is across Main
Street at the corner of Main and Pleasant
Streets.

The artistically painted building which houses the active Marion Art Center was originally the Universalist Church.

Prior to 1833 Captain Noble E. Bates had gathered friends to see how many shared his radical religious views. Disapproving neighbors were not invited, including the other captain of his Two Captains' House!* Many were interested in a less Puritan-like religion in which a more comfortable future was possible in the doctrine of Universal Salvation. The Marion Universalist Church was thus born, meeting in people's homes before they built this church. It thrived for years until finally sold when support diminished.

For over two decades, the Marion Art Center has provided additional cultural dimensions for Marion and neighboring communities. Its Cecil Clark Davis* Gallery offers varied art programs. A community little theater group, many classes, and special events round out the program.

Early adaptive reuse has preserved this historic church in an artistically imaginative manner. Natural shingle contrasts neatly with white trim, orange doors, and subtle avocado soffits. The colors are repeated in the steeple.

#4
Old Stone Studio
46 Spring Street
1820
Open as antique shop

Return to your car and drive north on
Spring Street. The Old Stone Studio is at
46 Spring, just this side of the Fire Sta-
tion, on the left side of the street.

This ivy-covered square stone building started life in 1820 as one of the early saltworks in Marion. As the need for domestic salt declined, the bulding was converted and used by Captain Henry M. Allen for refining crude oil and making charcoal.

In the 1880s this building with the strong aroma of oil and charcoal was purchased by a new owner, and its entire complexion changed to one of artistry, perfume, and lavish social gatherings. For to this coastal town of sea captains, whalers, and shipbuilders had come Richard Watson Gilder,* editor of *Century Magazine*. Gilder had the stone building restored and adapted to serve as a studio for his wife, who was an artist in her own right.

The Gilders attracted people from the artistic and literary worlds and with them ushered in a new and exciting era. In this beautifully adapted salt and oil factory, set among stately Cathedral Pines, were entertained Charles Dana Gibson,* Joseph Jefferson, Ethel Barrymore, Henry James, Richard Harding Davis,* and President and Mrs. Grover Cleveland.*

During the 1880s famous Americans walked the roads of Marion. The people of Marion and those who came for rest from the public eye grew to know and respect each other, and both were richer for the experience.

#5
Old Landing
Front Street, opposite
Ryder Lane
1708
Open all year, no fee

Follow Spring Street north to Ryder Lane. Enroute you will pass the Tabor Academy Chapel on the left. Stop to enjoy this lovely chapel for which there is more information under #6. Ryder Lane is the first right turn at the end of the academy fields. Turn right and go one block to Front Street. Old Landing Wharf is on the harbor opposite Ryder Lane. Once this whole section of Marion was called Old Landing. Facilities: boat berths available, docking facilities, launching area limited to residents in season; parking.

As the new world entered the 1700s, settlers began moving from the initial settlement near Minister's Rock* on Little Neck here to the head of the harbor, where the sea served as their avenue of transportation and provided abundant food. By 1708 two stone wharves, Delano's and Hathaway's, had been built. Soon adjacent shipyards and ships' chandleries opened, and this early settlement known as Old Landing came into its own.

In 1887 Old Landing captains were surprised to find themselves host to the first lady when Mrs. Grover Cleveland* visited. The formal reception party given for her is still talked about. Soon both President and Mrs. Cleveland became regular summer visitors, graciously participating in local charity events, with the president obviously enjoying the fishing.

Now the harbor is quiet in winter and filled with a myriad of buoys and boats during warm months. In the 1700s and 1800s it teamed with excitement, as whalers unloaded cargo of whale oil and coasting ships loaded hulls with salt, produced here to be shipped to domestic and foreign ports. Notice the house across Front Street on the SW corner of Ryder Lane. During the 1800s it included one of the familiar windmills that pumped saltwater from the harbor to the many saltworks along the waterfront.

#6
Tabor Academy
Front, Cottage, Spring
Streets, Ryder Lane
1876
Open as private school

After leaving the wharf area, turn left and drive south on Front Street. The academy and its buildings are all along Front Street from Old Landing to Cottage Street.

On the shores of beautiful Sippican Harbor in Buzzards Bay, Tabor Academy is a warm, pleasant blend of old and new. The modern Academic Center complements historic buildings on the large campus.

In 1876 Marion's benefactor, Elizabeth Taber,* built the present Town House* as Tabor Academy, spelled so for Palestine's Mt. Tabor. Well into her eighties, this interesting lady was deeply concerned with young people and their education. She not only supervised the construction, she selected the first headmaster, and together the two designed goals the school would follow. Her unbeatable dedication continued as on the occasion when a ball field was needed and no land available. She eyed the two-story building occupying the ideal site and said, "Can't it be moved?" It was. In 1880 she built Taber Hall, now at 13 Cottage Street, as the headmaster's home, where she also lived in two rooms until her death in 1888.

On Spring Street, the chapel is a deeply reverent expression in modern form. Your eyes are drawn to magnificent stained-glass windows and focus is on the dominating plain cross above the open altar. Themes of religion and science are boldly portrayed in the stained-glass windows, and the unique needlepoint pew cushions add individually created nautical, educational, and patriotic symbols. The feeling is that all talent comes from God and with His help all can be explored, learned, and attained.

In warmer weather the waterfront becomes a center of activity and

learning, including voyages aboard the tall ship *Tabor Boy*. Here youth
go to sea and once again the sea makes adults of Marion's charges—a
feat that has continued in Marion since her early youth sailed off in
whalers to return proud, self-confident men.

#7   *Just before reaching Cottage Street, turn*
Bird Island Light   *left on Island Wharf Road and stop here to*
Entrance to Sippican   *enjoy* Island Wharf Park *and Numbers 7–*
Harbor   *12. Park facilities: bandstand, swim-*
1819, 1976   *ming, wharf and dock facilities, parking*
Island Wharf Park   *for park and town center (no fee), exten-*
Front Street   *sive harbor view can be enjoyed all year;*
Open all year, no fee   *open all year, no fee. From the wharf you*
                                                   can see Bird Island Light, which can be
                                                   seen over the wharves to the right of Ram
                                                   Island.

Lightkeeper-pirate, the title appears contradictory. Yet according
to local legend, the first lightkeeper of Bird Island Light was a pirate.
On the night of September 10, 1819, ex-pirate William S. Moore lit Bird
Island Light, which for the next 114 years would guide Marion's sailors
home from the frothy deep and welcome those from other ports. This
1½-acre island, named for the many birds that frequented it, must
have been a dramatic change for an adventurous pirate and his bride
from Boston. Possibly it was too much, for one day sorrow struck, and
the distress flag went up. The local minister walked across the frozen
harbor to help the keeper bury his wife.

Found with a bag of tobacco, an old letter dated October 10, 1833,
Bird Island, gives a little flavor of the morals of the day. "This bag
contains tobacco, found among the clothes of my wife after her decease.
It was furnished by certain individuals in and about Sippican, . . .
ignorant, malicious, and *loose*. May the curses of High Heaven rest
upon the heads of those who Destroyed the peace of my family, and the
health and happiness of a wife whom I Dearly Loved."[4] To the writer it
seems all sins were embodied in tobacco.

Only once in 114 years did the light go out, purposely extinguished
by the keeper, who was in desperate need of help for a dying child.
With a wrecked boat and a severe storm, his only hope was to
extinguish the light and pray that someone would understand the
signal. Help did come, but too late, and another soul perished on this
island with its light erected to save people.

In 1902 a thousand-pound fog bell and pyramidal tower were added. The complex of buildings was still standing on June 15, 1933, when the light shone for the last time. Three years later the complex was auctioned off. But before the new owner could consider making his home there, the hurricane of 1938 made a clean sweep of the island, leaving only the stone tower. Subsequently, the main inhabitants of the island have been roseate terns. It is still one of their main breeding grounds along the Atlantic coast.

During the nation's Bicentennial, the Sippican Historical Society had the light reactivated. Once again its light offers a friendly greeting to those who call Marion home and to those visitors from other ports who linger to enjoy this picturesque coastal town.

#8
Marion General Store
(Old Meeting House)
140 Front Street
1794–1799, 1841
Open as store

Walk up Island Wharf Road to Front Street and turn left. Notice the VFW Hall on the corner of Front and Cottage Streets. It was originally the Music Hall *built in 1892 by Elizabeth Taber to provide a place for the performing arts in Marion. As you continue south on Front Street notice the building at 152 Front. This was once the popular* Handy's Tavern, *built in 1812 by Captain Caleb Handy. Here, in earlier years, seamen gathered after their ocean voyages, and the Concord–New Bedford stage made regular stops. Continue on to the General Store on the corner of Main and Front Streets.*

This friendly General Store and Old Meeting House has long served as a focal point for the people of Marion. By 1794 those living in Sippican felt it was time they had their own church and began this meetinghouse, only to run out of money. Captain George Bonum Nye said he would complete the construction on the condition that he would then own the property. Thus it became one of the few individually owned meetinghouses in New England.

As was the custom of the day, the building, with raised pulpit and sounding board, was also used for town meetings. At one time children attended a private school held in the gallery.

By 1841 Captain Nye had died; a new meetinghouse was sought; and this one was bought by Deacon Stephen Delano. Now named Delano Hall it served as a center for local social gatherings. In 1856 Delano sold it for $1,000 to Andrew J. Hadley, who further remodeled it to house a store on the main floor, three shops on the second floor, plus a hall for social events. Hadley was also ship's agent, paying crews as they returned from their long voyages. This was indeed a busy place.

Proprietors' claim that the store sold everything anyone could want was tested when someone bet the owner $5 the store didn't have a pulpit for sale. The storekeeper searched and returned with the old pulpit, which he sold for $10. The store remained true to its claim.

#9
Congregational Church of Marion
28 Main Street
1841
Open for services

Across Main Street is the Congregational Church.

"But it did not fall, because it had been founded on the rock."[5]

The white man's first church in the lands of the Sippican had the sky as its roof and a rock for an altar, for the first services were held at Minister's Rock* on Little Neck. In 1699 a meetinghouse was built near today's Rochester Common, and in 1703 the church was officially organized under the Reverend Samuel Arnold. Members from today's Mattapoisett, Marion, and Wareham all attended services until their members left to form: the Mattapoisett church in 1736, the Wareham church in 1739, and the North Rochester church in 1753. Parishioners in Rochester and Marion remained in the mother church until 1798, when the church in Marion was established.

In 1841 they built this beautiful Greek Revival church here on Main Street. The church, with steeple in the Christopher Wren mode, was designed by Solomon K. Eaton of Mattapoisett, who between 1837 and 1845 designed a new building for each of the five sister churches that descended from the original meetinghouse.

Over the years the congregation has grown, and changes have been made to the building. In 1872 a clock was installed with only three faces. Donations were requested for the clock. George Kelley, who lived close to the church, refused to contribute. His neighbor, Captain Henry Allen, said he would contribute his own share and give $50 for Mr. Kelley, providing there would not be a face on the side of the clock viewed from Kelley's house. Spite won out, and the three-faced clock was added to the belfrey as you see it today.

In appreciation for her many generous gifts to the church, a stained-glass window was installed behind the pulpit in 1894 as a memorial to Elizabeth Taber.* Then in 1915 the present Hathaway Memorial windows were given to the church. Contrasting dramatically with the white woodwork, light walls, and red carpeting, these inspirational windows of Mary and Martha remind the viewer that there are different ways of serving God. In installing the Hathaway windows the Taber Memorial window was removed. In 1976 it was rediscovered and placed in the Congregational Chapel as the focal point of the fellowship hall.

As the church bells ring out over Marion, listen to them carefully, for they are carolling the continuity of a faithful congregation that goes back to 1703.

#10
Sippican Historical Society
Museum
Dr. Ellis House
27 Main Street
1834
Open seasonally and by
appointment, no fee

Diagonally across Main and Front Streets is the Sippican Historical Society Museum.

This home of the Sippican Historical Society was Sippican's second post office and home to Dr. Walton Nathan Ellis. Few men in Sippican wore as many hats as Dr. Ellis—physician, postmaster, town clerk, library founder, choir director, and poet, to name a few.

Ellis, a dedicated doctor, made house calls on foot and charged the amazing fee of fifty cents. He was one of the original ten men to pledge $1,000 for the new Congregational Church in 1841. He started the first lending library in town, using a large closet in his home, and supported the library as it expanded. Ellis wrote his correspondence in rhyme, served as town clerk and postmaster, and was instrumental in having Marion set off as a separate town in 1852.

During Dr. Ellis's tenure as postmaster, Democrat President Franklin Pierce appointed fellow Democrat, Captain Nathan Briggs, to replace Ellis. Republican Ellis refused to give up his position, which resulted in two post offices, each with its own political following. Ultimately Captain Briggs resigned and Dr. Ellis left Marion.

In spite of the temporary hard feelings, Captain Nathan Briggs maintained a special place in the hearts of the people of Marion as one of their famous sea captains. His family, as so many others in Marion, were clothed and fed by profits from the sea. Ultimately, five of his children would perish at sea, and ironically, he would be struck down by lightning while standing at his own front door.

A cloud of mystery surrounds the death of Captain Briggs's son Benjamin. On November 4, 1872, Benjamin sailed from New York as captain of the *Mary Celeste*, with wife and baby daughter aboard. A month later his ship was found sailing west as a ghost ship. The longboat was gone; there was water in the holds; the cargo was intact; and the ship's papers were gone. Yet there appeared no real cause of trouble. There have been many theories, from an extreme drop in barometric pressure to the possibility of fumes from the cargo of alcohol which may have threatened explosions. The fear of explosions could have caused the captain to hurry his family and crew to the longboat which was probably connected to the ship by a line. When they felt the danger of explosion over, they would return to the ship. But somehow the line parted, and their ship and hope of survival sailed away, leaving them fifty miles from nowhere in a tiny, unprepared boat to perish at sea.

Return to this historic home, which in later years was owned by Dr. Ellis's daughter, Annie. She married Sylvanus Hall, who was appointed postmaster by Abraham Lincoln in 1860. Mr. Hall must have been a very formal man for he wore a starched shirt and collar night and day, changing only on Saturdays to be ready for church on Sundays. One can hardly believe any form of starch would be sufficient to keep a shirt looking neat for seven days and seven nights unless the wearer slept standing up and very rarely moved during the day.

Step inside this historic home with its remembrances of bygone days. See the old post office, early kitchen, Gerard Curtis Delano's Indian paintings, *Mary Celeste* exhibit, scrimshaw done by early seamen, Elizabeth Taber's* doll collection, Charles Dana Gibson* sketches, paintings by Cecil Clark Davis,* Victorian furniture, a china collection, and more. All have been lovingly preserved by the Sippican Historical Society so that Marion's interesting past may yet remain alive.

#11
Main Street
14 Main, 1760
9 Main, 1780
2 Main, 1794
0 Main, pre-1820
1 Main, 1806
99 Water, 1806
All private

From the Historical Society walk along Main Street toward the water.

As you walk down Main Street from the church toward the water, notice the picturesque historic homes, many of which are tidy Capes with weathered shingles. In earlier times, when called Wharf Village, wharves bustled with shipbuilding, sail making, ships' stores, and the excitement of docking whalers and coasters, seamen and cargoes.

The house at *Number 14 Main*, built about 1760, once contained a tiny dry goods shop and housed artist Charles Dana Gibson* when he summered here. The separate small shed in back long ago served as a town schoolhouse. The fourteen-year-old teacher, Elizabeth Pitcher, later became the town's benefactress, Mrs. Elizabeth Taber.*

Number 9, built about 1780, is where Richard Harding Davis,* worldwide adventurer-reporter and author of *Gallagher* and *Soldiers of Fortune*, did much of his writing in Marion. Davis married artist Cecil Clark* in one of Marion's grandest occasions for which Ethel Barrymore was maid of honor and Charles Dana Gibson an usher. Davis was the idol of Booth Tarkington and recognized by Winston Churchill. Other summer residents were Franklin Delano Roosevelt and Admiral Richard Byrd.

In the Two Captains' House,* *Number 2*, one of the captains hosted the first meeting of Universalists for which he had to borrow chairs from distant friends as his neighbors abhorred his radical beliefs.

At the foot of Main Street, *Number zero*, is the old "Watch-Out House" where the steep garret stairs were climbed to watch for returning whalers. The house was built so close to the water that ropes were attached to its neighbors to deter high tides from floating it out to sea.

Number 1 Main Street, the northernmost building bordering number zero, was a sail loft where sails were made for mighty whaling ships and coastal traders. The small building across was a cooper's shop, where barrels with iron hoops or birch bands were made for whale oil or cranberries.

Turning the corner at *99 Water Street*, you see the Beverly Yacht

Club on the left, which in earlier days was the village inn where shipbuilders lived, stagecoaches stopped, and churchgoers rushed to warm up between services. Whaling ships docked and now pleasure boats tie up by the clubhouse, which still offers warm welcome to modern-day mariners.

#12
Saint Gabriel's Church
124 Front Street
1847, 1874
Open as church

Turn right and walk south along Water Street to South Street; turn right, and walk up South to Front Street. The church is on the corner of Front and South Streets.

The dainty open bell tower appropriately resembles a school bell as the church was constructed in 1847 as Sippican Academy to provide suitable education for captains' children. By 1860 Dr. Ellis's library was housed here until moved to the present library. In 1874 the empty Academy building was greatly modified to become Saint Gabriel's Church, with its steeply pitched roof, weathered shingles, and featured ascending dove stained-glass windows.

#13
Minister's Rock
Oakdale Avenue
c.1679
Open all year, no fee

Return north on Front Street to your car. As you leave Island Wharf Road, turn right on Front Street. Follow Front Street to Route 6 and turn right. Take the second right onto Hermitage Road, then first left on Oakdale Avenue. The rock is after the first house on the right.

You can almost picture the twenty-nine courageous families as they gathered around this huge boulder to worship. These new proprietors arrived in 1679 to begin a new settlement. With the rock as their pulpit, they unknowingly linked hands with even more ancient times when the Sippicans, a village of Massasoit's* Wampanoags, held ceremonies here. Reaching further back, possibly as long as 4,000 years ago, the rock was the center of Indian worship.

#14
Great Hill estate, farm, and
greenhouse
Off Delano Road
1909-1911
Open all year, no fee

Return to Route 6 and turn right. Take the first right on Creek Road; drive to end and turn right on Point Road. Drive 1.7 miles to Delano Road and turn left. The estate entrance is .3 mile in on the right, with stone gate house and black iron gates. Drive through gates about one mile to greenhouses and estate.

The greenhouses of Great Hill are open for business. Here you can stroll through greenhouses, gardens, and on paths throughout the grounds, though the mansion and houses remain private. Visitors are treated to a view of a spectacular peninsula of open lawns, stately trees, azaleas, rhododendron, acacia, daffodils, and dogwood. All, capped by a fantasy-land stone castle, are nearly surrounded by the waters of Buzzards Bay.

A legendary meeting occurred nearby, prior to 1676, featuring Indian fighter Benjamin Church* and Indian Queen Awashonks. The queen and her warriors, with elaborate ceremony, agreed to support Church and the English cause. This alliance directly led to Philip's defeat in 1676 and ended the violent horror called King Philip's War.

Wampanoags camped here, leaving artifacts for collectors and a large rock hollowed into a bowl in which to grind corn. Another large boulder features a carved hand which has led to a variety of pirate-treasure stories.

The 1800s brought appreciation of the sheer beauty of the site, and in 1860 the Marion House, a three-hundred-guest hotel, was built near the present mansion. When a visiting millionaire, Albert Nickerson, was asked to remove his contagious family, sudden scarlet-fever victims, he bought the hotel instead. Next, sugar-king John Searles owned the vast estate, and finally the Stone family, who in 1909 began the momentous changes culminating in today's dream estate.

An average of 125 workmen, fed and housed here, ten teams to deliver supplies, and forty-two stonecutters to shape blocks for the walls were required to create the thirty-room, fifteen-bathroom, magnificent mansion completed in 1911. The grounds, farm, woodlands, gardens, and greenhouses grew to be legendary and now include a unique collection of prizewinning acacia exhibited throughout eastern United States.

Though the mansion has been reduced in size and the yacht requiring a crew of twenty-seven is no longer berthed here, the remaining castle and 750 acres of splendor encompass a vast estate in an era when few such remain.

This ends the guided tour section of Marion. Return to Delano Road and turn left. Take Delano Road to first right on Point Road and follow Point Road to Route 6. Turn right and continue tour to Wareham.

Marion Beaches and Parks

(A) **Silvershell Beach**
    end of Front Street

Open sandy beach with harbor views and swimming; open all year, parking by sticker only in season

(B) **Island Wharf Park**
    Island Wharf Road
    off Front Street

Open park on the harbor with extensive harbor views; facilities: bandstand, swimming, wharf and dock facilities; parking; open all year, no fee

(C) **Old Landing**
    Front Street
    Opposite Ryder Lane

Views of harbor; facilities: boat berths, docking, launching area for residents only in season; open all year; parking

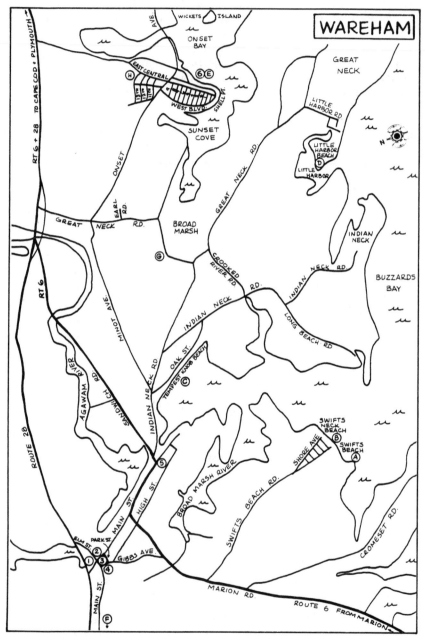

WAREHAM

WICKETS ISLAND
ONSET BAY
GREAT NECK
EAST CENTRAL
(H) ⑥(E)
WEST BLVD.
SHELL PT.
SUNSET COVE
LITTLE HARBOR RD.
LITTLE HARBOR BEACH
(D)
LITTLE HARBOR
N
RT 6 + 28 TO CAPE COD + PLYMOUTH →
ONSET
EARL RD.
GREAT NECK RD.
GREAT NECK RD.
BROAD MARSH
INDIAN NECK
(G)
CROOKED RIVER RD.
RD.
INDIAN NECK RD.
BUZZARDS BAY
RT 6
MINOT AVE.
INDIAN NECK RD.
LONG BEACH RD.
AGAWAM RIVER
SANDWICH RD.
OAK ST.
TEMPEST KNOB BEACH
(C)
ROUTE 28
INDIAN NECK RD.
SWIFTS NECK BEACH
(B)
SWIFTS BEACH
(A)
SHORE AVE.
⑤
BROAD MARSH RIVER
SWIFTS BEACH RD.
HIGH ST.
MAIN ST.
ELM ST. PARK ST.
②
①③ GIBBS AVE.
④
CROMESET RD.
MAIN ST.
MARION RD.
ROUTE 6 FROM MARION →
(F)

96

WAREHAM

DIRECTIONS:
Enter Wareham by way of Route 6 from Marion. After passing the Town Hall bear left on Gibbs Avenue, where road sign points to Route 28 Middleborough.

#1
Fearing Tavern Museum
Elm Street
c.1690, 1765, 1835
Open seasonally and by
appointment, small fee
HABS

Continue on Gibbs Avenue about three blocks. You will see the Old Town Square on the right, and the First Congregational Church on the left. Park on the far side by the Old Town Hall. Leave your car here to see numbers 1–4. Walk in front of the Old Town Hall, cross the railroad tracks to the Fearing Tavern on the left on Elm Street.

This intriguing tavern provides a field day for architecture, history, and preservation interests. A modest 1690s Cape is totally contained within the grand 1765 renovation, which was made around the original two-story, four-room home. Original timbers, walls, fireplaces, and chimneys were retained. In 1835 an ell was added. All periods are distinctly preserved to provide a unique tour through time.

It is interesting to walk from formal front parlor to the 1690 section, noting lower ceiling, wider floorboards, whitewashed plaster, and original fireplace. The 1690 public room is followed by the 1765 taproom.

Fascinating multiple levels of the second floor provide an extensive secret passage through former windows into closets and tiny halls. Here a British soldier was successfully hidden in this nest of patriots by a Tory wife, according to family history.

The attic presents an intriguing study of Yankee ingenuity in the building of one house around another. The sturdy stairs leading to skylights suggest fire access to the roof as well as an avenue up which cannon were hauled to fire from this height.

The original 1690 Cape was home to miller Isaac Bump, who sold it to Israel Fearing. Son Benjamin Fearing inherited it in 1757. He made the grand renovations in 1765 and became the first tavern keeper.

Fearing Tavern Museum

Early customers came to Fearing Tavern on foot or horseback as paths were not yet wide enough for stagecoach travel. The tavern became the center of town activity, where selectmen met and were served grog at town expense. Here Squire Fearing held court and decided the fate of lawbreakers. During the mid-1800s the small rooms next to the public room became the town's first post office. Fearings retained ownership of the tavern for nearly two centuries.

During the War of 1812, the British ship *Nimrod** terrified coastal residents. One of the few land battles occurred here in Wareham when 220 marines from the *Nimrod* landed and attacked Wareham on June 13, 1814. They fired a brig being built for tavern-owner William Fearing at his shipyard behind the tavern, and the nearby cotton factory was damaged.

Fearing Tavern has been painstakingly restored. The taproom is complete with the grill amazingly found nearly intact in the attic. A rare open closet with rounded interior walls remains, as do beautiful wide floorboards and panelling, ancient fireplaces, and most walls and timbers.

#2
Tremont Nail Company
Elm Street
1819, 1867

Across Elm Street is the Tremont Nail Company.

**Open limited factory
observation and company
store, no fee
NRHP**

The Tremont Nail Company survives as the strong representative of the many mills of Wareham. On this site once stood an old cotton mill, destroyed by the British in the War of 1812. Earlier, the town's beloved minister, the Reverend Noble Everett,* augmented his meager income with his fulling mill here, to clean, shrink, and thicken homespun and woven cloth. Prior to these mills, the first recorded here was the c. 1668–1690 gristmill of Isaac Bump, builder of Fearing Tavern.*

Iron ore was discovered here by colonists trying to till the difficult soil, and many households included furnaces and forges to produce nails and other ironware. In 1819 Tremont's predecessor began a larger scale nail manufacturing plant and rolling mill at this site in the former fulling mill of the Reverend Everett. The Tremont Nail Company name dates from 1858 and the present mill building from 1867. It remains the last of this major Wareham industry and one of the few companies in this country making ancient design cut nails.

The Tremont Nail Company is a complex of mill houses, herring fish ladder, and company store in addition to the factory. Visitors observing at the factory feel they are stepping back into the late 1800s— machinery and methods seem ancient, fascinating in this world of modern technology—a rare opportunity to see so vividly an earlier way of life.

**#3
Old Town Square
Old Methodist Meeting
House**

Walk back across the railroad tracks to the Old Town Square, bordered by Gibbs Avenue, Park and Main Streets.

**Old Town Hall,
505 Main Street**

**Benjamin Fearing House,
1 Park Street**

**Everett School
Gibbs Avenue**

**Not open to public at this
time**

Let your mind slip back to 1739 when Wareham was incorporated as a town, and the four-year-old First Meeting House stood on the square. The dirt road in front of the Meeting House was the settlers' main route to Rochester, Plymouth, and Sandwich. Homesteads were scattered throughout the surrounding forests. Issac Bumpus lived in the original home from which the Fearing Tavern* later developed with his all-important mills operating on adjacent rivers. As Wareham developed so did this historic town square.

Moving clockwise you see the *Old Methodist Meeting House* on Main Street opposite Park Street. Now owned by the Historical Society, it is slated for restoration to its original appearance as the first Methodist Meeting House, built circa 1825 on Tihonet and Carver Roads. To avoid vandalism the meetinghouse was moved here circa 1835, where it served the faithful each Sunday until 1842 when the newer, larger Methodist Church on Main Street was built.

From the Methodist Meeting House move across Main Street to the *Old Town Hall.* This small white-clapboard building, constructed in 1901, served for over thirty years as the Town Hall. Following a period of neglect and deterioration, the Historical Society, with the help of federal and state grants, restored the building to once again house town offices.

On the corner of Park and Main Streets stands the beautiful old *Dr. Benjamin Fearing House* built before 1800 by Benjamin, grandson to Israel Fearing of the Fearing Tavern.* The spacious old home became an inn in 1920, when the back two ells of stables and carriage sheds were converted to inn rooms.

Walk up Park Street to Gibbs Avenue. Across the street is the *Everett School,* originally built as the high school in 1890 and moved here in 1908. It was named for the Reverend Noble Everett,* who served the meetinghouse from 1782 to 1819 and the school committee for twenty-five years. Today, an ideal setting for kindergarten classes, this traditionally red schoolhouse, with its varied, shingled facade, continues to serve Wareham's young.

#4
First Congregational Church of Wareham
Gibbs Avenue and Main Street
1735, building 1914
Open for services

The First Congregational Church is found on the far corner of Gibbs Avenue and Main Street, adjacent to the Everett School and opposite Old Town Square.

An early independent streak in 1735 sparked the building of Wareham's first meetinghouse, where you now see the war memorial. The church was organized in 1739 with forty-three members under the name of the First Congregational Church in Wareham. Harvard graduate Rowland Thacher was ordained as their first minister. (C. 1739 parsonage still standing on Route 28 behind Old Town Hall).

The meetinghouse was the central focus of life. Here in the small wooden building, with front porch and turret topped by a whale weathervane, they worshipped, held town meetings, posted notices, met socially, and stored their ammunition. Under the devoted leadership of the Reverend Thacher that first meetinghouse served until 1770 when a larger one was built on the same site. Following his death, in 1775 the church hired three different ministers before they found in the Reverend Noble Everett* the type of strong, industrious, and reverent man they needed to lead their church.

The Reverend Everett, who would serve for forty years, came to Wareham in 1782 at an annual salary of fifty-six pounds. Even though his salary was eventually raised to four hundred pounds, he still found it necessary to moonlight by running a fulling mill and teaching in a school where he prepared many young men of Wareham for college. This amazing man was for all practical purposes a full-time minister, farmer, miller, and teacher—which gives evidence of the type of physically strong and spiritually tough men these frontier preachers were.

An anecdote from *Glimpses of Early Wareham* by Daisy Washburn Lovell shows Noble Everett as a worthy peacemaker. He was asked to settle a difference between two women, each of whom would not attend church if the other were there. His perfect solution was that whoever was most at fault should not appear in church. From that day forth, they were both ever present.

In 1828 a controversy arose over whether to hold on to the old church or build a new, larger one. With many abstaining, seven voting for, and four against, the die was cast. The old one was torn down in record time, in case someone should change his mind. The new ten thousand dollar steepled church was built where you see the church today. That same year saw the separation of church and state, the town giving up all control of the church as well as financial support.

This new financial burden proved doubly hard on the congregation when their beautiful, yet uninsured, church burned to the ground in 1904. Undaunted, they erected a new one in 1906, only to see it go up in flames in 1913. Again their church arose from the ashes, but this time, in 1914, it was made of stone. This present stone Gothic-style church, with its square bell tower and intricate stained-glass windows, gives a feeling of strength, permanency, and stability as it commands the old historic Town Square. Notice at the front of the adjacent Fellowship Hall, built in 1967, the roughhewn wooden cross with an evergreen planted at its base. This memorial speaks eloquently of the spiritual strength of the church, while symbolizing eternal life.

#5
Captain John Kendrick
House and Maritime
Museum
102 Main Street, opposite
Sandwich Road
c.1745
Open by appointment
through Wareham
Historical Society

Return to your car, turn right on Main Street and follow it through town to just beyond where Sandwich Road and Route 6 turn left. Parking is available behind the Kendrick House which is next to the Tobey Medical Center.

Many early New England sea captains and merchants owed their wealth to Captain John Kendrick of Wareham and his second-in-command Captain Robert Gray of Tiverton, Rhode Island, who made naval history in 1787-1790. They made the first successful trade run between Boston and China by way of the Pacific Northwest, opening what would become the very lucrative China Trade.

In 1787 six Boston entrepreneurs learned that Russians were buying Alaskan furs and trading them with China. Wishing to capitalize on this, they asked Captain Kendrick, a daring privateersman, to command a new trade venture which would include the ship *Columbia*, and Captain Gray in command of the sloop *Washington*. The expedition left Boston on September 30, 1787, arriving in Nootka Sound on the Pacific Northwest one year later. After trading for furs the ships sailed for Canton, China. There they successfully completed the second leg of the trading triangle, exchanging furs for tea, fine porcelain, and beautiful silks. In February of 1790 Captain Gray, commanding the *Columbia*, left Canton, arriving in Boston on August 9, 1790, to a hero's welcome after a total trip of 48,889 miles. The expedition, under the command of Captain Kendrick, had opened the door and proved the worth of the very profitable China Trade.

Kendrick remained in the Pacific, trading between China and the Pacific Northwest, and opening the sandalwood trade between Hawaii and China. His ship became the first American ship to carry the stars and stripes to a Japanese island. Today on the island of Shimo near

Nagasaki, there is a museum dedicated to Captain Kendrick and other early visitors. A memorial service is held on the island once a year in his honor.

In December of 1794 Kendrick was accidentally killed during a victory celebration following an Hawaiian War he had been involved in at Pearl Harbor. A friend, Captain Brown, acknowledging Kendrick's victory, fired a cannon salute. Unfortunately in his zeal he forgot to order the guns unloaded, and a shot hit Kendrick at his moment of triumph. He was honored in death by receiving the first Christian burial service on the Hawaiian Islands, thus ending the career of a man dedicated to the sea, international trade, and high adventure.

The *Columbia* went on to further fame on her second Boston-to-China run in 1790–1793, when Captain Gray discovered and named the Columbia River. Gray's and Kendrick's discoveries on the Pacific Northwest coast established a legal foothold for United States claims to Washington, Oregon, and Idaho.

Kendrick's home is appropriately situated on the edge of a river—Kendrick's natural roadway to the ocean and the world. Step inside to see how a successful Revolutionary War privateersman lived with wife and six children during the Revolutionary days. Notice the low ceilings, well-preserved paneling, wide floorboards, and large all-purpose essential fireplace. Wander through the furnished house and maritime museum and once again be at sea in the exciting days, when independent adventurers were willing to navigate untried routes and knock on unopened doors.

#6
Onset Beach and Bluffs
Off Onset Avenue
Open all year, facilities in season

As you leave the Kendrick House, turn left on Main Street; then immediately right on Sandwich Road, Route 6. Go over the bridge; take the first right on Indian Neck Road. Where road forks take middle road staying on Indian Neck Road. Follow Indian Neck Road to end and turn left on Great Neck Road. Follow Great Neck Road to Minot Avenue. The next right, almost a continuation of Minot, is Onset. Turn right on Onset and follow it to the Bay. The beach is on the right just before the pier and bridge. Facilities: bathhouse, rest rooms, snack bar, adjacent town pier, launching area, bandstand, summer concerts, parking (fee at beach), swimming, sailing lessons, picnicking, lifeguards.

Beautiful Onset Beach offers its natural beauty any season of the year. Here on this open smooth, sandy beach, nestled against Onset Bluffs, you can enjoy the constantly moving waters of Onset Bay—sometimes calm and smooth, sometimes rough and turbulent, yet with a consistent ebb and flow, a feeling of permanency, quiet power, and beauty. The sun plays on the windblown waters like a thousand dancing mirrors. Across the bay is Great Neck with its untouched landscape, and immediately offshore is Wicket's Island, named for its early Indian owner, Jabez Wicket, who was friendly to the white men. Above the beach is Onset Bluffs where concerts and shows are held during the summer. This land, once owned by the church, is now permanently protected to remain open for the enjoyment of all.

In earlier days, between 1775 and 1825, saltworks and their picturesque windmills dotted the shore between Onset Beach and Shell Point. This was a thriving industry until 1825 when trade restrictions were lifted on foreign salt. For years after, picnickers would find old salt pans lying around, giving the beach the nickname of "Old Pan."

Today "Old Pan" is still the focal point of Onset, drawing thousands each year to enjoy its natural beauty and ideally protected setting on Onset Bay.

This ends the guided tour section of Wareham. To continue tour, return on Onset Avenue to Great Neck Road and turn right. Go to Routes 6 and 28. Turn right and follow Routes 6 and 28 north, staying on Route 6 through Bourne, along the Cape Canal to the Sagamore Bridge for the Cape Cod Tour.

Wareham Beaches and Parks and Additional Points of Interest

Note: parking stickers are available free at the Town Hall for parking by day or season

(A) **Swifts Beach**
   Off Swifts Beach Road

Open sandy beach, view of bay; facilities: concession stand, lifeguards, swimming; seasonal sticker parking; open all year, no fee

(B) **Swifts Neck Beach**
   Off Shore Avenue

Open sandy beach, view of bay; facilities: lifeguards, swimming; parking; open all year, no fee

C Tempest Knob
　　Oak Street

Open sandy beach, view of bay; facilities: boat ramp, lifeguards, moorings, picnicking, swimming; seasonal sticker parking; open all year, no fee

D Little Harbor Beach
　　Off Little Harbor Road

Six acres of open sandy beach, quiet nontraffic area, extensive Buzzards Bay views; facilities: lifeguards, rest rooms, swimming and lessons; seasonal sticker parking; open all year, no fee

E Onset Beach and
　　Onset Bluffs (see #6)

Large open sandy beach and park; facilities: bandstand, bathhouse, concession stands, fishing, lifeguards, picnicking, pier, rafts, rest rooms, scenic tours; parking (some free); open all year, no fee

F Tremont Dam Park
　　Main Street northwest to
　　Mill Street, turn left,
　　follow dirt road to dam

Ruins of Tremont Nail Company when briefly located here in mid-1800s; also 1919 design dam: earth, concrete, gates, machinery restored to produce hydroelectric power which town will sell; facilities: picnicking, walking; parking; open all year, no fee

G Cranberry Bogs
　　Great Neck Road example

During 1800s farmers tamed wild cranberries; small perennial evergreen bushes which produce eatable berries; planted in sunken rectangular fields; flooded in winter to protect from freezing and thawing, in summer from insects and drought, in fall to aid harvesting; important part of Wareham's economy

H On-i-set Wigwam
　　13th Street, Onset at East
　　Central Avenue

Onset's unspoiled beautiful beaches were developed by unusual combination of business people and Spiritualists; Onset Bay Grove Association bought land from Fearing family, divided into house and business lots—early planned community development; summer visitors now outnumber Spiritualists, but this strangely shaped Wigwam, dedicated to "The Memory of the Redmen," remains

Cape Cod Canal Cruises　　Onset, (947-6051)

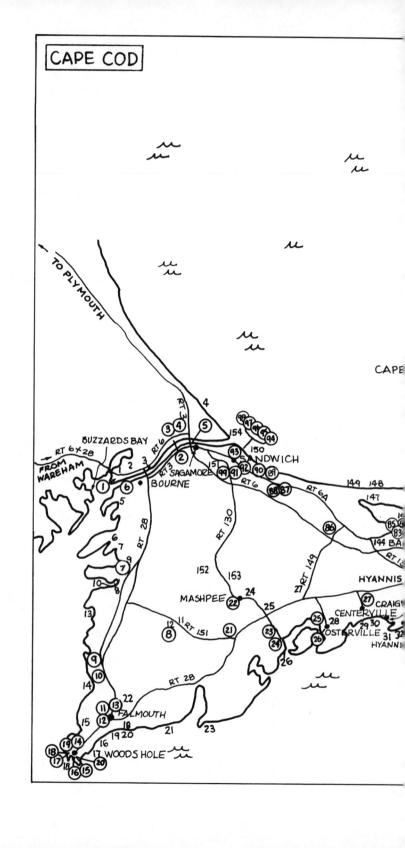

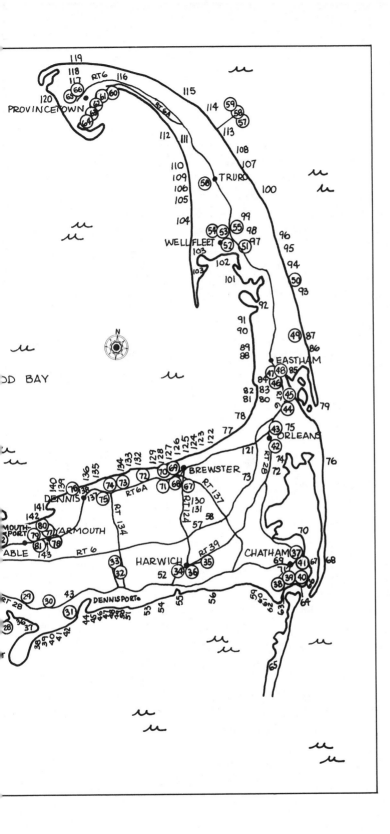

CAPE COD

Following are the beaches, parks, performing-arts centers, and points of interest on the Cape which are open to the public. As you enjoy Cape Cod be sure to take time to meander the less-traveled backroads and byways for a true feeling and insight into Cape Cod life. The beaches listed are open to the public either by a direct fee or by obtaining a parking sticker from the local town hall. See map for general locations of listings.

DIRECTIONS:

The tour begins at Bourne actually entering the Cape by the Sagamore Bridge. It then runs south on Route 28 to Woods Hole, then east on Route 28 to Chatham, north on Routes 28 and 6 to Provincetown, returning on Routes 6 and 6A west to Sandwich and the Sagamore Bridge.

Bourne

1. *Cape Cod and Hyannis Railroad,* Main Street and Academy Drive, open seasonally, fee. A scenic and historic train ride from Buzzards Bay over the unique 200-foot-high vertical-lift railroad bridge to Sandwich and Heritage Plantation and onto Hyannis or to Monument Beach, Cataumet, and Falmouth; also connects with the Cape Cod Canal Boat Ride.

2. *Cape Cod Canal Visitors Center,* Opposite Herring Pond Road on Route 6, open all year, no fee. Informative displays relating to construction and use of Cape Canal, short walk along canal, rest rooms, parking, picnicking, additional overlooks along Route 6; Canal, widest in world, begun 1909, 17.4 miles long.

3. *Indian Burial Hill,* Left on Herring Pond Road, immediate left, Burial Hill on right, open all year, no fee. Ancient burial ground of Wampanoag Indians, and site of First Meeting House for Indians in Plymouth Colony in 1637.

4. *Bournedale Herring Run and Carter Beal Conservation Area,* From Route 6 second left off Herring Pond Road, open all year, no

fee. Herring run in use since early settlers, alewives still run April
and May, parking, picnicking.

(5) *Pairpoint Glass Works*, 1967, Sandwich Road, Route 3 almost
under Sagamore Bridge, open weekdays all year, no fee. Craftsmen demonstrate world-famous hand-blown glassware.

(6) *Bourne-Aptucxet Historic Site*, 1627, Aptucxet Road, open seasonally, fee. Replica of trading post on original foundation built by
Plymouth men, funds originally used to repay Merchant Adventurers' loan, saltworks, windmill open as gift shop, and Grover
Cleveland's private railroad station.

(7) *Cataumet Methodist Church*, 1765, near intersection of Shore and
Old County Roads, open for services. Built as Indian meetinghouse, moved twice, still used as Methodist Church, windmill
across the street.

Beaches and Parks

1. Buzzards Bay Beach, off Electric Avenue.
2. Queenswell Pond, Cherry Street, freshwater.
3. Bourne Scenic Park, Route 6 east side of Bourne Bridge, open
   seasonally, fee, camping, picnicking, parking, rest rooms, tidal
   pool.
4. Sagamore Beach, off Plymouth Road at end of Clark Road.
5. Monument Beach, off Shore Road on Emmons Road.
6. Barlows Landing Beach, Barlows Landing Road.
7. Hen Cove Beach, Circuit Avenue.
8. Squeteague Harbor, off Megansett Road, clamming.
9. Picture Lake, County Road, freshwater.

Falmouth and Woods Hole

(8) *New Alchemy Institute*, Hatchville Road, open all year, no fee.
Tours, environmental, experimental farm, solar and wind power,
aqua-culture.

(9) *Friends Meeting House*, 1841, Main Street, Route 28A, West
Falmouth, Open for services. Quakers moved to the area in 1660s
to escape persecution, still-active meetinghouse.

(10) *Saconesset Homestead*, 1678, end of Old Homestead Road, off

Route 28A, Sippewisset, open seasonally, fee. Built by uncompromising Quaker, Thomas Bowerman, rainbow roof, early American architecture, 15 acres demonstrating premechanized farming, special events, exhibits.

(11) *Highfield of Falmouth*, Highfield Drive at end of Depot Avenue off Route 28, open all year, fees. 500-acre estate, Cape Cod Conservatory, Beebe Woods Art Center for learning and performing arts, lectures; college Light Opera and Falmouth Theater Guild open seasonally for performances.

(12) *Bates House Museum*, 16 West Main Street, Falmouth Village, open seasonally, fee. Birthplace of Katherine Lee Bates, author of "America the Beautiful," two-story Colonial.

(13) *Falmouth Historical Society Wicks-Wood House*, 1790, adjacent *Conant House Museum*, 1770, Palmer Street just off town center, open seasonally, fee. Built by sea captain and doctor, gracious home and museum, lovely gardens open all year.

(14) *Bradley House*, Woods Hole Road before library, open seasonally, fee. Woods Hole Historical collection, third oldest building in town.

(15) *Woods Hole Oceanographic Research Center*, 1871, Water Street, combines Woods Hole Oceanographic Institution and Marine Biological Laboratory, center of marine research, *Dolphin*, *Alvin*, research ships.

(16) *Candle House*, 1836, Water Street, Marine Biological Laboratory Administration Building. Built as spermaceti candle factory during whaling days, 2-foot stone wall, whaling ship's prow on street side.

(17) *Woods Hole Aquarium*, Albatross Street, open seasonally, no fee. Exhibits of sea life from Cape Cod and surrounding waters as far as Georges Banks.

(18) *St. Margaret's Garden*, Millfield Street opposite St. Joseph's church, open all year, no fee. Quiet garden on bank of Eel Pond, St. Joseph's bell tower.

(19) *Woods Hole Oceanographic Exhibit*, School Street, former church, open seasonally, no fee. Current research project, slide show.

(20) *Nobska Light*, 1829, Church Street and Nobska Road, grounds open all year, no fee. Stationary blinking light, appears red if mariner is in dangerous waters, beautiful views, limited parking.

Beaches, Parks, and Performing Arts

10. Megansett Beach, off County Road, North Falmouth.
11. Ashumet Holly Reservation, Ashumet and County Roads, off Route 151, open all year, fee. Self-guided nature walks.
12. Falmouth Playhouse, Theater Drive off Boxberry Hill Road off Route 151, performance fee.
13. Old Silver Beach, Quaker Road, West Falmouth.
14. Woodneck Beach, from Woodneck Road off Sippewisset Road.
15. Beebe Woods, Highland and Terheun Drives, trails.
16. Trunk River Beach, Oyster Pond Road.
17. Shining Sea Bikeway, Falmouth to Woods Hole, access Woods Hole Road past Mill Road and Steamship Authority Parking lot at Woods Hole.
18. Boats to the Islands, from Falmouth Heights Road, Falmouth and Woods Hole Road, Woods Hole.
19. Surf Drive Beach, Surf Drive and Shore Street, bird and wildlife reserve.
20. Falmouth Heights Beach, end Clinton Avenue.
21. Menauhant Beach, off Central Avenue and Menauhant Road, East Falmouth.
22. Goodwill Park, Goodwill Park Road off Route 28, freshwater.

Mashpee

(21) *Old Indian Meetinghouse*, 1684, Route 28 east of Route 151 rotary behind cemetery, open by appointment and for summer services. Oldest standing church on Cape, originally used for Indian worship, meetings, and social activities.

(22) *Mashpee Wampanoag Indian Museum*, 1793, Route 130 opposite herring run, open seasonally, fee. Museum centers on Wampanoag life, Mashpee Indian reservation was first one in country.

Beaches and Parks

23. South Cape Beach, end of Great Oak Road.
24. Ataquin Park and Beach, Lake Avenue off Route 130 on Mashpee Pond, freshwater.

Cotuit, Osterville, Centerville, Hyannis

㉓ *Cotuit Library*, Main Street, north of School Street, open all year, no fee. Ship models and Sydney A. Kirkman book collection.

㉔ *Dottridge Homestead*, c.1790, 1148 Main Street, Cotuit, open seasonally, no fee. House moved here from Harwich, 1800–1850 period furniture, behind its Santuit-Cotuit Historical Society Museum.

㉕ *Osterville Historical Society Museum and Houses*, 1795, West Bay and Parker Roads, open seasonally, fee. Period rooms, Sandwich glass, boat models, photos, Majolica and Lowestoft pottery, antiques.

㉖ *Crosby Yacht*, 1850, end of West Bay Road, Osterville, open all year. Here Horace Crosby designed and built the famous "Crosby Cat" boat, pleasure boats still built, display of Crosby half-models at Osterville Historical Society #25.

㉗ *Centerville Historical Society—Mary Lincoln House and Clark Lincoln Tin Shop*, 1850, 507 Main Street, open seasonally, fee. Fine varied collections, marine exhibit, glass, and period furniture and clothing.

㉘ *John F. Kennedy Memorial*, 1966, Ocean Street, Hyannis, open all year, no fee. Memorial in parklike setting, connected to Veterans Park, see below.

① *Cape Cod and Hyannis Railroad* (see #1 Bourne), Hyannis Depot on Centre Street.

Beaches, Terminal, and Performing Arts

25. Lovells Pond, off Santuit-New Town Road, Santuit, freshwater.
26. Loop Beach, Oceanview Avenue, Cotuit.
27. Hamblin Pond, off 149A, Marston Mills, freshwater.
28. Joshua's Pond, off Pond Street, Osterville, freshwater.
29. Craigville Beach, Craigville Road, Centerville.
30. Covell's Beach, Craigville Road, Centerville.
31. Keye's Memorial Beach, Sea Street, Hyannis.
32. Kalmus Beach, Ocean Street, Hyannis.
33. Veteran's Park Beach, Ocean Street, Haynnis, bathhouse, parking, play equipment, picnicking.

34. Nantucket/Martha's Vineyard Terminal, Ocean Street Dock, Hyannis.
35. Melody Tent, West Main Street, Hyannis, performance fees.

West and South Yarmouth

(29) *Baxter Mills*, 1710, Route 28 just before Mill Pond Road, open seasonally, no fee. Rare underwater turbine-powered mill, built by John and Shubael Baxter, still operating.

(30) *Aqua Circus*, west of Parker River bridge on Route 28, open nine months, fee. Performing dolphins, seals, chickens, petting zoo, wild animals, Chandler Shell Exhibit.

(31) *Judah Baker Windmill Park*, 1791, Willow and River Streets, open all year, no fee. Ran as grist mill until 1891, bought by Charles Henry Davis and made part of fifty-room house. In earlier days flag was raised atop mill to signal arrival of ships and barrel placed upside down to indicate departures. Small park on Bass River, pleasant views.

Beaches

36. Colonial Acres Beach, end of Standish Way, West Yarmouth.
37. Englewood Beach, end of Berry Avenue, West Yarmouth.
38. Sea Gull Beach, end of South Sea Avenue, West Yarmouth.
39. Thacher Park, end of Sea View Avenue, South Yarmouth.
40. Seaview Beach, South Shore Drive, South Yarmouth.
41. Parkers River Beach, South Shore Drive, South Yarmouth.
42. Bass River Beach, end of South Street, South Yarmouth.
43. Long Pond Beach, Wing's Grove, Indian Memorial Drive, South Yarmouth, freshwater. Cairn for last Indian in Yarmouth just beyond entrance to beach.

West Dennis, Dennisport

(32) *Jericho House Museum*, 1801, Main Street and Trotting Park Road, West Dennis, open seasonally, no fee. Barn museum, household artifacts, driftwood zoo.

(33) *South Parish Congregational Church*, 1835, Main Street, South Dennis, open for services. Known as "Captains Church," 1835 Sandwich chandelier, 1762 London organ.

Beaches

44. West Dennis Beach, Davis Beach Road, West Dennis.
45. South Village Road Beach, South Village Road, West Dennis.
46. Glendon Road Beach, Glendon Road, Dennisport.
47. Sea Street Beach, Sea Street, Dennisport.
48. Haigis Street Beach, Haigis Street, Dennisport.
49. Raycroft Parkway Beach, Raycroft Parkway, Dennisport.
50. Depot Street Beach, Chase and Depot Streets, Dennisport.
51. Inman Road Beach, Inman Road, Dennisport.

Harwich

(34) *Brooks Academy Museum*, formerly Pine Grove Seminary, 1844, Route 39, Sisson Road and Parallel Street, museum open seasonally, no fee. Historical Society and museum on second floor, Indian artifacts, antiques. First school of navigation in America held in this building 1844.

(35) *Brooks Free Library*, Route 39 and Bank Street, open all year, no fee. Large private collection of John Rogers, "the People's Sculptor."

(36) *Cranberry Bogs*, Along Bank Street, can be observed all year. Harwich a leader in cranberry production since 1840s.

Beaches

52. Sand Pond, off Great Western Road, North Harwich, freshwater.
53. Pleasant Road Beach, Pleasant Road, West Harwich.
54. Earle Road Beach, Earle Road, West Harwich.
55. Bank Street Beach, Bank Street, Harwich Port.
56. Red River Beach, Deep Hole Road or Uncle Venies Road, South Harwich.

Massachusetts Department of Commerce and Development, Division of Tourism

Windmill House

57. Long Pond, Long Pond Drive off Route 6, freshwater.
58. Wixon Memorial, Long Pond, Cahoons Road, freshwater.

Chatham

(37) *Railroad Museum*, 1887, NRHP, Depot Road, open seasonally, no fee. Museum housed in Victorian Depot active from 1887 to 1937, railroad memorabilia.

(38) *Atwood House*, 1752, NRHP, 347 Stage Harbor Road, open seasonally, fee. Joseph C. Lincoln room; Murals Barn contains religious murals by Alice Stallknecht-Wight, period furniture and special exhibits, Chatham twin light turret in garden; memorial for nearby unmarked grave of Squanto.

(39) *Godfrey Windmill*, 1797, NRHP, end of Shattuck Place, open seasonally, donations. Wind-powered gristmill which still operates.

(40) *Chatham Light,* 1808, Shore Road and Bridge Street, grounds open all year, no fee. Earlier two lights known as "Twin Sisters of Chatham," bluff offers exceptional views, marker indicates battle of Chatham Harbor, parking.

(41) *Chatham Fish Pier,* Shore Road and Barcliff Avenue, open all year, no fee. Active fishing fleet can be observed from observation deck above pier; headquarters for commercial and sport fishermen.

Beaches, Parks, and Performing Arts

59. Forest Beach, Forest Beach Road, South Chatham.
60. Cockle Cove Beach, Cockle Cove Road, South Chatham.
61. Ridgevale Beach, Ridgevale Road, South Chatham.
62. Harding Beach, Harding Beach Road, West Chatham, trails.
63. Oyster Pond Beach, Stage Harbor Road, Chatham Village. (Children's Beach)
64. National Wildlife Refuge, Morris Island, Morris Island Road, trails, parking only on Morris Island Road.

Surf Fishing, Nauset, Cape Cod

Massachusetts Department of Commerce and Development, Division of Tourism

65. Monomoy Wilderness Area, access by boat only, contact Audobon Society.
66. Lighthouse Beach or Coast Guard Beach, Main Street, opposite Coast Guard station.
67. Andrew Harding Lane Beach, Andrew Harding Lane.
68. Nauset Beach or North Beach, access through Orleans, need four-wheel drive.
69. Schoolhouse Pond, off Sam Ryder Road, freshwater.
70. Fox Hill walk, off Fox Hill Road, park at town landing on Strong Island Road.
71. Monomoy Theater, Main Street, Chatham, theater and concerts, fee.

Orleans

(42) *The Meeting House Orleans Historical Society*, 1834, Main Street and River Road, open seasonally, no fee. Was First Universalist Meeting House, now museum of sea, farm, and Indian artifacts, Orleans memorabilia.

(43) *French Cable Station Museum*, 1890, NRHP, Cove Road and Route 28, open seasonally, fee. From 1880 to 1940 station source of international communications, messages sent direct to Brest, France.

Beaches and Performing Arts

72. Pilgrim Lake, Herring Brook Road, freshwater.
73. Baker's Pond, Baker's Pond Road, freshwater.
74. Meetinghouse Pond, Barley Neck Road, freshwater.
75. Academy Playhouse, Main Street opposite Monument Road, fee.
76. Orleans or Nauset Beach, off Beach Road.
77. Skaket Beach, Namskaket Road.
78. Rock Harbor, naval encounter during War of 1812, packet ships between Boston and Cape.

Eastham

(44) *Old Cove Cemetery*, Route 6 opposite Hay Road, open all year. Site of first meetinghouse shortly after 1644, *Mayflower* passengers buried here and other 17th-century graves.

(45) *Edward Penniman House*, 1876, Fort Hill Road off Governor Prence Road, closed at present. Built by whaling captain, whalebone gateway, 19th century Victorian. Continue short distance on Fort Hill Road for panoramic view.

(46) *1741 Swift-Daley House*, Route 6 before Samoset Road by post office, open seasonally and by appointment, fee. Nathaniel Swift of Swift meat-packing company lived here, antiques, Eastham Historical Society.

(47) *Eastham Windmill*, 1793, Route 6 and Samoset Road, opposite town hall, open seasonally and by appointment, no fee. Old hand-hewn machinery still operative.

(48) *Schoolhouse Museum*, 1869, off Route 6 on Nauset Road, opposite Visitor Center, open seasonally, fee. Used through 1905, now museum housing Eastham Historical Society and collections.

(49) *Nauset Lighthouse*, 1838, end of Cable Road. Originally three lights known as "Three Sisters," tower 114 feet, 25,000 candlepower light, present light brought from Chatham 1923; parking at adjacent Nauset Light Beach.

Beaches

Cape Cod National Seashore
   79. Fort Hill, near Penniman House, Fort Hill Road, extensive bike and nature trails.
   85. Salt Pond Visitor's Center, Route 6 and Nauset Road, museum, extensive nature and bike trails, paved bike trail from Center to Coast Guard Beach.
   86. Coast Guard Beach, Doane Road, Environmental Education Center in old Coast Guard Station, beautiful views.
   87. Nauset Light Beach, Cable Road.
80. Herring Pond, Herring Pond Road, freshwater.
81. First Encounter Beach, Samoset Road, where Pilgrims first encountered Indians and exchanged fire.
82. Cole Road Beach, Cole Road.

83. Great Pond, Wiley Park, off Herring Brook Road, freshwater.
84. Salt Pond Beach, Route 6 just before Visitor's Center.
88. Kingsbury Beach, Kingsbury Beach Road.
89. Campground Beach, Campground Road.
90. Cooks Brook Beach, Silver Spring Beach Road.
91. Sunken Meadow Beach, South Sunken Meadow Road.

Wellfleet

(50) *Marconi Wireless Station Site*, Off Route 6 past Cape Cod National
Seashore Headquarters, open all year, no fee. Guglielmo Marconi
built his telegraph towers here and in 1903 sent first two-way
wireless communication between U.S. and England, message from
President T. Roosevelt to King Edward VII. Displays at National
Seashore Headquarters, interpretive shelter at site, trails to
White Cedar Swamp.

(51) *Museum of American Architecture*, Route 6 and Main Street,
open seasonally, fee. Evolution of New England architecture from
1600s to present illustrated through diorama and models.

(52) *Joseph's Garden*, Main and East Commercial Streets. Symbolic of
Reverend Joseph Metcalfe's dory. His church would not allow him
to fish, so left dory in yard. Storm filled it with soil and flower
seeds, which grew into a garden. Symbolic dories found on Cape.

(53) *First Congregational Church*, 1850, Main Street, open for services. Church clock believed to be only one in country striking
ship's time, Tiffany window depicting ship of *Mayflower* era, Hook
and Hastings 1873 organ.

(54) *Historical Society Museum*, Main Street, past Methodist Church,
open seasonally, fee. Originally village shop, now houses Wellfleet
memorabilia.

(55) *Samuel Rider House*, c.1800, NRHP, Gull Pond Road, open
seasonally, fee. Restored Cape farmhouse with changing exhibits,
owned by Historical Society.

Beaches

Cape Cod National Seashore
93. Marconi Beach, off Route 6, enter by National Seashore
Headquarters, trail.

103. Great Island Trail, Chequesset Neck Road, trails on Bound Brook and Griffin Island, 8-mile trail to end of Great Island and back.

92. Wellfleet Bay Wildlife Sanctuary, off Route 6 near West Road, trails, fee.

94. Lecount Hollow Beach, Lecount Hollow Road.

95. White Crest Beach, Ocean View Drive north of Lecount Hollow Beach.

96. Cahoon Hollow Beach, Cahoon Hollow Road.

97. Great Pond, off Cahoon Hollow Road, freshwater.

98. Long Pond, off Long Pond Road, freshwater.

99. Gull Pond, off Schoolhouse Hill Road, freshwater.

100. Newcomb Hollow Beach, off northern end of Ocean View Drive.

101. Indian Neck Beach, Pilgrim Spring Road.

102. Mayo Beach, Kendrick past town pier.

Truro

(56) *Bell Church*, First Congregational Parish of Truro, 1827, Town Hall Road, open for services. Named for Revere bell, has Sandwich glass windows and miniature whale-shaped window latches, on Hill of Churches in old cemetery.

(57) *Truro Historical Museum/Highland House*, Off South Highland Road, open seasonally, fee. Restored inn housing maritime and agricultural exhibits, artifacts back to Pilgrim days.

(58) *Cape Cod Light*, At Highland Light Station, Coast Guard Road past Highland House, tours arranged through National Park Service. Oldest light on Cape, first built 1798, present structure 1857, first light seen approaching Boston, most powerful on New England coast, path to scenic overlook.

(59) *Jenny Lind Tower*, 1927, Seen from Highland Station parking lot. In 1850 Jenny sang from top of tower then part of Fitchburg Railroad Depot Hall. She performed free as concert oversold and customers rioting. Tower moved here 1927 by Harry Aldrich as memorial to father.

Beaches

> Cape Cod National Seashore
> 114. Head of the Meadow Beach, Head of the Meadow Road, access to High Head Bicycle and Dune trails, glacial end of Cape.
> 115. Pilgrim Heights Area, High Head Road, interpretive shelter about spring discovered by Pilgrims, Pilgrim Lake Sand Dunes, trails.
> 104. Ryder Beach, Ryder Beach Road.
> 105. Fisher Beach, Fisher Road.
> 106. Pamet Harbor, Depot Road.
> 107. Ballston Beach, South Pamet Road, trails on north side of parking area running north to Pamet River.
> 108. Long Nook Beach, Long Nook Road.
> 109. Corn Hill Beach, Corn Hill Road, plaque for Pilgrims found Indian Corn here.
> 110. Great Hollow Beach, Great Hollow Road.
> 111. Encampment Park, Off Pond Road, plaque commemorating Pilgrim camp.
> 112. Pond Village Beach, Pond Road.
> 113. Coast Guard Beach, Highland Road.

Provincetown

(60) *Provincetown Art Association and Museum*, 460 Commercial Street, open seasonally, fee. Founded 1914 for artists and sculptors, art collections. Across the street a saltworks windmill is being reconstructed.

(61) *Provincetown Heritage Museum*, 1860, NRHP, 356 Commercial Street, open seasonally, fee. Art gallery and museum, marine artifacts, antique fire equipment, originally built as Methodist church.

(62) *Macmillan Wharf*, Route 6A and Lopes Square, open all year, no fee. Annual Blessing of Fleet, over 50 fishing vessels, annually about 10 million pounds of fish landed, boat rentals, parking.

(63) *Provincetown Marine Aquarium*, Commercial Street at foot of Carver Street, open seasonally, fee. North Atlantic fish and sealife collection.

(64) *Seth Nickerson House*, 1746, 72 Commercial Street, open seasonally, fee. Good example of ship's carpenter's work, ballast bricks in
chimney, antiques.

(65) *Oldest Cemetery* in Provincetown, Off Winthrop Street. Four
Mayflower passengers who died during brief stopover in 1620
buried here, other 1700 graves.

(66) *Pilgrim Monument and Museum*, 1910, Winslow Street off Brad-
ford Street, open all year, fee. 252-foot tower commemorating
Pilgrim landing, November 11, 1620, maritime, natural history,
Provincetown exhibits, collections of arctic explorer Donald Mac-
Millan.

Beaches

Cape Cod National Seashore
   117. Beach Forest Trail and Picnic area, Race Point Road.
   118. Province Lands Visitor Center, Race Point Road, bike
        paths, observation deck, information, films, hiking trails,
        displays, horse trails.
   119. Race Point Beach, Race Point Road, Rescue Museum in
        old Coast Guard Station.
   120. Herring Cove Beach, extreme end of Route 6.
116. Provincetown Dunes, Dunes parking sign just west of Pro-
     vincetown/Truro line on Route 6.

Brewster

(67) *Bassett Wild Animal Farm*, Tubman Road, open seasonally, fee.
Unusual and common animals and birds, picnicking and rides.

(68) *Joseph C. Lincoln's Birthplace*, Plaque on house south side Route
6A, just east of Route 137, private. Beloved author of Cape Cod
novels.

(69) *Brewster Historical Society Museum*, Second floor Town Hall,
Route 6A west of Route 137, open seasonally, fee. In depth
exhibits changed annually in dramatically restored Queen Anne
styled building.

(70) *New England Fire and History Museum*, Route 6A, ½ mile west
of Town Hall, open seasonally, fee. Diorama of Chicago fire, fire

memorabilia, Brewster blacksmith shop, Ben Franklin Philadelphia firehouse, apothecary shop, working museum.

(71) *Stony Brook Mill and Herring Run*, 1873, Stony Brook Road, east of Satucket Road, open seasonally, no fee. Was gristmill, then ice-cream plant, private home, now town-owned, and again a working gristmill.

(72) *Cape Cod Museum of Natural History*, Route 6A West Brewster, open all year, fee. Animal collections, artifacts, ecological exhibits, saltwater aquarium, lectures, films, trails—100 feet west is John Wing trail to Wing Island.

(73) *Drummer Boy Museum*, Route 6A West Brewster, open seasonally, fee. Life-size panoramic oil paintings of revolutionary scenes, 18th-century Smock Windmill on grounds, open in summer, no fee.

(74) *Sealand of Cape Cod*, Route 6A West Brewster, open all year, fee. Interesting marine park and aquarium, performing dolphins, shows, and exhibits.

Beaches and Parks

121. Nickerson State Park, Route 6A, camp sites, picnicking, fishing, trails, and swimming.
122. Crosby Landing Beach, Crosby Lane.
123. Linnell's Landing Beach, Linnell Landing Road.
124. Ellis Landing Beach, Ellis Landing Road.
125. Point of Rock's Landing Beach, Point of Rocks Road.
126. Breakwater Beach, Breakwater Road.
127. Saint's Landing Beach, Robbins Hill Road.
128. Robbins Hill Beach, Robbins Hill Road.
129. Paine's Creek Beach, Paine Creek Road.
130. Sheep Pond, Fishermans Landing, off Route 124, freshwater.
131. Long Pond, Landing Drive, freshwater.

Dennis

(75) *Scargo Tower*, Scargo Hill Road, open all year, no fee. 28-foot tower is highest vantage point on mid-cape, tower given to town as memorial to Charles and Francis Bassett Tobey 1929, overlooks Scargo Lake named for Indian legend.

76 *Josiah Dennis Manse,* 1736, NRHP, Nobscussett Road and Whig Street, open seasonally or by appointment, donations. Restored Colonial house museum with period exhibits, oldest existing Dennis schoolhouse on property.

Beaches, Parks, and Performing Arts

132. Sea Street Beach, Sea Street.
133. Cold Storage Beach, end Salt Works Road.
134. Harbor Road Beach, Harbor Road.
135. Howes Street Beach, Howes Street.
136. Corporation Road Beach, Corporation Road.
137. Princess Beach at Scargo Conservation area, Scargo Hill Road, freshwater, nature trails, playground, picnicking, parking.
138. Cape Playhouse Cinema, Route 6A, playhouse has stage plays with name performers, cinema said to have second-largest ceiling mural in world, shows old and new films, restaurant on property.
139. Bayview Road Beach, Bayview Road.
140. Horse Foot Path Beach, Horse Foot Path Road.
141. Chapin Memorial Beach, Chapin Beach Road.

Yarmouthport and Yarmouth

77 *Church of the New Jerusalem,* 1870, opposite Strawberry Lane and Village Green on Route 6A, open seasonally for services. Unusual Italianate architecture, Swedenborgian Church, outstanding organ.

Park at Post Office on Route 6A to see #78 through 80. Path behind post office goes by Botanic Trails Gate House on way to #78.

78 *Captain Bangs Hallet House,* 1740, 1840, 2 Strawberry Lane & Village Green, open seasonally, fee. Greek Revival, Historical Society of Old Yarmouth, 1740 kitchen, home of China trade Captain Thomas Thacher, sea-oriented collections, lovely old European weeping beech tree in rear.

⑲ *Colonial John Thacher House*, 1680, SPNEA, Route 6A and Thacher Road opposite Post Office, presently closed. Family heirlooms from many generations of Thachers who lived here.

⑳ *Winslow-Crocker House*, c.1780, SPNEA, Route 6A next to Thacher House, open seasonally, fee. Authentic, unspoiled Colonial architecture, furnished with antiques.

㉑ *Yarmouthport Village Pump*, 1886, Route 6A and Summer Street, open all year, no fee. Typical public water supply in Cape towns during 1800s.

Beaches and Parks

142. Bass Hole Beach, Center Street.
143. Botanic Trails of Yarmouthport, Faith S. Tufts Memorial Gate House, contributions, at rear of Post Office on Route 6A.
144. Dennis Pond Beach, off Summer Street, freshwater.

Barnstable

㉒ *Cape Cod Art Association*, Gallery and Studios, Route 6A, open seasonally, no fee. Exhibits by Cape Cod artists.

㉓ *Donald G. Trayser Memorial Museum*, 1856, Route 6A east of Hyannis Road and Mill Way, open seasonally, fee. Customhouse until 1913, Barnstable historic artifacts and memorabilia, fishing and tool exhibits in rear building.

㉔ *Sturgis Library*, c.1645, 3090 Route 6A, open all year, no fee. East side of house original home of the Reverend John Lothrop, Barnstable minister 1639–1653, also served as first meetinghouse, said to be oldest building in U.S. still used as library, Henry Kitridge maritime reference collection, extensive Cape Cod genealogy.

㉕ *Colonial Court House*, 1774, Route 6A and Rendezvous Lane, open by appointment and for special events. Earlier used as King's Court, later as a church, now houses Bicentennial memorabilia, flags, lectures.

㉖ *West Parish Meetinghouse*, 1717, Route 149 just north of Route 6, open for services. Outstanding example of Colonial ecclesiastical architecture, Revere bell, 5-ft. rooster atop cupola, congregation gathered under the Reverend Lothrop in 1639.

Beaches

145. Mill Way Beach, Mill Way Road.
146. Hathaway's Pond Beach, Phinney's Lane, West Barnstable, freshwater.
147. Sandy Neck Great Marshes, Sandy Neck Road, trails fourteen miles to Beach Point and back, parking fee in season.
148. Sandy Neck Beach, Sandy Neck Road.

Sandwich

(87) *Sandwich State Game Farm*, off Route 6A east of Pine Terrace Road, open all year, no fee. Raises pheasant and quail, opportunity to observe life cycle of game birds.

(88) *Benjamin Nye Homestead*, 1685, Old County Road, open seasonally, fee. Authentically restored and preserved, many family pieces, adjacent to Nye Pond where six generations of Nyes ran a mill until 1867.

(89) *Quaker Meetinghouse*, 1810, Gilman Road off Spring Hill Road, open for services. Oldest continuous Quaker Meeting in America, established 1657.

(90) *Steven Wing Fort House*, 1641, NRHP, Spring Hill Road opposite Juniper Hill Road, open seasonally, fee. Steven settled in Sandwich 1637, member of first Friends Meeting in America, persecuted by Plymouth, house owned and lived in by same family for three centuries.

(91) *Sandwich Fish Hatchery*, Route 6A just east of Main Street, open all year, no fee.

(92) *Daniel Webster Inn*, 1692, 149 Main Street, open as restaurant. Present Inn rebuilt after fire which destroyed Inn, where Daniel Webster* had retained a room year-round.

(93) *Yesteryear Doll Museum*, Building 1833, 143 Main Street, open seasonally, fee. Outstanding collection of dolls displayed in old First Parish Meetinghouse, church clock gift of Jonathan Bourne* of New Bedford Whaling fame.

(94) *Sandwich Glass Museum*, 1907, Route 130 and Tupper Road, open seasonally, fee. Sandwich Historical Society, houses collections of Sandwich glass and historic artifacts.

(95) *Dexter Grist Mill*, 1654, Grove and Water Streets, open season-

ally, fee. Restored active gristmill, built by Thomas Dexter, original Sandwich settler.

(96) *Thornton Burgess Museum/Eldred House*, 1756, Water Street, open seasonally, no fee. Memorabilia of Thornton Burgess, author of Peter Rabbit, Mother West Wind Books, and other children's books; born in Sandwich, he visited his Aunt Arabella Eldred Burgess in this home. Briar Patch Trails and Green Briar Nature Center and Jam Kitchen off Discovery Road, which is near four-mile marker on Route 6A.

(97) *Shawme Pond*, Water and Grove Streets, open all year, no fee. Burgess Museum on shore of pond where wildlife so familiar to Burgess stories are ever present, peaceful setting, pond dammed for early waterpower, 1683 cemetery on Grove Street side.

(98) *Hoxie House*, 1680s, Water Street opposite School Street, open seasonally, fee. Classic saltbox, tiny leaded windows, restored to 1680–1690 period with period furnishing by Boston Museum of Fine Arts, overlooks Shawme Pond.

(99) *Heritage Plantation*, 1917, Grove and Pine Streets, open seasonally, fee. Property of Charles Dexter who hybridized the Dexter Rhododendron, 76 acres of Americana, Shaker Round Barn, automobiles, windmill, military miniatures, antique firearms, tools, arts, spectacular gardens, picnicking and trails.

Beaches and Parks

149. Sandy Neck Beach, Sandy Neck Road.
150. Sandwich Town Beach, Town Neck Road.
151. Shawme-Crowell State Forest, Main Street, campsites, trails.
152. Snake Pond Beach, Snake Pond Road, freshwater.
153. Lowell Holly Reservation, South Sandwich Road on Wakeby Pond, also known as Wakeby Reservation Sandwich Conservation Recreation area, parking, picnicking, sandy beach, parking fees seasonally.
154. Scusset Beach, Phillips Road.

This ends the Cape Cod tour, leave the Cape by way of the Sagamore Bridge and drive north on Route 3 toward Plymouth.

MARTHA'S VINEYARD

To those who know and love her, Martha's Vineyard is a land of history and hospitality, surrounded by an untamed yet fascinating ocean with ever-changing moods and vistas. She has been home to whaling captains, intrepid fishermen, and competitive anglers. She has been a welcome residence for prominent men and women and generations of Vineyard natives, as well as adopted home for those captured by her beauty and charm.

Founded by Indians, named by Bartholomew Gosnold, settled by Thomas Mayhew in 1642, Martha's Vineyard has its own unique place in island history. Here from the very beginning White men and Red men, in mutual respect, learned to live in peaceful harmony. From here Vineyard whalers plied the seven seas in search of the lucrative whale. Beautifully preserved captains' homes speak eloquently of those historic years. During the Revolutionary War this small island was blockaded by the British, whose raiding parties captured powder, livestock, and other goods until she declared herself a neutral land. When whaling declined in the mid-1800s Oak Bluffs became a popular place for religious camp meetings. First known as Cottage City, the area attracted thousands of visitors each year, thus opening the door for later tourism. Today the Vineyard's main industry is her summer visitors, though each year more and more, captured by her unique spirit and peaceful beauty, remain as permanent residents. For she is an island with unmatched coastlines and beaches, picturesque fishing villages, rolling hills and farmland, quaint weathered homes, stately captains' mansions, guardian lighthouses, rose-covered fences, sturdy stone walls, and the ever-present wild grapes for which she was named.

Vineyard Haven

Tisbury Town Hall. 1844, 21 Spring Street, open as town offices and Katherine Cornell Memorial Theater. Built as Congregational-Baptist church, neoclassic architecture, restored for Vineyard's Haven's three-hundredth anniversary, wall murals of Vineyard life in theater.

Tisbury Museum. 1796, NRHP, Beach Street, opposite fire station, open seasonally, fee. Georgian with Federal touches, seven museum rooms representing Vineyard life in 1800s, changing displays, molding in parlor carved by sailors while at sea, special Portuguese exhibit.

Seamen's Bethel. 1893, Union Street, open all year, fee. Started as refuge for sailors by missionary Madison Edwards, here seamen found rest, food, and spiritual support, chapel, museum of artifacts brought back by seamen.

DAR Museum. 1828, Main Street and Colonial Lane, open by appointment through DAR Chapter. Built as school, used as Congregational church, now owned by Daughters of the American Revolution, used as museum: artifacts, scrimshaw, china, and costumes.

West Chop Lighthouse. end of Main Street, closed to public. Picturesque setting.

Windfarm Museum. Edgartown-Vineyard Haven Road, open seasonally, fee. Living museum illustrating wind, solar, and alternate power showing practical use of power produced, many unusual and historic type windmills, solar building, farm animals.

Oak Bluffs

Flying Horses Carousel. 1884, NRHP, Oak Bluffs and Circuit Avenues, open seasonally, fee for rides. Wooden horses carved by Charles W.F. Dare in New York c. 1876, one has Coney Island #4 written on inside panel, can still grab for the brass ring and earn a free ride, said to be oldest running flying horses in country, excellent example of American folk art.

Civil War Memorial Statue. 1892, Ocean Avenue, open all year, no fee. Entitled the "Chasm is Closed," dedicated by Union soldiers and patriotic citizens, rare flesh-toned statue honoring Confederate soldiers, unusual to be found north of Mason-Dixon.

Martha's Vineyard Camp Meeting Association, Trinity Park, Tabernacle. NRHP, access Siloam Ave., area open, no fee, houses private. First camp meetings by Methodists 1835, land bought by Wesleyan Grove Camp Meeting Association 1839, first pitched tents, high fence built, 1860s tents replaced by small gingerbread Gothic-type cottage, Gospel tent replaced by Tabernacle 1879. Illumination Night on a

Wednesday evening each summer, begins with concert at Tabernacle, then each building lights antique Oriental paper lanterns until entire campground is aglow.

East Chop Lighthouse. Highland Drive, grounds open all year, no fee. Also known as Telegraph Hill, site of earlier semaphore signal tower, now benches and beautiful view of Nantucket Sound and Cape Cod.

Hansel and Gretel Doll Museum. New York Avenue, open seasonally and by appointment, fee. Dolls and doll furniture from nineteenth and twentieth centuries.

State Lobster Hatchery. Shirley Avenue off County Road, open weekdays seasonally, no fee. Interesting opportunity to observe egg-laden females and the early life of young lobsters.

Edgartown

Old Whaling Church. 1843, Main Street, open as performing arts center, fee. Reflects architecture and wealth of whaling era, large beautifully restored interior with 160 box pews, 92-foot tower seen from the ocean.

Vincent House. 1672, Pease's Point Way behind Old Whaling Church, open seasonally, fee. Oldest known house on island, shows original hardware, brick and woodwork, clay insulation, fine example of early architecture, owned by Martha's Vineyard Historical Preservation Society, along with Old Whaling Church and Dr. Fisher House.

Dr. Daniel Fisher House. 1840, Main Street next to Old Whaling Church, open as professional offices. Large, impressive Greek Revival built by Dr. Fisher, physician and wealthiest man on island, house shows excellent adaptive reuse.

Town Wharf. Dock Street, open all year, no fee. Earlier owned by Dr. Daniel Fisher, site of his whale oil refinery. Believed he supplied, at one time, all the lighthouses in the country with whale oil. Today On-Time ferry leaves for Chappaquiddick—only public contact with island. Observation deck.

North and South Water Streets. Lovely old captains' homes with white fences and colorful gardens take you back to days of prosperous whaling era. Edgartown was first settlement and county seat since 1642.

Dukes County Historical Society. Cooke and School Streets, Thomas Cooke House, 1765, open seasonally. Francis Foster Museum, library, and grounds open all year, fee in season. Thomas Cooke was Customs Collector, twelve rooms furnished with Vineyard antiques, costumes, scrimshaw, and ship models. Museum features "Vineyard and the Sea." Gay Head light tower, whaleboat and shed, 1854 fire engine, and try-works are on grounds.

Edgartown Lighthouse. Starbuck Neck Road, open as beach, no fee. Light is on Lighthouse Beach at edge of harbor, views of Chappaquiddick, Nantucket Sound.

Chilmark

Menemsha. End of North Road, open all year. Quaint picturesque fishing village created when Menemsha Creek dredged 1905, center of Vineyard scalloping, lobstering, and fishing both commercial and sport, Coast Guard base.

Gay Head

Gay Head Cliffs and Lighthouse. End of Lighthouse and South Roads, open all year, no fee. Mile-long cliffs of multi-layers which have been altered over millions of years forming unique colors and geological lines holding archeological finds, cliffs NHL. Light built 1799 was one of first revolving type. Spectacular views of Elizabeth Islands, Cape Cod, and Nomans Land. Small shops, some run by descendants of Wampanoag Indians who make wampum jewelry from quahog shells.

West Tisbury

Mayhew Chapel and Indian Burial Ground. One mile in on South Indian Hill Road, Chapel open Sunday afternoons in summer, Burial Ground open all year, no fee. Small well-preserved chapel built 1839, at one time school for Indians, religious services held here until 1903, memorial to Thomas Mayhew, Jr., 1621–1657, and the community of Praying Indians he converted to Christianity. Burial Ground of unmarked field stones, early pulpit rock behind. Wildflower Sanctuary planted by Martha's Vineyard Garden Club.

Chicama Vineyards. 1971, State Road ¼ mile south of West Tisbury/ Vineyard Haven line, open all year as commercial vineyards. Cultivates European and Vineyard grapes, first winery licensed in Massachusetts, wine tasting and tours available.

BEACHES AND PARKS

Vineyard Haven
  Lake Tashmoo Town Beach, on Lake Tashmoo off
    Herring Creek Road
  Owen Park Beach, Main Street
  West Chop Woods, Franklin Road, 83 acres, trails
Oak Bluffs
  Joseph Sylvia State Beach, Beach Road
  Oak Bluffs Town Beach, Sea View Avenue
Edgartown
  Felix Neck Wildlife Sanctuary, Vineyard Haven Road, 350 acres,
    visitor center, trails
  Lighthouse Beach, Starbuck Neck Road
  Sheriff's Meadow, Planting Field Road, 16 acres, trails
  South Beach or Katama Beach, Katama Road on Norton Point
Chappaquiddick Island
  Cape Pogue Wildlife Refuge and Wasque Reservation (East
    Beach), Dyke and Wasque Road
Chilmark
  Menemsha Public Beach, North Road
  Menemsha Hills Reservation Beach, reached by walking mile from
    Menemsha Public Beach
Gay Head
  Lobsterville Beach, West Basin Road
West Tisbury
  Cedar Tree Neck Nature Preserve, Indian Hill Road, trails

NANTUCKET ISLAND

Once you have visited Nantucket Island, the Little Gray Lady of the Sea, she will beckon you back year after year. Twenty miles at sea, surrounded by Nantucket Sound and the Atlantic Ocean, she captures her visitors with a magic charm which seems to surround and isolate them from the worries of the real world.

Nantucket was settled by colonists, who believed in living in harmony with one another, and nurtured by whaling, which set her destiny as the first whaling capital of the world. Though Nantucket's golden years of whaling prosperity were in the late 1700s and early 1800s, the aura of the whaling ship and the "Nantucket Sleighride" is still felt on this picturesque, fourteen-mile long island with its endless beaches and colorful moors. Nantucket offers a look into those bygone days of whaling when men challenged the mightiest of all mammals. Victory meant high financial rewards, failure meant severe loss or death, for there was little compromise with a sixty-five foot, sixty ton sperm whale.

Whaling captains' mansions, cobblestone streets, rose-covered homes with weathered shingles, and docks mooring pleasure boats and working boats from up and down the east coast await the visitor. Here also can be enjoyed all types of land and water sports, as well as the ever-changing beauty of an island at sea.

Abiah Folger Franklin Fountain. 1900, Madaket Road one mile from end of Main Street, open all year, no fee. Erected in memory of Abiah Folger, mother of Benjamin Franklin, near site of her home.

1800 House, Mill Street. Open seasonally, fee. Home of High Sheriff, a typical Nantucket central-chimney home of the 1800s, Windsor chairs, Chinese export porcelain, English dinnerware, and period furniture.

Friends Meeting House and Historic Museum. 1838, Fair Street, open seasonally, fee. Built as school for active Quaker community, today summer services, art gallery, and museum.

Greater Light. Howard Street, open seasonally, fee. Artist Hannah Monihan converted old barn into ostentatious home filled with decorative and unusual rooms and furnishings.

Brant Point Light, Nantucket Island

Hadwen-Satler Memorial House. 1845, 96 Main Street, open season-ally, fee. Neoclassic home of wealthy whaling merchant during Nan-tucket's golden years. Appropriately furnished and maintained.

Jethro Coffin House. 1686, NHL, Sunset Hill, open seasonally, fee. *Oldest House.* horseshoe chimney, period furniture.

Lightship "Nantucket." Straight Wharf, open seasonally, fee. Once guarded treacherous South Shoals off Nantucket, living museum.

Maria Mitchell Birthplace, Observatory, and Library, and Hin-chman House. On Vestal Street near Milk Street, open seasonally, fee. Birthplace of astronomer Maria Mitchell shows Mitchell furnishings, library holds many of her papers, observatory in her memory for research and observation, Hinchman House is a natural science mu-seum and aquarium.

Nantucket Life Saving Museum. 1874, off Polpis Road, open season-ally, fee. Reconstructed Surfside Life Saving Station built in 1874. Lifesaving memorabilia.

Nathaniel Macy House. 1723, Liberty Street and Walnut Lane, open seasonally, fee. Originally built in Sherborne, first settlement on island, moved in 1741, gunstock corner posts.

Old Fire Hose Cart House. Gardner Street, open seasonally, donations. Collection of early fire equipment.

Old Gaol. 1805, Vestal Street, open seasonally, fee. Built of oak logs and iron bolts with fireplaces, cell, stocks. It is said prisoners were allowed to go home at night.

Old Windmill. 1746, Mill and Prospect Streets, open seasonally, fee. Beautiful illustration of early working mill, still grinds corn by wind with wooden machinery.

Pacific Club. 1772, Main and Washington Streets, private. Built by whaling merchant William Rotch* as warehouse and countinghouse. Seamen's club organized in 1854 for those who had sailed the Pacific.

Peter Foulger Museum. 1971, Broad Street, open daily, fee. Contains exhibits of early Nantucket, whaling, ship models, navigational equipment, paintings, fire equipment, and Indian artifacts, plus maritime history and genealogy library.

Three Bricks. 1838, NHL, 93-97 Main Street, private. Three mansions built by Joseph Starbuck, wealthy whaling merchant, for his sons during Nantucket's golden years.

Whaling Museum. 1847, Broad and South Beach Streets, open seasonally, fee. Built by William Hadwen of the Hadwen-Satler House as a candle factory, now houses whaling memorabilia honoring Nantucket's golden era, exhibits of whalecraft shop, shipsmith shop, sail loft, rigging loft, cooperage shop.

PUBLIC BEACHES

Nantucket Town
   Jetties Beach, off North Beach Street.
   Children's Beach, off South Street.
   South Beach, off Washington Street.
Siasconset
   Sconset Beach, end Sconset Road.
Surfside
   Surfside Beach, Surfside Road.
Cisco
   Cisco Beach, Hummock Pond Road.
Madaket
   Madaket Beach, Madaket Road.
   Dionis Beach, Eel Point Road.

HISTORY OF PLYMOUTH

Here in the middle of a New England winter one hundred ocean-weary, hungry, and lonely settlers came ashore and laid the stonework for the greatest nation on earth. They reached down into the very depths of their souls. They had been tried and tested for this mission—through years of religious persecution in England, struggle in Holland to retain their own identity and faith, and a sixty-six day cramped, harrowing crossing—to find the God-given will not only to survive, but to grow, to build, and to create.

The seeds that ultimately grew into the Plymouth Colony were sown in England in the early 1600s. (see *Setting The Stage*) By 1608 a group of Separatists who had been meeting secretly in William Brewster's* manor house in Scrooby,* England, became tired of continued religious persecution. They took the first step along the arduous road that would finally lead to the New World, settling in Leyden, Holland, under the spiritual leadership of the Reverend John Robinson* and lay leader William Brewster. However, as the years passed they found the freer Dutch way of life influencing their children and political unrest developing between the Netherlands and Spain. Many began to look to America, where they might settle—keeping their own English customs, establishing a Separatist church, and having a better opportunity for economic prosperity.

After several discouraging attempts, the Leyden Congregation made an agreement through Thomas Weston* with the London Adventurers. It called for all supplies to be purchased through the Adventurers and all lands, profits, and capital to be owned by joint stock which would be divided after seven years, providing all debts were paid. It would be twenty-eight years before this obligation would finally be terminated.

The Pilgrims left Leyden aboard the *Speedwell* and in Southhampton joined forces with the *Mayflower** sailing from London with fellow Separatists and others recruited by Thomas Weston. Unfortunately, the *Speedwell* proved unseaworthy. The *Mayflower* gave refuge to as many as possible and left for the New World on September 16, 1620.

The Pilgrims sighted Cape Cod on November 9, 1620, and anchored off what is now Provincetown. Aboard ship on November 11 the historic Mayflower Compact was signed, spelling out the initial agreement by which the Plymouth Colony would be governed. John Carver* was chosen first governor in this new and yet untried world.

On December 21 the weary voyagers finally landed at what is now Plymouth. Though midwinter, the site still looked inviting, and one hundred thankful settlers began the awesome task of turning a wilderness into a home. It is interesting to note that of those one hundred fewer than half were from the Leyden congregation and only three—William Bradford* and Elder and Mrs. Brewster—were from the original Scrooby group. Yet it would be the strong influence of these few, with their constant faith in the goodness of their God and the belief that He would sustain them, that enabled the colony of Plymouth to survive and eventually to prosper.

That first winter took its gruesome toll; only half lived to greet the beautiful New England spring of 1621. Their spirits were lifted in March when the first supposedly feared Red man entered their camp and said, "Welcome." Indian Samoset introduced the Pilgrims to Squanto and to Massasoit, chief of the Wampanoag Indians. With the support of Massasoit and the guidance of Squanto the settlers were able to tame the wilderness.

During the summer of 1621 this industrious, God-fearing group of farmers and craftsmen planted and harvested crops, filled their larders for winter, and improved their living conditions. Fall saw the Pilgrims so thankful for their deliverance that Governor William Bradford, who had succeeded Governor Carver following the latter's death in April, declared a week of harvest celebrations to be jointly shared and enjoyed by settlers and Indians alike. The colony began to prosper.

As word of the success of the Plymouth Colony reached England more and more craftsmen left their futureless positions in England to seek land and possible wealth in the New World. These craftsmen brought much needed skills to Plymouth and her colony. During the 1630s settlers began to develop towns in the surrounding countryside, thus strengthening the colony but weakening the town of Plymouth. Even the leaders began to move—Myles Standish,* John Alden,* and Elder Brewster to Duxbury, Edward Winslow* to Marshfield, and William Bradford, at least part time, to Kingston. By 1645 the colony had grown to a population of 2,500 and included ten outlying towns. The once-ragged settlers had become self-sufficient self-governing colonists, who, having once set a tentative foot in the New World, had remained to see it tamed.

Friendly relations and the pact of mutual protection between Massasoit's Indians and the Pilgrims remained in effect for over forty years. With the death of the chief in 1661 and the rise to power of his son, King Philip,* relations became strained. All-out war erupted in 1675 into King Philip's War, the first and one of the bloodiest in the long series of Indian Wars. Following Philip's death in 1676 peace returned to the area. Plymouth had survived another trial in the determined colonization of New England.

The Plymouth Colony was never as powerful or as wealthy as its northern sister, the Massachusetts Bay Colony. Following a series of political maneuvers, Plymouth became part of the Bay Colony in 1691. Though the Massachusetts Bay Colony became a more lasting political entity, it was the unforgettable courage, faith, and fortitude of the smaller Plymouth Colony and its heroic leaders that became part of the living heritage of every American.

With the passing of the first generation of Pilgrims and the dissemination of their descendants, Plymouth went through a natural transition from prime settlement to being one of the many small fishing and farming communities along the Massachusetts coast. The early 1700s saw the building of boatyards at the mouth of Town Brook,* launching a shipbuilding business that was prosperous until the Civil War. At that time Town Brook was open to the harbor and provided an ideal location for building and mooring vessels. The mid- to late-1700s saw the rise of cod fishing, which added significantly to Plymouth's economy. The Revolutionary War, War of 1812, and a variety of embargoes and duty regulations created peaks and valleys in the fishing economy, but it survived all obstacles and remains a permanent part of Plymouth.

Modes of transportation improved with the introduction of a steamship line between Boston and Plymouth in 1828, the running of the stage from Boston to Plymouth and the Cape in 1834, and the opening of the Old Colony Railroad in 1844. With this increased mobility businesses prospered, banks and hotels opened, and a greater social awareness developed through cultural exchange.

The mid-1800s brought change to Plymouth. The Gold Rush lured many seamen and craftsmen from Plymouth to seek quick wealth in California. The Civil War took its toll. The decline of whaling and the changes of duties on foreign fish and salt caused the center of activity to shift from the waterfront to the already functioning mills and factories along Town Brook and Nathans Brook. From the mid-1700s through the 1900s, Town Brook provided waterpower for a succession of textile mills, gristmills, ironworks, wireworks, and tack and rivet factories. Plymouth Cordage Company,* which opened its doors in 1824 on Nathans Brook, was probably the single most influential company, providing steady employment for 125 years. As these industries expanded, many immigrants from Portugal, Ireland, Italy, France, and Germany, seeking new opportunities, came to Plymouth to work in the factories. Plymouth remained true to the spirit of its first immigrants in 1620, once again offering refuge and opportunity to people seeking a better way of life.

Today, yet another industry is important in Plymouth, that of tourism. Here, through restoration and reconstruction and a myriad of exhibits and events, you can experience the rich heritage of the founding fathers. In the surroundings of modern day Plymouth, with all its comforts and conveniences, you are able to go back in time and almost touch, feel, and know the world of the Pilgrims. You come away with a deep sense of pride and rededication to the principles and beliefs that have made this country strong.

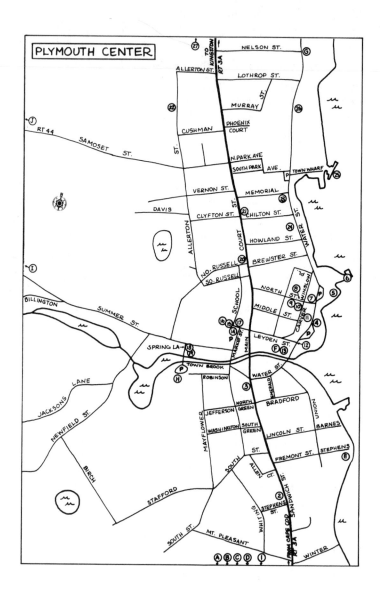

PLYMOUTH CENTER

PLYMOUTH

DIRECTIONS:
Leave Cape Cod by the Sagamore Bridge and drive north on Route 3 toward Plymouth. From Route 3 take exit 4 to Route 3A and turn left going north on Route 3A. Or drive north on Route 3A along the coast past Manomet. Where Plymouth Plantation Highway to Route 3 bears left from Route 3A stay straight on Route 3A; continue .7 mile to Plimoth Plantation on the left.

#1
Plimoth Plantation
Warren Avenue, Route 3A
1945
Open April through
November, fee charged

Plimoth Plantation is on the left side of Route 3A, shortly after passing Plymouth Beach. Facilities: gift shop, museum, parking, rest rooms.

Since earliest childhood you have heard the story of the Pilgrims and the first Thanksgiving, and in many ways it has become almost fairy tale in nature—how much truth, how much myth? Here at Plimoth Plantation, the Pilgrims and the reasons for their first harvest celebration (which evolved into Thanksgiving) become a reality. The Pilgrims take on flesh and bone; their homes and fort are made of real wood, with wattle and daub construction and thatched roofs. You can see, feel, smell, and be part of what life was like in 1627. Few historic events have been as documented or as thoroughly researched and implemented as Plimoth Plantation.

Thanks to the foresightedness of its originator, Ralph Hornblower, the visitor can now understand the true significance of the founding fathers. Beginning at the Plymouth Waterfront, where still remain two replica Pilgrim Houses (see #5), the foundation moved here to the Hornblower Estate and established a replica of the original Plymouth Village.

As you leave the warm, inspiring, introductory slide presentation and start down the hill to the old Meetinghouse Fort, you are quickly back in 1627. The plain benches and pulpit with roughhewn timbers speak eloquently of the simple, dedicated, God-centered life of the Pilgrims. The cannon atop the fort speaks of the hardships, dangers,

141

Massachusetts Department of Commerce and Development, Division of Tourism

Plimoth Plantation

and trials the Pilgrims met, accepted, and conquered. From here they could look out over their village and harbor—their immediate small world some three thousand miles from home, family, and friends.

Walk through the village and visit the homes of those first settlers. Reality is everywhere from the furnishings, stored foods, ways of cooking and tending crops and animals to the very people themselves, who speak with the accents and knowledge of 1627. You are surprised to remember that the Pilgrims spoke with differing English dialects. Suddenly drums sound and men rush to the Bradford House for their matchlock muskets. They form their militia group, ever ready to defend their village if necessary—a very real and important part of those early days.

Thanksgiving will never be quite the same again. For after having visited Plimoth Plantation, you come away filled with a new pride in the founding fathers, a new understanding of their determination, sacrifice, and dedication, supported by an unalterable faith in the goodness and strength of their God.

#2
Harlow Old Fort House
119 Sandwich Street
1677
Open extended season, fee charged
NRHP

Continue north toward Plymouth on Route 3A, which becomes Sandwich Street. The Harlow Old Fort House is on the left just past Stephens Street.

The ancient Harlow House dates even further back in time to the Fort on Burial Hill. (see #16) The Old Fort was dismantled after 1676. Its timbers were awarded to Sergeant William Harlow for his services in the King Philip's War and later used in the construction of this house. The scarfing of some of the beams in the Harlow Old Fort House supports the idea.

For 243 years Harlows, relatives, or in-laws lived here until 1920, when the house was purchased by the Plymouth Antiquarian* Society. Modifications made by succeeding generations were removed, historic posts and rafters were preserved, and outer clay-and-straw walls were reconstructed to original plans under the guidance of noted architect Joseph E. Chandler, himself a Harlow relative. Now this working-museum house closely depicts life as it was in the time of the William Harlow family, a fine example of the second-generation Plymouthian who received the torch to carry on from the Pilgrims. Harlow was a cooper, a selectman, a member of the General Court, and an inspector of inns and ordinaries, as well as an early dabbler in real estate.

The house is a working museum where the costumed, knowledgeable hostesses demonstrate spinning, dyeing, weaving, candlemaking, and other early household arts. Classes for all ages are a long tradition.

The house itself is weathered shingle, with gambrel roof and central chimney. The rustic interior rooms—great hall, workroom, buttery, scullery, and bedrooms—are appropriately furnished with seventeenth-century pieces similar to those on the inventory of William Harlow's possessions. The doorstep was verified to be a cutting from Plymouth Rock, then carefully cut further and the pieces sold to raise funds to restore the house.

The grounds include a separate kitchen where the hostess makes jellies and another building which houses classes and a small gift shop. Herb gardens, and the area in which corn is planted as part of a traditional event of long standing, complete the setting.

#3
Howland House
33 Sandwich Street
1666
Open extended season,
fee charged
NRHP

Continue north on Sandwich Street. The Howland House is on the left between North Green and Water Streets.

In this weathered-clapboard Colonial home, Pilgrims talked, ate, and shared the daily joys and concerns of Plymouth life during the last

Howland House interior

half of the 1600s. The house was built by Jacob Mitchel in 1666 and sold the following year to Jabez Howland, son of *Mayflower** travelers, John and Elizabeth Tilley Howland,* who at one time lived here with their son.

John Howland, patriarch of the Plymouth Howlands, left England at age twenty-seven aboard the *Mayflower* as a steward-servant to John Carver.* During the crossing, the Pilgrims believed John was saved by the Grace of God as his grasping hands caught the topsail halyard when he was suddenly washed overboard. John's long and useful life proved the value of this miraculous rescue. He was one of the exploratory shallop crew who first found and recommended Plymouth. His marriage to Elizabeth was the second such ceremony performed in the Old Colony. He became an heir of Governor Carver's and earned his independence. He owned property in Kingston, Duxbury, and Plymouth, served on the Governor's Council, was one of the eight local "Undertakers" who assumed Plymouth's debts, and was agent for the

Pilgrims' trading post in Kennebec, Maine. He died during his eightieth year. John Howland was buried on Burial Hill overlooking the harbor he first saw on that historic December day, when he helped a small group of men decide that this was where the freedom-seeking Pilgrims should make their homes.

This carefully restored home illustrates the continuing evolution of a household in Plymouth from the mid-1600s through the mid-1700s. The right side of the home was begun in 1666 as a side-chimney house consisting of the front room with fireplace and room above. The rooms have been furnished with seventeenth-century pieces, with a chest and a Bible box believed to have belonged to the Howlands. The fireplace, beams, upstairs floor, and outside walls, made of local goat hair, clamshells, and beach sand, are original. Small pieces of original glass can be seen in the leaded windows.

The rear kitchen, with fireplace and adjoining borning room, plus the two rooms above, now a minimuseum, were all added c.1700. Notice the fireplace includes an oven. The kitchen holds an old, rare water bench, a large specially slanted cupboard, whale-oil lamps, tinderbox, and pewter ware—all illustrating improved living conditions.

You gain another fifty years as you step into the left side of the house, which was built c.1750. Now you see painted wood paneling, wood moldings, decorated wood, sash windows, pewter flatware, a closet and an upstairs with the more lavish furnishings of the eighteenth century. This section is a beautiful climax to a walk through more than a century of Plymouth living.

#4
Plymouth Rock
Water Street
1620
Open all year, no fee
NRHP

From Sandwich Street take next right on Water Street and follow it around to the water. Just past Leyden Street on the right are free parking areas. Park here to visit points #4-13. Plymouth Rock is at end of first parking area.

Though not the huge boulder your imagination expects, this small rock was a giant step for this country and the Pilgrims who landed here in 1620. The rock became the cornerstone of a new nation based on faith in God, with its churches founded upon a rock. Waves still lap the shore and tidal marks engrave the sand surrounding the historic rock upon which those early adventurers dared step to begin life anew in Plymouth.

It was recognized officially in 1742 as the Pilgrim landing site. When a proposed wharf would have hidden it, action was taken by Thomas Faunce, third elder of the Plymouth Church and last remaining person to have spoken with the first Pilgrims. The ancient Plymouthian gathered his children and grandchildren and many others about him. He became the link of oral history as he recounted the Pilgrims' own story of their landing on the rock.

Just prior to the Revolution, in 1774, with twenty yoke of oxen, the rock was moved to the Town Square as a shrine. Unfortunately, it broke in two; one part remained on shore. In 1834 it was ceremoniously moved to Pilgrim Hall.* Finally, in 1880, it was returned and cemented to its original piece. The sixteen-Tuscan-pillared portico, designed by McKim, Mead, and White, was given by the National Society of Colonial Dames of America in 1921. Easy and pleasant access is available to view the rock—so long a symbol of American invincibility and strength.

#5
Replica Pilgrim Houses   *Replica Pilgrim Houses are just north of*
1627 House & c.1657 House   *the Plymouth Rock along the water.*
Water Street
c. 1950
Open extended season,
fee charged

Here you can see the harbor filled with a myriad of masts outlined against the long sandy strip of Plymouth Beach with the Gurnet and Clarks Island in the background. In addition to the peaceful paths and beautiful view, you can easily walk to the Replica Pilgrim Houses, Governor William Bradford's statue, Plymouth Rock, State Pier, and *Mayflower II.*

The first house, the Replica Pilgrim House of 1627, was an initial project of Plimoth Plantation. (see #1) You can picture the four to eight people who lived in this roughhewn, cattail-reed-thatched cottage, with its oiled-linen-cloth windows and dominating fireplace. The second house, now housing a gift shop, is a replica of those built about thirty years later. It is interesting to compare the two. The passage of thirty years made glass for windows available, though in tiny pieces to avoid larger taxes. Clapboards replaced sawn timbers, and shingles replaced roof thatch.

#6
***Mayflower II* & State Pier**
Water Street
Open extended season,
fee charged for
Mayflower II

Just north of the Replica Pilgrim Houses is the State Pier where Mayflower II *is anchored. Facilities: ocean cruises, ferry service between Plymouth and Province-town, scenic tours with historic narrative, gift shop, rest rooms, telephones.*

Sixty-six days of rolling sea were marked with violent storms, no sanitary conditions, seeping water, a cracked main beam, twenty people in the Great Cabin (26 ft. × 18 ft.), eighty-two housed 'tween decks with no natural light or ventilation except when hatches were open, and limited food which developed worms and maggots. Yet the undaunted Pilgrims knelt on deck and thanked God for their deliverance when land was sighted November 9, 1620. Miraculously, of the 102 passengers who left Plymouth, England, September 6, 1620, only four died. Thanks to the birth of two, one hundred settlers arrived in the New World.

Today *Mayflower II*, a replica of a ship of the same period and tonnage as the first *Mayflower*, lies at anchor next to the State Pier. Going aboard you quickly forget it is a replica, for the guides are costumed and speak in English dialects with knowledge only up to and including their recent harrowing Atlantic crossing in the year 1620. Standing 'tween decks, as you feel the slight movement of the *Mayflower II*, imagine the pitching of the first *Mayflower*, the roar of waves and wind, and the darkness, dampness, and foul air with closed hatches. Where once weary colonists slept, ate, and passed the long hours, now walk wide-eyed kids, eager youth, and awed adults.

In 1954, so that all might truly understand the realities of the first *Mayflower* adventure, William A. Baker painstakingly designed plans for *Mayflower II*. Built by Stuart Upham of Devon, England, the vessel was authentically handcrafted, just as the first one would have been. The three-masted, square-rigged bark, captained by Alan Villiers with a crew of experienced sailors, left Plymouth, England, April 20, 1957, to follow the same course as the first *Mayflower*. The ship proved to be very seaworthy and capable of riding out the storms they encountered, but even the hardiest of sailors suffered sea sickness and found the accommodations very cramped for their thirty-three crew members.

#7
Pilgrim Mother
Water and North Streets
1920
Open all year, no fee

Across Water Street from the Replica Pilgrim House, on the corner of North and Water Streets is the Pilgrim Mother statue. Facilities: benches.

Standing serenely, contemplatingly, with yet a touch of sadness, this statue represents that first group of Pilgrim women who came on the *Mayflower*.* While Pilgrim men were the undisputed heads of family, it was the patience, understanding, love, and spiritual guidance of women that served as the essential mortar in the building of this new settlement in a strange land. The Plymouth settlement survived and succeeded, where others failed, because the settlers came as families. It was their feeling of family unity and strength which gave the Pilgrims the necessary foundation to survive and to grow. The continuing growth of America is indebted to the original strength of those Pilgrim women who bore the children, fed and clothed the family, tended the sick, worked in the fields with their men, and quietly endured suffering and hardships while sustaining the faith of all around them.

The statue, given in 1920 by the Daughters of the American Revolution on the three hundredth Anniversary of the Pilgrim Landing, is symbolically surrounded by gardens with special herb plantings. Each herb is representative of the many virtues of the Pilgrim Mother. Basil stands for love, thyme for courage, sage for immortality. You become aware of the qualities necessary to encourage the founding of a new nation.

#8
Mayflower Society House
Edward Winslow House
General Society of
Mayflower Descendants
Headquarters
4 Winslow Street
1754, 1898
Open extended season,
fee charged

Walk up North Street one block to the Mayflower Society House on the right at the corner of North and Winslow Streets.

This fascinating museum house was rescued from being leveled for a parking lot by the General Society of Mayflower Descendants, who have their headquarters here.

Massachusetts Department of Commerce and Development, Division of Tourism

Mayflower Society Edward Winslow House

The mansion expresses living in the grand manner in two eras, early Georgian of Colonial times and Victorian Colonial Revival of the turn of this century. The early Georgian front portion was built in 1754 by Edward Winslow, great-grandson of *Mayflower* passenger Edward Winslow,* third governor of Plymouth Colony. The fourth generation Winslow was also active in public office, but his strong Tory views necessitated his rapid departure at the time of the Revolution.

The next owners, the Jackson family, added interesting events to the house's history. In 1835 daughter Lydian married Ralph Waldo Emerson in the east parlor. In this same room, in 1842, son Dr. Charles Jackson used himself as the subject in an experiment which discovered the use of ether.

In 1898 the house became the property of Chicago millionaire Charles Willoughby, who secured architect Joseph Everett Chandler to enlarge the estate with a Victorian addition. The home was more than doubled, moved back from the road, raised five feet, and nearly surrounded by elaborate porches. The rear Victorian addition regally compliments the Georgian front rooms.

The eye is drawn to the elaborate front portico, the many columned porch, the tiers of balustrades, and the crowning cupola with its spectacular view. Inside, the magnificent flying staircase of the Georgian section is repeated to form a mirror image staircase linking the Georgian and Victorian periods. Lavish rooms take you to another world to experience the feeling of being entertained in the great fashion of past times.

Beautiful paneling and woodwork of the Georgian era, traditionally painted, is complemented by the gleaming natural finish of Honduras mahogany, sycamore, and cherry of the Victorian era. The unusual Delft tiles of the first section are carried throughout.

Museum-quality furnishings are mainly gifts of *Mayflower* descendants. The cover of a Bible box reputedly carried on the *Mayflower*, exquisite chandeliers, many notable ancient clocks, Sandwich glass, Wedgwood, costumes, quilts, and the 1670 Court cupboard of the Brewster family are among the priceless treasures furnishing this magnificent mansion of gracious living and interesting people.

#9   *Diagonally across North Street from the*
Spooner House   *Winslow House is the Spooner House.*
27 North Street
c. 1747
Open extended season,
fee charged

The Spooner House is a museum house of five generations of a Plymouth family. All furnishings are authentic, Spooner-owned, and accumulated over two hundred years. The total picture provides insight into the daily life, employment, and interests of a Plymouth family from pre-Revolutionary days across two centuries to 1954 when the house became a museum.

The house is late Colonial–Early Georgian style at a conservative level. Fireplaces and Oriental rugs appear in nearly all rooms. Wallpapers are varied and interesting, especially in the study—paper which once lined tea boxes from the Orient. Furniture includes pieces of country Chippendale, Queen Anne, Hepplewhite, William and Mary, and Duncan Phyfe. The influence of the sea is felt throughout. The sea captain's bedroom has a window to view the harbor, with neighboring houses recessed slightly so that each house has its harbor view. Treasures from the China trade are displayed, including rose medallion china and blue Canton ware.

The first Spooners to live here, Ephraim and Elizabeth, moved in when Elizabeth, in 1763, inherited the original right side of this house built in 1747. They added the left or eastern portion of the house later. Deacon Ephraim Spooner was a merchant, town clerk for over half a century, served on the Committee of Correspondence, was a judge, a member of the Legislature, and the Executive Council.

James, son of Ephraim and Elizabeth, was also a merchant and owned Grand Banks fishing schooners. He cut an east window to view the wharf area to observe his interests. His son married a Spooner whose brother, Bourne, founded the Plymouth Cordage Company* in 1824. The company grew to become the largest rope-making company in the country, outliving every concern then listed on the Boston Stock Exchange.

A later James, the last Spooner here, worked for the Plymouth Cordage Company for sixty-two years. He was accomplished in music and left funds to provide outstanding concerts at no cost. His civic benevolence included willing this house and furnishings to become an interesting museum house available to all. Costumed hostesses of the Antiquarian Society* share their extensive knowledge to further the society's purpose: "to give the present a better understanding of the past."[6]

#10
Plymouth National Wax
Museum
16 Carver Street
Open extended season,
fee charged

Walk back toward the harbor on North Street, bearing right to the Wax Museum on the corner of Carver and North Streets. Facilities: gift shop.

The Wax Museum is tastefully executed and amazingly realistic. Twenty-seven interestingly detailed tableaus, reenacted from ancient records or paintings, depict early life of the Pilgrims. Informative signs and recordings guide you to scenes of Pilgrims exploring the idea of leaving England, their life in Holland, experiences aboard the *Mayflower,** early Plymouth struggles, and finally the first Thanksgiving.

It is interesting to watch other visitors here—to see the enthusiastic attention and proud patriotism of all ages.

#11
Cole's Hill
Sarcophagus
Statue of Massasoit
Bordered by Carver, North,
Water, and Leyden Streets
1620
Open all year, no fee
NHL

Cole's Hill is directly in front of the Wax Museum. Facilities: benches, scenic view.

This prominent hill, symbolic of the Pilgrims, served as their first lookout, burial ground, and cornfield. First it offered a sense of security—a place from which they could oversee the harbor and surrounding area. Then, struck with the awesome hardships of winter Pilgrims all too soon used it to inter their dead. The unmarked graves were dug secretly at night so Indians would not know of their heavy losses. In time they planted corn atop the hill, which helped turn questionable existence into successful survival.

Cole's Hill was named for James Cole who came from England in 1633 and settled on the hill, where he ran an ordinary and lived until his death in 1692. Cole's Hill is still symbolic of the Pilgrims. Here can be found a granite Sarcophagus, given by the General Society of Mayflower Descendants in 1921, on which are named the almost forgotten half of God-fearing Pilgrims who died that first winter. Its inscription tells the story: "In weariness and painfulness, in watchings often, in hunger and cold they laid the foundations of a state wherein every man through countless ages, should have liberty to worship God in his own way." In close proximity stands the bronze figure of their friend and benefactor, Wampanoag Sachem Massasoit,* who signed a mutual assistance pact with the colonists that lasted over fifty years. This imposing statue was created by Cyrus Dallin and placed here by the Improved Order of Red Men in 1921.

As you stand atop Cole's Hill, sensing the age-old presence of indomitable forefathers, look out with Massasoit over his harbor and yours. Visualize one lonely ship full of fearful yet determined settlers. At the same time see today's harbor full of pleasure boats and a replica of the *Mayflower** docked at State Pier. Let the two visions become intermingled and more than 360 years slip away and the Pilgrim spirit is as fresh and vital today as it was in 1620.

#12	*Turn right on Carver Street and walk one-*
Leyden Street—First Street	*half block to Leyden Street. Walk this first*
Site of First Common	*street for a feeling of early Plymouth. The*
House	*site of the first Common House is on the*
Leyden Street	*SW corner of Water and Leyden Streets.*
1621	*There is a marker.*
Open all year, no fee	

Walk Leyden Street from the waterfront to Burial Hill and walk the street of Pilgrims, the first street in New England. Here were the first homes of the Pilgrims—Bradfords, Brewsters, Winslows. Today the road is paved; then it was dirt, surrounded by a stockade. Now clapboard and brick houses line the route to modern churches above.

Then thatched-roofed, daubed-chimneyed, rough-cut wood homes looked up at a flat-roofed meetinghouse fort with cannon atop.

On December 28, 1620, the Pilgrims scientifically and fairly planned the development. Lots were drawn by the nineteen household groups and single men. A Common House was constructed first, to shelter men working on shore, store their supplies, serve as a hospital, and provide a meetinghouse for worship and public meetings. Here, on February 27, 1621, the first recorded popular suffrage occurred with the election of Myles Standish as Captain.

As you walk, picture the original Pilgrim settlement of seven crude houses and four common buildings guarded by the Fort-Meetinghouse on the hill, all now carefully reproduced at Plimoth Plantation. (see #1) Plymouth, unlike the early settlements of Maine and Virginia, has never been abandoned. In spite of terrible hardships, men built this first street for their wives and families, and it has never been deserted by their descendants to this day.

#13   *Walk back down Leyden Street. On the SW*
Brewster Gardens   *corner of Leyden and Water Streets enter*
Pilgrim Pathways   *the Brewster Gardens. The Gardens ex-*
Entrances: Leyden and   *tend west, running along Town Brook.*
Water Streets (main); Main
Street next to Post Office;
Jenney Grist Mill
Open all year, no fee

Pathways wandering through Brewster Gardens provide opportunity for peaceful strolling in a pastorally pleasant and historically rich setting. The path follows Town Brook where Pilgrims gathered to collect reeds for thatching roofs and, in early spring, to catch herring for fertilizing cornfields.

Memorials along the way remind visitors of their heritage. The Pilgrim Maiden is a stone study of the dedication and courage of "intrepid English women." Determined, strong, yet compassionate, she stands firm against the winds of time and the ebbs and flows of life, with Bible in hand. At Pilgrim Spring you can drink from the fresh-water spring from which Pilgrims drank. Nearby is a memorial tablet to Lydian Emerson,* wife of Ralph Waldo Emerson. It also honors her brother, Dr. Charles Thomas Jackson, who discovered the first safe method of using ether as an anesthetic.

The tastefully landscaped gardens continue as the path wanders across a picturesque bridge and quietly ducks under several busy roadways following the brook. Wildlife is attracted to the brook, which adds to the peaceful atmosphere of Brewster Gardens.

#14
1749 Courthouse
Leyden and Market Streets
1749
Open daily in season and by appointment, no fee, donations accepted
NRHP

Return to your car and drive up Leyden Street to top of hill. The Courthouse is on the left side of the Town Square. Parking is available off Market Street, left just before Town Square. Park here for #14-17.

The 1749 Courthouse is the oldest wooden courthouse in the United States, yet its history reaches back even further. Probably as early as 1670 the court section was added to an already existing building called the "Country House." After 1685, when Plymouth became the "shire" of newly incorporated Plymouth County, court sessions were held here. In 1749 the court building was dismantled piece by piece and probably laid out in the town square. Much of its fine solid timber was used to reconstruct this building keeping the original courtroom, with new underpinings and a new first-floor added. Thus the present 1749 Courthouse, which also had provision for use as a town house, was created.

Spanning the times of both Country House and 1749 Courthouse, a Public Market similar to Faneuil Hall in Boston occupied the basement from 1722 until 1858. In 1820, with the construction of a new courthouse, the building became the Town House.

In 1970 the building was restored, with a museum of the town on the first floor and the original courtrooms on the second. The town museum is a fascinating collage of Plymouth. Archeological displays include a support "knee" of the William Palmer house, c.1622, and specimens of this building's earlier frieze work and wallpaper. The scaffolding components of a torturous-looking gallows are complete with a model and photo of the actual setup. Relics of Pilgrims and Indians, original town records, and ancient fire-fighting and police equipment complete the Plymouth collection.

As you climb the stairs to the restored courtroom, you walk back in time. The reproduction furniture reenacts the scene, and you expect to see the seven Pilgrim judges at the mammoth raised bench facing the entrance. The feeling of the ancient courtroom is heightened by raised clerks' desks, formal witness stand, and jury benches facing the judges. The room is surrounded by portraits of distinguished American judges. In recent years, when the Brockton Courthouse was being repaired, this courtroom again saw active service. Its historic solemnity impressed its modern counterparts.

#15
First Parish Church in
Plymouth
Town Square, Head of
Leyden Street
1606, building 1899
Open for services

The First Parish Church is at the head of Leyden Street, just up from the Courthouse.

"The Lord hath more truth and light yet to break forth out of His Holy Word."[7] Guided by these words from the Reverend John Robinson* in 1620, the ancestors of this First Parish Church in Plymouth set sail from Holland for the New World. Fourteen years earlier a small group, finding the rituals and hierarchy of the Church of England intolerable, had broken away from the established church and worshiped in secret at William Brewster's* manor house in Scrooby,* England. There in 1606 they joined together in a church body which has had a continuous fellowship from England to Holland to America to the present day, culminating here at the First Parish Church.

During their first year in Plymouth, they held services under the able leadership of Elder Brewster in the Fort-Meetinghouse atop Burial Hill. (see #16) Their first settled minister, the Reverend Ralph Smith, came in 1629. Two years later he was assisted by Roger Williams, who went on to establish the colony of Rhode Island. During the next one hundred years, from this mother church came equally strong and faithful sister congregations: First Church in Duxbury and First Church in Marshfield in 1632, First Church in Eastham in 1646, First Church in Plympton in 1698, First Church in Kingston in 1717, and the Second Church in Plymouth in 1738. In 1801 James Kendall, minister of the mother church, preached such Unitarian ideas, that part of the congregation withdrew a year later to form the Third Church in Plymouth, now known as the Church of the Pilgrimage. (see #17)

Today's beautiful, Norman Gothic style stone church, built in 1899, stands as the sixth meeting place and the fifth actual church building, their first meeting place having been in the fort. It stands symbolically at the head of Leyden Street,* where the Pilgrims first lived, adjacent to Burial Hill where many of the Pilgrims lie in eternal rest, and overlooking the harbor where the *Mayflower** first landed the dedicated charter members of this parish. The main doorways, arches, and towers of the church were appropriately fashioned after St. Helena's Church in Austerfield, England, where Governor Bradford* was baptised. The beautiful arched wooden interior is reminiscent of the castles of England where the Pilgrims first gathered. Brilliant Tiffany stained-glass windows abound. The window over the choir loft depicts the historic time when the Reverend John Robinson preached his farewell sermon to his congregation as they prepared to leave Holland aboard the *Speedwell.*

In this beautiful edifice you can feel the strong influence of its heritage reaching back to 1620 and beyond the sea to Leyden, Holland, and Scrooby, England.

#16
Burial Hill
Fort-Meetinghouse site
Head of Leyden Street at
School Street
c.1621, c.1637
Open all year, no fee

Behind the First Parish Church and along School Street is Burial Hill.

Follow the path from Town Square up the dignified steps lined with evergreen to Burial Hill, and walk back in history. Study historic and fascinating stones in this peaceful setting 165 feet above the sea, with the beautiful panoramic view much as it was in Pilgrim times. This hallowed land is the final resting-place of many brave, dedicated, faithful forefathers.

Shortly after landing, the Pilgrims fortified this hill with the help of the *Mayflower's** Captain Jones* and crew, who mounted guns from the ship. Ancient cannon of the same type are installed here now. The fort was repaired and rebuilt many times, in 1627 called a Fort-Meetinghouse, with cannon mounted on the barricaded roof above the meeting room. Here Pilgrims assembled immediately when called by drum beat. In 1643 a brick Watchhouse was constructed nearby. After the end of King Philip's War in 1676 the fort was dismantled, and its timbers given to Sergeant William Harlow. (see #2)

Probably by 1637 the hill became the burial place, with Elder Brewster,* Governor Bradford,* John Howland,* and many *May-*

flower forefathers believed buried here. The oldest dated headstone is 1681. The monument to Governor William Bradford is inscribed in Latin: "What your fathers attained with such difficulty, Do not basely relinquish," an admonition for every generation to consider. The stone for the last man of the *Mayflower* reads, "Here ended the Pilgrimage of John Howland." The last woman and final *Mayflower* survivor, Mary Allerton Cushman, widow of Elder Thomas Cushman, is buried near the Cushman monument.

War history is recorded here by the graves of Caleb Cook, who was with Captain Church* when King Philip* was killed in 1676; of Dr. William Thomas, who was at Louisbourg in 1745 in the French and Indian Wars; and of the twenty-two Revolutionary War graves. Near the Old Fort site is the General James Warren monument. He was president of the Provincial Congress and militia leader. Here also lies his wife, Mercy Otis Warren, literary leader and author.

Author Jane Austen immortalized others buried here in her books, *Nameless Nobleman,* about the mysterious Dr. Francis LeBaron,* and *Dr. LeBaron and His Daughters.* Dr. Francis LeBaron never revealed why he hurriedly escaped the continent, abanding all including his real name, his present name believed to be only his title. He arrived in Plymouth a prisoner, captured aboard a wrecked French ship. At the town's request he remained, served well as physician until his death, and founded the LeBaron family.

Many quaint and unusual messages can be found in this peaceful setting, which honors America's roots.

#17
Church of the Pilgrimage
Leyden and School Streets
1801, 1840, 1898
Open for services

At the corner of School and Leyden Streets on the north side of the Town Square is the Church of the Pilgrimage.

In 1801 the Unitarian views of the new minister at the First Parish Church (across the square) forced a group of people, one fewer than the majority, to separate from that church. They formed what is now the Church of the Pilgrimage. Here members feel, as inscribed on the church facade, they have "adhered to the belief of the fathers" and are the true successors of the original Pilgrim Congregation, which had its origins in England. That Separatist church, formed in Scrooby,* England, in 1606, became the basis of American Congregationalism, with each congregation having its own authority. This idea was a major contribution by Plymouth to American religion.

The 1840 Tuscan building, their second, has an architecturally strong Greek Revival interior. The large, open sanctuary features Corinthian pilasters in an extensive colonnade reaching to the elaborate ceiling molding. The altar is contrastingly simple. Recessed paneled woodwork and tall windows of tiny cathedral glass complete the effect of this church, which remains strong in its Congregational belief.

#18
Richard Sparrow House
42 Summer Street
c.1640
Open as pottery shop,
fee for historic house
NRHP

Drive south on Market Street (away from Square), turn right on Summer Street and then left on Spring Lane. Cross Town Brook and park in the parking area to see points 18 & 19. For the Sparrow House walk back to Summer Street and turn right. The house will be on the right. Facilities: pottery shop with exhibits.

It is believed the left half of this tightly clapboarded house was built circa 1640 by Richard Sparrow, which would make it the oldest house still standing in Plymouth. It was originally built with one room on the ground floor and a sleeping room above. Step inside to appreciate the seventeenth-century furnishings, charm, and practicality. The focus of early settlers' homelife was the large fireplace. Here meals were prepared and heat was given to warm occupants throughout long, cold New England winters.

During the fifteen years that Richard Sparrow lived here, he added the back rooms, giving the house a saltbox effect. In 1690 the next owner, Bonum, acquired the adjoining land and added the right side of the house, tying into the central chimney. Following the Bonum years the house passed through a series of owners until 1932 when Katherine L. Alden bought it. Through restoration the original red oak timbers allotted to Richard Sparrow in early Plymouth records were discovered, thus establishing the approximate date of initial construction.

Katherine Alden lived in one side of the house, using the other to develop a pottery school, business, and museum. She first used local clay and her own special glazing methods which produced a popular reddish earthenware. Her classes evolved into the first state-sponsored adult education classes in the country. The pottery school and business still continue today with new directors making a more advanced stoneware pottery.

#19
Jenney Grist Mill
Town Brook Park
Spring Lane
1971
Open All year, no fee

Walk back to Spring Lane, turn left onto it and the Grist Mill will be on your left. Facilities: gift shop, benches, paths, parking.

The Jenney Grist Mill is a reconstruction of the ancient gristmill operated by John Jenny possibly as early as 1636. The modern 1971 reconstruction was based on technology of three centuries ago. From outside you can see the quaint weathered millhouse, simple dam and waterpower controls, and the fish ladder, where herring run in early spring. The path along the brook leads to Brewster Gardens. (see #13) Inside, the waterpowered mill grinds corn, wheat, and rye daily, with the milled flours available at the gift shop.

The original mill was begun by Stephen Deane. At Deane's death, John Jenny (spelling of Jenny varies) completed this grinding mill and operated it until his death in 1644, when his son Samuel took over until 1683. The gristmill continued to operate for 212 years.

This quiet, peaceful brook once supported many active mills. In 1671 George Bonum erected a fulling mill nearby. Later industries included in 1838 the Robbins Cordage Company, in 1860 Loring's Mill which supported a tack and rivet works, and in 1890 the Bradford and Kyle Wire Works. Finally, in 1971 the Jenney Grist Mill was reconstructed as a working mill.

Nearby are additional craft-making and gift shops, as well as peaceful Town Brook Park. In the park well-kept lawns, towering copper beech trees, inviting paths and benches surround Jenney Pond. The pleasant setting is complete with a footbridge where children happily fish and wild water fowl abound.

#20
Captain Joseph Bartlett
House
Plymouth Federal Savings
Bank
32 Court Street
1803
Open as bank

Return to your car. Return to Summer Street and turn left. Take this first right on Russell Street, then take right at Police Station and follow around to Court Street. Turn left on Court. The bank will be on your left.

Plymouth provides an interesting study of the architectural development of the country it began. The steeply pitched, thatched-roof houses of the earliest period are accurately reproduced at Plimoth Plantation.* Other seventeenth-century Colonials—Capes, gambrels, and saltboxes—are found sprinkled throughout town, some among the Greek Revivals of North Street. Stately Georgians and Federals are not as common, with this possibly Bulfinch-designed Federal being an outstanding example of the period.

This magnificent Federal building retains much of its graceful proportions and elegant, delicate detail as when constructed in 1803 by Captain Joseph Bartlett. His grandson, John Bartlett, who was probably born here, is best known for his work *Familiar Quotations*. The mansion was purchased in 1827 by Nathaniel Russell, Plymouth's leading industrialist. He expanded his shipbuilding, owning, and trading interests to include industries such as rolling and slitting mills and nail manufacturing, thus spurring the industrial growth of Plymouth. Here lived succeeding generations of Russells for 125 years until the 1950s when the building became the Plymouth Federal Savings Bank.

#21   *Continue north on Court Street to Chilton*
Pilgrim Hall   *Street. Pilgrim Hall is on the NE corner.*
75 Court Street
1824
Open all year, fee charged
NRHP

Pilgrim Hall is one of the oldest public museums in the United States. It was constructed by the Pilgrim Society in 1824 to appropriately shelter Pilgrim artifacts for all generations to admire and share. The solid Greek Revival structure of Pilgrim Hall was designed by Alexander Parris,* creator of Boston's St. Paul's Church and Quincy Marketplace.* Originally of wood, the columned portico was created in granite in 1922, and the library wing was also a later addition. The cornerstone contains ancient treasures, among them a 1621 sermon and the first printed newspaper in the colony, dated 1786.

The museum houses the world's most extensive collection of Pilgrim possessions—the books they read and wrote and the tools, weapons, and furnishings they brought or fashioned. A special slide presentation is available, telling the story of the Pilgrims from England to Holland, and the voyage, landings, and arrival of those courageous forefathers. Paintings include one of Edward Winslow* in the only actual painting from life of a *Mayflower** passenger as well as later massive renditions of Pilgrim experiences.

The owners' names of these invaluable relics read like a well-known history book, which this museum actually depicts. The swords of Captain Myles Standish* and Governor John Carver,* chairs of Carver, Brewster,* Bradford,* and Winslow,* books of/or by Elder Brewster, Bibles belonging to John Alden,* Governor William Bradford, and John Eliot's 1685 edition in which he translated phonetically the Indian language are some of the priceless treasures. There are also models of a Pilgrim house and Old Fort-Meetinghouse, Wampanoag art and arrowheads, Champlain's 1605 map, Brewster's chart for the *Mayflower*, and Peregrine White's* cradle.

The *Sparrow Hawk* section is fascinating—the only relic of the tiny valiant ships which explored and colonized America. Bound for Virginia, in 1626 the *Sparrow Hawk* was wrecked off Cape Cod, buried in sand, and rediscovered in 1863. She was displayed on the Boston Common* until brought here for permanent preservation in 1889.

#22
National Monument to the
Forefathers
Allerton Street
1859–1889
Open all year, no fee
NRHP

Drive north on Court Street to Samoset Street, Route 44, and turn left. Follow Samoset Street to Allerton, second right, and turn right. The monument will be on the left side of Allerton Street.

From her impressive site above the harbor, the dominant figure of Faith, symbol of Pilgrim thoughts and deeds, surmounts the tallest solid-granite monument in the United States. Eighty-one feet high, the monument was a prototype for the Statue of Liberty. The noble figure of Faith is thirty-six feet tall, with smaller figures representing liberty, morality, law, and education. These in turn shelter other ideas depicted in granite. The *Mayflower** passengers are listed. The magnificent monument is dedicated to Pilgrims in remembrance "of their labors, sacrifices and sufferings for the cause of civil and religious freedom." Creation of the monument was one of the primary goals of the Pilgrim Society,* founded in 1820 to perpetuate appreciation of the Pilgrims.

#23
The Antiquarian House
126 Water Street
1809
Open extended season,
fee charged
NRHP

Return to Samoset Street and turn left. Follow Samoset Street through to Water. Turn right and park in the lot immediately on your right. The Antiquarian House is across Memorial Street from the parking area. Park here for points #23–25.

Major William Hammatt wanted a home unique in Plymouth, where the tidy Cape style reigned. In 1809 he built this basically Federal residence, with its unusual octagonal rooms and three-story, split-level ell.

Hammatt was a young, successful shipowner and merchant. He and his wife, a descendant of John Howland* and Dr. Frances LeBaron,* entertained lavishly. The War of 1812, which halted New England shipping, eventually caused the Hammatts' move to Maine, where they founded the town of Howland.

In 1830 Thomas Hedge purchased this house where his descendants were to live for nearly a century. Hedge, a coastwise and worldwide merchant, owned shares in fishing schooners and whalers. Hedge's Wharf was located where Plymouth Rock is today. The Hedges also liked to entertain, with musicals in the drawing room. Daniel Webster* was a frequent guest.

The delicate proportions of this unusual Federal house are highlighted in the balustraded full porch of the clapboarded exterior, which is capped with hip roof and four chimneys. From the reception hall, the graceful staircase rises between octagonal formal front rooms. Marble fireplaces, bronze cornices, furniture of Queen Anne, Hepplewhite, and Chippendale, and china from Canton and Bristol complete the scene portraying the life style of successful nineteenth century merchant-ship owners. Hardworking New Englanders hadn't the time to create this kind of art, so they appreciated and admired such luxuries.

Another featured room is the captain's bedroom, so called as it viewed the harbor where trade ships arrived. A McIntyre* bed, one of the twelve made by the architect of Federal Salem, dominates the room. Nearby, the pioneering 1863 bathroom is retained as it was. Furnishings throughout are all from Plymouth history, much from the Hedge family and their friends. Costumed hostesses enjoy sharing "their" house and their extensive knowledge, often with unusual anecdotes, to give you the feeling of knowing the family and their times and becoming part of their lives.

In 1919 the life of the mansion was threatened, and the Antiquarian Society* was formed to save it. Preservation included moving the entire building, which was accomplished by one elderly man with one horse over a full summer. The Society now owns and maintains a house to demonstrate life in each century: the 1677 Harlow Old Fort House (see #2), the 1749 Spooner House (see #9), as well as the 1809 Antiquarian House. The Antiquarian House was appropriately opened to the public on Forefathers' Day in 1920 when Calvin Coolidge,* then governor of Massachusetts, occupied Governor Bradford's chair here for the now traditional succotash, a hearty stew served every Forefathers' Day.

#24
Mayflower Experience
114 Water Street
Open extended season,
fee charged

Turn right and walk south on Water Street to the Mayflower Experience which will be on the right side of Water Street.

In three small theaters a reenactment of the *Mayflower** voyage is portrayed though slides, wax figures, and audio effects. Outside the theater a replica model, called the *Mayflower III*, is displayed. A candle factory outlet and extensive gift shop complete "The Mayflower Experience."

#25
Town Wharf
Water Street, foot of Park
Avenue
1800s, 1921
Open all year, no fee

Walk back by parking area and cross Water Street to the Town Wharf. Facilities: docking and mooring spaces available through harbor master, deep-sea fishing, scenic cruises, charter boats, and fishing.

Where today you see only Town Wharf and State Pier, during the 1800s you would have seen as many as eight wharves servicing whalers, merchant ships, and fishing vessels on Plymouth's busy waterfront. Passengers traveled by steamboat from Plymouth to the Cape and Boston. Water Street bustled with countinghouses, blacksmith shops, sail lofts, rigging lofts, cooper shops, and ships' chandleries. Water Street continues to be the busy center of Plymouth life, only now world-traveling seamen have been replaced by world-traveling tourists.

Plymouth's fishing fleets, which have sailed in and out of Plymouth harbor since the mid-1700s, have successfully weathered embargoes, wars, and tariffs. Though the ships are newer and the gear modernized, the fishermen are still clad in hip boots, work clothes, and slickers like their fathers before them. They still sail with the same tides, search out the same seafood (yellowtail and blackback flounder, cod, and lobsters), and face the same age-old dangers of the sea. Walking along the wharf you can see local fishing vessels and ones from as far away as St. Augustine, Florida. Here they take on ice and supplies or unload their catch to be sold in Plymouth or trucked to Boston and New York.

On warm sunny days the harbor is alive with motorboats, small fishing boats, visiting and local yachts, and sailboats with their colorful sails contrasting against the blue water and sky. At night light-houses—Duxbury Pier Light and Plymouth Gurnet Light—beckon to you with their flashing lights, each with its own special identifying sequence.

This picturesque harbor, now viewed by tourists and residents, was once entered by men and women looking for a home, a refuge, a new world, and a new life, all based on complete faith in their God.

#26
Cranberry World Visitors
Center
Water Street
Open extended season,
no fee

Return to your car. Exit from parking area and turn left on Water Street; drive north along water to Cranberry World Visitors Center, which will be on your right. Facilities: parking, museum, scenic views.

A fascinating cranberry museum is offered by Ocean Spray Cranber-ries, Incorporated, a fifty-plus-year-old cooperative.

Outside there are well-signed visual dioramas showing "What's in a Bog," an actual working bog, plus displays of old machinery and tools. Inside, well-labeled displays, many with audio-visual effects, tell the story of cranberries and the people who have worked with them since Colonial times. Cooking demonstrations, recipes, and cranberry re-freshments are included. Art exhibits, outdoor concerts, and an invit-ing parklike area with beautiful harbor views are featured at this well-executed cranberry museum.

#27
Commonwealth Winery
Cordage Park
383 Court Street
1899 Library, 1978 winery
operation
Open all year, no fee

Continue to end of Water Street, turn left and drive to Route 3A, Court Street. Turn right on Court Street. Follow Court Street one mile to Winery which will be on the right. Enter at Cordage Park's main en-trance and follow signs to Winery.

The building is an 1899 Colonial Revival, in its day a Plymouth showplace, with the beautiful panoramic view of Plymouth Bay. It was constructed by the Plymouth Cordage Company* as a library for its employees. The company was noted for its thoughtful, extensive provisions for its employees, though the building's present use could not have been envisioned then!

Now the library has been rescued, and the main room is gradually being restored. Here photos explain the wine-making process, related paraphernalia are displayed, and a free tasting bar and retail sales area are established.

A guided tour leads down a narrow stairway into a room full of fifty gallon oak barrels aging red wine. A modified coal chute is the grape transporter. The whole wine-making process is in action and explained—stemming and crushing of grapes, pumping must to fermentation areas, screening, heat control, storing, bottling, labeling, and shipping. All occur amid the fascinating contrast of elaborate woodwork and other architectural details of the past.

The new industry has been scientifically developed after careful study. Areas surrounding the numerous local cranberry bogs are ideal for grape growing. Much of the work is hand done, yet the industry is growing healthily in the space age. It is interesting to learn about the wine-making process and share the excitement of this new Massachusetts industry.

This ends the guided tour section of Plymouth.
To continue tour drive north on Route 3A to Kingston.

Plymouth Beaches and Parks

(A) **Priscilla Beach**
(south on 3A past Rocky Hill Road; left on Point Road to beach at end; next to White Horse Beach)

Beautiful sandy beach, with White Horse Beach creates sweeping crescent along open ocean; facilities: swimming; limited public parking, private (fee) lots between White Horse Beach and Priscilla Beach; open all year, no fee

(B) **White Horse Beach**
(3A south 1 mile past Plimoth Plantation turn left on Rocky Hill Road; follow to end; turn left and follow to beach; next to Priscilla Beach)

Inviting, open, sandy beach; facilities: lifeguards, swimming; private (fee) parking lots beyond beach, limited public parking; open all year, no fee

(C) Pilgrim Station Shore Front, Boston Edison Company; (south on 3A one mile past Plimoth Plantation turn left onto Rocky Hill Road, 1.4 miles to entrance on left)

Beautiful open ocean vista, framed with flourishing rose hips and beach plums plus well-maintained grassy areas; facilities: benches, fishing (no swimming), rest rooms, walking; parking; shore-front park of this nuclear plant is open all year, no fee

(D) Plymouth Beach Warren Avenue (at Bert's Restaurant parking-lot entrance)

Plymouth's longest beach, part sandy, part rocky; open panoramic water view; facilities: bathhouse, lifeguards, picnicking, rest rooms, swimming; parking; open all year, parking fee in season

(E) Stephens Field Park off Stephens Lane or Sandwich Street

Bay park with marshy beach; facilities: ball fields, bathhouse, concessions, picnicking, playground equipment, swimming, tennis; parking; open all year, parking fee weekends in season

(F) Brewster Gardens* (see #13). Entrances: corner Leyden and Water Streets; Main Street near post office; Jenney Grist Mill*

Pleasant park with path along Town Brook and several Plymouth memorials; open all year, no fee

(G) Nelson Street Park off Water Street (first street north of Cranberry World*)

Open harbor view and marsh beach; facilities: bathhouse, ball fields, play area, picnicking, rest rooms, swimming; parking; open all year, seasonal weekend parking fee

(H) Town Brook Park Spring Lane (see Jenney Grist Mill*)

Peaceful expanse of well-maintained grass and trees with millpond and ornamental bridge; nearby path connects with Brewster Gardens* along Town Brook; ample parking; open all year, no fee

(I) Morton Park off Summer Street (after cross Route 3 take first left, small sign for park)

Freshwater inland park; facilities: bathhouse, concessions, lifeguards, picnicking, rest rooms, swimming; parking; open all year, seasonal fee

Ⓙ **Myles Standish**
　　State Forest
　　Routes 3, 44, 58

12,000 acres of forest; facilities: campsites, bathhouse, boating, concessions, fishing, hiking, horse trails, hunting, picnicking, recreational vehicle trails, swimming; parking; open all year, fee charged

Plymouth Harbor Tours
Cape Cod Canal Cruises
Whale Watching Trips
Fishing

Town Pier or State Pier
Captain John & Son 224-8136
Plymouth Harbor Tours 746-4762

HISTORY OF KINGSTON

Master Christopher Jones'* agreement with the Pilgrims was only to transport them aboard the *Mayflower** to the New World. Yet when they landed at Plymouth, he, his ship, and his crew remained until April, supporting and helping the determined Pilgrims. Just as Captain Jones' essential support helped the Pilgrims to survive and establish a successful settlement, so has his namesake, the Jones River, served as the essential artery for Kingston, servicing her people from earliest settlers to today's modern residents.

As more colonists came to Plymouth, settlers reached out from compact Plymouth seeking more land and greater opportunities. The shores of the Jones River provided ideal grazing land with easy access by water. In the 1627 land-grant distribution, Governor William Bradford* received land along this Jones River. Here Bradford's sons and their sons built homesteads which soon prospered. By the 1720s grandson Major John Bradford* owned most of what today is north Kingston and gave part of his land for a meetinghouse, schoolhouse, burying ground, training green, and minister's home. Due to his leadership and generosity, Kingston was incorporated in 1726. Thus a century after the landing of the Pilgrims, the name of Bradford continued to be a strong guiding force.

During the early 1700s, Kingston was predominantly a farming community situated on the banks of this river which provided power for her mills as well as docking areas for small fishing vessels and a limited coastal trade. The year 1713 saw the widening of Kingston's scope as Samuel Drew and Caleb Stetson developed shipbuilding, which soon became the hub of Kingston's economy, continuing through the mid-1800s. During the Revolutionary War, a ship of Washington's Navy, the brigantine *Independence*, was built here in 1776. In 1806 Joseph Holmes,* who became one of the leading shipowners in the country, established his yards at the Landing.*

Shipbuilding continued on the lower part of the river until about 1874. The upper river and tributaries were busy supplying mill sites and power for Kingston's growing mills and factories, which were a dominant part of the economy from the 1820s into the 1900s. These industries in time brought a change to Kingston's way of life. Factory workers no longer needed large tracts of land for farming but settled in small homes, closer together. The mid-1800s saw the completion of the Old Colony Railroad, improved roads, antislavery and temperance movements, and the arrival of immigrants from Germany and Ireland to work in the factories. Today Kingston is an interesting combination of old world traditions, well-preserved Colonial heritage, and modern-day small industry.

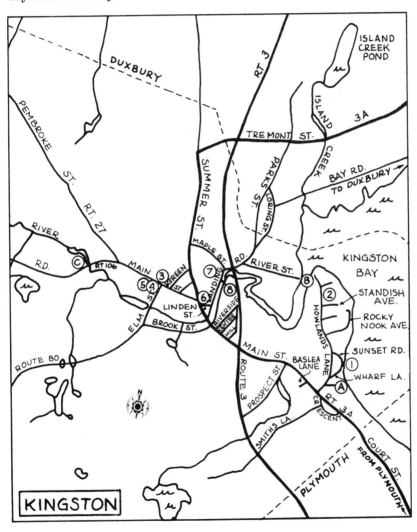

KINGSTON

DIRECTIONS:
From Plymouth continue north on Route 3A to Howlands Lane, or enter Kingston by Route 3, exiting at Route 3A. Go south on Route 3A or Main Street to Howlands Lane to start tour (sign for Grays Beach and Rocky Nook).

#1
Delano's Wharf
Rocky Nook
Wharf Lane
1802-1803
Private

Turn right onto Howlands Lane and take second right, which is Wharf Lane. Follow it to water's edge where you will see the stone wharf on the right.

Kingston's Rocky Nook has proven to be an ideal location for the servicing of ships since the 1600s, when wealthy merchant Edward Gray first built a wharf and warehouse here on the Nook's shoreline. During the 1700s the Sever family of prominent merchants and ship-owners added their wharves to Rocky Nook. Next, the 1800s saw the arrival of the Delanos with Benjamin Delano and Captain Peter Winsor building the present stone wharf in 1802.

Benjamin Delano and son, Joshua, were second only to Joseph Holmes* in ownership of vessels in Kingston during the mid-1800s. Their wharf was a beehive of maritime activity centering on fishing, trade, and rigging. Ships built on the Jones River were brought here to Delano's Wharf for final rigging before going to sea. Kingston's fishing fleet landed their fish here and at other wharves on the Nook. The fish were laid on local fish flakes to dry, then preserved with salt from the adjacent Delano saltworks, and later stored in warehouses, to be shipped throughout the world.

Today's peaceful residential atmosphere is a far cry from the busy commercial maritime center of the 1800s, when the wharf was set against a background of ships' masts, cargo-laden docks, and windmills pumping water to Delano saltworks.

#2
Howland Farm Site
Howlands Lane
1638
Open all year, no fee

Follow Wharf Lane, which becomes Sun-set Road, back to Howlands Lane and turn right. A short distance after Stand-ish Avenue on the right side of Howlands Lane on side of hill is the Howland Farm marker. On the left side of the lane is a marker for son Joseph Howland's home.

Here near this stone, appropriately marked with a relief of the *Mayflower*,* was the homestead of Pilgrims John and Elizabeth Howland.* (see Plymouth #3) In 1638, looking for wider horizons, John Howland bought this land on Rocky Nook extending from the stone marker to the water's edge. On this seashore land John and Elizabeth farmed and watched their nine children grow and become independent. In later years, when the main house burned, John and Elizabeth moved to Plymouth to live with their son, Jabez, until a home could be rebuilt. They later returned to Kingston where John died in 1673.

#3
First Congregational
Parish Church (Unitarian)
1851
Main and Green Streets
Open for services

Return on Howlands Lane to Main Street, Route 3A, and turn right. Follow Route 3A to intersection of Routes 3A and 106. Bear left on Route 106, drive two blocks to Green Street. Turn right and park on street for #3–5.

Where else but America, New England particularly, were so many towns founded because devoted churchgoers found traveling to their distant meetinghouses increasingly difficult? Thus it was in Kingston in 1717 that the first line of the petition of separation from Plymouth immediately refers to their distance from the meetinghouse and the desire of about forty-eight families to establish their own church.

The Reverend Joseph Stacy, a twenty-six-year-old Harvard gradu-ate, became the first minister. The initial meetinghouse, erected in 1721, was a small, simple structure, large enough to hold the entire population. The men's benches, women's benches, and rare family pews, though Spartan, were separated from the galleries at each end where Indians and Negroes sat.

The church quietly progressed under the Reverend Stacy for twenty years until his death, when the Reverend Thaddeus Maccerty was called. Maccerty's leadership was brief, due to his inviting to Kingston the controversial, fiery Reverend George Whitefield. This eloquent evangelist stormed through many New England churches in the mid-eighteenth century. Kingston shut its meetinghouse doors to White-field and its own minister Maccerty. Later, ardent patriot the Rever-end William Rand led the flock from 1746 through the Revolution, to be replaced at his death by the Reverend Zephaniah Willis, who would serve Kingston for sixty-seven years. A devoted record keeper, he became the town's first historian.

During the Willis ministry, in 1798, the second meetinghouse was built—a magnificent structure. The building had impressive twin towers, which flanked the grand columned portico. While this new church was being constructed, the congregation met in an unusual temporary shelter made from the roof of their first meetinghouse supported on posts on the Training Green and irreverently called the "Quail Trap."

The present church was constructed in 1851. Greek Revival and Italianate combine in the dominating bracketed pediment, quoined corners, rounded arch doors and windows, and gleaming white shiplap facade.

#4   *Continue one-half block west on Main to*
Joseph Holmes House   *Elm Street. The Holmes house is on the*
Elm and Main Streets   *SW corner facing Elm Street.*
1797
Private

A quiet, devout man of commanding physical and spiritual stature, Joseph Holmes, born in 1771, prepared for the ministry and served a church on Cape Cod. Soon, feeling his true talents lay in the building of ships rather than the saving of souls, he leased a shipyard on the Taunton River.

Returning to his hometown in 1805 he bought this house, built by his brother Lemuel, and a shipyard at the Landing. He commenced a career in Kingston that would cover fifty-seven years. He oversaw the building of seventy-eight more vessels, culminating in his being the leading shipbuilder and owner of packets, fishing vessels, and mer-chant ships in Kingston between 1830 and 1855.

When Joseph and his wife, Lucy, bought Lemuel's home they also took over his store, located in the front northeast room. While Joseph oversaw the building of ships, guided his many trade ventures, and corresponded with foreign and domestic merchants, Lucy was busy turning a failing store into a prosperous business. Their dignified yet conservative Federal home spoke of their financial success. The indomitable Mr. Holmes, never retiring, continued to oversee his shipyards until his death in 1863 at age ninety-two.

#5
Washburn Tavern
234 Main Street
c.mid-1700
Private

Next door to the Holmes House on Main Street is the former Washburn Tavern, now a private home.

Beautifully maintained, this late Colonial appears more like early Georgian, perhaps due to its interesting arrival here. For arrive it did, transported by oxcart and packet boat from Marshfield, where it had been built by a Winslow about mid-1700. About 1795 stonecutter Bildad Washburn purchased the house and dismantled it in preparation for its move here. The handsome house was reassembled and opened soon after as Washburn Tavern. When the second meetinghouse was built in 1798 pew-owner Bildad Washburn was able to host the celebrating workers in his new tavern.

#6
Squire William Sever House
2 Linden Street
c.1768
Private

Return on Main Street to Route 3A and turn right. Take first left which is Linden Street. The Squire Sever House is on the left.

This beautifully preserved home provides architectural interest in addition to telling the story of the dynamic Sever family. When Squire William Sever built his home about 1768 on Linden Street, it was a gambrel-roofed, twin-chimneyed Georgian country mansion house. It was greatly modified during the Federal Period with the addition of a third floor and roof balustrade. In 1842 the squire's son, Captain James Sever, removed the third-floor addition which was in need of repair. By 1942 the roof balustrade was gone also, and the original classic Georgian again dominates.

Squire William Sever was representative to the General Court in 1750 at the age of twenty-one, a member of the Provincial Congress of Massachusetts Bay, and state agent supervising the building of the brig *Independence*.* Much later, his great-granddaughter, Martha Sever, pioneered as a nurse during the Civil War and died serving this cause.

Squire William was also a very successful merchant, shipowner, and land baron, continuing and expanding his father's interests and later joined by his sons. The Severs owned an ironworks and furnace and engaged in whaling.

#7
Major John Bradford House
Landing Road at Maple
Street
1674
Open seasonally and by
appointment, fee charged

Continue a short distance on Linden Street to Landing Road and turn left. Follow Landing Road along the river to Maple Street. The entrance to the Bradford House is on the left off Landing Road just before you come to Maple Street.

Often referred to as the principal inhabitant of Kingston, Major John Bradford led in the establishment of Kingston's own church and the new town itself when they broke from Plymouth in 1726. Major Bradford, grandson of Governor William Bradford* who was granted land in Kingston a century earlier, was a prominent landowner and very generous in donating land for the town center and other needs. A successful merchant, John Bradford exported local products and owned a gristmill as well as being a Plymouth deputy, state representative, selectman, moderator of the first town meeting, and military leader during King Philip's War.

On a rise overlooking the Jones River, from which he could oversee his domain, Major John Bradford built the first (west) portion of this house as a half house in 1674. Here he and his wife Mercy raised their seven children and lived for over half a century. In 1720 the Bradfords added the rest of today's house and rebuilt the fireplaces. During the 1850s, publisher Walter Lippincott rented the house to Kingston's first Irish immigrant family. Here a traveling priest celebrated the first mass in Kingston.

In 1920, historian George Francis Dow* guided the restoration, and a year later this historic house was opened to the public. Period furnishings, most from the area, help recreate the image of family life of a seventeenth-century "principal inhabitant." The architecture is classic First Period—a plain facade, low to the ground, with small diamond-paned windows, unobtrusive entry door, massive central chimney, and saltbox gable roof.

Here was once housed the original manuscript of Governor William Bradford's history *Of Plymouth Plantation* in the beautiful ancient

Major John Bradford House

script of the governor's hand. This unique, irreplaceable treasure was lent to interested researchers by Major John Bradford. In 1728 one of the borrowers left the manuscript at the library of Old South Church in Boston. Here it remained for fifty years. During the Revolution, the manuscript disappeared. Another half century passed before chance found the work at the library of a London palace. It returned to its native land in 1897 and is now carefully preserved in the Boston State House.*

#8
Holmes Shipyard Site
Landing Marine
Landing Road
1765
Open for business

Across Landing Road from the Bradford House is Landing Marine, which is the site of the Holmes Shipyard. Next door to Landing Marine is the Stephen Drew House.

Stephen Drew House
51 Landing Road
1785
Private

In 1776 the famous Revolutionary sixteen-gun brig *Independence* was built here at the Landing. What is today called the "Landing Place" on the Jones River was for more than a hundred years the center of Kingston's most profitable industry, shipbuilding. Don't let this river, which is reduced to a stream at low tide, fool you. For here stood busy shipyards and wharves exchanging trading goods from the mid-1700s until the last Holmes ship was sold in 1887.

The Landing area was originally owned by Major John Bradford.* From 1765 when Samuel Foster built a wharf here down through shipyard owners Lysander Bartlett, Joseph Holmes,* and John Drew to today's Marine Landing, the Landing has continually hosted a working boatyard.

From 1806 to 1883 the renowned Holmes yard turned out one to three vessels per year, sending the larger ones to Delano's Wharf* on Rocky Nook for rigging. The smaller vessels fished the Grand Banks and carried on a prosperous packet trade between Kingston and Boston. The larger barks and schooners carried cotton from southern ports to England and Europe, returning with iron, salt, coal, and Irish immigrants escaping the potato famine of 1845–1847.

The house next door at 51 Landing was built by Stephen Drew c.1785 when he was building vessels at the Landing. It was known as the Landing House, and Joseph Holmes later used it as a sail loft with a ship's chandlery in the basement. He also served crackers, cheese, and coffee here to celebrate the launching of his ships.

This ends the guided tour section of Kingston. Follow Landing Road under the bridge at the base of Maple Street to continue tour to Duxbury.

Kingston Beaches and Parks

(A) **Gray's Beach**
   Howland Lane

Small, sandy tidal beach from which can see Delano Wharf* with facilities: bathhouse, lifeguards, picnicking, open ball-playing area and playground, rest rooms, swimming, tennis; open all year, seasonal parking fee

(B) **Ah De Noh**
   End of River Street off
   Landing Road

At the mouth of the Jones River, town boat launching with harbor master's office, ample parking; open all year, annual launching fee

(C) **Sampson Common and**
   Memorial Forest
   Wapping Road west of
   bridge

Natural park with developed paths, facilities: fishing, parking, picnicking; open all year, no fee

HISTORY OF DUXBURY

Duxbury has been home to four giants in the world of men—two founding Pilgrims in the 1600s and two merchants extraordinaire in the 1800s.

In 1630, as Plymouth opened her doors to more and more settlers, the confines of the stockade settlement became too claustrophobic for Captain Myles Standish* and Elder William Brewster.* Seeking more land, they settled on a fertile peninsula, Captain's Nook Hill,* in Duxbury. One, Elder Brewster, helped sustain the indomitable inner courage and indestructible belief in God that the Pilgrims had, allowing them to face any and all adversaries with a faith that did not know the meaning of the word defeat. The other, Captain Standish, took a band of fewer than thirty questionably trained and armed men and, through his own bravado and courage, obtained the respect and friendship of the local Indians and put fear into the hearts of the unfriendly ones. Their determined leadership allowed a fledgling settlement to ultimately grow into a mighty nation.

By 1631 these families, along with other Plymouth settlers, had moved permanently to Duxbury, named in honor of Standish's ancestral home. Here their first church was gathered in 1632 under the able leadership of Elder Brewster.

The town of Duxbury was a farming community for its first hundred years, until 1719, when Thomas Prence opened a shipyard on the Nook. Soon Duxbury was launched on a new and exciting way of life.

The year 1764 witnessed the commercial beginning of two other Duxbury giants, Ezra Weston* and Ezra II,* who dominated the Duxbury maritime world until 1857. Ezra Weston at age twenty-one bought Benjamin Prior's yard on the Nook, soon called the "Navy Yard" because Weston built so many ships there. Ezra and son, Ezra II, created such a successful maritime conglomerate that they were known locally as King Caesar I and King Caesar II.

Weston shipyards, at the Nook and later on Bluefish River, built Weston ships using wood from Weston-owned forests or brought from Maine on Weston ships. Sails were made at Weston sail lofts, anchors at

Weston Forge, and even food eaten aboard Weston ships was produced on Weston farms. Weston profits were invested in the Duxbury Bank where Ezra was president. In the "Weston World" of the Northeast, father and son alike were all powerful and wealthy, yet were benevolent employers well ahead of their time.

From 1820 to 1870, along with the world-famous name of Weston, there were other prosperous shipyards run by Sprague, Drew, Sampson, Turner, Hall, Delano, and Cushing. Shipbuilding and coastal and foreign trade touched every life. Duxbury men took pride in the ships they built and in the local crews who sailed them. When a ship was launched, schools and businesses closed, flags flew, and all gathered to help and/or watch the graceful ship slide off her stocks and float freely and easily.

Two other industries, fishing and shoe manufacturing, were important factors in Duxbury's nineteenth-century economy. Fishing vessels plied the Georges and Grand Banks for cod and mackerel. During the winter months seamen turned to shoemaking, first in small one-room shops by their own homes and later in factories where more modern mass production added to their financial success.

As the need for larger ships grew, the shallow harbors of Duxbury proved inadequate, and craftsmen moved to other ports to continue their trade. The discovery of gold and the building of the railroad turned men's thoughts westward, and many families left Duxbury. However, the railroad proved an asset, bringing summer people to enjoy Duxbury's natural beauty and ocean-side recreation.

Today Duxbury is a stately, picturesque, New England coastal town which takes pride in its unique history, preserves its historic merchants' and sea captains' eighteenth- and nineteenth-century homes, and welcomes year-round and summer residents to enjoy its sandy beaches, peaceful harbors, and beautiful countryside.

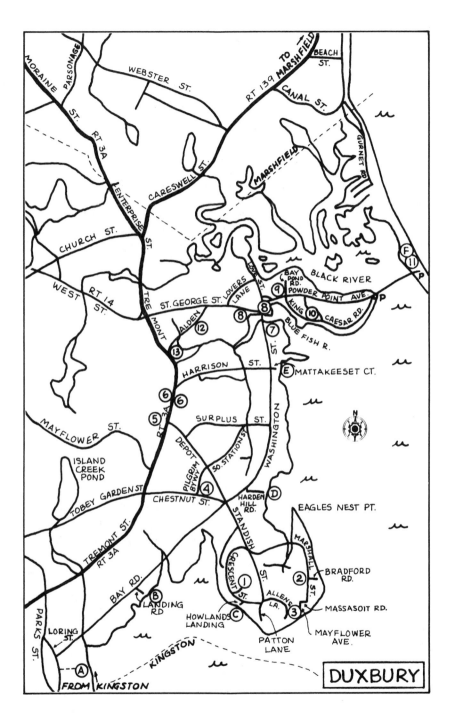

DUXBURY

DIRECTIONS:
From Kingston travel north on Landing Road, which becomes Loring Street in Duxbury; .3 mile after crossing town line bear right on Bay Road (sign for Duxbury Business Area). Drive 2.1 miles to Standish Street. Or, take Route 3 to Duxbury and exit at Route 3A, Tremont Street. Drive east on Tremont to Chestnut Street and turn right. Follow Chestnut Street to Standish Street for beginning of tour.

#1
Standish Monument
State Park
Crescent Street
1872
Open all year, no fee

From Bay Road or Chestnut Street at five-way intersection with flagpole turn right on Standish Street. Follow Standish Street. Note stone marker at corner of Captains Hill Road (first street on right). This marks early gate which kept cattle on the Nook. Take next right on Crescent Street. Drive one-half mile, take first paved left, which is entrance to State Park. Facilities: scenic view, rest rooms, parking.

A statue of the first commissioned military officer in the New World, Myles Standish,* stands high above Captain's Hill, overseeing the harbor and land he spent the last thirty-six years of his life protecting. His leadership in fortifying Plymouth and creating a perpetual show of strength outmaneuvered what easily could have been a vicious enemy. Due to his efforts, a strong bond of mutual respect developed between Pilgrims and Indians.

As you approach this national memorial to a military leader, notice how the fourteen foot statue of Myles depicts him with sword sheathed and hand outstretched in a civil act—holding the royal charter he was instrumental in having transferred from England to Plymouth. Entering the 116 foot granite shaft, you see stones given by the New England states, with the keystone from President Grant on behalf of the American people.

The circular climb to the open windows at the top is well worth the effort. Here, while being refreshed by ocean breezes, you can enjoy

Myles Standish Monument

spectacular views in all directions. *To the east* is Clark's Island, named for John Clark of the *Mayflower* crew. He was the first to land on the island December 11, 1620, when the *Mayflower* shallop, carrying a small exploratory party searching for a permanent place to settle, found shelter during a severe storm. Over the years Clark's Island has been used for a saltworks, for Plymouth's poorhouse, as grazing land for sheep, a bird sanctuary, and home to a few hardy islanders.

Behind Clark's Island, at the southern end of the long sandy bar known as Duxbury Beach, are Saquish Neck and the Gurnet. Saquish (Indian for clams) Neck, now privately owned, was the site of Fort Standish, active during the Civil War. On the outermost part of this sandbar, at the Gurnet (named for its resemblance to the head of a gurnet fish) stands Plymouth Light. In 1776 a six-gun fort was built here to protect the harbor from the British. At that time the light, erected earlier in 1768, became the only light in lighthouse history to be hit by a cannonball when the fort was attacked by the British ship *Niger* during the Revolutionary War. During the War of 1812, the Gurnet was garrisoned and enlarged, and during the Civil War a new fort, Fort Andrews, was built.

To the south is Plymouth. Notice the old Plymouth Cordage buildings,* and on a clear day follow the coastline out along Cape Cod to

181

Provincetown. *To the west* look across Kingston Bay to the mouth of the Jones River. *To the north* is a sea of green trees sprinkled with church steeples, ponds, and beautiful countryside.

Looking out over this 360-degree panoramic view of history and natural beauty, you can still feel that sense of freedom that was so vital in the lives of the early Pilgrims and so strongly supported by Captain Myles Standish.

#2
Brewster Home Site
Eagle's Nest
off Marshall Street
c.1631
Open all year, no fee

Exit from Standish Monument Park and turn left on Crescent Street, which becomes Standish Street. Continue on Standish Street to first right, Marshall Street, and turn right. Follow Marshall around to Bradford Road, third left, which comes in on left. Opposite Bradford Road is a stone marker. The site of the home is a short distance in on the dirt lane by the marker. Park on Marshall Street or Bradford Road and walk lane to the end, where there is a large group of lilacs on land now owned by the Duxbury Rural and Historical Society.

William Brewster* struck a spiritual spark in Scrooby,* England, which he nurtured and sustained through persecution in England, exile in Holland, and tribulation on the high seas until it burst forth into flame in a small settlement in the New World. Here he inspired the souls of his fellow Pilgrims as they withstood the rigors of their early arduous years in Plymouth. Arriving at age fifty-six, William Brewster led and encouraged his flock for a decade before moving to Duxbury.

Sometime prior to 1631 widower Brewster purchased this land and built his home near where you see these beautiful lilacs. Many believe the lilacs were brought to the New World by Brewster's son, Jonathan, as a gift for his father or at his father's request.

The homestead was divided between sons Love and Jonathan upon Brewster's death in 1645. Love Brewster's share ultimately went to Josiah Standish, while grandson Deacon William Brewster inherited Jonathan's share. Thus future generations of Standishes and Brewsters continued to live side by side, helping to develop the land and carry on the dreams of their ancestors.

#3
Myles Standish Homestead
Site
End of Mayflower Avenue
1627 grant
Open all year, no fee

Continue south on Marshall Street. At end turn right on Massasoit Road. Follow it to Mayflower Avenue, the first left turn. The Standish site is at the end of Mayflower Avenue. Facilities: parking, view

In Duxbury Myles Standish raised his family and ran his 120-acre self-sufficient farm. His land grant of 1627 consisted mainly of the southern half of Captain's Nook, where on this bluff he built his home overlooking Plymouth Harbor.

To this early homestead Myles and Barbara Standish brought their three children—Charles, Alexander,* and John. Four more soon joined the family on the Nook—Myles, Jr., Josiah, Charles, and Lora. Alexander and Josiah were the only ones to survive their parents. Following Captain Standish's death, Barbara lived on in the house until it burned about 1665. It is believed the hearthstone, some doors, timbers, and latches from the home were used in building son Alexander's 1666 home, still standing at 341 Standish Street.

Duxbury historian Laurence Bradford relates that Captain Standish carried an unusual Persian sword made of meteoric iron and inscribed by Mohammedans. This sword put special power into the hand of the user, who could not lose if he raised it against enemies of the faith. Whether it was the sword, or the man who carried it, doesn't really matter. For with the passing of Myles Standish went an extraordinary man. An officer and a man of English gentry, he left wealth and estate behind to join a small band of dissenters who had a dream, an unshakable faith in their God, and a desire to live free in a new world. He helped make that dream come true.

#4
Old Burying Ground
First Meetinghouse Site
Chestnut Street and
Pilgrim By-Way
c.1635
Open all year, no fee

Retrace your route to Standish Street and turn right. Continue on Standish Street back to five way intersection. Drive around flagpole taking third road, Chestnut Street, at the 11:00 position. The Old Burying Ground is on the corner of Chestnut and Pilgrim-By-Way, first right.

Quiet, peaceful, tree-shaded, the Old Burying Ground is one of the oldest and most fascinating in the country. The area is simply marked, making it easy to explore and experience the sense of unity with the past.

This land was once the center of Duxbury life, as the marked sites of the first two meetinghouses attest. The very plain First Meetinghouse was raised about 1635 in the southeast corner near the Chestnut Street entrance. Further east, in 1706, the next meetinghouse was built.

The center monument draws immediate attention, surrounded by a fortresslike stone wall, cannons, and cannonballs. Inside the memorial is a simple boulder inscribed "Myles Standish."* Unmarked, rough, pyramid-shaped fieldstones mark the graves of Captain Standish, his daughter Lora, and daughter-in-law Mary.

John and Priscilla Alden* are buried in the Alden Corner (near Chestnut and Pilgrim-By-Way corner.) Near their unmarked graves, the Ground's oldest gravestone honors their son Jonathan who died in 1697. The stone has not always rested so peacefully here. At one time the Old Burying Ground had become overgrown through neglect. Ezra Weston* found the abandoned Jonathan Alden stone and took it to his home for safekeeping. Thirty years later, at Ezra Weston's death in 1852, the stone went to his brother, then at his death, to Miss Lucia Bradford who died before realizing her intent to replace it. Finally, her nephew found the Alden corner, matched the stone to its foundation, and, in 1886, returned the wandering stone after more than half a century.

#5
Town Center
First Parish Church
Old Town Hall
Duxbury Town Offices
Tremont Street
c.1840
Open all year, no fee

Continue on Chestnut Street to Route 3A, Tremont Street, and turn right. The Town Center is on the left opposite Depot Street, just past the cemetery.

In 1840 the meetinghouse of the First Parish Church was built, commensurate with the prosperity brought during shipbuilding prime. Built by ships' carpenters with Weston* guidance, this massive structure's huge sanctuary is starkly angular and rectangular. Sturdy, hidden framing supports one of the largest wooden-trussed assembly rooms in the United States. It is the fourth building of this ancient congregation gathered in 1632.

Their first meetinghouse, one of the first two formed after Plymouth, was at the Old Burying Ground* and probably a very plain, simple structure, twenty-eight by eighteen feet. During worship men sat on one side and women on the other. However, men had all the narrow, backless benches for themselves during town meetings as women couldn't vote.

The first regular minister was the Reverend Ralph Partridge, an able, scholarly man, who peacefully led his pioneering congregation in simple, austere worship from 1637 until his death in 1658. Money problems, particularly in paying the minister's meager salary, plagued the young church. Ministers often appealed to government leaders or courts to obtain their living. When the Reverend Robinson in 1737 sought funds promised him he was locked out of his church. These pious Pilgrim descendants often boldly settled their differences with strong actions.

This same Reverend Robinson was openly heckled during worship. On one occasion, a frequent opponent, who often made faces at him, provided his own retribution when the pipe he had been smoking before service and tucked into his pocket suddenly ignited, causing his hurried departure amid appropriate expressions from the pulpit. Robinson eventually left for Connecticut to join his daughter and son-in-law, Governor Trumbull, founder of the family of artists, writers, and civic leaders.

Unfortunately, serious disagreements continued. The next minister, the Reverend Samuel Veazie, came under the influence of Whitefield's* "New Lights," a revival doctrine not shared by his congregation. Finally, during the ministry of the Reverend Charles Turner from 1754 to 1775, the congregation settled and united in contented worship.

Religion, education, and government were united here on this land at the Town Center since the early 1840s when an impressive triumvirate of Greek Revival structures arose. White clapboard, wide pilasters, and plain, dominating pediments are featured in all three. The church commands on the left, with Mayflower Cemetery adjacent. The *Old Town Hall* is in the center, and a modern replica of Partridge Academy is on the right. Partridge Academy was established with a gift from the Honorable George Partridge, descendant of early settlers, delegate to the Second Provincial Congress, Continental Congress, and United States Congress. After the Academy burned, the Duxbury *Town Office Building* was constructed on the same site to the same design, and Partridge insurance funds still aid Duxbury students through college scholarships. Thus the intent remains, and the impressive buildings, surrounded by open greens and backed by stately trees, appear much as the original three did when first constructed in the early 1840s.

#6
Captain Gershom Bradford House
931 Tremont Street
1808
Open by appointment with the Duxbury Rural and Historical Society, or limited hours seasonally fee charged

Captain Gamaliel Bradford House
942 Tremont Street
1807
Private
NRHP

Continue a short distance north .2 mile on Tremont Street. The Captain Gershom Bradford House is on the right, with the Captain Gamaliel Bradford House next on the left.

A classic house museum, the *Captain Gershom Bradford House* beautifully illustrates gracious living at the successful shipmaster level in this sea-oriented town. The house was built by a Bradford,* lived in only by Bradfords, and the furnishings are entirely from the four generations of Bradfords who lived here. Descended from Governor William Bradford, the family carried on the tradition of Duxbury seafaring adventure.

Captain Gershom served with his older brothers and soon rose to command his own vessels. He built this home in 1808. The delicate Federal entry is featured, with original fan and glass retained, though brick ends of the house have been clapboarded over. The walk is formed of lava blocks brought from Sicily's Etna volcano by Captain Bradford.

Inside, the woodwork detail is arresting. The delicately carved moldings of varied geometrical patterns immediately draw your attention. Each design is different. The interior remains much as it was in Captain Bradford's time, with original colors and carefully reproduced wallpaper completed with Bradford furnishings, paintings, and fine library.

Diagonally across the street is the *Captain Gamaliel Bradford House* built by Captains Gershom and Gamaliel's father in 1807. The large wing was constructed earlier by their father in the 1700s and attached to the 1807 house. The Captain Gamaliel House is more grandly Federal, similar to their sister Jerusha's house, the King

Caesar House.* Impressive brick sides, delicate frieze molding, quoined corners, graceful fanlights, and later Greek Revival porticos are featured.

#7
Blue Fish River area
Washington Street near St.
George Street
Open all year, no fee

Continue north on Tremont Street, make the first right turn onto Harrison Street, and continue to Washington Street. Turn left and drive north on Washington Street to the bridge over the Blue Fish River. There are two markers and limited parking just before the bridge on the right. On the far or north side of the bridge there is a small park on the left side of Washington Street.

Today this peaceful setting belies the feverish activities of one and two centuries ago. This now quiet riverside, bathed twice daily by the tidal Blue Fish River, has known the sweat and toil of shipbuilders and the rhythmic throb of gristmills powered by changing tides. Israel Sylvester and Captain Samuel Delano built their shipyards on the river's edge during the 1760s. They were joined about 1766 by Joseph Drew's Grist Mill. In 1803 a drawbridge and dam were built across the river, providing a pond for the mills. From 1830 to 1845 the shores from the millpond and bridge to the outer river mouth were lined with shipyards. The largest of them all, Ezra Weston* at one time had one hundred ships listed with Lloyds of London. The Duxbury Rural and Historical Society has landscaped a small riverside area where you can relax and enjoy the peaceful river of today while contemplating those past centuries.

#8
Duxbury Bank, 1833
Cable Office, 1869
Washington and St. George
Streets
Private

Just beyond the Blue Fish River at the next corner, Washington and St. George Streets, is the former Duxbury Bank. Across Washington Street from the bank is the Duxbury Rural and Historical Society's Drew House.

Duxbury Rural and
Historical Society
Charles Drew, Jr., House
685 Washingon Street
c.1826
Open by appointment

Now a private home, this quiet Greek Revival building, with Ionic-columned entrance, corner pilasters, and frieze across the front has played a role in two powerful, enthusiastic periods in Duxbury history. Weston-led shipowners and sea captains were so successful this *Duxbury Bank* was incorporated to handle their business. Ezra Weston II* was president from its beginning in 1833 until his death in 1842. As clippers eased Duxbury away from her shipbuilding prime, the bank closed. In 1869 the building became the Cable Office and shared the excitement of the trans-Atlantic cable which came from France to the shores of Duxbury.

Across the street, are the office and library of the *Duxbury Rural and Historical Society* in the late Georgian–early Federal Charles Drew, Jr., House owned by the society. The research library is available to serious researchers.

#9
Monument to Dick
Spar Soak
Bay Pond Road
Open all year, no fee

Bear right on Powder Point Avenue. Take the first right on King Caesar Road and park along the road. Walk back across Powder Point Road to Bay Pond Road to see the Monument to Dick and the Spar Soak. The Monument is on the left side of Bay Pond Road a short distance in from Powder Point Road, behind the granite school marker. The old Spar Soak is just beyond the marker on the same side of the road.

Dick was a favorite horse who worked three generations in Weston service. Boys looked forward to the chance to ride old Dick as he patiently walked in circles in the cellar of the ropewalk to supply the required power. His service is honored here.

Nearby you can see one of Duxbury's Spar Soaks. Here a stream was dammed to form a spar soak where masts were stored underwater until needed in shipbuilding.

#10
King Caesar House
King Caesar Road
1808–1809
Open seasonally and by appointment, fee charged
NRHP

Continue on King Caesar Road. White finial-topped gateposts mark the King Caesar House on the left with its wharf directly across the street.

King Caesar House

From this imposing mansion King Caesar II, born Ezra Weston II,* commanded his empire. From here he could oversee the Weston shipyards and control almost all phases connected with building ships and merchandizing their cargoes. For Ezra Weston II owned rope walk, spar yard, blacksmith forge, sail loft, warehouses, general store, timber, and lumber. His farm supplied food for the long voyages, and Weston coastal schooners, packets, and oxteams transported goods to his wharves to sail on his ships to their faraway destinies.

His father, Ezra Weston I,* started life as a farmer but grew to become the first major American shipbuilder after he initiated his yard in 1764 at age twenty-one. He revealed a human note when, as storekeeper, he wrote "kauphy"—a commodity known as coffee—spelled without benefit of a single letter of the word.

Weston ships were Duxbury ships—commanded by Duxbury captains and manned by Duxbury lads, who followed the natural progression from early years of work on the rope walk and wharf to the deck. The Weston-owned *Smyrna* in 1830 was the first to carry the flag of the United States to the Black Sea. Here the *Hope* was launched in 1841, then the largest merchant ship in New England. The next year King Caesar II died, and his sons tried to carry on the business. But the mightly clipper era arrived, ships outgrew Duxbury rivers, and the empire of Weston shipbuilding dissolved about mid-1800.

This impressive Federal mansion provided the appropriate throne for King Caesar II across from the massive stone wharf where Weston ships were rigged and fitted. Effectively framed by original fence and ornate post finials, the house features quoined corners, dentils at roof line, and front entry with original delicate, elaborate leaded tracery in fan- and sidelights.

The furnishings are in keeping with the period in this most lavish house in town. Some are original: Ezra II's chair from which he watched Duxbury sunsets and a portrait and inkstand of Daniel Webster,* a friend and frequent visitor here. Jerusha, wife of Ezra II and sister of Captains Bradford,* had the parlor wallpapers imported from France. Beautifully restored, they are attributed to DuFour. Much of the interior woodwork was beautifully carved by the ships' carpenters who created the house.

A wing features a special Weston-Duxbury museum and gift shop. Exhibits include the Weston house flag, ship's log, ships' carpenters' tools, and treasures brought from faraway lands. Even the belfry atop the studio roof has a story. It came from a Spanish mission. It had been stolen by pirates who attacked a Weston ship and were in turn stood off and boarded.

This many-faceted museum-mansion provides interesting displays at every turn and the opportunity to share the life-style of King Caesar II.

#11
Duxbury Beach
Across Powder Point
Bridge
Open all year, no fee

Duxbury Access: *Continue on King Caesar Road to Powder Point Avenue, where bridge begins. Parking before bridge is limited and across bridge is for resident sticker parking only in season. Open all year, no fee.*
Main access through Marshfield: *Take Route 139 off Route 3A; follow it to Canal Street. Turn right; continue as Canal becomes Gurnet Road and continues to beach. Facilities: boat launching, bathhouse, fishing, parking, picnicking, rest rooms, snack bar, swimming; Open all year, seasonal parking fee.*

This beautiful, dreamlike beach is the first vacation spot in the country, for here Pilgrims summered. Over eight miles of clean, sandy, dune-guarded beach stretch from Marshfield across Duxbury Bay to Saquish* and the Gurnet.*

Great storms have sent the sea surging through cuts in the beach and dunes created by the sea's relentless power. Cuts have been closed and barricades erected to trap sand and prevent further breaches.

Some restoration work resulted from the persuasive urging of Daniel Webster.

The town section of the beach (access from Duxbury) is worth the nearly ½-mile walk across century-old Powder Point Bridge, believed to be the longest wooden bridge in the country. The walk itself is enjoyable at anytime or season, with pauses to watch fishermen, study tides, or appreciate the setting sun.

The beach is everything you could want—a spectacular sandy beach which seems to go on forever. To the north is Green Harbor and to the south, a clear day brings the Gurnet with its lighthouse into view. The clean, fine sand of Duxbury Beach is protected by grass-covered dunes, and the open ocean in its many moods invites recreational enjoyment or quiet contemplation.

#12   *Leaving the Bridge take right-hand road,*
John Alden House   *Powder Point Avenue, back to Washing-*
105 Alden Street   *ton Street. At flag pole turn right on St.*
1653   *George Street. Follow St. George past li-*
Open seasonally and by   *brary to first left on Alden Street. The*
appointment, fee charged   *entrance to the Alden House is on the left*
NRHP   *opposite Railroad Avenue.*

This interesting historic site spirits you back to the time when hardy Pilgrims lived right here—on land you can walk, in a house you can see.

Tall, blond, strong, cooper, master carpenter, and farmer, John Alden* lived here with his wife Priscilla until his death at age eighty-nine. They were immortalized by Alden descendant Longfellow in his poem of Myles Standish's* asking John Alden to propose to Priscilla for him. Priscilla is purported to have replied, ". . . Speak for yourself, John." Whatever the real story, it is known that the two young Pilgrims married in 1621 in Plymouth and developed into Colonial leaders. John served as agent of the colony, as its treasurer, and pledged his English land holdings to help cover the colony's indebtedness. They remained friends with the Standishes, and ironically, their daughter Sarah married Myles Standish's son Alexander.*

John and Priscilla Alden's house is just as intriguing as their lives. In 1653, with son Jonathan, they built their second Duxbury home, this classic First Period Colonial house. The front portion, with large central chimney; small, unobtrusive door; small, unbalanced windows; and steeply pitched roof, is separately framed from the obviously older back portion of kitchen, buttery, and borning room. What is the story here? Questions about the first Alden Duxbury house resulted in a scientific dig led by Roland Wells Robbins,* recognized archeologist. Inch by inch they dug and sifted until the entire foundation of the first house emerged. This circa 1628 site can be reached by a short walk along a path from the 1653 house. The path leads through woods to an open field behind a school. The site is fenced, and a granite memorial is nearby. Interestingly enough, the dimensions of this 1628 house are equal to those of the older added rear portion of the 1653 house. Additional clues lead to the conclusion that the 1628 house was moved soon after the 1653 house was built, and attached to it.

Here have lived ten generations of Aldens—a remarkable heritage. Centuries of Alden living made modifications, such as the 1850 rear ell addition, but most of the basic structure, walls, floors, and fireplaces are original.

The early section—kitchen, buttery, and borning room—is clearly defined. You feel like a Pilgrim in this section of wide-boarded floors and wall panels, board and beam ceilings, and beehive-oven fireplace. All furnishings are Alden family pieces. Flax- and wool-spinning devices catch your eye, such as the spinning wheel of Pilgrim John Alden's granddaughter Elizabeth. A special display features artifacts found in the archeological dig.

The house stands alone on a knoll as if in quiet reflection of the 1600s, untouched by the twentieth century. Here John and Priscilla Alden and their fellow Pilgrims walked these paths and founded a small settlement that would grow to be part of a yet unheard of mighty nation.

#13   *Return to Alden Street and turn left. The*
Art Complex Museum   *Art Complex is on the left just before*
189 Alden Street   *Tremont Street.*
1971
Open limited hours and by
appointment all year, no fee

This fascinating museum complex is housed in a beautiful modern interpretation of Duxbury's rolling hills, woods, and sea. Galleries benefit from northern-exposure skylights and great walls of glass.

Initiated and directed by the Weyerhaeuser family, the museum complex offers an amazing array of cultural events and charges no admission. An authentic Japanese Tea House is the scene of formal tea ceremonies in the summer. The galleries feature permanent collections of paintings, drawings, prints, ceramics, glass, and Shaker furniture augmented by special exhibits. Regular concerts and lectures are given, and the extensive library, with its outstanding Japanese section, is available to the public.

This ends the guided tour section of Duxbury. To continue tour drive north on Tremont Street, Route 3A, to Marshfield.

Duxbury Beaches and Parks

(A) **Bay Farm**
Loring Street
Dirt road off east side of
Loring Street
Just past town line

Walkways to ocean through conservation lands shared with Kingston—open fields, trees, saltmarshes, ledges, small beach area—beautiful views overlooking Duxbury Bay; limited parking on dirt access road and Bay Road; open all year, no fee

(B) **Landing Road Beach**
Landing Road
Off Bay Road

Small, sandy beach with beautiful view of Duxbury Bay, Standish monument, Duxbury Light, and Plymouth; facilities: boat launching, picnicking, swimming, very limited on-street parking; open all year, no fee

(C) **Howland's Landing Beach**
Howland's Landing
Off Crescent Street

Small, sandy and rocky beach with view across Duxbury Bay to Plymouth and Kingston; facilities: boat launching, swimming, no parking; open all year, no fee

(D) **Harden Hill Beach**
Harden Hill road
Off Washington Street

Small, sandy beach with view across protected bay to Duxbury Beach and Saquish; facilities: boat launching, swimming, no parking; open all year, no fee

(E) **Mattakeesett Court**
Town Landing
Off Washington Street

Facilities: boat launching, Harbor Master, moorings, parking, no swimming; open all year, no fee

(F) **Duxbury Beach***
See #11 for accesses from
Duxbury and Marshfield
and details

Over eight miles of open sandy beach, dune-guarded, with endless vistas; facilities: boat launching, bathhouse, fishing, parking, picnicking, rest rooms, snack bar, swimming; open all year, seasonal parking fee at Marshfield access

HISTORY OF MARSHFIELD

Marshfield has been home to two outstanding American statesmen who played key diplomatic roles during delicate times in the country's history—Edward Winslow* during the 1600s and Daniel Webster* during the 1800s.

Edward Winslow's essential diplomacy kept open the avenues of understanding between the tightly knit, self-disciplined, religious Pilgrims and the outside world of tough-minded businessmen in England and impetuous, free-living Indians in the New World. The support of both groups was imperative for the success of the Plymouth Colony.

Daniel Webster, lawyer, orator, and congressman for a quarter of a century, stood for strong federal government. He supported it against Nullification Acts, and through brilliant oratory preserved the nation in his defense of the Compromise of 1850. Though Winslow and Webster lived two centuries apart, their estates joined each other in a town they both cherished, and their lives were both cut from the same rich cloth of wisdom, sensitivity, and service.

As early as 1632 people gathered at a meetinghouse in Green's Harbor, near where Governor Edward Winslow built his cherished home "Careswell"* a few years later. These first settlers established homesteads along Green's Harbor and North River, using the waterways as avenues of transportation and sources of seafood. By 1636 ships were wintering on the North River. Here, in 1645, Thomas Nichols built the first ship, heralding what would become one of the famous shipbuilding centers of New England—active between 1670 and 1871.

The War for Independence put a temporary damper on Marshfield's shipbuilding industry and divided the town into two camps, each equally loyal to its own cause. Marshfield's many wealthy landowners, appointed to important Provincial offices, felt a strong loyalty to the British Crown. On January 31, 1774, they carried by one vote a reaffirmation of allegiance to the Crown, becoming the only town in New England to take such a stand. At the same time Marshfield had

194

many farmers and merchants who believed in controlling their own destiny and were passionately loyal to the patriot cause. Thus one group sought strength from a known way of life, while the other was willing to step out into an untried world of freedom where future government powers would "come from the consent of the governed."[8]

The "shot heard round the world" might well have been fired in Marshfield. Just prior to Lexington and Concord, patriot General John Thomas of Marshfield sent troops to capture a British force garrisoned at loyalist Nathaniel Ray Thomas' home in Marshfield. However, the patriots delayed their arrival, reaching the Thomas home after the British had escaped by boat to Boston. Thus what might have been the first encounter was avoided. With this step Tory power ended. Marshfield publicly declared June 19, 1776, that it would support independence from England if the Continental Congress voted for such a move.

With the culmination of hostilities, Marshfield returned to her own destiny, that of shipbuilding on the North River. Now you hear birds singing, but in those golden days of sail you heard the striking of hammers, the strain of saws on hard oak, the groan of ropes as tension mounted, the flapping of halyards against new masts, and at break time the call of "Grog O" for thirsty men. This was a way of life for two centuries. Then as the lumber supply dwindled, larger ships were needed, and steamships and railroads claimed coastal trade, the shores of the river became strangely silent. In 1871 the *Helen M. Foster* slid down the ways, to be the last ship built on this mighty river.

Marshfield had other smaller industries such as grist- and lumber mills and shoe, nail, cotton, and woolen factories, yet it was her superior shipbuilding that took the name of Marshfield and the North River around the world. Today Marshfield is a way of life, loved and cherished by summer and year-round residents, whether they be local merchants and farmers or famous people like Edward Winslow and Daniel Webster.

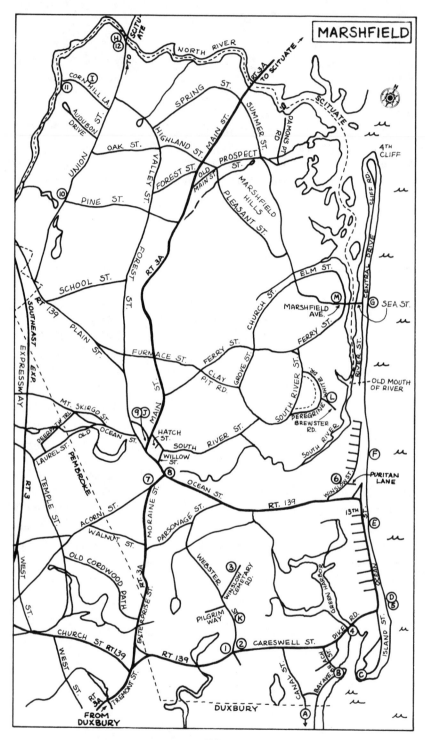

MARSHFIELD

MARSHFIELD

DIRECTIONS:
From Duxbury drive north on Tremont Street, Route 3A, to Careswell street, Route 139. Turn right onto Careswell Street. Or, from the Southeast Expressway, Route 3, take Exit 12 for Route 139 in Marshfield.

#1
1699 Isaac Winslow House
Daniel Webster Office, NHL
Blacksmith Shop
Careswell and Webster
Streets
Open seasonally,
fee charged

Drive east on Careswell Street 1.4 miles to the Winslow House, which is on the left at corner of Careswell and Webster Streets.

Edward Winslow* was one of the guiding forces of the early Plymouth settlement. He was among the exploring party who agreed on Plymouth as the place to establish their settlement. He first met the approaching Chief Massasoit* and remained as hostage while Massasoit met with Governor Carver. Winslow, with his naturally diplomatic ways, found favor with the chief and served as an able negotiator. In 1623 he sailed for England, returning with much-needed cattle and sheep, which established an economic basis for future trade with other colonies. Along with many others, Winslow felt the sting of death when his wife, Elizabeth, died during that first terrible winter. At the same time Susanna White, mother of Peregrine the first white child born in the New England, lost her husband. In 1621 Susanna and Edward were united in the first wedding ceremony performed in Plymouth.

The confines of Plymouth bore in on the ambitious Winslow, and in 1636 he moved to Marshfield and built his home, "Careswell," between the present Winslow house and Duxbury marshes. Unfortunately, nothing of the house remains, though "Careswell" was considered one of the largest manorial farm estates in the colony. From there he served as governor of Plymouth Colony, member of the General Court, and commissioner to the New England Confederacy.

1699 Isaac Winslow House

Edward's son, Josiah, also lived at "Careswell" and was appointed Chief Military Commander of the Plymouth Colony in 1657. He served as governor from 1673 to 1680. His son, Judge Isaac, built the present house circa 1699 on the Winslow estate. From Isaac the homestead passed to son General John Winslow, active during the French and English wars. His son, Dr. Isaac, though a loyalist during the Revolutionary War, was allowed to remain in Marshfield in appreciation for his devoted medical services. Dr. Isaac was the last of the Winslows to live in this old mansion, dying in 1819.

As you walk through this 1699 house, you catch a glimpse of how the Winslow families lived when Marshfield was but a frontier town. To the left of the front door is the common room with seventeenth-century rough, hand-hewn beams, exposed natural wood, and large fireplace. Here Judge Isaac entertained the leading men of Plymouth Colony. Behind the common room is the old kitchen with its adjoining buttery and root cellar, early kitchen utensils, walk-in fireplace, and exposed beams. Entering the front parlor you advance into the eighteenth century. Notice the wallpaper, painted paneling and woodwork, plastered ceiling, eighteenth-century furnishings, and the smaller, more formal fireplace with Delft tiles.

Upstairs was the office of Dr. Isaac where many a Tory meeting was held during the Revolution. Across the hall is the Bridal Chamber, decorated with the finest paneling in the house for the first Isaac's bride, Sarah Wensley. The fireplace was used as a model for the brickwork in the fireplace of the Governor John Wentworth home in Portsmouth, which is now on display in the Metropolitan Museum of Art in New York.

Webster's Law Office: To set the stage for the Webster Law Office, you must go back to the year 1641. At that time Edward Winslow's contemporary William Thomas was granted two miles of land adjacent to "Careswell." Thomas developed his lands into a thriving estate, leaving it to his son and his son's sons who held important civic and military positions down through the years. In 1827 statesman Daniel Webster came to Marshfield and purchased lands that had belonged to the Winslow and Thomas families to create his over two-thousand-acre estate. Here Daniel lived in baronial splendor in the house that had first been built c.1754 by Nathaniel Ray Thomas, fifth descendant of William Thomas. The actual house, which burned in 1878, was on a rise of land off Webster Street opposite Pilgrim Way. The present Victorian home, which rests on the original foundation, was built by Webster's daughter-in-law, Mrs. Fletcher Webster.

When Daniel Webster rode through the gates of his estate, he left political problems behind and entered his cherished world of farmer and agriculturist. He stocked the farm with prize cattle, Chinese poultry, South American llamas, and peacocks, and added one hundred thousand seedlings to the many plantings. From 1827 until his death, Daniel spent as much time as his demanding public life would allow in his home, said to resemble Sir Walter Scott's Abbotsford in England. In addition to the main house were workers' cottages, barns, a blacksmith shop, and his beloved office.

In 1852, in full awareness of his approaching death, Daniel Webster detailed his epitaph—sharing his belief in Jesus Christ. He bid his family, friends, and workers farewell, and uttered his final words, "I still live."[9]

Sadly, when the house burned, only his office remained for future generations to visit. In 1966 the office was moved here to the Winslow complex. Step inside this unassuming, small yellow building in which worked a genius of a man dedicated to the laws and welfare of his country. In his office can be seen paintings of the Webster House, special collections, his desk and table, his favorite beaver skin hat, and other memorabilia of Webster's personal life.

Blacksmith Shop: This small, naturally aged clapboard and wood shingle-roofed structure was a shed attached to the Josiah Winslow homestead. It was moved to the Winslow grounds and is now a working blacksmith shop operated on special occasions.

#2
Old Winslow School House
Careswell and Webster
Streets
1857
Open limited hours in
season and by appointment,
no fee

The schoolhouse is across Webster Street from the Winslow House.

As you enter through the double doors, you are back in the school days of the 1800s, the building structurally just as it was when built on Webster land. The schoolroom remains as originally used, with dual student desks, covered glass inkwells, original clock, and organ. The old stovepipe still travels the length of the room, and the original blackboard still has the eraser cupboard nearby. Additional collections, donated from Marshfield family treasures, include old kitchen utensils, costumes, and century-old Marshfield Fair memorabilia. Built in 1857, it was one of eight early district schools of Marshfield.

Much earlier, in June 1642, the first recorded move for public education was made in Marshfield, when Edward Winslow* and eleven others pledged to pay for their children's education and to supplement others' as well. The old South School (marker at Webster and Parsonage Streets) was established in 1645. By 1660, at the colony level, the idea of public education became a general law, with the actuality of schools and teachers following later. Marshfield's pioneering educational interests are preserved here by the Marshfield Historical Society.

#3
Winslow Cemetery
Winslow Cemetery Road
c.1641
Open all year

Drive north on Webster Street to Winslow Cemetery Road, first paved right. Turn right. The cemetery will be on the left opposite Presidential Circle.

At Winslow Cemetery are memorials to Marshfield's sons who helped lay the stonework and establish the guidelines for this country.

As you enter the cemetery, on your left, enclosed within a wrought-iron fence, are the graves of Daniel Webster* and his family. Appropriately, above Daniel's grave flies the Stars and Stripes representing the country he strengthened and preserved through his oratory, his writings, and his legal defenses.

A short distance behind the Webster enclosure is a monument to the early settlers of Green Harbor (Marshfield's first settlement) with such familiar names as Winslow, Thomas, and White. Near the Green Harbor monument is the Governor Edward Winslow* grave, marked with the family crest. Other Winslow graves, including Edward's son Governor Josiah Winslow, lie in close proximity.

Adjacent to the Webster compound is a marker indicating the site of Marshfield's first meetinghouse. (see #8) Here on the hill c.1641 a small thatched-roof building was erected to the glory of God and for the spiritual support and growth of Marshfield's early settlers.

#4
Green Harbor Dike
Dike Road
1872
Open all year, no fee

Return on Winslow Cemetery Road to Webster Street and turn left. Follow Webster back to Careswell Street and turn left. Follow Careswell, Route 139, over a mile to where it crosses over Green Harbor Dike.

This peaceful setting was a source of enormous dissension and creator of feuds which rivaled the intensity of those in the Tennessee Mountains and lasted nearly a century! The Green Harbor Dike, which supports the road across Green Harbor River, was the cause of this agony and antagonism. In 1872 the dike was constructed to enable salt meadows and marshes to be used to grow crops. The resulting production of hay and vegetables was amazing, without added fertilizers, and the richness was retained for years. Unfortunately, the dike wreaked havoc with fishermen who could no longer use the shallow harbor and river which had gradually filled as a result of the dike.

A thriving lumberyard was choked off as the river shoaled. Many legal and illegal battles resulted, including attempts to blow up the dike in this "holy war against the unholy dike." Finally, at the turn of this century, jetties were built at the mouth of Green Harbor River to prevent sand buildup within the harbor and river, and dredging operations continue to this day.

#5
Brant Rock Beach
Ocean Street
Open all year, no fee

Continue on Dike Road to end, turn left on Ocean Street and park. Beach is across from Union Chapel. Facilities: lifeguards, swimming, parking along wall and in village behind Bud's store.

Weathered shingled houses and rugged stone bulkheads line this crescent-shaped sandy beach. To the north the Scituate coastline extends into the distance. The unbroken horizon fills the east, with breakwaters and rocky outcroppings to the south.

Brant Rock Village was once two islands of several names, finally named after Brant Geese. The area remained dormant until ocean-loving vacationers and modern rail transportation combined to usher in the resort hotel era. Soon the occasional gunhouse and lobster fishing shelters were replaced by Pioneer Cottage in 1861, the Churchill in 1866, Brant Rock House in 1874, Ocean House in 1875, Fair View in 1877, and later Peace Haven. Times changed, the grand hotels are no longer, and now the quiet winter village in summer hosts day trippers.

#6
Kenelm Winslow House
Winslow Street
c.1645
Private

Drive north on Ocean Street, Route 139. Past 13th Road the road turns sharply left; then continue one half mile to Winslow Street on the right. Turn right on Winslow Street. The Winslow House is .3 mile in on left opposite Puritan Lane.

The Kenelm Winslow House is a centuries-old "Mansion House" built by a family of substantial means. More lavish than most, it was possibly built about 1645 as a half-house and added to. Over the years the house has been modified to the needs of each generation, though it retains many period features.

The first Kenelm Winslow in this country received a one-hundred-acre grant in 1637 and settled here. A carpenter, he made caskets and furniture for Plymouth Colony. Brother of Governor Edward Winslow,* he represented Marshfield in the General Court of the Colony. His son, Nathaniel, was also a town leader, being captain of the militia, selectman, deputy to the Plymouth Court, and three times representative to the Combined Colonies. Many generations succeeded, often with a member named Kenelm, the last to live here a daring patriot amid a family and town of Tories.

#7
Tea Rock Hill
Moraine Street
Open all year, no fee

Return to Route 139 and turn right. Continue on Route 139 to traffic light and intersection with Moraine Street, Rt. 3A. Park in this vicinity for #7-8. Walk south on Moraine Street to opposite the Tea Rock Apartments. On the right side of the street is a marker to Tea Rock Hill.

Little of the hill remains, the land is privately owned, but the marker for Tea Rock Hill invites you to remember Marshfield's own tea party. It was shortly after the Boston Tea Party, on December 19, 1773, that a group of daring patriotic men, women, and children sprang into action in this Tory-strong town. They confiscated known stores of British tea and carried the tea by oxcart to Tea Rock Hill. In the eerie lantern light on that winter night, they knelt to pray. Jeremiah Lowe offered his torch to the tea, completing the Marshfield Tea Party. He and his family soon evacuated to the safety of New York, where, four generations later, his descendant Seth Lowe became mayor.

#8
First Congregational
Church
Ocean at Moraine Street
1838
Open for Services

The First Congregational Church is at the intersection of Moraine, Route 3A, and Ocean Street, Route 139.

The present simple white-clapboard Greek Revival building, with unadorned pilasters, pediment, and steeple, is the fifth meetinghouse of the congregation gathered in 1632. The first thatched-roof building was located near the Winslow Cemetery.* It was sold in 1657 for fifty shillings when the new meetinghouse was built near the site of the present church. Several meetinghouses followed on this site, with some of the timbers of the fourth building used in the construction of the present church in 1838.

The first regular pastor was the Reverend Richard Blinman, who had been removed from his English church and came here at the invitation of Governor Winslow. An able, scholarly man, he was possibly too advanced, for he defended infant baptism. He soon left for Cape Ann where he played a significant role not only as spiritual leader but as canal and bridge designer of a system still present today and still bearing his name, though spelled Blynman.

Life in the seventeenth century can be pictured through excerpts from church records: a disagreement over the dwelling house built by the second minister brought Standish and Alden from the court of Plymouth to remind Marshfield to support its minister. Dedicated parishioners carried arms to meeting, always aware of possible Indian attack. Justice was harsh and nondiscriminating—Kenelm Winslow,* brother of Edward, was imprisoned for slander; he purportedly called the Marshfield congregation "all liars." Church and state began to separate, with town meetings discussing worldy affairs and the church focusing on spiritual matters. The close of the 1600s was highlighted by the memorable day in 1698 when Peregrine White* joined the church at age seventy-eight.

Early in the 1800s, gradual "backsliding" led to a critical condition and a point of decision—to remain orthodox or join the current Unitarian drive. They decided in favor of Trinitarianism, keeping the First Church of Marshfield one of the few Old Colony churches to resist the Unitarian movement. Dartmouth, Amherst, and Andover Theological graduates led successful revivals of Evangelism here in Marshfield, and the church survived the doldrums. Daniel Webster* attended faithfully when in town as did Adelaide Phillips,* musical idol of a century ago.

#9
Veterans Memorial Park
Ocean and Main Streets
Open all year, no fee

Make a left as if coming from Moraine Street and drive west on Ocean Street, Route 139, to Main Street, Route 3A. The Memorial Park is at the intersection. Facilities: benches, paths, picnicking.

Veterans Memorial Park is a beautifully landscaped living memorial to veterans of World War II, Korea, and Viet Nam. It is a giant park in a tiny area, a quiet interlude at a busy corner. Stone benches for resting, a shelter for inclement weather, a willow-shaded pond, a tiny covered bridge, and well designed and maintained gardens of shrubs and flowers invite you. South River flows through the park; a decorative, waterpowered mill wheel turns; a small waterfall murmurs sedately; and interesting wildlife enjoy the quiet millpond.

A marker indicates the site of Ford Mill, the first gristmill in Marshfield, built before 1657 by Josiah Winslow and William Ford.

#10
Hatch Mill
Union Street
1812
Open by appointment, no
fee

From intersection of Routes 3A and 139 drive north on Route 139 2.6 miles to Union Street. Turn right on Union and drive 1.1 miles to Pine Street which will be on right. Turn left on dirt road opposite Pine Street and park for Hatch Mill. Follow dirt lane into mill area.

Peacefully floating mallards gracefully rise as you approach the quiet millpond opposite Hatch Mill. Not long ago the screech of a saw could be heard and will be heard again as the Marshfield Historical Society restores and reactivates this waterpowered mill. Once again rough-cut boards of old, fashioned by the up-and-down saw, will be available to the public and to groups, such as Plimoth Plantation, who value old methods.

Over one-hundred-fifty years old, the mill was in use until 1965. From 1670 on, other mills owned by the Hatch family operated from time to time on this same brook system at other locations.

#11
Gravelly Beach
North River shipyards
End of Corn Hill Lane
Open all year, no fee

Return to Union Street, turn left and drive north 1.4 miles to Corn Hill Lane. Turn left. As you follow Corn Hill Lane, notice on the right access to conservation lands and woods trails in Corn Hill Woodland,* with Gravelly Beach at end of road.

From 1645 through 1871 the North River was more than a river. During nearly two centuries of shipbuilding the yards along this meandering waterway turned out over 1,025 vessels. (see Marshfield history)

At the end of Corn Hill Lane on the North River is what was known in earlier days as Gravelly Beach, a busy herring fishery station, where herring were taken in early spring as they made their run upriver to spawn. On the Marshfield banks, near this present peaceful open marshland dotted with islands of trees, once stood a Rogers shipyard, turning out schooners and merchant ships called "snows" from 1790 to 1819. Down river on the Scituate side the Wanton yard was active even earlier, from 1670 until 1840. Here many a privateer was built as well as some of the largest vessels on the river. The *Lagoda*,* owned by Jonathan Bourne,* was built here in 1826. Today the river flows by at its steady determined pace, as if still eager to carry a new hull down its picturesque way to the ocean beyond.

#12
Brooks-Tilden Shipyard
Preserve
Union Street Bridge, 1801
Union Street at North River
Open all year, no fee

Return to Union Street and turn left. Drive north to just before North River, .9 mile. On the left is the entrance to the preserve. Union Street then crosses over North River at Union Street Bridge. Preserve facilities: canoe launch, fishing, picnicking, parking

Today cars rush over the Union Street Bridge at fifty-plus miles per hour with drivers hardly looking to right or left. Back in 1644 people traveled at a slower pace and could enjoy the beauty of the river as they crossed on Elisha Bisbee's ferry. The ferry ran until 1801 when the Union Street Bridge was built, a toll bridge until 1850.

During the shipbuilding era, upriver on the Scituate side was the Block-House Shipyard, named for a garrison which offered protection to early settlers during King Philip's War. Upriver on the Marshfield side were the yards of Brooks and Tilden, active from 1784 to 1860.

Today, where once 70-to-280-ton vessels were launched, you can launch any hand-carried craft. You can feel the same fast-flowing ebb tide, which in earlier days carried new hulls downriver, or feel the incoming flood tide which once brought supply ships upriver. Where you now navigate the river with a small paddle, the vessels of old were captained by a special breed of men—the North River Pilots.

This ends the guided-tour section of Marshfield. Follow Union Street over North River to Route 123. Turn right and follow Route 123 for Scituate tour.

Marshfield Beaches and Parks and Additional Points of Interest

(A) **Duxbury Beach***
  Marshfield Access Canal
  Street to Bay Avenue to
  Gurnet Road
  See Duxbury #11

Over eight miles of open sandy beach, dune-guarded, with endless vistas; facilities: boat-launching, bathhouse, fishing, picnicking, rest rooms, snack bar, swimming; parking; open all year, seasonal parking fee

B **Burke's Beach**
Bay Avenue and Beach
Street

Inviting, open sandy beach, protected by stone jetty lining Green Harbor,* panoramic ocean view; facilities: bathhouse, lifeguards, swimming, walking; parking; open all year, parking fee in season

C **Green Harbor Marina and**
Town Pier

Active snug harbor for fishing and pleasure boats, picturesque; facilities: boat facilities; parking; open all year, no fee

D **Brant Rock Beach**
(See #5)
Ocean and Dike Road

Half-mile sandy crescent, open ocean views; facilities: lifeguards, swimming; parking along wall and in village behind Bud's store; open all year, no fee

E **Fieldston Beach**
Ocean Street

Shingle beach, sandy only at low tide, full ocean-horizon view; facilities: swimming, walking; parking usually allowed at restaurant with occasionally fee charged in season; open all year, usually no fee

F **Rexhame Beach**
Winslow Road

Peninsula of open sandy beach with marsh and South River on west, inviting full ocean view; facilities: swimming, walking, only sticker parking in season or walk on; open all year, no fee

G **Humarock Beach**
Whites Ferry
Sea Street

Inviting, open, sandy beach, spectacular ocean views; facilities: swimming, walking; parking limited to residents of Marshfield and Scituate only in season; open all year, no fee

H **Brooks-Tilden Shipyard**
Preserve (See #12)
Union Street just before
bridge on North River

Fifteen acres of natural woods and marsh along North River, can study ebb and flow of tide and effect of marsh land, see distant view along river; facilities: canoe launch, fishing, picnicking; parking; open all year, no fee

I **Corn Hill Woodland**
Corn Hill Lane

Eighty-three acres, trails through beech trees to North River and view; facilities: picnicking, walking; limited on-street parking; open all year, no fee. At end of Corn Hill Lane is Gravelly Beach* and site of a Rogers shipyard, view of marsh, and North River, with parking available; open all year, no fee

Ⓙ Veterans Memorial Park*
(See #9)
Routes 3A and 139

Beautifully landscaped tiny park with walks and benches, no nearby parking; open all year, no fee

Ⓚ Cherry Hill
Webster's Wilderness
Webster Road

Eighty-seven acres containing leaf-carpeted trails and conservation areas, especially well marked and maintained; overlooking a small pond is a granite marker indicating location of Webster's last speech July 24, 1852; facilities: ball fields, playground, picnicking, Recreation Center building, self-guided nature trails (guide booklet at Center or Town Hall); parking, open all year, no fee

Ⓛ Peregrine White Homestead
Site
Peregrine White Drive
c.1648
private

Boulder marks site of Homestead, present farmhouse could contain parts of historic original; Peregrine born November 20, 1620, on *Mayflower* in Cape Cod Harbor, first white child born in New England, widowed mother married Edward Winslow* as first New England bride; Peregrine was Pequot War volunteer, ensign for Myles Standish, member of Council of War, General Court

Ⓜ White's Ferry Site
Humarock Beach
Ferry and Sea Streets
Open all year
No fee

Site of court-ordered ferry to Boston 1638, first ferry captain Jonathan Brewster, son of Elder Brewster,* 1712 ferryman Benjamin White; area known as White's Ferry, also shipbuilding scene; across bridge is beautiful open sandy Humarock Beach*

HISTORY OF SCITUATE

Scituate, historically founded by "men of Kent celebrated in English history as men of gallantry, loyalty and courtly manners,"[10] has much to offer the present-day visitor. It is a town whose water tower has been converted to look like a fifteenth-century Roman tower and whose harbor is symbolically protected by picturesque Scituate Light.* It is the home of the "Old Oaken Bucket"* made famous by poet Samuel Woodworth and a town once saved from British attack by the courage and ingenuity of two lightkeeper's daughters.

Here on lands already cleared by Indians men from Kent, England, established homesteads before 1628. By 1633 they had laid out a village along Kent Street. The fledgling settlement officially organized its church under the Reverend John Lothrop and in 1636 became an incorporated town.

A year later a grant of land, known as the Conihassett Grant, which included the harbor, was assigned to Timothy Hatherly and three other gentlemen. Hatherly, known as the father of Scituate, had long been interested in the area. He first realized its potential in 1623 when he came to Plymouth aboard the *Anne*. As a member of the London Adventurers, when he returned to England he sided with the Plymouth Colony in their business negotiations and himself offered financial assistance. He returned to Scituate in 1632 where he became assistant to the General Court, treasurer of the colony, and commissioner of the United Colonies.

The Scituate area, whose name evolved from the Indian name for Satuit Brook which flows into Scituate Harbor, was not conducive to farming. Thus the townsfolk realized their main support from the North River and the sea. The North River, with its immediate access to lumber, its abundant shoreline for shipyards, and its protected waters, provided the ideal location for shipbuilding—Scituate's main industry from 1640 to 1872. In 1773 James Briggs built the famous ship, *Columbia*, later captained by John Kendrick* and Robert Gray.* (see Wareham #5)

Scituate's active fishing fleet brought in seafood for local consumption and domestic and foreign trade. Her brooks provided waterpower for grist, saw, and clothing mills. An active iron forge and the manufacturing of bricks and nails also added to the economy.

The abundant natural supply of Irish moss, which when cleaned and dried produces a commercially desirable high-quality gelatin, formed the basis of yet another industry. In 1847 two Irish fishermen, Daniel Ward and Myles O'Brien, began gathering moss from rocks and bringing it to shore on flat dories—later known as the moss fleet. They dried the moss on open sandy beaches, baled it, and shipped it to Boston for sale. With a few modern technical improvements, this industry is still active today.

Scituate has perpetuated the tolerant approach to life set by her first "Men of Kent." In earlier days, while Boston expelled Quakers, Scituate allowed them to live in peace. While Salem hung alleged witches, Scituate asked for a public apology. While Scituate was passionately loyal to the patriot cause during the Revolutionary War, she did not necessarily persecute her Tory sympathizers. While many of her wealthier citizens kept slaves, her most-admired citizen, Justice William Cushing,* defended the legal case which prepared the way for abolition of slavery in Massachusetts. While others lived in disunity, the Unitarian First Parish Church lived in harmony with her offspring, the Trinitarian Congregational Church, during the doctrinal controversy that sent shock waves throughout New England. In later years the Scituate atmosphere of creative and intellectual curiosity provided an ideal home for men and women of the literary and musical worlds.

Today Scituate's people are proud of their past, eager to recognize and presesrve their historic sites, and appreciative of the varied natural wonders of their coastline. Her four cliffs resemble the Cliffs of Dover in Kent, England—reminiscent of early founders, the "Men of Kent."

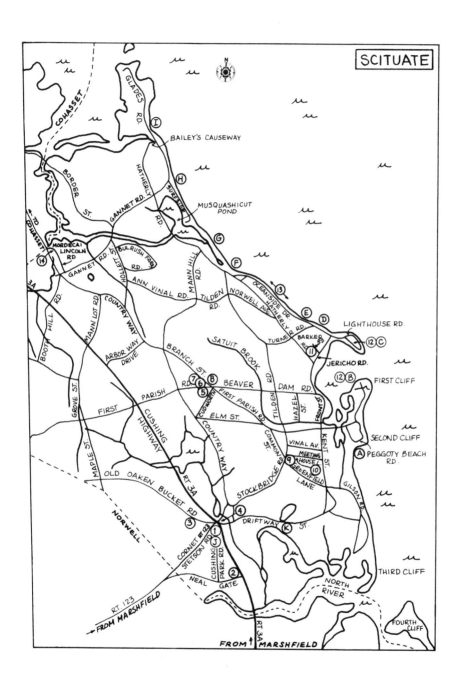

SCITUATE

DIRECTIONS:
Enter Scituate from Marshfield, following Union Street over the North River to Route 123. Turn right onto Route 123. Or exit from Route 3 at Route 53. Drive north to Route 123 and turn right.

#1
Cushing Memorial State Park
Cushing Park Road off
Neal Gate Street
1954
Open all year, no fee

Drive NE 1.1 miles on Route 123. Just before the Norwell-Scituate border make a right turn onto Neal Gate Street. The entrance to the Cushing Park will be on the left in .6 mile. Drive to the end of Cushing Park Road and park on the right side of the circle. The enclosed graveyard can be seen from the road.

The final resting place of Scituate's most famous son is the focal point of Cushing Memorial State Park, a lovely, wooded, small retreat. An unbeaten path leads to the stonewall-enclosed Cushing family cemetery.

Judge William Cushing* was a giant among a family of outstanding lawyers, judges, ministers, diplomats, elected officials, and military leaders. His vast achievements appropriately expanded the Scituate tradition of tolerance and personal freedom.

Judge Cushing succeeded his father as judge of the Superior Court of Massachusetts in 1772, where he was the only patriot during the troubled period prior to open rebellion. After the Revolution he became chief justice. Throughout this difficult and demanding period of unrest and untried democracy, Judge William Cushing picked up the torch and led his state and nation to a sound and just judicial system, providing the solid foundation necessary to support future generations. In 1783, during the Quaco case, he made such a positive charge to the grand jury opposing the whole idea of slavery that the direct result was the abolition of slavery in the state of Massachusetts. He helped frame and interpret the constitution of the Commonwealth of Massa-

212

chusetts and helped ratify and interpret the United States Constitution. With the formation of the federal government, President George Washington in 1789 asked him to be a justice of the United States Supreme Court. Here he frequently presided in the absence of Chief Justice Jay. He later declined his confirmed appointment as chief justice for health reasons.

Much of Judge Cushing's time was spent riding the circuit, even at the Supreme Court level. He was accompanied by his wife whose totally devoted, ladylike demeanor earned her the rarely bestowed title, Madam, indicating a rank earned in her own right. Their travels, often in a one-horse shay, carried them as far as Portland, Maine, and Atlanta, Georgia.

Madam Cushing remained a thrifty New Englander. In spite of the opulent entertaining which occurred at their political and social level, Madam Cushing thriftily used invitations to dine at the White House and calling cards of history's famous people as winders on which to roll her embroidery silk thread. She carried on a warm, mutually respecting correspondence with Abigail Adams,* Mercy Warren, and Mary Pinkney.

#2	*Return to Neal Gate Street and turn left;*
Belle House	*go .1 mile. The Belle House will be the last*
Neal Gate Street	*house on the left before reaching Route*
1742	*3A.*
Private	

The first Scituate Cushing, John senior, in 1662 bought a farm built circa 1635 on Belle House Neck from the heirs of William Vassall. John[1] was Deputy of the Colony Court, Assistant to the Colony, and later representative to the court at Boston. His son, John[2], was chief justice of the Inferior Court at Plymouth, Counsellor of Massachusetts, and judge of the Superior Court. His son, John[3], was Scituate's representative, probate judge, judge of the Superior Court, Counsellor of the Province, and father of Judge William Cushing.*

In 1742 John Cushing[3] built the current Belle House here where Judge William was born. They soon moved to another mansion house built in 1743. Now only Belle House remains, a stately Colonial set on a rise overlooking the North River.

#3
Old Oaken Bucket, Well,
and Homestead
Old Oaken Bucket Road
1675, 1835
House private
Museum open by
appointment
Fee charged

Continue on Neal Gate Street to Route 3A, and turn left. At the first traffic light turn left and immediately take the right fork, the Old Oaken Bucket Road. The Old Oaken Bucket can be seen alongside the house which will be on your left in .2 mile.

The old oaken bucket, the symbol of Scituate, was made famous in verse by Samuel Woodworth as he looked back in fond memory on his childhood home.

> How dear to this heart are the scenes of my childhood
>   When fond recollections presents them to view;
> The orchard, the meadow, the deep tangled wildwood,
>   And every loved spot which my infancy knew;
> The wide spreading pond and the mill that stood by it,
>   The bridge and the rock where the cataract fell;
> The cot of my father, the dairy house nigh it
>   And e'en the rude bucket that hung in the well.
> The Old Oaken Bucket, the iron bound bucket,
>   The moss covered bucket, which hung in the well.[11]

This vivid picture of Woodworth's early surroundings can still be seen near the site of the Northey homestead where he lived with his father and stepmother, Betsy Northey. As the boy worked long, hot hours in the fields he grew to appreciate the gifts of cool well water brought up by the old oaken bucket. Years later, in 1817 when he was a well-known editor, author, and poet in New York, his sensitive nature remembered those carefree days of youth when nothing tasted as good as the cool water drawn from this well. Beside the house is the famous well with its graceful sweep, which can still raise an old wooden bucket full of cool clear water.

The small 1675 house attached to the rear of the present house speaks eloquently of Scituate's early settlers. Here in this one-room home with sleeping loft lived ancestor John Northey. Possibly because his baby son was a sound sleeper, he was saved from a brutal Indian death. It was during the King Philip's War. The baby was asleep in a crib at his grandmother's nearby house, when suddenly a howling group of Indians broke cover and rushed the unguarded house. The grandmother fled the building, desperately seeking help at the nearby Stockbridge garrison.* The Indians burst in, but seeing no one and smelling fresh baking bread, they momentarily forgot their blood-thirsty pursuit and enjoyed the warm bread before abandoning the house and attacking the garrison. During the ensuing encounter the grandmother stole back into the house, and much to her relief and surprise, found the baby sleeping quietly in his crib. Quickly gathering him up, she returned to the garrison. Within a few hours the Indians burned the house to the ground.

This historic 1675 building was found in an adjacent field and moved to this location circa 1835, when the present home was built. The 1675 building has recently been carefully restored under the guidance of Mrs. Kathleen Laidlaw and the Scituate Historical Society. It now serves as a museum housing old Northey pieces, artifacts of early Scituate, and original Currier and Ives and early engravings of the "Old Oaken Bucket," plus photographs, song sheets, postcards, and other memorabilia relating to Samuel Woodworth.

#4
Stockbridge Mill
Country Way
c.1640
Open on tour days and by
appointment, fee charged

Return on Old Oaken Bucket Road to traffic light. Cross Route 3A and bear left on Country Way, not toward Scituate Harbor. The Stockbridge Mill is immediately on the right across from Old Oaken Bucket Pond.

The nation's oldest, still-operating, waterpowered gristmill is the Stockbridge Mill. The framing, including gunstock posts, rests on foundation stones laid mid-seventeenth century. The gate wheel, base millstone, and crane are original dating to the 1600s. The grain chest was featured in a special exhibit in the Museum of Fine Arts in Boston, the only one yet found from this early period.

Sometime before 1640 Isaac Stedman, a miller from England, dammed the First Herring Brook which created the millpond immortalized in "The Old Oaken Bucket."* It powered the gristmill he built here about 1640, probably the first waterpowered gristmill in Plymouth Colony. Some of the machinery which still operates today he brought with him from England, a mere two decades after the first Pilgrims arrived.

By 1650 John Stockbridge acquired a part-ownership, and later his son Charles owned the mill outright. Charles Stockbridge expanded, built other mills, and handled much of the grist and lumber milling needed by the colony.

Across the road, the circa 1656 Stockbridge "mansion," built on the shores of the millpond, became the very important scene of an attack during King Philip's War. Strategically garrisoned as the main blockhouse by Cudworth,* it safely sheltered women and children during the day-long battle. King Philip aimed to destroy all mills and all people he found. Scituate's well-trained, well-armed militia successfully repulsed the invading Indians, held an important line of resistance, and saved the Stockbridge Mill, one of the few to survive. Sadly, the garrison-mansion burned in 1830.

The mill was owned by Stockbridges until 1830 and operated and owned by Clapps into this century, when given to the Scituate Historical Society in 1922. The mill is totally restored and operates on tour days. It is fascinating to see all the parts and procedures involved in grinding corn and to realize how much of the operation is exactly as it was over three hundred years ago.

#5	*Follow Country Way north 1.7 miles to*
Cudworth House, Barn,	*First Parish Road, traffic light, and turn*
and Cattle Pound	*right. Go .2 mile; First Parish Church*
333 First Parish Road	*will be on left and school on right. Drive*
1797	*into school lot; Cudworth House is on left*
Open seasonally and by	*side of entrance. Park at school for #5–8.*
appointment, fee charged	

Now home to Scituate's impressive Historical Society, the Cudworth House also tells the story of an interesting founding family of Scituate.

The first James Cudworth was a fascinating man. A well-educated, wellborn, natural leader, with a strong sense of right and wrong, he served his new land in a unique variety of ways. He was a founding father of Scituate, an influential leader of Plymouth Colony, captain of Scituate's first military company, and later commander of the whole colony's forces to the successful end of King Philip's War. In 1681 he was Deputy Governor and agent for the colony in England.

Though not himself a Quaker, he strongly opposed their persecution and drew the Old Colony to a more tolerant view at heavy personal cost. "As I am no Quaker, so am I no persecutor."[12] Ringing words of General Cudworth still admired today and taught in Quaker schools. In 1658, when he was captain of militia, he urged tolerance for Quakers, and the intolerant Governor Prence had him removed. His ranks were stripped from him, and he was disfranchised. His election the following year as deputy to the Court was rejected by the Massachusetts government. His peaceful and dignified perserverance prevailed, and the next governor, Josiah Winslow, immediately reinstated him.

It is curious for one family to be associated in such a variety of religious supports. James Cudworth's first home was the first meeting place until the Meetinghouse was built. He strongly defended the rights of Quakers. Later, the bench-lined shed of this Cudworth House offered appreciated warmth and hospitality to hardy members of First Parish Church* between services. In 1821 the attic room here hosted the fledgling Baptist Society for four years and later welcomed the Unitarians at the time their church burned.

This Cudworth House was purchased by a direct descendant of the first James, also named James Cudworth, in 1728. His grandson, Zephaniah, removed the original Cape and built the current gambrel in 1797 around the earlier circa 1636 chimney.

You enter a home of yesterday and first see the entry shed which contains a working loom over 250 years old. The operator demonstrates and explains so well you finally understand how a loom works and what linsey-woolsey is (linen set up with cross threads of wool). Next, the kitchen focuses on the ancient fireplace and beehive oven surrounded by quaint but cumbersome utensils of old. The house contains furnishings from Scituate homes dating to early Colonial times. Featured are a special Cushing* room, genealogy library, a kettle forged by Mordecai Lincoln,* a London piano over 250 years old, ancient pewter and china, and samplers as old as the house. All curtains in the house were created on the ancient loom.

The barn is a museum which could stand alone. Its recognized collection of tools and implements dates to early Colonial times. Lafayette's* coach from Philadelphia and Judge Cushing's* one-horse shay are featured. The nearby cattle pound was constructed in 1671 and moved to its present site in 1953, with careful regard for its original specifications: "Horse high, bull strong, and hog tight."[13]

#6
First Parish Church of
Scituate
330 First Parish Road
Gathered c.1636, building
1881
Open for services

The church is across the road from the Cudworth House.

With its roots in England, its first building of chinked planks and board roof, its fifth church spire a landmark to mariners at sea, the First Parish Church of Scituate has served the spiritual needs of its parishioners since 1635.

On January 8, 1635 the First Parish Church of Scituate was organized under the Reverend John Lothrop, who had earlier been imprisoned in London for his nonconforming ideas. Their first meetinghouse was built a year later on Meeting House Lane. (see #10) The Reverend Lothrop served his flock well until 1639 when a doctrinal disagreement over the methods of Baptism caused him to leave Scituate for Barnstable, taking a group of followers with him.

Baptism continued to be a bone of contention in this frontier community. Their third minister, the Reverend Charles Chauncey, called to the church in 1641, believed in total immersion with no exceptions. A sufficient number strongly disagreed and left to form in 1642 the Second Church of Christ in Scituate, now the First Parish in Norwell. Much of the heated controversy ended in 1654 when the Reverend Chauncey left to become the second president of Harvard College. He replaced the Reverend Henry Dunster, who in turn was called to First Parish here in Scituate.

As the congregation grew, new meetinghouses were built in 1682, 1708, and 1737. The fifth meetinghouse was built on the present site at the time of the American Revolution in 1774 and served for over one hundred years. It burned on July 4, 1879 due to the overexuberant use of firecrackers. The 100-foot spire of that fifth meetinghouse stood high above the countryside and guided many a seaman into Scituate Harbor. The meetinghouse was affectionately called "The Old Sloop."

In 1825, under the Reverend Nehemiah Thomas, the New England-wide controversy over the doctrine of Unitarianism verses Trinitarianism came to a head in Scituate. The Reverend Thomas, being from Harvard, home of Unitarianism, was himself a strong advocate. However, an equally strong group remained loyal to their Trinitarian beliefs and left to form what is now the First Trinitarian Congregational Church.

The congregational split divided families. Deacon Ward Litchfield took his five sons to the new Congregational Church while his wife, Betsey, with one son, remained at First Parish. It is told that one night Deacon Litchfield asked his wife to prepare a "light" supper for a meeting he was hosting for members of "his" church. She complied by serving at the table only twelve "lighted" candles.

Returning in thought to today's First Parish, step inside the Italianate style church. This, their sixth building, was dedicated in 1881, and the sanctuary now has pale blue-gray walls, white woodwork and wainscoating, angled pews trimmed in dark stain, all set against a background of red carpeting. Notice the ship under full sail in the vibrantly colored Waterman memorial stained-glass window. It speaks eloquently of Scituate's lifelong connection with the sea.

#7
Lawson Tower
First Parish Road
1902
Open tour days and by
appointment
NHM

The Lawson Tower is directly behind the First Parish Church.

In the center of Europe's Rhine River stands a fifteenth century Roman tower—the model for Scituate's most unusual, horizon-dominating water tower. The 153-foot structure was given to the town in 1902 by copper king Thomas W. Lawson.* Lawson, who had made a fortune through his cornering of the copper market, was esthetically

Lawson Tower

Charlotte Parsons

offended by the appearance of the town water tower across from his magnificent estate, Dreamwold.* The fascinating, staunch, Roman-style tower still effectively hides the active water tower within.

Standing at the base and looking skyward you see the round, natural-shingled tower capped by a heavily bracketed overhang, higher windows, then more brackets, and finally the roof, molded to cone shape and pierced by dormers capped by spires. The whole is crowned by a single spire and weathervane.

As you climb the stairwell within the solid structure, you hear wind whipping but feel no sway. Once aloft, you find the ten-bell carillon surrounded by copper bell deck and original cypress-shingle-lined walls. You look out over the array of varicolored trees sprinkled with church steeples and outlined by the seemingly endless ocean. This gorgeous view from the top-of-the-world Lawson Tower makes it well worth timing your visit to tour days when the tower is open. On those days a bell concert is also featured, including of course the "Old Oaken Bucket."*

#8
Dreamwold
Branch Street
c. 1900
Open for business

Walk from Lawson Tower in front of school toward Branch Street. Dreamwold is on the other side of Branch Street. More of the Dreamwold Estate can be seen by traveling NW on Branch Street.

Now the scene of gala local awards dinners and receptions, Dreamwold was once the culmination of the dreams of Thomas Lawson.* The architecture is eclectic, featuring rambling though balanced Victorian styles. Chimneys rise from distinctly shaped roofs; a modest columned portico frames the entry. The estate once included more than five hundred acres, containing its own road and fire department systems, grand racetrack, horse stables for one hundred or more, prize livestock, pigeon-dove house, and even a hotellike housing arrangement for English bulldogs.

Copper King Lawson arrived in Scituate in 1898 and reached baronial heights of living here. An avid sailor, he built unique yachts, one to race in the America cup, the only seven-masted yacht known then. She was not accepted for the race, so he destroyed her. He attracted long friendly visits from world journalists of the muckraking era. He wrote *Frenzied Finance*, an expose of the stock exchange which had been a source of his riches and then became the cause of his downfall in 1922.

#9
Mann Farmhouse and
Historical Museum
Greenfield Lane
late 1600s, mid-late 1700s,
1825
Open seasonally and by
appointment, fee charged

Return to your car, exit from parking lot and turn right. Follow First Parish Road staying on right of monuments, one mile past fire station to "Y" in road. Bear right onto Common Street which runs into Stockbridge Road. Turn right and immediately left on Greenfield Lane. The Mann Farmhouse is on the left corner.

This beautifully restored Cape spans three centuries. It is interesting architecturally with its late 1600s foundation supporting the mid- to late-1700s main house with the attached 1825 ell. It has the rare experience of sharing the lives of only one family since the arrival of the first English settlers. And, even a fascinating tale of pirate treasure unfolds within these walls.

The first clue to the treasure was the wearing of a huge old coin on his watch chain by the last Mann, Percy. Percy had become an eccentric. He felt himself ill-used when the town took his gravel pit by eminent domain. He announced his withdrawal from town support and his plan to let his home deteriorate so that the town would get nothing when they took it for back taxes. He carried out his plan for forty years until his death at ninety-three in 1967. He was successful; the house was a sadly neglected wreck.

But the story continues. His distant relative heirs gave the priceless family furnishings to the Scituate Historical Society with the stipulation that they restore the house. The Society accepted the challenge. Through careful planning, painstaking craftsmanship, and amazing patience and fortitude, the Mann Farmhouse and Museum emerged as you see it today.

To get back to the treasure, at Percy Mann's death the heirs searched with metal detectors. Finally, almost accidentally, attic floorboards were raised to reveal two rusty cans filled with mid-1700s coins! And how had they gotten there? Speculation concludes that a coin-holding bag stamped "Holmes" could refer to the known Scituate pirate of that name. He commandeered a Spanish vessel, reaped a treasure, and buried it. He was captured, tried, and hung before he could return to his cache. It is likely that a member of the Mann family discovered the treasure, near where once the Mann property extended to the sea at Third Cilff.

The natural-shingle full Cape is pleasantly set amid three acres highlighted by special projects of the Scituate Garden Club. Lovely old sycamore, horse chestnut, and black-walnut trees and magnificent crocus beds are surrounded by picturesque stone walls.

Inside, some furnishings date to the 1600s and almost all are from the Mann family, actually used in this home of long tradition. A child's high chair, marked "PW 1620 TM 1650" indicated the first user was Peregrine White* and that it passed to Thomas Mann at his birth. Other treasures include 1720 slat-backed chairs, a Rodney Brace clock, and an early Chippendale mirror. Above, a sail loft is rigged and outfitted appropriately, reminiscent of the days when a working sail loft was here in 1821. A sound film briefly recounts some of the valiant steps taken by the Scituate Historical Society in the restoration of this remarkable Mann Farmhouse and Museum, which is well worth visiting.

#10
Men of Kent Cemetery
Meeting House Lane
1628
Open all year, no fee

Go back to Stockbridge Road, turn right and go one block to Meeting House Lane. Turn right, the cemetery will be on the right, past the newer one on the left.

Scituate was the only town in the Plymouth Colony that was not originally settled through the natural expansion of the Plymouth settlement. Before 1628 people from Kent, England, had established homesteads on Scituate's shores. Her high cliffs with cleared land for grazing and farming were a welcome sight to those early ocean-weary travelers. The "Men of Kent" as they were known were in most cases cultured, well-educated, wealthy, ambitious people who left their comfortable homes in England to invest their knowledge, talents, and wealth in the New World.

This cemetery is dedicated to those early pioneers. Notice the central monument to the "Men of Kent," which lists the names of founding settlers. A descendant of each family contributed to this stone memorial. Wander this old cemetery whose earliest graves were laid adjacent to the first three meetinghouses, which stood on this hilltop. Note one of the earliest—the 1628 grave of John Vinal. Here indeed was laid the cornerstone of Scituate.

#11
Barker Tavern
21 Barker Road
c.1634
Open as restaurant and to
visitors, no fee

Continue on Meeting House Lane to Kent Street and turn left. Follow Kent Street, which becomes Front Street, through town along the harbor. At traffic light turn right on Jericho Road, take third left onto Barker Road. Tavern is on the left.

Heavy beams, thick wooden walls lined with rare handmade brick, and a remaining garrison porthole begin to tell the story of this unusual old tavern. A modified section remains from the circa 1634 house built by John Williams, which served as a staunch garrision in the 1675 King Philip's War.

John Williams' son, John, Jr., who was a leader in the final pursuit of King Philip and deputy to the Colony Court, inherited this well-built house. His conflicting personality produced records of civic and military leadership yet vicious behavior toward wife, Elizabeth—daughter of first pastor the Reverend John Lothrop—and children and wards. The courts finally removed his family to safety while requiring him to support them. When not fighting Indians he fought family and neighbor as sixty-three lawsuits testify.

John Williams, Jr., left his house to his grandnephew Williams Barker, where it stayed in the family for nearly two centuries. Time added many changes to the house which was later called the Hatherly Inn, Garrison Inn, and now Barker Tavern.

The original circa 1634 John Williams house is easily distinguished as you enter the tavern, for it is the central entrance area dominated by huge dark beams and massive central chimney. The room to the left includes a wall believed to be one of the oldest in the country. In the basement the seaward wall was pierced to allow entrance to an underground railroad tunnel leading to the shore. Situated on a rise above the harbor, the Barker Tavern provides a fascinating opportunity to dine amid antiquity or simply to visit.

#12
Scituate Light
Scituate Harbor
Lighthouse and Rebecca
Roads
1811
Open tour days and by
appointment, fee charged

Return to Jericho Road and turn left. Follow along the harbor to end of road. Turn right and drive to the Light. Facilities: parking, views, rock walking.

If you have ever wondered if one or two people can accomplish anything, just remember the "Army of Two" in Scituate. The United States was at war with England. The year was 1814. The British had already made one attack on Scituate harbor, burning ten vessels. For months Rebecca (19) and Abigail (14), daughters of lightkeeper Simeon Bates, had watched and listened while Colonel John Barstow and his regiment paraded and trained on the green near the light. Then on September 1, 1814, while the militia was away and the girls were alone at the light, they saw two landing boats with British Marines approaching the harbor. Grabbing a fife and drum they ran outside and from behind a clump of cedar trees played with loud bravado "Yankee Doodle" and other marching tunes. The men on the frigate *La Hogue* and in the landing boats heard the music. Believing a regiment was waiting they quickly reversed oars and returned to their ship. The "Army of Two" had been victorious. (The Bates Home, where they lived in later years, is still standing at 6 Jericho Road)

In 1811 Scituate Light and the keeper's house were built at the entrance to the harbor in an attempt to prevent repetition of the many wrecks that occurred each year along the adjoining coastline. Unfortu-

Scituate Light

Massachusetts Department of Commerce and Development, Division of Tourism

nately, following her light captains often confused Scituate Light and Boston Light and ran full force into Minot's Ledge. Thus in 1850 a light was constructed on Minot's Ledge. Sadly it succumbed to the fury of the sea a year later. Scituate Light continued to shine until the present Minot's Light* was completed. On the morning of November 15, 1860, Keeper Thomas Richardson extinguished Scituate Light for the last time.

Though her beam no longer shines out to sea, the light is illuminated at night, adding to the picturesque setting of the harbor. In 1917 the town bought the light for $1000. Thanks to her historically minded citizens it was completely restored in 1967 and its care turned over to the Scituate Historical Society. When the house is open you can see the fife Rebecca used on that fateful day in 1814 and the documents from Congress referring to the sale of the light and the "Army of Two." This snug keeper's home has stood against storms for over 170 years, while neighboring houses—and even the covered walk to the light—have blown away.

Though officially inactive, Scituate Light still guards her historic harbor where shipyards were active from 1673 to 1864. Along with newly christened ships of yesteryear, fishing vessels have sailed in and out of the harbor since circa 1680. Mackeral fishing was the main catch during the 1700s and 1800s when thirty- to thirty-five vessels were fitted out annually. Scituate's fishing fleet continues to serve the area with fresh fish unloaded daily at Town Pier.

This picturesque harbor still offers protected refuge to sailboats, yachts, and other small craft, as well as the time-honored fishing vessels. Masts, though sleeker and often made of metal instead of wood, are still seen silhouetted against the setting sun, as they have been for over three hundred years.

#13
Scituate beaches
Sand Hills Beach—D
Hatherly Beach—E
Egypt Beach—F
Mann Hill Beach—G
North Scituate Beach—H
Minot Beach—I
Open all year, in season
sticker parking

Return on Lighthouse Road, bear right along water on Turner Road. Follow Turner Road to Oceanside Drive. Travel north along Oceanside Drive to see Scituate beaches. See map for locations. Follow Oceanside Drive to end, turn left, go one block and turn right on Hatherly Road. Follow Hatherly Road 1.7 miles to Gannett Road. Turn right here for a scenic beach drive along the water. Go to end, turn around and return via Bailey's Causeway. Facilities: lifeguards, swimming.

Scituate's beautiful and varied coastlands urge you to stroll their length. From the cliffs on the south, the edge of the sea continues along the rock-strewn cliff base to sandy and shingle beaches. These beaches, formed within a protective crescent, extend their reach as far as the massive granite ledges of the northern border of Scituate.

#14
Colonial Boundary Line,
Country Way, 1640
Mordecai Lincoln Mill and
Homestead,
Country Way and Mordecai
Lincoln Road
c. 1691
Historic markers on road,
land private

At end of Causeway turn left and follow Hatherly back to Gannett Road traffic light, and turn right. Follow Gannett about .8 mile to traffic light and Country Way; turn right, go .3 mile to left-hand bend in road, Mordecai Lincoln Road goes off to right. Over the bridge on the left is the Lincoln Homestead. The historic marker for the boundary line is on Country Way just south of the intersection.

The beginning of a significant and unusual Colonial Boundary Line is marked by a sign on Country Way near Mordecai Lincoln Road. The longest straight line boundary within the state, it originally separated the Massachusetts Bay Colony from Plymouth Colony and is now a county boundary. It was established in 1640 by John Endicott,* Israel Stoughton, William Bradford,* and Edward Winslow.* The prestige of the group indicated the importance of this line. For it was the first time two colonies had set their own boundaries without seeking help or receiving intervention from England. Another paving stone in the road to a democratic America was laid. It was only the second artificial boundary in the New World and must have presented many difficulties in walking this straight line through all landscapes, and in Pilgrim dress!

Nearby Mordecai Lincoln built his home and began his mills about 1691. First shingle-, then iron-, then gristmill were efficiently powered by the unusual three dam setup Lincoln devised which allowed double use of the same water. Originally a blacksmith, he established what was probably the first iron works in the colony. His father came to Hingham in 1640, and his son, also Mordecai, became a founder of Pennsylvania's iron industry. Lincolns migrated to further wilderness areas, and five generations later produced President Abraham Lincoln.

The beautiful old house still impressively commands the site above the ancient gristmill. Well-built circa 1691, the Colonial remained in the Lincoln family until the early 1800s. The steeply pitched roof and central chimney dominate the house as it overlooks the peaceful scene, complete with mallards on the millpond contentedly practicing noisy, crash landings.

This ends the guided tour section of Scituate. Drive north on Country Way to continue with Cohasset tour.

Scituate Beaches and Parks

Beaches listed from south to north, open all year, no fee, parking in season restricted to town stickers only

(A) **Peggotty Beach**
Peggotty Beach Road

Deep, open sandy beach, protected by Scituate's cliffs, with clear view of cliffs and open sea, named for nurse in *David Cooperfield;* here John L. Sullivan trained for fight with Paddy Ryan and won World Boxing Championship

(B) **Scituate Harbor**
Front Street
Jericho Road
(see #12)

Picturesque harbor, views, boat launching and mooring, fishing, free parking along Cole Parkway

(C) **Lighthouse Point and beach**
Lighthouse and Rebecca
Roads
(see #12)

Picture the "Army of Two,"* enjoy ocean and harbor views, walk the stone jetty, study the famous lighthouse; ample parking, open all year, no fee

(D) **Sand Hills Beach**
Ocean Side Drive at
Turner Road

Small, protected sandy beach, just north of harbor, good ocean views

(E) **Hatherly Beach**
Ocean Side Drive at
Kenneth Road

A shingle beach connected with Sand Hills Beach

(F) **Egypt Beach**
Egypt Beach Road

Southernmost part of gently curving crescent, sandy with protecting rocky barrier, nearby parking lot restricted in season, open ocean views

(G) **Mann Hill Beach**
end of Mann Hill Road

Climb the beach stone barrier to this shingle beach, excellent views of granite ledges and Minot's Light off Cohasset

(H) **North Scituate Beach**
end of Gannett Road
Glades Road

Extended sandy beach, some shingle areas, excellent beach walking and views of Minot's Light and open sea

(I) **Minot Beach**
Glades Road—end of
public section

A small shingle beach overpowered by granite ledges

(J) **Cushing Memorial State**
Park
Cushing Park Road
(see #1)

A small memorial park, a peaceful wooded area surrounding the Justice William Cushing grave site; facilities: trails, parking; open all year, no fee

(K) **Driftway Conservation and**
Recreation lands
Driftway Street

Planned combination of conservation and recreation; facilities: canoe launching, hiking trails, parking, playing fields, picnicking, viewing platform; open all year, no fee

HISTORY OF COHASSET

The glacial age left Cohasset literally standing on a rock, creating rugged ledges, protruding granite fingers, and treacherous yet beautiful rock-strewn coastline. As if to soften this severe exterior, nature covered much of Cohasset with lush fertile marsh grass. These two natural phenomena have strongly influenced the town.

Her picturesque Common beautifully illustrates the life of Cohasset. The open green symbolizes open marshland, her natural bounty, which first attracted settlers to Cohasset. The eighteenth-century sea captains' homes surrounding the Common speak of the natural role the sea has played in her life. The earlier modest historic houses tell of Cohasset's years of frugality, hard work, and self-sufficiency.

In 1670 the Hingham town fathers divided the area now known as Cohasset into seven hundred shares, though little real growth occurred until after 1700. Circa 1704 Mordecai Lincoln, ancestor of Abraham Lincoln, built an ironworks on Bound Brook. In 1708, George Wilson and Joseph Souther were granted the right to build vessels at the Cove. Charcoal pits, local sawmills, and ironworks soon supported this industry, and small vessels were built for local use in cod fishing and coastal trade. The fishing and shipbuilding industries served as the mainstay of Cohasset's economy until the mid-1800s.

Following a long battle with Hingham, in which intervention from the General Court was finally needed, Cohasset became a separate precinct in 1717. A meetinghouse was built, Daniel Lincoln was moderator, and visiting preachers ended the necessity for long journeys on the Sabbath to Hingham. This also ended an ingenious custom which illustrated Yankee cooperation called "Riding and Tying." One couple would ride the horse halfway to the meetinghouse while another couple started walking. At the halfway mark, the first couple tied the horse and walked the remainder of the way. When the walking couple reached the tied horse they would mount and ride the last half to the meetinghouse, where the news of the week was eagerly shared along with the spiritual uplift of the long service.

Not long after becoming an independent town in 1770, Cohasset men were called to fight for an even-greater independence, that of separation from England. While the men were at war, the staunch Cohasset women carried on. One, Persis Tower Lincoln, whose husband had been taken by the British at sea, skippered her brother's boat, running the British blockade to obtain sorely needed supplies from Gloucester.

Several decades later, on June 16, 1814, Militia Captain Peter Lothrop received word that the British had burned ships at Scituate. Not taking time for hat, coat, or saddle, he leaped astride his horse, as Paul Revere had done nearly forty years earlier. He alerted men in town and on farms, calling all to the meetinghouse. Riders were sent to other towns for help, and by the next morning twelve hundred men were entrenched along the Cove as eleven British barges and a sloop tender hove into sight. One look at those bristling armed countrymen, and the British reversed oars and rowed a fast retreat.

The South Shore Railroad, which came to Cohasset in 1849, helped support a transitional economy as fishing and shipbuilding declined. During the latter half of the 1800s and into the 1900s, Cohasset changed from a self-sufficient farming and seafaring town to a suburb of Boston, where more and more people lived in Cohasset but worked elsewhere. During summer months, she opened her doors to summer residents, who discovered the natural beauty and wonder of Cohasset's rock-lined coast. Beautiful homes and summer hotels were built along Jerusalem Road*—one of the most scenic drives in all New England.

Cohasset also attracted well-known theatrical personages. From 1889 until 1905, the six Hanlon brothers, English pantomime actors and aerialists, headquartered in Cohasset. Here with their cast and crew, they prepared colorful sets, rehearsed, and staged performances which opened each fall at the Old Boston Theater. The sounds, sights, and enthusiasm of those performances brought a special aura and excitement to this unique seaside town. Today the South Shore Music Circus* brings Broadway's and Hollywood's finest, creating in Cohasset a colorful center of performing arts.

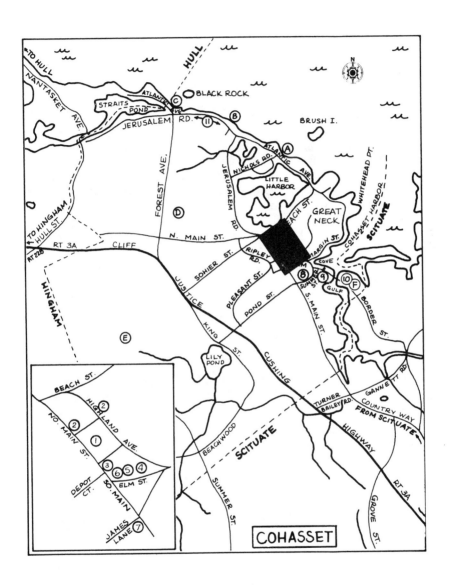

COHASSET

COHASSET

DIRECTIONS:
Leave Scituate by Country Way, which becomes South Main Street in Cohasset. Follow South Main Street to the Common, where South Main Street meets North Main Street. Enroute after 1 mile notice oldest remaining house in Cohasst at 179 South Main Street. The small Cape was built by Joshua and Rachel Tower Bates c.1695 and altered by later generations. Both husband and wife were descendants of original Cohasset settlers. Or enter Cohasset by following Route 3A to Sohier Street. From Sohier turn right on North Main to the Common.

#1
The Common
North Main Street and
Highland Avenue
1683
Open all year, no fee

The Common is just beyond the modern day center of town between North Main Street and Highland Avenue past Depot Court. Park along Common to see #1-7.

Crowned by her churches, Cohasset's *Common* is a jewel among picturesque New England commons. The broad green, complete with pond, is surrounded by some of Cohasset's finest historic homes as well as three churches and the Town Hall. All white with black or green shutters, the buildings are examples of the best of the eighteenth and nineteenth centuries. Colonial, Georgian, Federal, Greek Revival, Italianate, and Second French Empire homes provided the havens from which early ministers, sea captains, and merchants emerged to conduct the affairs of Cohasset.

The harbor was the working center for many of the people who lived near the Common in the 1700s and 1800s, but it was the Common itself that was the stabilizing center of their lives. Here families lived and attended church, which was their social as well as religious center. From the early days of hardship and toil, through the more productive years of farming and fishing, to today when many a citizen lives here but is employed outside of Cohasset, this church-centered Common has provided a peaceful unifying atmosphere for all those whose lives have been touched by it.

In the center of this picturesque Common is the imposing First Parish Unitarian Church.* Just east of it stands an ecclesiastical offspring, the Second Congregational Church,* and beside it the Town Hall built in 1857.

As you walk around the Common slip back in time and become acquainted with Cohasset's earlier settlers. Be aware of such names as Tower, Bates, Nichols, Lincoln, and Beal, for these are the family names of the original share owners of Cohasset.

Begin at *19 North Main* with the modified early Georgian style *Unitarian Parish House.** It was built in 1722 by First Parish's initial minister, the Reverend Nehemiah Hobart, who was the central figure of Cohasset's early life. Continuing north away from the center, notice the Georgian and Federal Period homes. At *35 North Main* is an 1857 Greek Revival with Italianate features. This is home to *Gilbert S. Tower*, descendant of original settler Ibrook Tower, who it is believed built the first house on the Common. In 1802 *Abraham Hobart Tower* erected the present modified Georgian style home at *45 North Main*, at which time the first Tower house was taken down.

Continue your walk in history beyond the Common to the majestic 1713 *Joseph Bates* house, which overlooks Little Harbor at *67 North Main*. Joseph Bates, one of the original share owners, died in 1713 before living in this early Colonial home he had built. The house then passed to his son, Joseph Bates, Jr., one of the seven members of First Parish who signed the initial covenant December 13, 1721. Across North Main at #72, Joseph Junior's grandson, *Major Jonathan Bates*, built a small Cape, which has been greatly expanded and remodeled over the years into the gracious home it is today at the head of Little Harbor.

Return to Highland Avenue on the east side of the Common. The early Federal style house at *63 Highland* was built in 1793 by *Samuel Bates*, brother to Major Jonathan Bates. Samuel, Revolutionary soldier, ships' owner and captain, drowned off Brush Island in 1801. The house was later bought by Levi Nichols, descendant of Israel Nichols, who settled in Cohasset prior to 1695. The next three homes add their own architectural charm to the Common, in order: Greek Revival, Second French Empire with mansard roof, and Federal.

The modified Georgian-style home at *31 Highland* was built by *James Hall* in 1750, using some of the lumber from the original First Parish Meeting House. His son, Captain James Hall, who also lived here, was a gallant Revolutionary soldier. He helped drag cannons from Fort Ticonderoga to Boston, served at Yorktown and Valley Forge, and was aide to General Washington. Following the war he married Cohasset heroine Persis Tower Lincoln. (see Cohasset history) The house was later bought by *Zenas D. Lincoln*, great, great, greatgrandson of Daniel Lincoln, original Cohasset share owner and first moderator of First Parish.

Behind St. Stephen's Church* stand two more historic homes. The Reverend *Josiah Crocker Shaw* built *#23* in 1794, two years after he was called to First Parish. The Reverend Shaw was a recipient of one of four gold medals given by a grateful King of Denmark to men in Cohasset for unselfish aid and comfort to shipwrecked Danish sailors of the *Gertrude-Maria*, which went down off Brush Island in 1793. Next door the central chimney *#7* was built by *Adam Beal* in 1756, and owned during the 1800s by sea captain *George Hall*. Adam Beal's uncle had built a home in Cohasset as early as 1690.

Returning to *3 North Main Street*, you see the large, adapted *Elisha Doane House*, now the Community Center. This house was built in the Georgian manner by James Stutson in 1750 and sold in 1792 to Elisha Doane,* who added the third floor. Elisha Doane, son of one of New England's wealthiest men, whose estate was valued at 125,000 pounds sterling, came to Cohasset in 1786. His wealth, influence, and business acuity were strong factors in the growth of this small coastal town. He invested in a tide mill at the Cove, building floodgates across Mill River to provide power. He supported a project whereby Little Harbor was dammed and drained, providing acres of lush marsh grass for nearly fifty years, until the dam was destroyed in the storm of 1851. He owned a fishing fleet, Doane's Wharf and fish house, and merchant ships, and served his community as justice of the peace, moderator, and selectman. Elisha sold the house to Thomas Smith, who ran a successful tavern in this ideal location during the 1800s.

Cohasset's Common speaks quietly yet eloquently of the spiritual, economic, political, and historical life of this unique town by the sea.

#2
First Parish Meetinghouse
23 North Main Street
1747

First Parish Meetinghouse and Second Congregational Church are found on the Common. The Town Hall is adjacent to the Second Congregational Church.

**Second Congregational
Church
43 Highland Avenue
1824
Open all year for services**

"The inhabitants of Conahasset shall have liberty to get up and erect a meeting-house. . . ."[14] With this commission in 1713 the settlers were given permission to build their own church. Their first meetinghouse was a small unadorned 35 ft. × 25 ft. building with raised pulpit, gallery, and pews made of hand-planed boards. Yet to the eyes of those first seven members, who on December 13, 1721, signed a covenant stating their commitment to their Lord and offering mutual concern for one another, the meetinghouse must have seemed like a precious cathedral.

Today's church was built in 1747 to accommodate their growing congregation. The porch was added in 1768, and in 1799 the present picturesque steeple completed the building. The clock was added in 1846 with the stipulation that it would be forever under the control of the town. Cushions, stoves, and carpeting were added over the years to the joy of the parishioners. Pause for a moment in this light, open sanctuary. Notice the box pews and red carpeting in eloquent contrast to the Doric columned gallery. The imposing raised wooden pulpit is beautifully flanked by pilaster-guarded windows, and covered by an ornate sounding board.

The first minister was the Reverend Nehemiah Hobart, grandson of Hingham's first minister, the Reverend Peter Hobart. Nehemiah Hobart wrote the basic covenant, which laid the solid spiritual foundation for the infant church. Their third minister, the Reverend John Brown, served a growing congregation for over forty-four years, seeing them through the French and Indian Wars and the Revolutionary War, serving as chaplain in both. A story is told of his first meeting with the congregation. All were for him, save one. When the Reverend Brown asked him why, he answered, "I like your person and your manners, but your preaching, sir, I disapprove." Mr. Brown replied, "There, is where you and I are agreed. My preaching I do not like very well myself, but what folly for you and I to set up our opinion against that of the whole parish!"[15] Needless to say the opposition was withdrawn.

The Reverend Jacob Flint served from 1798 to 1835. As his teachings became more Unitarian in doctrine, in 1824 twenty members separated from First Parish and built the Second Congregational Church.* Controversy and bitterness followed, but First Parish's seventh minister, the Reverend Joseph Osgood, healed the breach with such words as, "We should be rivals only in Christian charity and good works."[16]

Second Congregational Church

Following the separation, the newly formed Second Congregational Church dedicated their meetinghouse in January 1825 on land given by Captain Nichols Tower. Within a year they called the Reverend Aaron Pickett as their first minister. Within thirty years it became necessary to add onto the Highland Avenue side of the building. In 1878 the building was further enlarged by raising it and adding a first floor, which was called Bates Hall in honor of the Bates family, who served the church faithfully for three generations. At that time a new entranceway was added and a three-stage steeple built, which still flies the same banner-style weathervane as its mother church on the Common.

January 19, 1928, saw the awesome destruction of the interior by fire. Within six months devoted parishioners turned tragedy into progress, and on July 1, 1928, a rededication service was held in their enlarged, restored, and redecorated church.

Today the two white churches at the center of the Common stand in mutual support and respect as members of a revered family.

#3
St. Stephen's Episcopal
Church
Common, South Main
Street and Highland Avenue
1899
Open all year for services

St. Stephen's Church is the stone church at the southern end of the Common between South Main Street and Highland Avenue.

In beautiful, complete compatibility with the granite ledges from which it arises, St. Stephen's stands stoically at the edge of the Common. The English perpendicular Gothic style, in massive Quincy granite, contrasts and complements the white clapboarded New England Common.

The reverent, peaceful sanctuary is smaller and warmer than expected, with boldly colored Biblical stained-glass windows. Solid hand-

carved oak pews face the carved, oak-paneled altar, reflecting dignified, elegant craftsmanship. The font shaft was a gift from Hingham,
England. It was their original one dated circa 1346 and believed
damaged by Cromwell's men.

St. Stephen's is noted for the fifty-one bell carillon given in memory
of Jessie Barron, wife of Wall Street's Commodore Barron,* by her
daughter Jane Bancroft in 1924. St. Stephen's organist Mrs. Edward
Stevens then became the first woman in the United States to play a
carillon. It is fascinating to climb the bell tower to gaze up at the array
of bells ranging from the huge five-and-one-half-ton bourdon bell to the
twelve pound ship bell. The expert carillonneur stretches to reach
across the clavier (keyboard) using pad-protected fingers or palm
edges, and nimble feet. The carillon is played every Sunday before
services and during special summer concerts which magnificently ring
across the Common, bringing feelings of peace and contentment.

#4
Maritime Museum
Cohasset Historical Society
Museum
4 Elm Street
c.1760
Open seasonally and by
appointment, fee charged

From St. Stephen's Church walk back, or
south, on South Main Street a very short
distance to Elm Street. Turn left for the
three Cohasset Historical Society Muse-
ums. For historical continuity visit first
the Maritime Museum at 4 Elm Street.

Allow time to explore leisurely this fascinating museum of seafaring
days relived. The museum is housed within the historic Bates Ship
Chandlery built about 1760 at the Cove.* Moved from the Cove in the
1950s, the chandlery's plain Colonial exterior is enhanced by tiny
gardens, carefully tended by the Cohasset Garden Club.

Inside, a myriad of sea treasures awaits you. You find scrimshaw,
ship models, weights and measures, photos, paintings, whaling implements, shipwright tools, wood from the original *Constitution*, and the
nameboard of the Weston* owned *Smyrna*, the ship which opened the
Black Sea. The plate was washed off the brig while in Cohasset waters
and preserved here. The collection also includes a log pipe from
Nathaniel Treat's saltworks, part of the lens of Minot's Light,* and a
model of the pioneering ironworks of Mordecai Lincoln* with memorabilia of Abraham Lincoln, his descendant. While discovering the many
fascinating relics of the sea, enjoy the feeling of Cohasset's past and the
flavor of an old ship chandlery.

#5
Historic House
Cohasset Historical Society
Museum
2 Elm Street
c.1810
Open seasonally and by
appointment, fee charged

The Historic House is next to the Maritime Museum at 2 Elm Street.

Next door to the Maritime Museum is another interesting gray-clapboard structure also preserved for posterity by the ambitious Cohasset Historical Society. Built right onto granite ledge, surrounded by neat fences and the compact, cheerful gardens of the Cohasset Garden Club, the Colonial Georgian-style Historic House presents a way of life in the early 1800s.

The house was built for Captain John Wilson, who commanded schooners to Malaga, St. Thomas, and other ports, and who operated a ship's chandlery on the first floor. Captain Wilson was captured during the War of 1812 while sailing his packet *Cohasset* to Boston. Fortunately her cargo of fish didn't interest the British man-of-war, and Wilson and his ship were released to fine-paying owner Levi Tower. This house stayed in the Wilson family until 1912 and has since housed a tea shop, tailor, and photographer before acquisition in 1936 by the Cohasset Historical Society.

Inside, the former chandlery has beautiful, exceptionally wide-board wainscoting and a unique settle where the family gathered by the fire at night for warmth and light when the chandlery was closed. Paintings and furnishings from Cohasset families complete the portrait. The family lived upstairs where the quaint kitchen, cheery bedroom, doll-filled children's room, and borning room complete with model of mama and baby can be found.

#6
Independence Gown
Museum
Cohasset Historical Society
Museum
Elm and South Main
Streets
c.1848
Open seasonally and by
appointment, fee charged

The Independence Gown Museum is adjacent to the Historic House on the corner of Elm and South Main Streets.

This unusual museum claims to have the most extensive collection of gowns north of the Smithsonian. The neat, modest, brick-and-clapboard structure is from the Greek Revival period. It is nestled, Old World style, into the ledge, seemingly under the wing of St. Stephen's Church above.

About 1848 it was built as a fire station to house the Independence Fire Company and later became a police station. The first floor remains a small fire and police museum, where you can see the old jail cells, one complete with model prisoner.

In striking contrast, the stairs take you to another world—a grand background with elegant models in historic gowns. Featured are a profusion of gowns, laces, fans, and parasols spanning nearly two hundred years. It all began with a trunk full of gowns found in the barn of Mrs. Thomas Francis Richardson. The collection also includes the presentation suit worn by her son the Honorable Charles Richardson at the Court of Queen Victoria.

#7
Red Lion Inn
71 South Main Street
c.1704
Open all year as restaurant
and inn

Walk south on South Main Street one block. The Red Lion Inn is on the right, on the corner of James Lane and South Main Street.

Tradition permeates the whole atmosphere of this quaint yet practical inn. Three generations of modern-day innkeepers proudly continue the hospitality first offered by the pioneering James family.

The inn began as the home built by Thomas James about 1704 for his bride Patience, daughter of Ibrook* and Margaret Tower.* Thomas James was active in the 1721 founding of the church and had an interest in Mordecai Lincoln's* smelting of iron at Turtle Island. 175 years of James' ownership of this building followed, with modifications by each generation. Thomas James' grandson Christopher became a storekeeper, expanded the building, and was the first to accommodate guests for bed and drink at the sign of the Red Lion. Located on the Plymouth to Boston road, it has served as an inn almost continuously, with a variety of names, hosting a variety of people.

In 1840 the inn was the haven for Danish sailors rescued from the wreck of the *Copenhagen*. Cohasset earned her reputation for unusual honesty when every bale of cargo from the *Copenhagen* was eventually found and returned. Here also stayed the Hanlons, forerunners of modern musical comedy and Cohasset's summer theater.

Much of the small, original, circa 1704 building remains in the main dining room. You can see centuries-old timbering, paneling, fireplaces, and the massive central chimney. A portion of wall is open to display the very early clay brick insulation packed between studding. Upstairs, one of the fireplaced guest rooms, probably added about 1825, was once used as a dance hall. This second oldest remaining building in Cohasset is well worth a visit and provides a warm and interesting background to a good meal.

#8
Caleb Lothrop House
14 Summer Street
1823
Open limited seasonal
hours and by appointment,
fee charged
NRHP

Return to your car and drive back or south on South Main Street. Notice the Pratt Memorial Library on your left. Here are found beautiful murals of early Cohasset life. Take next left on Summer Street. The Lothrop House is first house on left. The offices of the Cohasset Historical Society are located here, along with a small research library.

This stately white-clapboarded Federal, with its twelve-inch brick ends, is the only one of its kind in Cohasset. It retains its gracious-living features without the grand elegance of the Salem Federals, marking a difference between north and south shores of Massachusetts. The Cohasset Historical Society heroically rescued and beautifully restored the Lothrop House, and the Community Garden Club of Cohasset created the lovely granite-walled, brick-pathed landscaping.

Within, the house is elegantly practical. It is outstandingly decorated with period-painted original wainscoting, a Dorothy Waterhouse wallpaper over original plaster, carefully coordinated draperies, and unique stenciling. Appropriate period furnishings include an Eli Terry clock and interesting brass-plate fireplace fender.

During the despised War of 1812, Captain Peter Lothrop became Cohasset's Paul Revere. (see Cohasset history) Peter's son Caleb was the builder of this house where only Lothrops have lived. He was a shipowner and ship chandler, owner of trading and fishing vessels and a wharf within the Cove. He was treasurer of the Cohasset Savings Bank, town treasurer, and selectman. His cousin Captain Daniel Lothrop retired from the sea to become a salvage and insurance expert, a challenging field here where so many tragic wrecks occurred. He made a careful list of the losses over thirty years, which proved the convincing evidence to build the first Minot's Light. The Lothrops, an important part of Cohasset's history, are interesting to remember as you visit their pleasant Federal home.

#9	*Continue on Summer Street to Border*
Captain John Smith	*Street and turn right driving along the*
Commemorative	*head of the harbor. The Smith Commemo-*
Town Landing	*rative is on the left before Hugo's Restau-*
Border Street	*rant. Facilities: benches and roofed pavil-*
Open all year, no fee	*ion. Adjacent Town Landing for boat*
	docking and fishing.

In the summer of 1614 Captain John Smith's two ships lay anchored off the coast. While his men fished, Smith and several others set out in a small boat to explore the New England coast. Thanks to the unquenchable curiosity of Captain Smith, his group were undoubtedly the first white men to pass through the treacherous granite outcroppings and enter beautiful Cohasset Harbor. Afterward he wrote, "We found the people in those parts verie kinde; but in their furie no lesse valiant. For, vpon a quarrell we had with one of them, hee onely with three others, crossed the harbor of Quonahassit to certaine rocks whereby wee must passe; and there let flie their arrowes for our shot, till we were out of danger."[17] Unfortunately one Indian was killed and one wounded, thus marring the first red man–white man encounter in Cohasset. Nevertheless Smith came away with such a favorable impression of the Massachusetts coast as to write "The Countrie of Massachusets . . . is the Paradise of all those parts."[18] Returning to England he wrote of his New England adventures referring to himself as Admiral of New England.

The boulder commemorating his discovery stands in front of a columned, roofed pavilion overlooking the harbor with its fishing, lobster, and pleasure boats. Adjacent to the memorial is the *Town Landing*. On the far side of the Landing is a modern day ships' chandlery, reminiscent of earlier chandleries, which serviced the active fishing and boat-building industries here during the 1700s and 1800s.

#10	*Continue on Border Street. Entrance to*
Government Island	*Government Island is a sharp left imme-*
Minot's Light	*diately after crossing bridge. However*
Beacon Rock	*there is only sticker parking on island, so*
Access from Border Street	*park along street on island side of bridge.*
Open all year, no fee	*Facilities: mementos of Minot's Light;*

path to Beacon Rock leads from east side of entrance up behind old shed and house to top of rocky ledge overlooking harbor. Facilities: boat docking and mooring, fishing, Harbor Master, Cohasset Sailing Club offers lessons and races.

Here on Government Island, a small peninsula forming the southern border of the harbor, was the focus of the remarkable creation of the present *Minot's Light*. Cohasset is known for her dangerous granite ledges, causes of untold wrecks, and known also for her daring, dedicated people who responded immediately to battle any sea to rescue life and property. In 1807 the Massachusetts Humane Society stationed the first lifeboat in the United States here in Cohasset. Heartbreaking disasters off Cohasset rocks, sometimes over forty in less than a decade, led to the building on Minot's Ledge of the first United States offshore lighthouse, which itself met disaster.

In 1847 the wildly hazardous job was begun, and three years later a sixty-five-foot light and keepers' quarters shone above the support of nine iron pilings. Tragically, it took less time for the sea to destroy the light than for man to build it, and in 1851 the tower plunged into raging seas, taking two keepers to their deaths.

Cohasset Harbor with Minot's Light templates in the foreground

Authors

The lightship replacement proved not as effective a warning, and careful planning began for the construction of Minot's Light. The plan of chief engineer, General Joseph Totten, modified and supervised by Captain Barton S. Alexander, gradually became a reality. Ingenious practices were devised to conquer each obstacle as it arose. Truly artistic carving of the best Quincy granite produced the exact dimensions required to grip the challenging ledge. On Government Island 3514 tons of granite were painstakingly hewn into 1079 dovetailed blocks, matched to the templates you see here, and transported by barge to Minot's Ledge. The tiny ledge was only above calm sea level 130 hours in 1855, the first year of construction, and not many more working hours were available in each of the next three years. At the exact combination of tide and wind, stonecutters were ferried to the ledge to begin, supervised by a full-time lifeguard and an alert watchman who shouted "roller coming" to alert the workers to grasp the lifeline when a wave broke over the ledge. Finally, the solid tower was safely completed in 1860, rising 114 feet above the dangerous ledges and raging seas off Cohasset.

For over a century the sturdy sentinal has survived, withstanding storms such as the gale of 1888 which cast a wave breaking over the top of Minot's Light. Its 1,4,3-flash, now automated, continues to warn mariners and also deliver a message interpreted by many who read the 1,4,3 as "I love you." Captain Brennock, who worked on the light, best reflects the feelings: "The new Minot's Tower was almost an idol with me. I watched it rise, knew and handled every stone in it, and now I love to sit and watch it from my window, on a stormy night, when it shines like a huge star."[19]

Government Island now belongs to the town and provides a place for all to enjoy. It serves as a living museum for the amazing lighthouse. The small building next to the Cohasset sailing club once held kerosene for the light. The lighthouse bell and the template patterns used in the light's construction are easily visible, and an old keeper's house remains, now privately rented. Just above, reached by a path is *Beacon Rock*. Here, when it was time to change batteries (which had replaced kerosene), tenders signaled the lighthouse with flags by day, with lights by night. Be sure to save enough energy and time to climb to the top of Beacon Rock, elevation eighty feet. The path leads up ledge to stairs carved into the rock. The fantastic view is well worth the small climb, making you want to gaze in all directions at once.

Immediately below, at the Gulf/Border Street Bridge, rapids froth at the meeting of fresh and saltwater as currents of the Gulf River confront the tide. The Gulf River once supplied tide-powered mills here, such as Elisha Doane's* tidal gristmill of 1792, sited across the river where today's boatyard stands. The river was regulated by dam and floodgates, the remains of which can be seen from the bridge at low tide and provide part of the rapids. Now kayakers treasure the racing, brackish water. The battle of tide and current is dramatic at any time.

Beyond the Doane Mill Site is Hugos Restaurant, site of the old Bates and Tower fishing wharves. Across the street was the Bates Ship Chandlery, now the Maritime Museum* on Elm Street. Directly across the Cove is another site of once-active boatyards, now a grand estate. The magnificent neo-Georgian brick mansion is home to the grand-daughter of Clarence W. Barron, the *Wall Street Journal* publisher, whose ample mansion was replaced by this one. To the right is the yacht club. Another estate at White Head Point, site of the first United States lifeboat station, marks the open sea where Minot's Light stands guard. Nearby, in earlier days, a windmill drew seawater through pine-log water pipes (see one at Maritime Museum) to huge drying vats, which eventually produced about four ounces of salt from a gallon of seawater.

On the Scituate side, continuing to the right, the outer point, the Glades, is dominated by the Charles Francis Adams estate and the smaller estates of his descendants. Further to the right the woods of Scituate are broken only by a church steeple, and the Gulf opens to view.

#11
Jerusalem Road and Atlantic Avenue Coastal Drive
Little Harbor Sandy Beach—Ⓐ
Moors' Rocks Reservation—Ⓑ
Black Rock Beach—Ⓒ
Open all year for walk on

Return on Border Street keeping next to harbor, bear right at triangle and right on Margin Street. Take third left from Margin Street onto Atlantic Avenue, follow Atlantic Avenue until it becomes Jerusalem Road. No parking allowed along Atlantic Avenue or Jerusalem Road, Sandy Beach parking off season.

Along the ridge of Cohasset's granite shores runs Jerusalem Road, a noted scenic coastal drive. Here breathtaking glimpses of endless ocean vistas, the Boston skyline, and intriguing lighthouses compete with lovely seacoast homes and estates for your attention.

It was to Jerusalem Road that summer visitors first came. By the mid-1800s Cohasset was known as a proper summer residence for Bostonians, among them, in different centuries, John Quincy Adams and John Fitzgerald Kennedy. The grand summer hotel era dawned with an interesting sidelight. One of the earliest, the Black Rock Hotel built in the 1700s, was a special retreat for coot hunters. This migratory saltwater duck (black butterbill) drew seasonal visitors to Cohasset. Some remained to build homes along Jerusalem Road. The latest Black Rock House remained a huge towered and turreted giant on the ledges above Black Rock Beach until it was removed in the 1960s.

The drive begins as Atlantic Avenue crosses Little Harbor Bridge at the tiny outlet to the sea. Here from 1804 to 1851 Cuba Dam held back the ocean, making Little Harbor a productive source of lush marsh grass. Near the bridge is Deadmen's Rock, a boulder on the ocean side where victims from the wrecked brig *Saint John* were piled. Ninety-nine people lost their lives when the *Saint John*, an Irish immigrant ship, dashed to bits within an hour on the ledge near the nearly completed Minot's Light. Henry D. Thoreau wrote a moving account of the scene with perceptive commentary.

Across Little Harbor Bridge, Atlantic Avenue continues along a narrow strip of land to *Sandy Beach* and your first glimpse of the open sea. The open sandy-shingle beach has a great view of Minot's Light and offshore ledges, powerfully beautiful and equally dangerous, the scene of so many shipwrecks. The beach is protected by granite outcroppings which have so dominated land and sea here for millions of years. The land side is bordered by gracious coastal homes, well designed to hug their granite ledges and use the natural contours of this magnificent shore.

Jerusalem Road comes in on the left, ending Atlantic Avenue. *Moors' Rocks Reservation* on the ocean side, just past Jerusalem Lane and before Deep Run private way, is on the rocky ledges of Cohasset's rugged shore. At Moors' Rocks the whole open vista emerges. Here is the breathtaking panorama of the Boston skyline, with a clear view of bridges, the Hancock Building, the Prudential. You see Boston Light, Graves Light, other harbor lights, and beyond to Massachusetts's North Shore as far as Cape Ann. Ships dot the far horizon, with smaller sailboats and fishing boats nearer shore. To the south, Cohasset ledges and Minot's Light, and everywhere the ebb and surging tides of the constant sea. Moors' Rocks Reservation, three acres under the supervision of Cohasset Historical Society, is open to all to appreciate this view.

Opposite Forest Avenue is *Black Rock Beach*, a sandy or rocky beach, depending on tide. Jerusalem Road now follows Straits Pond away from the open sea.

This ends the guided tour section of Cohasset. Follow Jerusalem Road to Hull border to continue tour.

Cohasset Beaches and Parks

(A) Sandy Beach*
Atlantic Avenue

Parking is the problem at this semipublic sand and shingle beach, ample parking but sticker required in season; Walk-on facilities: bathhouse, swimming, view; open all year, no fee

(B) Moors' Rocks Reservation*
Jerusalem Road

Spectacular views from bold granite ledges, three acres controlled by Cohasset Historical Society; no parking; open all year, no fee.

(C) Black Rock Beach*
Off Jerusalem Road

Though a town owned beach there is no parking anytime, .3 acres of sandy-stony beach; Walk-on facilities: swimming; open all year, no fee.

(D) Wheelwright Park
Entrances: Forest Avenue, North Main Street

Well-signed entrances lead to peaceful, wooded park of mainly passive recreation; facilities: paths, picnicking, riding ring; can park along road; open all year, no fee.

(E) Whitney and Thayer Woods,
Route 3A at head of Sohier Street

750 acres preserved for conservation, education, and recreation by the Trustees of Reservations; twelve miles of paths, woods, glacial boulders called erratics, view of harbor from Turkey Hill; facilities: cross-country skiing (degree of difficulty marked), hiking, nature study, parking, picnicking, riding, scenic viewing, snowshoeing; open all year, no fee

(F) Government Island*
Border Street just past Gulf River Bridge (See #10)

A varied, interesting site for scenic and historic appreciation and summer recreation; Beacon Rock has excellent views, Minot's Light history here; facilities: path to Beacon Rock, picnicking, sailing club, town docks and mooring; sticker parking only on island, park on street on island side of bridge; open all year, no fee

HISTORY OF HULL

Fishhook in shape, originally a storehouse for the Plymouth settlement, Hull was set aside as an early fishing station and incorporated in 1647.

During the American Revolution, Hull's strategic location made her an integral part of the war. Batteries built on Telegraph Hill* were instrumental in breaking the British blockade of Boston in 1776, and striking at British forces when they landed at Boston Light.*

Adjacent to Boston Harbor, her unique position has also made her the unwilling site of hundreds of shipwrecks. As a result, the mid-1800s saw the development of the Massachusetts Humane Society at Hull. Here their most active member and ultimately most-decorated lifesaver in United States history, Joshua James,* lived and guided the rescues of more than six hundred people.

In 1826 the "Sportsman," Hulls' first public house, was built, heralding Hull's most prosperous and famous era—that of the gala summer hotels from the mid-1800s into the early 1900s.

Today the silks and piazzas of the hotel era are gone, as are the grand hotels, but gracefully curved, four-mile long, Nantasket Beach still welcomes the refreshing waters of Massachusetts Bay and continues to lure thousands each summer to enjoy the sea breezes and escape the heat of the cities.

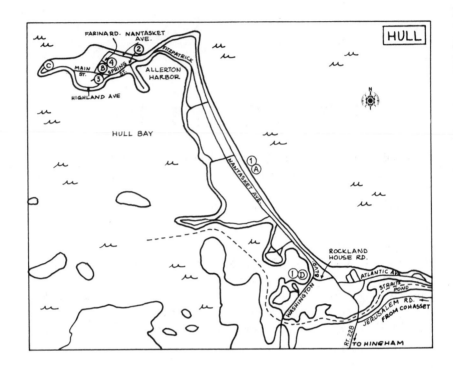

HULL

DIRECTIONS:
From Cohasset follow Jerusalem Road to Nantasket Avenue, Route 228, and turn right for the Hull peninsula. Or Take Route 3A north through Cohasset to Route 228, turn right and follow Route 228 to Hull and Nantasket Avenue.

#1
Paragon Park
Nantasket Beach
Beach open all year
Park and facilities open
seasonally, fee charged

Paragon Park is on the left side of Nantasket Avenue, at the beginning of the peninsula. For Nantasket Beach stay on Nantasket Avenue and the beach will be on the right. Facilities: bathhouse, refreshments, rest rooms, swimming, walking; parking

Paragon Park is your introduction to Hull. Called a Yankee Coney Island, it offers a huge array of amusements, eateries, souvenir shops, games, and rides. *Nantasket Beach* is adjacent, with four miles of gradually sloped, hard-packed sand and tiny rocks where once carriages and strollers promenaded at low tides. It has been a favorite summer retreat for over a century, where bathers still enjoy the gentle surf. The clear ocean vista is guarded to the north by Boston and Graves Lights and to the south by Minot's Light.

#2
Lifesaving Museum
Nantasket Avenue and
Spring Street
1889
Open seasonally, fee
charged

Follow Nantasket Avenue taking left fork, where road divides to the end of the peninsula. Bear to extreme left on road going over causeway. The main road becomes Spring Street and Nantasket Avenue turns right. Turn right onto Nantasket Avenue, the Lifesaving Museum is on the left.

This Lifesaving Museum is a monument to dedicated, courageous people. It began as "Old" Point Allerton Lifesaving Station, built by the Federal government after the unbelievable actions of Joshua James* and his lifesaving crews during the great storm of 1888. Again and again they set out that wild night to rescue crews of four separate, storm-stranded vessels. Captain James was appointed keeper at age sixty-two, receiving the only age waiver in the service granted by Congress. During his twelve years as keeper, he and his teams raced to rescue crews of eighty-six shipwrecks with amazing success.

Lifesaving is a tradition in Hull since the days when Colonial Boston was one of the country's busiest ports, and Hull placed a lighthouse on Great Brewster Island in 1681. The Nantasket Roads channel, most often used, passes through Hull waters where seventy percent of Boston Harbor's major wrecks happened.

The Massachusetts Humane Society began in 1785, and over the years lifesaving rescuers evolved useful equipment and team-spirited drill techniques similar to those of New England's volunteer firemen. Their success is their reward, as on the chilling winter Sunday in February of 1927 when the huge five-masted schooner *Nancy* floundered off Nantasket Beach. Led by Captain Oceola James, son of Joshua James, rescuers headed into monstrous waves after tying a rope to the shore. Finally reaching the troubled ship, they timed the waves to painstakingly rescue the crew one by one.

Today the New Point Allerton Coast Guard Station continues to be one of the country's most active, averaging 850 search and rescue missions annually.

The abandoned old Point Allerton Station gradually became a sad derelict. Concerned citizens and community development funds have joined to rescue this proud institution.

#3   *Return to Spring Street and turn right.*
Hull Public Library   *Follow Spring to Main Street, bear left on*
Main Street   *Main, and the library is on the left at the*
Site c.1644, house c.1888   *corner of Main and Highland Avenue.*
Open all year, no fee

This library site has several interesting stories to tell. It was first recorded about 1644 when the church was formed, and there were only twenty houses in Hull. Here lived the Reverend Marmaduke Matthews in the unofficial parsonage as the colony did not support a minister for Hull until 1670.

A later occupant, the Reverend Samuel Veazie, sued the town for back wages, unfortunately, a not-uncommon circumstance. The story is told that he was in such desperate straits he raced to the beach to salvage a hide from a dead horse only to be beaten in the race by townspeople. He was allowed the shoes which he sold for twenty-five cents to the village blacksmith. After Veazie's death, in 1767, British officer William Haswell settled here with his daughter, Susanna Rowson, who became noted in the fields of acting, teaching, and writing. Here they nursed, then buried a British soldier mortally wounded in an attack on Boston Light.

About 1888 the rectory was removed by professional Irish-American John Boyle O'Reilly, patriot, poet, and editor of the *Pilot*. He and his wife designed and built this building as their summer home, and it became home to the Hull Public Library in 1912.

#4   *Continue on Main Street past library,*
Fort Revere Memorial   *take the second right on Nantasket Ave-*
Park, NHS   *nue, then second right on Farina Road,*
Fort Warren   *and go straight to reach the fort.*
Boston Light, NRHP, NHL
Farina Road
1600s
Open all year, no fee

Perhaps the most spectacular view of Boston Harbor is found at the end of Hull, atop Fort Revere Memorial Park. You can clearly see the stately buildings of Boston to the west. The island-studded harbor is right at your feet, with George's Island* and its Fort Warren* the nearest to the north. Moving to the east you see the Brewster Islands, with Boston Light on Little Brewster. Harbor lights and islands lead your eye to Boston's north shore, Cape Ann, and the Two Lights of Thacher's Island off Rockport. The total panorama emerges as you look back at Nantasket Beach and the southern coastlines of Hingham and Cohasset.

This elevation has been fortified since Colonial times as it commands the harbor entrance. In the 1600s beacons were set and a watchhouse was erected. During the French and Indian Wars, in 1704, Colonel Benjamin Church* assembled 550 New Englanders and Indians here to assault the French in Maine and Acadia. During the Revolution, minutemen and French united here when invasion threatened, as when Lord Howe's fleet entered Boston Harbor. Surprisingly, it was the French who, under Count D'Estaing, Admiral of the French fleet, garrisoned this key harbor defense post with marines and sailors during the Revolutionary War.

During the War of 1812 the American *Chesapeake* and British ship *Shannon* fought a spectacular naval duel off Hull. *Chesapeake* Captain James Lawrence, though dying, ordered his often-quoted command, "Don't give up the ship!"[20]

Fort Warren on George's Island, immediately north, played a leading role in the Civil War. There the song "John Brown's Body" developed, and southern prisoners of war were held, including James Mason, John Slidell, and Confederacy Vice-President Alexander Hamilton Stephens. Here also arose the legend of the Lady in Black, a southern bride who managed to reach her incarcerated husband. She was caught trying to escape and hung as a spy.

In the 1800s the site became known as Telegraph Hill when it became part of one of the earliest telegraph systems. When an incoming ship was sighted a wood signal apparatus indicated which ship. The message was relayed visually via an island to Boston's Central Wharf to notify the owners. Later a system of 112 flags, one for each Boston skipper, was used. Now the water tower built in 1903 serves as an important landmark and interesting observation post.

From here you have the best view of picturesque, historic *Boston Light*, dating to 1716 when a tonnage tax, like today's road tax, was collected to pay for it. It is ironic that America's first lighthouse was a Revolutionary War battlefield and attacked by both sides. When the British controlled the light and harbor, several American attacks were led to destroy the light. When the British were finally driven out, they mined the light—its final destruction. In 1783 Boston's beloved light was rebuilt and has remained undaunted.

Fort Revere continued to protect the coastline through World War II, with present ruins dating from the early 1900s fortification. As you walk the paths among the old fortifications and relive their history, you are engulfed in the total panoramic views, especially spectacular on a clear day near sundown when distant points catch the last rays of the sun.

This ends the guided tour section of Hull. Return on Nantasket Avenue and Route 228 into Hingham to continue the tour.

Hull Beaches and Parks

(A) Nantasket Beach*
    Nantasket Avenue

About four miles of hard-packed sand and small stone beach, gradual slope, open ocean vista; facilities: bathhouse, refreshments, rest rooms, swimming, walking; parking; open all year, seasonal parking fee

(B) Fort Revere Memorial Park*

Can drive nearly to top; magnificent panoramic view of Boston Harbor and north and south shores; walk paths among old fortifications; climb tower weekends in season; parking; open all year, no fee, donations accepted in season

(C) View of Boston Harbor and skyline
    End of Main Street

Fascinating water-level view; just beyond high school at western tip of Hull; small parking area

(D) Paragon Park
    Washington Boulevard

Amusement park on a huge scale, rides, games, souvenirs, food; parking; open seasonally, fees charged

Boston Commuter and Tour Service

Mass Bay Line 542-8000
Pemberton Pier, end of Hull

Boat launch or rentals

Pemberton Pier

HISTORY OF HINGHAM

Hingham is a town where all church steeples reach skyward to the same God. While others were worrying about denominational differences, Hingham's citizens were benefiting and growing from shared pulpits, open discourse, and the sharing of God's love for all. Hingham's legacy to her children has been the free, nourishing air of tolerance.

Descendants of Hingham's early families brought inspired, dedicated leadership to the Massachusetts Bay Colony, New England, and the United States. John Hancock,* whose mother Mary Hawke was born in Hingham, served this yet unborn nation as president of the Massachusetts Provincial Congress and the Continental Congress and as first governor of Massachusetts. James Otis, descendant of John Otis, one of Hingham's early settlers, was a powerful spokesman in the determined stand against British taxation which culminated in the American Revolution. Native son General Benjamin Lincoln* was a renowned leader of troops, aide to Washington, secretary of war under the Articles of Confederation, and the man who received General Cornwallis' sword in final victory at Yorktown. Eighty years later President Lincoln, descended from Hingham Lincolns, held the nation together through the terrible internal conflict of Civil War.

The ancestors of those dedicated patriots, along with other early settlers in Hingham, came mainly from England's middle class. In 1633 Edmund Hobart and Nicholas Jacob and families settled at Bare Cove, so called because, when the tide was out, the shallow harbor did indeed look bare.

In 1635 Edmund Hobart's son, the Reverend Peter Hobart—tolerant of others' beliefs in a day when that was uncommon—arrived in Bare Cove with twenty-eight settlers from England. From that day forward the settlement grew. House lots were drawn along North and South Streets, a meetinghouse was built and church organized, and the settlement was incorporated as Hingham, named for their homeland of Hingham, England.

The year 1645 saw the first growing pains of independence and a dramatic test of future democratic ways. Lieutenant Anthony Eames had long commanded the town's militia. His name was sent to the town council to be approved as captain of the militia. But before this was accomplished, Lieutenant Eames unfortunately commented on the ineptness of his troops. They reacted by submitting the name of Bozoan Allen to be their captain. The council voted in favor of the more experienced Eames. By now the independent militia would not follow Eames and insisted on picking their own leader. In equally strong fashion the General Court, headed by Deputy Governor John Winthrop,* reminded the town that military authority was in the hands of the magistrates.

The case was ultimately brought before the General Court in Boston, where townsmen supported the militia and accused Deputy Governor Winthrop of criminal offenses. Following heated court sessions, the men in question were fined, and Governor Winthrop was acquitted of his charges. In his summation Winthrop spoke of two liberties— natural (doing what one wished) and civil (moral and political law). If man lives by the first the country will fall, but if man lives by the second, the country will prosper. Here was laid down another milestone in the acceptable road to freedom and democracy.

For Hingham's first hundred years, she was basically an agricultural community of self-sufficient homesteads with a few ships built at the harbor and local fishing supplementing their food supply. The 1700s saw the growth of mills on local ponds, the establishment of ironworks, shipyards built along Hingham's protected harbor, and the beginning of commercial fishing under Captain Francis Barker at the foot of Ship Street.

With such descendants as John Hancock, James Otis, and General Benjamin Lincoln, Hingham took a strong stand for independence during the Revolutionary War. Her men could be found fighting on all the major battlefields, bringing honor to their town and their new country.

During the 1800s Hingham moved from self-sufficient farmers and seamen and one-family artisans to small industries manufacturing nails, guns, woolen goods, leather articles, furniture; rope and sail making; and coopering items such as the well-known "Hingham Bucket." Surplus goods were traded in Boston and other New England towns.

However, manufacturing never really caught on as a major life-style. With the coming of the railroad in the last half of the 1800s, and the growth of industries in Boston and neighboring towns, more and more of Hingham's wage earners worked outside the town with their beloved Hingham serving as a sanctuary to return to after the workaday world.

HINGHAM

DIRECTIONS:
Enter Hingham from Hull by way of Rockland Street from Route 228. Or enter Hingham on Route 3A from Cohasset. Or from Route 3 take Route 228 north to Route 3A and turn left and drive to rotary.

#1
World's End Reservation
End of Martin's Lane
Open all year, fee charged

From Route 3A at rotary take first right off rotary which is Summer Street. Drive to first traffic light, which is Martin's Lane and turn left. Coming from Hull on Rockland Street turn right on Martin's Lane. Drive to the end for entrance to World's End. Facilities: hiking, fishing, nature study, scenic views, cross-country skiing, snow shoeing—no swimming or picnicking—parking available.

World's End Reservation is a peaceful oasis, aptly named, for here you leave worldly cares behind you as you wander this picturesque peninsula with its interesting combination of untamed and cultivated lands.

Wooden pathways allow entrance to the fascinating environment of the marshes. Well-maintained trails lead over Pine and Planters Hills from which, to the West, you can view Hingham Harbor, where the three islands of Ragged, Sarah, and Langley seem close enough to touch and Button Island lies close to Hingham's protecting shore. As the tides recede channels become obvious, and anchored boats are left in isolated pools of water or resting at awkward positions on the open mud flats, waiting forlornly for the returning tide. As your eyes move northward, Boston bursts into view with its own unique architectural skyline. To the East, beyond the Weir River, are the hills of Hull, Nantasket Beach, and the amusement rides of Paragon Park. Farther out on the horizon are the shoulders of the North Shore reaching to Cape Ann.

Continue your walk across the narrow bar at the end of Planters Hill and onto World's End itself—truly a green oasis with green roadways guiding you around the tip of the peninsula. As the water laps quietly

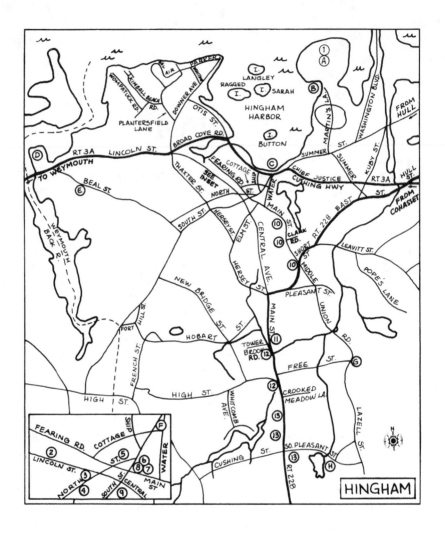

on the shore you feel a thousand miles away from the worldly cares of the businesses that can be seen on the distant shores of Weymouth, Quincy, and Boston, and you are thankful that this area was saved and set aside.

In 1856 John Reed Brewer bought most of this land, creating one of the largest farms in the area. In the 1890s, plans were formulated to develop the area with famed naturalist Frederick Law Olmsted guiding the landscaping. But, luckily for future generations, the housing part was abandoned. In later years the area narrowly escaped being the site for the United Nations and a nuclear power plant. Finally in 1967, when the Brewers proposed to sell the land, devoted friends and neighbors on the South Shore united, raising enough money in one weekend to cover the down payment. The land was ultimately turned over to the Trustees of Reservations who now maintain it for the enjoyment of all.

#2

The Old Ordinary

21 Lincoln Street

c.1680

Open seasonally and by

appointment, fee charged

Return to traffic light at intersection of Martin's Lane, Summer, and Rockland Streets and turn right. Follow Summer back to rotary on Route 3A. Go around rotary going west or right on Route 3A. At traffic island bear left onto North Street and follow it about three blocks. Bear right just past St. Paul's Catholic Church and park in lot for #2-9. From parking lot turn right and walk up Lincoln Street past the New North Church to the Ordinary which will be on your right. Notice the neighborhood of historic homes, notable Colonials and classic vernacular Greek Revivals.

One of Hingham's greatest assets is the Old Ordinary, an original First Period treasure which commands the hill above Lincoln Square. Warmly aged clapboards and white-trimmed twelve over twelve windows are capped by the wood-shingled roof, whose interesting lines reflect the modifications of many centuries.

It all begain in the 1680s when Thomas Andrews built a house, one room down and one up. By 1702 his son, also Thomas Andrews, was granted a license "to sell strong waters . . . provided he send his customers home at reasonable hours with ability to keep their legs."[21]

Francis Barker—master mariner, captain of horse, and successful tavern keeper—bought the Ordinary in 1740 and made extensive additions. Half a century later, the tavern was again owned by a descendant of the first owner. Named Andrews Tavern, it was the scene of a "Grand Peace Ball" celebrated when privateersman Captain Andrews returned from the War of 1812. In 1817 the name changed to Wilder's Tavern, with new owners, the Abiel Wilders. Mrs. Wilder's spiced wine was a favorite of frequent guest Daniel Webster.* His portable writing desk and good-luck fishing cup are displayed here. The Ordinary returned to life as a private home in the twentieth century, and in 1922 Dr. and Mrs. Wilmon Brewer gave the Old Ordinary to the Hingham Historical Society in memory of his father, Francis Willard Brewer.

Before you enter this "extraordinary Old Ordinary" notice the

The Old Ordinary

prizewinning Colonial garden designed by Frederick Law Olmsted, uncle of a previous owner, and maintained by the Garden Club of Hingham. Once inside you immediately feel great age and history. On the left you enter the 1740 section, with gleaming, wide floorboards, chestnut summer beam, beautiful wainscoting painted authentic green, and Papillon wallpaper, one of the first continuous patterns.

The furnishings throughout contain outstanding period pieces. Paintings, clocks, and collections of china, glass, pewter, and clothing are featured. Handwork is abundantly displayed as well as unique documents, a *Mayflower* treasure, and a Chinese tea chest containing some remains of the tea from the Boston Tea Party.

Toward the back, in the 1760 part, is the taproom with fascinating mementos of tavern keeping. You can almost hear the keeper's closing warning, "Gentlemen, mind your p's and q's" (pints and quarts). Next is the warm, hospitable kitchen with its fascinating array of items.

The tool collection room contains an impressive, well-labeled and well-organized display of every imaginable hand tool.

Coming around to the dining room, you are in the 1680s portion, though the room is Federal as modified in the early 1800s. The small adjacent library spans both the seventeenth and eighteenth centuries and contains the keepers' note from the Minot's Light* tragedy found in a bottle in Massachusetts Bay by Gloucester fishermen.

Upstairs the bedrooms of both centuries contain more valued relics, including cradles of both Hingham governors of Massachusetts, Andrews and Long, and an early Bradford cradle. One bedroom closet reveals the exterior of the original 1680s house when the 1740 addition was made. You can see the original bracket from the overhang and the size of the clapboards so well preserved. The Old Ordinary is a fascinating historical and architectural treasure, beautifully preserved and maintained by the Hingham Historical Society.

#3
Lincoln Historic District
Lincoln and North Streets
Lincoln Square
General Benjamin Lincoln
Home, 181 North Street, c.
1673, 1715, 1790
NRHP, HABS, NHL,
private

Samuel Lincoln House
182 North Street, pre 1740
private

Samuel Lincoln House
172 North Street, possibly
c.1667 private

New North Meeting House,
1 Lincoln Street, 1806, open
for services

Cross Lincoln Street and walk back down the hill to intersection of Lincoln and North Streets, keeping to the right of traffic triangle with Lincoln statue. On the right at corner of North and Lincoln is the General Benjamin Lincoln House. Samuel Lincoln House at 182 North is opposite the General Lincoln House. Samuel Lincoln House at 172 North is opposite statue with side to road.

Here Lincolns yet live and have for over three centuries! This name of local and national distinction arrived with so many Lincolns among the earliest settlers that they were identified by their trades. Some of the historically rich Lincoln homes remain today here around *Lincoln Square* dominated by a pensive-visaged statue of Abraham Lincoln.

One of the most fascinating Lincoln houses is the *General Benjamin Lincoln Home*. The land was granted to Thomas Lincoln, cooper, about 1640, and he or his son probably built the small two-over-two-room beginnings of the General Benjamin Lincoln Home about 1673. Bold additions were made during the early Georgian Period (1715) and again in early Federal times (1790) to create the unified, grand Colonial-Georgian home of Revolutionary War General Benjamin Lincoln.

General Lincoln served locally as selectman, treasurer, and Collector of the Port of Boston, and nationally as an aide to General Washington and secretary of war. He was honored to receive the sword of Cornwallis as symbol of British surrender at Yorktown.

His lovely home, with gray clapboards, black shutters, and two large chimneys supporting nine fireplaces, is set amid beautiful tall trees. Within, the older rooms in the rear are rich with wide-board, deep-patina paneling and contrast interestingly with the more formal later period front room. Different eras of living are reflected here where continuously lived generations of Lincolns, from a simple cooper to a politically wise military man, and home still to a modern day Lincoln descendant.

Across North Street very close to the road is a *Samuel Lincoln House* at 182 North Street. Built prior to 1740, the house with the interesting roof line has sheltered Lincolns, Barkers, and Thaxters, and was once owned by the Society for the Preservation of New England Antiquities.

At 172 North, with its side to the road, is another *Samuel Lincoln House* built before 1700. An historic marker points out the weathered clapboarded home with its irregularly spaced First Period windows. The land was purchased in 1649 by one of the eight early Lincoln families. Seven generations of Samuel's line followed, and one of his great, great . . . grandsons was Abraham Lincoln, though he did not live here.

Across is the *New North Meeting House* built in 1806 from adapted plans of Charles Bulfinch, plans which are now in the archives of the Smithsonian. It is a beautiful, classic Federal with delicate fanlights over entries capped by a Palladian window. Full-height plain pilasters grace the white clapboarded facade crowned by clock tower, cupola, and banner weathervane. The church was formed by a group from the Old Ship Meeting House* led by "Deacon in uniform" General Benjamin Lincoln. Worshippers here included Governors John Andrews and John Davis Long.

The varied histories and architecture of these buildings provide interesting study within the rich tapestry of Hingham's proud heritage.

#4
Odd Fellows Hall
196 North Street
1829
Open as business

Walk up North Street past the General Benjamin Lincoln House. The Odd Fellows Hall will be on the left at number 196.

Among interesting period homes is the Odd Fellows Hall. This simple Greek Revival building rose in 1829 as the First Universalist Church. Here, in 1868, the first woman in New England was ordained, the Reverend Phebe Hanaford. This pioneer was soon followed, elsewhere in Hingham, by the Reverend Anna Howard Shaw, who was the only applicant for the pulpit of the then-struggling Methodist Society in 1877. The Reverend Shaw was hired and within a year had the church back on its feet. She went on to earn a medical degree, to become a leader for women's suffrage, and to earn national honor with the United States Distinguished Service Medal.

#5
Reverend John Norton
House, 103-105 North
Street, c. 1650

Reverend Ebenezer Gay, 89
North Street, c. 1722

Nye Tavern, 79-81 North
Street, c. 1680

Waters Tavern, 73 North
Street, c. 1793

Waters Tavern, 71 North
Street, c. 1753

Historic Marker for first
landing
Homes all private

Walk back past where you parked the car, turn left and walk east on North Street. After crossing Fearing Road, the Norton House is second on left after post office. The Gay House and Taverns follow in order on the left as you walk north.

Walking along North Street you experience a living flashback into Hingham's early history. At 103 is the greatly altered home of Hingham's second minister, the *Reverend John Norton,** great grandfather of Abigail Adams. Unfortunately all that remains of the original home is possibly a part of the center section. It was during the pastorate of this congenial and pious man, from 1678 to 1716, that the Old Ship Meeting House* was built in 1681.

Next door at 89 is the home of Norton's successor, the *Reverend Ebenezer Gay,** whose descendants have always lived in this central chimney, early Georgian–style home. Sitting high above North Street, facing in the direction of Old Ship Meeting House, where Gay served from 1718 until 1787, the house symbolizes Gay's pastorate. He was a man revered and loved by his congregation, whom he taught by example as well as the word. During the years of this liberal-thinking intellectual there began a slow movement away from the conventional Puritan theology to a more liberal interpretation that set the stage for Unitarianism in the next few decades.

It was to the Reverend Dr. Gay's credit that prior to and during the Revolution, even though he strongly believed the Colonies should not separate from England, he was able to retain the respect and loyalty of his politically diverse congregation. The story is told of members from the Committee on Safety calling on the Reverend Dr. Gay to see if he was harboring any arms. He calmly put his hand on the Bible and said, "There, my friends, are my arms, and I trust to find them ever sufficient for me."[22] Thus ended the encounter and question of where his ultimate loyalties lay.

His ready wit was shown one day when traveling with a friend to Boston. The friend said humorously as they passed the Boston gallows, " 'Where would you be, my friend, if that gallows had its due?' 'Riding alone to Boston!' was Dr. Gay's prompt response."[23]

Continue east to the house at 79–81, formerly the *Nye Tavern*, where British officers, captured during the Revolutionary War, were served their meals. The next two houses on the corners of Ship Street were the early *Waters Taverns*. Here, as well as at the Nye Tavern, many a tired traveler was served and many a Hinghamite gathered for a mug of ale or rum. In even earlier days, when the harbor extended farther inland, this was the site where the Reverend Peter Hobart* and his band of settlers landed in 1635 and held their first religious service of thanksgiving. Events of this historic part of North Street seem a far cry from today's busy street, where many of those taverns and homes of yesteryear have been altered and made into single and multiple residences.

#6
Hingham Cemetery
Old Fort
Main Street and South Street entrances
1600s
Open all year, no fee

Walk back to the Gay House and cross North Street to where South Street begins. Walk up South Street a short distance to the entrance to the Cemetery on the left. Walk toward the administrative building and take the first path to the right. The Monument to the early settlers and the Old Fort earthworks are at the top of the path.

The hill on which today stands the cemetery, Derby Academy,* and the Old Ship Meeting House,* once extended farther west. When a section was cut away to build today's Main Street early graves were reinterred within the circular earthworks of the Old Fort on Burial Hill* behind the Academy. There a simple granite obelisk was erected in 1839 to honor the "First Settlers of Hingham." Three centuries ago the Old Fort had been built on the summit of this now-peaceful hill by some of those same first settlers during King Philip's War.

The site of the Old Fort is an ideal starting place for a walk back through Hingham's history as you visit the graves of her sleeping sons and daughters. Two cemetery roadways run behind Derby Academy and the Old Ship Meeting House. Follow the upper one. On your left before the roadway bends away from the church is a raised grave covered with a granite slab on which is carved an inscription to the first three ministers of the Old Ship Meeting House, the Reverends Hobart,* Norton,* and Gay,* who served a total of 150 years. A short distance beyond is the fenced tomb of Major General Benjamin Lincoln,* who served during the Revolutionary War.

Continue on this pathway, passing under a magnificent beach tree, which seems to create a natural temple. Then on the left you will see the statue and grave of the loved and respected "war governor" John Albion Andrew, commander-in-chief of Massachusetts during the Civil War. Across the side pathway is a monument to another well-known governor of the commonwealth, that of John Davis Long.

At every turn you will see familiar names of Hingham's town family, which all quietly tell the story of Hingham's growing years.

#7
Old Ship Meeting House of
the First Parish
90 Main Street
1681
Open seasonally and by
appointment, no fee
NHL, HABS

After viewing the governors' graves retrace your steps to the General Benjamin Lincoln grave. From there, you an see the Old Ship Meeting House. Exit from the cemetery to the meetinghouse.

"Let the Work of Our Fathers Stand" is rightfully inscribed on the First Parish seal, and well the Old Ship Meeting House has stood for more than three centuries and fifteen generations.

During the pastorate of the second minister, the Reverend John Norton,* the present Old Ship Meeting House was erected in 1681 on land given by Captain Joshua Hobart. At a cost of 430 pounds and using lumber from the first church building, inspired carpenters and ship

Old Ship Meeting House

builders combined talents to erect this building. It was styled after the Elizabethan Gothic churches of England, which had remained in the minds of the settlers as symbols of their ancestral homes. The fact that it is the oldest wooden church in continuous use in the country is a lasting tribute to the dedicated efforts of her builders.

As you observe the solid, imposing lines of the Old Ship Meeting House, your eyes are drawn upward by the commanding sweep of the hip roof capped by balustrades setting off the delicate lines of the spire, which seems to reach like a connecting link to heaven. If today, among wonders of architectural achievements, this building seems impressive, imagine the feelings of awe, pride, and humility that must have been experienced by its first worshippers.

Step inside. Picture that first Sunday, January 8, 1682, when over three hundred parishioners filled the church. Warmed by a few foot warmers, the mutual warmth of one another, and the words of the Reverend Norton,* the townsfolk watched the hourglass on the pulpit turn many times during that first daylong service. The wood still glows with the spiritual warmth and fortitude of those early days.

Originally hard wooden benches faced a pulpit on the easterly side of the building. About 1729 a fourteen-foot addition was added to the east side. In 1755 the church was balanced with a similar addition to the

264

west side, the seating arrangement changed, the first square pews installed around the perimeter, and the present pulpit built.

During the next hundred years, the benches were gradually removed and pews substituted. In 1869 major interior changes were made in accord with the Victorian mode of the day. Curved cushioned pews were installed, carpeting laid, velvet hangings added, furnace installed, and the meetinghouse rededicated. Two years earlier an organ had been added, replacing individual instruments, and in 1870 oil lamps were hung paving the way for evening services.

In 1930 the Old Ship Meeting House was restored with the generous financial aid of Eben Howard Gay, great, great grandson of the parish's third minister, the Reverend Ebenezer Gay.* Today we see a beautiful wooden edifice which combines the simplicity and strength of its seventeenth-century exposed naturally curved trusses and ceiling beams with the aroma and soft patina of its eighteenth-century wooden pews and pulpit. The rope from the bell, high above in the belfry, still hangs intriguingly in the center of the church, just waiting for eager hands to call the faithful to worship.

As the First Parish moved from the conservative discipline of her earlier Puritan and Calvanistic ways to the more liberal doctrines of Unitarianism, her doors and her pulpit remained open to the faithful and to the free exchange of ideas.

Adjacent to the church is the 1912 Hingham Memorial Bell Tower, housing eleven bells copied from ones in Norfolk, England. With one rope for each bell, eleven trained people combine talents to play bell concerts for special occasions.

#8
Old Derby Academy
Building
Main Street
School 1791; building 1818
Open by appointment and
on tour day, fee charged

As you leave the Old Ship Meeting House, turn right on Main Street and walk down the hill to Old Derby Academy, which will be on the right.

Derby Academy's founder, Madam Sarah Hersey Derby, was one of the most interesting people produced by Hingham. Legend tells of Sarah Langley, a beautiful but ragged daughter of a fisherman living on Langley's Island, who met the wealthy, talented Dr. Ezekiel Hersey and immediately captured his heart. The islands of Hingham Harbor perpetuate the legend with their names: Ragged, Sarah, Langley.

When she was twenty-four, Sarah did marry the dashing Dr. Hersey in 1738. Their large farm-estate became the social center where the Herseys entertained at levels which drew frequent references in the diaries of John Quincy Adams and Massachusetts Chief Justice Benjamin Lynde.* Dr. Hersey died in 1770, and Sarah inherited his whole estate, except for his legacy endowing a chair for anatomy which created Harvard Medical School. (A Hersey family house remains at 229 North Street, a large Georgian with impressive Greek Revival entry, given by family, now housing community activities.)

Ten months later Sarah married wealthy Salem widower Captain Richard Derby,* with their pioneering nuptial agreement protecting her holdings. Derby was a very successful merchant in the triangular trade, member of the General Court and Governor's Council and father of Elias Haskett Derby* who developed the lucrative East India trade.

In 1783, a widow again, now sixty-nine, she returned home to Hingham. The next year she began arrangements to make her dream a reality—a school for both boys and girls. She defined her revolutionary ideas creating the oldest coeducational school in the country. Here girls were to study classical subjects as well as needlework.

The Derby School formally opened in 1791 and was incorporated as Derby Academy in 1797. In 1818 the old buildings were removed, and this elegant Federal was built. Now the school occupies its new buildings on Burditt Avenue and this Old Academy building is home to the Hingham Historical Society.

Steep steps lead from the road to the impressive yellow-clapboard, three-stories-tall, grand Federal which commands its historic site. Inside, where students once struggled toward higher education, now the grand formal reception room hosts weddings, concerts, receptions, and meetings. Soft blues, pale yellows, and muted golds reflect the original colors. The first two floors have interesting paintings and a few museum-quality displays.

#9
Ensign John Thaxter House
Hingham Community
Center
70 South Street
c.1695
Open for center activities

Continue downhill to first left at corner of South and Main Streets and turn left. Go one block and the Thaxter House will be on the far left corner of South and Central Streets.

As early as 1680, the land on which the Hingham Community Center now stands was bought by Ensign John Thaxter. It is possible that

some of the present building predates 1680. It is recorded that a four-
room early period dwelling, possibly part of the center section, was
standing in 1695. Upon the marriage of great, great grandson, Quincy
Thaxter, in 1786, the western side was added.

The fourth John Thaxter was born here in 1755. He later read law
under John Adams and subsequently served as his private secretary
when Adams went to France to secure the peace treaty. In 1783 it was
John Thaxter who hand-carried the vital document to Congress.

The house remained in the Thaxter family for another century until
the death of Norton Q. Thaxter in 1873. It later served as the rectory
for St. Paul's Catholic Church, home to the Wompatuck Club, and now
serves the community as its Community Center. In spite of changes
and additions many of the fine old details have remained, such as ceiling
beams, woodwork, and especially the beautifully painted panels done
by John Hazlitt about 1785. John, who became a well-known English
miniature artist, was the son of the Reverend William Hazlitt, who
often substituted for Dr. Gay at the Old Ship Meeting House during the
1780s.

#10
Main Street Houses to
Hingham Center
Private

*Return to your car by walking north on
Central Street one small block to the cor-
ner of North and Lincoln Streets. You will
exit from the parking lot onto Fearing
Road. Turn right and follow it across
North Street where it becomes Main
Street. Follow Main Street south for the
interesting houses listed.*

Main Street offers an excursion through New England's historic
architecture. It is abundantly endowed with a variety of architectural
periods in pleasant harmony with each other, complemented with
magnificent trees. One of the oldest houses is now the kitchen portion
of the *Daniel Cushing House*, at 209 Main Street. Built circa 1690, it
has been modified through the centuries, and now Greek Revival
features dominate. Daniel Cushing's father, Matthew, was the patriarch and founder of the United States Cushing family, arriving in
Boston in 1638. (see Scituate #2) Daniel was town clerk, magistrate,
and delegate to the General Court. A careful record keeper, he was a
reliable source of Hingham history. Across from the Daniel Cushing
House was the Matthew Cushing House, built in the late 1600s. Now
only the foundation and well sweep remain.

The 1809 *Nye House* at 235 Main Street, opposite Clark Road, is a stately yellow clapboarded Federal with brick ends. The house at 243 Main Street was constructed in 1808 as a double house and remains a pleasant, staunch Federal. Both houses feature delicate front entries and quoined corners.

At the next corner, Main and Leavitt Streets, is a magnificent *Old Buttonwood Tree* with graceful limbs reaching skyward as they have since 1790. It is now over 16 feet around and 90 feet tall.

The *Fearing Burr House* at 289 Main Street in Hingham Center was built in 1806. This lovely house reflects late Georgian influence highlighted by Federal features of delicate dentils along cornice and pediment, quoined corners, and brick sides.

Across from the Common and Training Field, the triple house at 303-309 Main is the *Hawkes Fearing House* built in 1784. Different architectural styles tell of later editions to this home of town leader and state representative Hawkes Fearing, whose wife was a Lincoln of Samuel's line. (see #3) Once a tavern and inn, in the early 1800s it hosted ecclesiastical conventions.

#11
John Tower House
Main Street
c.1664
Private

Continue south on Main Street one mile. The John Tower House is a small Cape on the left past 518 Main, three houses before Tower Brook Road enters on right.

Set back from the road sits a simple Cape, warm with memories of over three hundred years of the Tower family. Here early settler John Tower built his home and dug his well, and both have survived to shelter and nourish his descendants. Flowers line the path to the house with its modest door and small, unbalanced windows of early period design.

#12
Joseph Wilder House
557 Main, c.1875

Edward Wilder House
597 Main, c.1650
Private

The Joseph Wilder House is on the right side of Main Street, just after Tower Brook Road. Then continue south on Main Street to the next corner, High Street. The Edward Wilder House is second on right on Main past High.

The unusual roof line of this handsome Cape drew the nickname, The Rainbow House. It is the *Joseph Wilder House*, the first visible house on the right after Tower Brook Road. An even older Wilder house is the circa 1650 *Edward Wilder House* at 597 Main Street. Wilders have played historic roles in Hingham since Edward Wilder came here with his widowed mother in 1638.

Before the Revolution a Wilder named Molly was instrumental in saving a mysterious young surgeon called Francis LeBaron.* When law officers arrived to arrest him for illegal entry into the colony, Wilders hid him in the attic behind a featherbed Molly was stuffing. The house was searched, but the attic air full of feathers turned back the searchers and saved Dr. LeBaron, who later married Molly.

The famous Hingham bucket was first a "cottage industry" when buckets were made by hand in homes and small shops about town. Hingham's "Bucket Mill" at nearby Cushing Pond off Mill Lane began when a Wilder bought the site in 1845. The Wilder Wooden Ware Manufactory produced the first wooden buckets with brass hoops and bails. In 1902 its fifty employees were still turning out one thousand buckets a day when the main building was destroyed by fire. This oldest bucket-producing mill in the United States was never rebuilt. Hingham buckets were recognized by Dana in his *Two Years Before the Mast* when a crew member from Hingham was immediately called "Bucket Master."

#13
Second Parish in Hingham
Church, 685 Main, 1742

Cushing Houses
753 and 757 Main Street

Reverend Daniel Shute
House, 768 Main, 1763
Church open for services,
houses private

Continue south on Main Street .4 mile; the church is on the right. Cushing Homes are .3 mile further south on same side of street. The Shute House is on the far left corner of South Pleasant and Main Streets.

Traveling south on Main Street, after passing Crooked Meadow Lane and a rise in the road, you see before you what looks like a mile-long common transversed by Main Street. On the right side is the imposing Federal-style *Second Parish Church*. This, the third off-spring of the Old Ship Meeting House* of First Parish, was born in controversy but, with the wisdom of both ministers, soon grew into a oneness of spirit with its mother church.

For nearly twenty years the people of South Hingham had agitated for a church. Finally in 1742 they built this meetinghouse four years before actually becoming a separate parish. To picture that early building, imagine the present one without the front facade or tower and with the main entrance on the parking lot side. In 1829 the facade was changed to today's Bulfinch design. Step inside to appreciate the lovely interior—with specially grained wood pews, balconies whose panelings incorporate wood from the original pews, raised pulpit with organ behind, all surrounded by pristine white walls trimmed in gray.

In 1746, when the Reverend Daniel Shute became their first minister, Dr. Gay, rector of the First Parish, gave the following wise advice to the new offspring: "Build not for faction nor a Party, but for promoting Faith and Repentance in communion with all that love our Lord Jesus Christ in sincerity."[24] Dr. Gay and the Reverend Dr. Shute became lifelong friends, exchanging pulpits and philosophy. They established the mold by which both churches worked together from an early Puritan background to today's Unitarian philosophy.

Continue south on Main Street; observe the houses set well back from the busy road as if holding onto the tranquility of yesteryear yet a little longer. The eye sweeps over homes of varying sizes and architectural styles from small early Capes and modest farmhouses to more elegant Federals, Greek Revivals, and Victorians—all illustrating that special charm that is unique to New England.

Pause at 753 Main at the old *Theophilus Cushing Homestead* built before 1690. Here son Theophilus, Jr., who became one of the wealthiest men in South Hingham, was born in 1703. Theophilus, Jr., later built the house at 757 as an addition to his birthplace. Theophilus, Jr., played a vital part in the early life of the South Hingham Parish. He gave the land, plus part of the materials used in building the first meetinghouse, was instrumental in forming the parish itself, and served as a lay leader for many years. His son, Theophilus III, served as a brigadier general during the Revolutionary War and later as state representative and senator. During the war years the Cushing home was known as *Cushing Tavern* and served many a weary traveler.

Diagonally across Main Street at the corner of South Pleasant Street, is the regal Georgian-style home of the *Reverend Daniel Shute*. This spacious home, composed of nineteen rooms in all, was built circa 1763. The front shows quoined corners and ashlar panels cut to resemble stone. The balanced facade of the Georgian Period is complemented by the columned front portico. Here lived the venerable

Reverend Daniel Shute, who in addition to being the first pastor of Second Parish from 1746 to 1802, was chaplain during the French and Indian War and member of the state constitutional convention and the convention which ratified the federal constitution. He received a Doctor of Divinity degree from Harvard College in 1790 at age sixty-eight. In order to supplement his small salary, he also boarded and tutored students in his home, among them the son of the future Governor John Hancock, as well as the sons of General Benjamin Lincoln.*

Shute's son, Dr. Daniel Shute, respected surgeon during the Revolutionary War, served under General Benjamin Lincoln at the Battle of Yorktown. Dr. Shute was the second of many generations of Shutes to live in this their paternal homestead. During his long and devoted career as a physician he recorded the delivery of 1,274 chldren, which was equal to more than a third of the entire population of Hingham when he died in 1829.

It is interesting to note that the Reverend Dr. Shute's two wives were Cushings, his son married a Cushing, and three of his grandchildren married Cushings—creating a continuing merger of two family lines which played vital roles in the history of South Hingham.

Drive north on Main Street and follow Route 228 signs back to Route 3A. Turn left on Route 3A and follow it through Hingham to Weymouth.

Hingham Beaches and Parks and Additional Points of Interest

(A) World's End Reservation*
Martin's Lane Off
Summer Street
(See #1)

Well-maintained paths and platforms lead through marshes and tree-lined meadows around peaceful 249-acre peninsula to fascinating vistas of Hingham Harbor, Boston skyline, and beyond; cross-country skiing, nature study, walking; parking; open all year, fee charged

(B) Martin's Lane Beach
Martin's Lane at entrance
to World's End
Reservation*

Small tidal beach; boat launching, float; limited parking; open all year, no fee

(C) **Hingham Harbor Parks***
Grand Old Bandstand
Park
Hingham Bathing Beach
Town Pier
Route 3A

Parks line the harbor allowing public access to Hingham Harbor for scenic enjoyment, historic remembering, plus active and passive recreation; band concerts, benches, boat facilities, biking, fishing, picnicking, swimming, walking; parking; open all year, no fee, sticker parking only at Hingham Bathing Beach.

(D) **Stodders Neck Park**
Route 3A (sign to
Hingham Pumping
Station)

Small neck of land on Hingham side of Weymouth Back River Bridge, pleasant oasis along river with paths, scenic views; ample parking; open all year, no fee

(E) **Bare Cove Park**
Beal Street near Route 3A

461 acres, former Navy ammunition depot now passive recreation area on Weymouth Back River; biking, bird-watching, fishing, nature study, picnicking, sunbathing (no swimming), trails, walking; parking; open all year, no fee

(F) **Mill Site**
Mill Street
c.1643
Restaurant open

Mill Street once path over dam which powered historic mills beginning c.1643; Ye Olde Mill Grille was old painter's mill, contains original timbers, exposed beams, pegs, and display case of mill memorabilia

(G) **Wompatuck State Park**
Access Free Street

Land deeded in 1633 by Algonquin Indians to farming settlers, in World War II an ammunition depot, now a 2,700-acre park with large visitor center complex, camping area, self-guided nature trails, paved biking-hiking trails, Mount Blue Spring where pure water once bottled and sold; biking, cross-country skiing, hiking, horseback riding, nature study, snowmobiles; parking; open all year, no fee except for camping area

(H) **Fulling Mill Pond**
South Pleasant Street

Small pond, peaceful pleasant retreat, noted for ducks, public access to most of waterfront; canoeing, picnicking; limited parking; open all year, no fee

Boston Commuter Boat
Service

Massachusetts Bay Lines, Inc. 542-8000
Hingham Shipyard

HISTORY OF WEYMOUTH

Early Weymouth was a town influenced by the Church of England and Puritanism and by loyalty to the King of England and loyalty to a colonial governor. Like good steel, she was tempered in the fires of controversy and emerged stronger for it.

The first founder, wealthy London merchant Thomas Weston, was concerned with immediate trade and financial return and could not see the long-term value of a family-settled, religiously strong colony such as Plymouth. In September of 1622 Weston's two ships, *Charity* and *Swan*, arrived in Weymouth, then called Wessagusset, to set up a fishing station and trading post of men only. They built a blockhouse, homes, and stockade, but neglected the essential ingredient needed for success, that of planting crops for a continuing food supply.

Unusual retribution occurred when the settlement became so desperate for food that some of the settlers stole food from the Indians. According to legend, one of the thieves was caught by the Indians, who demanded punishment. The settlers formed a court. The culprit was tried, found guilty, and sentenced to be hung before the Indians to appease their anger. One enterprising settler suggested that instead of hanging the real thief, they dress a sick man, who had no hope of recovery, in the thief's clothing and hang him instead. Discussion ensued, but history does not tell whether the strong thief or the sick man was used for appeasement. A sad commentary on how desperate the settlers had become. Difficulties continued to plague the settlement, which was soon abandoned. Weston's dream for a successful colony had to wait.

In 1623 Sir Ferdinando Gorges, who dreamed of establishing the most powerful settlement on the New England coast, obtained a land grant which included Boston Bay. Gorges learned from Weston's mistakes. He sent out two ships, *Katherine* and *Prophet Daniel*, laden with 120 men and women—including clergy, craftsmen, farmers, and traders—under the command of his son, Captain Robert Gorges. They landed at Wessagusset and used the deserted Weston buildings. Under their charter, Sir Ferdinando Gorges was to be governor and the Reverend William Morrell of the Church of England was to be the overall religious leader. These two facts did not invite eager support from Plymouth. However, they survived the winter, but along with the welcome warmth of spring came news that Sir Ferdinando's position in England had weakened. Consequently, Captain Gorges returned to England, leaving the colony on its own.

A small band of English families arrived from Weymouth, England, in 1624, joining the remaining community at the mouth of the Fore River. With no governing head, the settlers governed themselves and thus was born the first American town government, which evolved into the familiar New England town meeting. Here began those radical ideas of government by the people, open elections, and free speech. In 1635 Wessagusset was incorporated as the Plantation of Weymouth.

What started out as a Church of England colony to be governed by the absentee Sir Ferdinando Gorges became caught between the Pilgrims on the south and the strong influence of Governor John Winthrop* and his no-nonsense Puritans on the north. Weymouth was soon purged of its questionable Church of England leanings by the General Court, who either banished, whipped, or disfranchised anyone who had other than Puritan beliefs. "The people went into the prison house of Puritanism and had the key turned upon them."[25] Puritanism and Colonial control had won over the Anglican church and absentee royal authority.

The 1600s and 1700s saw slow growth in this plantation by the sea, where farming was the mainstay with lumber, salt, mackerel, and iron ore used as trade items with Boston. Shipbuilding was a limited part of Weymouth life from the late 1600s through the 1800s.

During the 1800s shoemaking became one of the town's most important industries, growing from family industry through small cooperatives to huge industrial complexes by 1875. At that time large numbers of European workers were imported to work in the factories, thus changing the complexion of Weymouth's population. Sadly, by 1930, the cost of labor and raw materials along with increased competition from abroad ended Weymouth's eminence in the shoe industry.

Today Weymouth is a residential city with light industry. Many of her wage earners work outside of Weymouth, but enjoy homelife in this comfortable, unpretentious town by the sea.

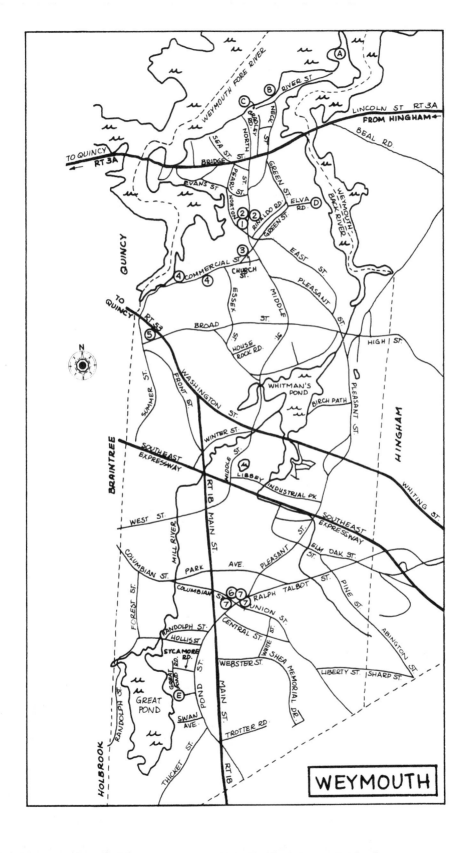

WEYMOUTH

WEYMOUTH

DIRECTIONS:
Enter Weymouth on Route 3A from Hingham. (Lincoln Street becomes Bridge Street in Weymouth.) Continue on Bridge Street .8 mile to North Street; turn left, drive .8 mile to Norton Street, which is just beyond cemetery, sharp right on Norton. Or exit from the Southeast Expressway (Route 3) going north at Route 18 (Main Street, Weymouth). Drive north to Washington Street; turn right and go to Middle Street; turn left and follow Middle Street to Norton Street and turn left.

#1
Abigail Smith Adams
Birthplace
Abigail Adams Historical
Society
180 Norton Street
1685
Open seasonally, fee
charged

On Norton Street the Abigail Adams House is immediately on the right. Park here for #1–2.

This wandering "ell" house has finally found a permanent resting place here on Norton Street only three hundred feet from its original building place. Back in 1685 the fifth minister of the First Church in Weymouth,* the Reverend Samuel Torrey, built this house at the corner of North and East Streets. Fifty-three years later, the eighth minister, the Reverend William Smith, bought the house and added a large main wing, creating one of the mansions in Weymouth. Here he lived with his wife, Elizabeth Quincy Smith, and their four children. Abigail, one of the four, born in 1744, enjoyed the warmth and security of this parsonage until her marriage to John Adams* in 1764.

Adams came first as a friend of Richard Cranch, suitor to Mary Smith, but he returned on his own, as the pert, intelligent, younger sister Abigail, or Nabby as her friends called her, sparked his interest. For nearly three years John Adams traveled the dusty roads to this parsonage until he won the heart and hand of Abigail Smith. They were married October 25, 1764, and thus were united the well-known Quincy/Smith family and the yet unknown Adams family. Together they would launch a family line that would serve their country as few families have done.

Abigail spent her early life in three homes which prepared her for the role she would play in history as the wife of intelligent, dynamic John Adams, mother of independent, devoted John Quincy Adams, and grandmother of magnetic negotiator Charles Francis Adams. She grew up in this clapboarded, dormered early Colonial on Norton Street. Here she learned of religious and moral affairs. Her father encouraged her use of his extensive library, giving her a chance to read Shakespeare and the classics in a time when most women did not worry about such academic pursuits. She enjoyed long visits with her Aunt Elizabeth and Uncle Isaac Smith in Boston, where she learned the ways of a socially prominent merchant family in a bustling seaport. There she felt the heartbeat of the colony, as well as the protective arms of Mother England, all seasoned by the constant flow of international visitors and goods. Pleasant weeks were spent with her grandparents, Colonel John Quincy and Elizabeth Norton Quincy, prominent leaders in Braintree and the colony. There she was exposed to lively political and legal discussions as well as being swept up in the local social whirl.

Even though Abigail was nine years younger than John Adams and had had no formal education, by the time they were married, she was undoubtedly one of the best educated ladies of her time in New England. She had a mind worthy of parrying with John's. Over the years he listened to and was influenced by her astute observations of the political scene. She was equally able to handle the farm, all the accounts, and raise a family of four. John spent much of his time in his legal practice, involved in political affairs in New York and Philadelphia, and later on national missions to France, Holland, and England. She served at home so that he might be free to give of his talents to a fledgling nation.

Abigail joined her husband in Paris after the signing of the Peace Treaty and then spent three years with him in London, where she was the first woman of the United States to be presented at the Court of St. James. They returned to the United States in 1788 where some of her happiest years were spent in New York while John was vice-president. During John's term as president she served as the first hostess of the newly built, as yet unfinished, White House in Washington. When his term was over they retired to Quincy where she lived in declining health, as the beloved wife and mother of a challenging family, until her

Abigail Smith Adams Birthplace

death in 1818. Abigail Adams was one of the unsung heros of the American Revolution and of the formative years of the country.

By 1838 the old parsonage was in such poor repair that the church decided to build a new one at 8 East Street. The Smith wing was torn down and the small "ell" was sold to Farmer Ford who moved it to Bridge Street, where it housed farmhands. Here it served for over one hundred years until 1947 when the government bought the farm and prepared to remove all the buildings. A group of Weymouth women, realizing the historic importance of this "ell," formed the Abigail Adams Historical Society and saved the building. They had it moved to its present location on land donated by the town for one dollar, paid by a young blind lad, Edwin McCaw.

The house was painstakingly restored under the enthusiastic leadership of the society. The front parlor, with its lovely wide-board paneling, the carefully utensiled kitchen, the narrow stairway to the quaint bedrooms above, and the furnishings authenticated to the years 1740 to 1760 are all part of the nostalgic charm you feel here. As you walk through this historic home where Abigail grew up, you feel a little richer for having caught a glimpse of Abigail Adams' life in the mid-1700s.

#2
North Weymouth Cemetery
North and Norton Streets
1600s
Open all year, no fee

The North Weymouth Cemetery is adjacent to the Abigail Adams Birthplace. It fronts on Norton Street and on both sides of North Street.

Adjacent to the Abigail Adams House is the old burying ground. Here you will see familiar Weymouth names such as Bicknell, Lovell, Tirrell, Torrey, and Bates. One unusual stone from this century even has a pair of dice engraved on the back.

Across North Street can be seen the older part of the cemetery. On the right of the entrance are the graves of the beloved Reverend William Smith* and his wife, Elizabeth Quincy Smith, parents of Abigail Adams.* Opposite is the tomb of Dr. Cotton Tufts,* neighbor of the Smiths and dedicated Revolutionary leader, statesman, and doctor. The Tufts' tomb was permanently sealed following the death of the last Weymouth Tufts, Susannah, in 1877. Susannah and her brother, Quincy, donated the Tufts Library.*

Atop the rise, where the Soldiers' Memorial now stands, was in earlier days Watch House Hill. Here by 1628 it is very probable a meetinghouse was built. Now a quiet peaceful oasis, this was once the center of Weymouth life.

#3	*Return on Norton Street, keeping to right*
First Church of Weymouth	*of island. Drive through railroad under-*
17 Church Street	*pass and take first right at traffic light.*
1639, 1833	*Drive up Church Street one-half block to*
Open for services	*the First Church of Weymouth on the*
	right.

Weymouth takes the prize for the combination of its confusing ecclesiastical origins and the notable scholarly achievements of its pastors. The first attempted settlement by Thomas Weston* had no religious ties, to which some historians attribute its rapid demise. With the next attempt, Captain Robert Gorges brought the Reverend William Morrell, with the aim of establishing the Church of England in this Pilgrim locale. Then in 1635 the arrival of the Anglican minister Joseph Hull and his party brought definite religious activity, which soon blossomed into one meetinghouse and three dissenting ministers. The disputing ministers were products of the unsettled times when Puritans disputed doctrine among themselves, and Pilgrims and Church of England Episcopalians added diversity.

The Reverend Hull left officially in 1639, ending the Church of England form. That same year the Reverend Samuel Newman was called and managed to unify the church as well as to create a scholarly concordance. Probably the first concordance of the English Bible, it eventually formed the basis of *Cruden's Concordance*, still used today.

He was followed by American-educated Thomas Thacher, who was also a physician, wrote a lexicon of Hebrew, and was ordained in Weymouth. Next, the Reverend Samuel Torrey, adviser to top leaders, became one of the few men to decline the presidency of Harvard College.

A later minister was the Reverend William Smith whose daughter Abigail married the unknown country lawyer-farmer John Adams on this site in 1764.

The first meetinghouse was probably a simple, crude structure on Burying Hill. Other meetinghouses were built as the parish grew or when destroyed by fire, as in 1751 when three barrels of the town's gunpowder stored in the loft added to the excitement. In 1833 the present meetinghouse was built, a beautiful example of New England church architecture, built by a committee, following no particular form but selecting appealing features from many. Simple, yet impressive, the all-white meetinghouse has Greek Revival and Georgian qualities dominating.

The soft, peaceful colors of the sanctuary draw focus to the cross above the massive mahogany pulpit. Numbered box pews of old have doors which once protected worshipers from drafts, and long-handled collection boxes are still used. The stately grandfather clock was created and given by Elmer Stennes. Recently the church was literally rolled away while Sunday School rooms, a gym, and a kitchen were built under. Then it was rolled back to remain the tall landmark of Weymouth's past, present, and future.

#4
Deacon Thomas White
House
449 Commercial Street
c.1660

Quincy Tufts Homestead
246 Commercial Street
c.1696
Houses private

Continue on Church Street to Commercial Street blinker, and turn right. The Deacon White House will be .4 mile on the left behind stone wall and heavy greenery; .5 mile further on, just over railroad tracks on the right, is the Tufts Homestead.

A classic, snug Cape-style house symbolizes the early economy of Weymouth, and many examples can be found along this section of Commercial Street. A particularly fine Cape is the *Deacon Thomas White House*, circa 1660, at 449 Commercial. Nearly hidden by stone walls and shrubs, the Deacon's charming Cape is simple, naturally aged clapboard, remarkably unchanged by time.

Overlooking the Fore River at 246 Commercial is the *Quincy Tufts Homestead* begun circa 1696. The house is now primarily Georgian with added sheds and outbuildings. This beautiful river setting was home to Quincy Tufts and his sister Susannah, founders of the Tufts Library in 1879. Their grandfather, Dr. Cotton Tufts, was born in 1731 to one of Weymouth's earliest families. His great grandfather was representative to the General Court in 1684, and Dr. Tufts continued the family leadership tradition. Graduating from Harvard at age fourteen, he became a charter member and president of Massachusetts Medical Society, a member of the Committee of Correspondence, and a member of the convention which adopted the United States Constitution.

#5
Town Museum, Tufts
Library
Weston Park, Waterloo
Grave
46 Broad Street
Open all year, museum
usually by appointment, no
fee

Continue on Commercial Street to Washington Street, traffic light, and turn left on Washington, then next right on Broad Street at traffic light. The library will be on the right. Weston Park is directly behind the library and the Waterloo grave is in the Ashwood Cemetery, across from the library, opposite Franklin Street. The grave is at the rear, above the ground tombs.

A twentieth-century drought revealed a rare fifteenth-century American Indian dugout canoe in Weymouth Great Pond, which itself had been formed by a receding ice glacier over 12,000 years before. This unique find is carefully preserved in the Tufts Library ground floor *Town Museum* of the Weymouth Historical Commission and the Weymouth Historical Society. The dugout, one of only two known in North America according to Harvard anthropologist James Dietz, has been permanently preserved by an innovative use of polyethyleneglycol. Tests indicate the ten-foot long dugout was made from an eastern white pine approximately 150 feet tall about six hundred years ago. It is beautifully displayed in a mood-setting diorama. The perspective of Great Pond is so realistic you almost expect an Indian to emerge, retrieve the dugout, and paddle away. Murals reenact the making of a dugout, and paintings record episodes of Weymouth history, created by talent within the Weymouth school system.

The museum also features four separate collections from Weymouth's past. In "Grandma's Attic" are an Elias Howe 1860s sewing machine, a Civil War era carpetbag, heart decorated foot warmers, and other items which come together to tell of life from 1870 to 1920. A "Nineteenth Century Doctor's Office" plus a well-labeled surgical instrument collection tell of Weymouth's many doctors. The "Old Shoe Shop" appears to be waiting for the shoe craftsman to step back to work. The "1700s Colonial Kitchen" is a wealth of functional utensils, many with strangely appropriate names.

Another display is a trubute to a local Thomas Edison—Edmund Soper Hunt. Hunt, in addition to his fireworks factory, created such diverse inventions as imitation ivory for ladies' fans and the lifesaving gun to fire a breeches buoy for rescues from the sea.

The *Tufts Library* itself is a modern, full service facility. In the Weymouth section are books and historical records, Carroll Bill paintings of early scenes, and a Willard clock which had been stolen, was found burning in the marshes, and has been rescued and restored.

Behind the library is *Weston Park* named for the family name of Marie Weston Chapman, an outstanding abolitionist who worked with William Lloyd Garrison on the *Liberator* and helped found the Boston Female Anti-Slavery Society. It is also the scene of the long traditional July Fourth picnic immortalized in the rare folk-art treasure of Weymouth's Susan Torrey Merritt, now displayed in the Art Institute of Chicago.

Diagonally across Broad Street is another of Weymouth's interesting old cemeteries, with a particularly unique grave, that of John W. Gillion, believed to be the last veteran of Waterloo. When he was the final living survivor, he chose to remain here in the country which had welcomed him, rather than accept his native country's invitation to return for an award.

#6
Old South Union Church
25 Columbian Street
1854
Open for services
NHL

Return on Broad Street, cross Washington Street, and continue 1.4 miles to Middle Street, traffic light. Turn right, immediately on left is the old Jefferson School (NRHP), a beautifully balanced 1888 Queen Anne–style building, which is historically and architecturally valuable. Continue 2.3 miles on Middle Street, passing under expressway, to Main Street, Route 18, traffic light. Turn left and drive .9 mile to Columbian Street

Chester B. Kevitt

Old South Union Church

(traffic light, South Shore Hospital and sign for Rockland), turn left. Shortly on left is the Old South Union Church. Park along street for #6–7.

"Old South" is the beautiful result of New England committee architecture, with dominating steeple reaching grandly toward heaven. The raised front facade of shiplap boarding is highlighted by stately Corinthian pilasters capped by a boldly denticulated pediment. Above, the clock tower is topped by a bell tower supporting the strong, graceful spire. Painted white, impressive Old South remains Congregational, qualities shared with its northern Weymouth counterpart from which it officially separated in 1723.

Old South's first two ministers logged ninety-three years between them. There followed a continuing history of piety, strong leadership, and the usual doctrinal disputes.

Not long after the new 1854 (present) meetinghouse was built, the unique bell was silenced. Its "silver-tone" quality was attributed to the one hundred dollars worth of silver believed cast into it by Captain Eliphalet Loud who brought it from London in 1788. It cracked dramatically in 1865 while tolling President Lincoln's death. Its broken pieces were incorporated within the replacement bell which continues to invite worshipers to today's services.

#7
Columbian Square
Fogg Shoe Factory, early 1800s
Fogg Building, 1888
Fogg Library, 1897, NRL
Open all year as public buildings, no fee

Next to the church is the Fogg Library. On the far left corner of Columbian Square is the old Fogg Shoe Factory, and across Pleasant Street on the right is the Fogg Building.

Here at Columbian Square, where two ancient Indian trails once met, industrialist and philanthropist John Fogg built three very different structures. The oldest is the *Fogg Shoe Factory*. The practical, bluntly rectangular style building was typical of Weymouth's important shoe industry and now houses street-level shops.

Across the street is the 1897 Italian Renaissance *Fogg Library*. Solid, staunch, it is built of Weymouth seam-face granite, a special granite once much in demand and still quarried on a smaller scale in Weymouth on Washington Street near Hingham. Interesting architectural detail focuses on chimney wall caps and roof line, and includes Brissi stained-glass windows. Much of the original interior remains, including furnishings. Once private, now a branch of the public library, the Fogg Library also houses the Weymouth Historical Society library.

In fascinating contrast, across the square is the dramatically Richardsonian 1888 *Fogg Building*, which once hosted the Opera House and functioned as a city cultural center. Here turrets, towers, chimneys, and spires rise in unbalanced glory from the steeply pitched roof crowning the massive, powerful core. Sandstone, brick, and granite provide variations in color and texture.

This ends the guided tour section of Weymouth. Return on Main Street, drive back up it to Route 53, Washington Street. Turn left and follow Route 53 through Braintree to Quincy Avenue in Quincy.

Weymouth Beaches and Parks

(A) **Webb Memorial State Park**
End of River Street

Once Indian summer camping site, most recently a Nike missile base, now thirty-six-acre park with spectacular views from its many paths along well-maintained grounds; interesting views of Boston, harbor condominiums, uninhabited islands; see Grape Island, scene of "false alarm" British Revolutionary War Invasion which was actually only a hay-cutting expedition as recorded by Abigail Adams; facilities: parking, paths, picnicking, rest rooms; open all year, no fee

(B) **Wessagussett Beach**
End of Neck Street

Sandy beach along harbor with variety of views of Quincy industry, moored boats, harbor islands; facilities: bathhouse, lifeguards; parking in season is sticker only; open all year, no fee

(C) **Great Hill Park**
off 3A
End of Bradley Road

Small park, unexpected open panoramic views across water to Quincy and Boston; along Fore River; facilities: benches, parking; open all year, no fee

(D) **Great Esker Park**
Elva Road access

Unusual park, natural gravel hill esker extends above marshes along Weymouth Back River; miles of trails follow old Indian trail; ideal for biking, nature study, walking; guided nature walks in season; parking; open all year, no fee

(E) **Great Pond Reservoir***
Access: Park at Alice E.
Fulton School off Pond
Street past Sycamore. Or
at treatment plant off
Great Pond Road

Weymouth Great Pond, formed over twelve thousand years ago by receding glacier remains peaceful scene which attracted Indians to hunt and fish here along Indian trail linking Massachusetts Bay and Rhode Island. (See #5 about dugout found here.) Later bog iron, which can still be seen today along the shore, was harvested by white men for Weymouth's pioneering ironworks. Now a protected water supply, the pond is surrounded by natural beauty with paths allowing access to walkers; parking at back of school or on street; path from side of playground leads to pond; open all year, no fee

HISTORY OF QUINCY

Quincy, which went from the frivolity of the Maypole to the solemnity of the White House, has an interesting history to tell. In 1625 Captain Richard Wollaston sailed into what is now Black's Creek and started a small settlement of men. Within a year Wollaston left the area, which retained his name as Mount Wollaston. The next spring one Thomas Morton, a London lawyer, arrived on the scene. He took command of the settlement, making it a trading post with himself in charge, exciting others to support him and forget the authority of Wollaston.

To say the least, Morton was a colorful character. Far from the laws and harassments of England, these men led by Morton felt the headiness of sudden freedom. To celebrate May Day in the fashion of Merry Old England, in May of 1627 they erected the now famous flower-wreathed and antler-topped Maypole. Around it they danced, drank, and made merry for days, much to the disgust of their more austere Pilgrim neighbors. Plymouth sent messages to Morton asking him to lead a more temperate and restrained life and to stop trading guns and liquor with the Indians. Morton turned a deaf ear to all entreaties. Still Plymouth tolorated him until they realized he had traded more firearms to the Indians than they possessed collectively.

Finally, in 1628, Governor John Endicott* put an end to this blight on their wilderness landscape. Morton was sent back to England. The Maypole was cut down, and the settlement ended. Thus concluded the colonies' first recorded "wild party."

By 1634 Mount Wollaston was annexed to Boston and permanent settlement began. The General Court encouraged people to move from crowded Boston to uninhabited Mount Wollaston by offering land grants. Grants went to William Coddington, Edmund Quincy,* William Hutchinson, Atherton Hough, and the Reverend John Wheelwright.* All would leave their courageous marks.

Two especially, John Wheelwright and Anne Hutchinson,* wife of William, left their footprints on the rocky road to freedom of speech, conscience, and religion. In 1636 the Reverend Wheelwright was appointed to gather a church at the Mount. Within a year his liberal sermons had aroused the ire of the Puritan Church led by John

Winthrop.* He was ultimately banished from the colony for contempt and sedition. Within the same year, his sister-in-law, Anne Hutchinson, was tried for having meetings in her home where religious attitudes were discussed and voiced. She, too, was banished for promoting dissension. Coddington, who had supported Wheelwright, also left and later became the first governor of Rhode Island. Sadly, narrowness of thought had deprived a community of talented freethinkers.

However, Quincy continued to be a town blessed by outstanding personages. Her history has been played out as a great drama on a life-size stage, where as one leading figure exited another of equal ability entered.

The 1630s saw the settlement of the Adams and Quincy families in Mount Wollaston. Their descendants played leading roles in the lives of their town, commonwealth, and country for over three centuries. Rarely would there be a time when any town group of significance would meet without a Quincy or Adams present. From these two unique families came authors, architects, historians, leaders of commerce, military men, statesmen, ambassadors, mayors, and the pinnacle of all—two presidents, John Adams* and son, John Quincy Adams.*

In 1640 Mount Wollaston was incorporated as the town of Braintree, with the North Precinct becoming Quincy in 1792, named for Colonel John Quincy, and a city in 1888.

Quincy was not only a town of distinguished people but one of hard work and innovative industry. The 1700s saw the beginning of tanneries and leather work, which evolved into boot and shoe manufacturing in the 1800s. In 1750, the peninsula of Germantown was the site of the first planned industrial development in this country. Eight industries were planned and skilled German workers recruited.

Though these were important industries, it was granite that transformed Quincy and brought her worldwide fame. The mid-1700s witnessed the start of the granite industry, where their natural granite resources were used to build King's Chapel* in Boston, followed roughly fifty years later by the building of the Bunker Hill Monument.* The first commercial railway (see #12) in the United States was built in Quincy in 1826 and carried Quincy granite from the quarries to the Neponset River. This marked a turning point in the activities of quiet, sedate, Anglo-Saxon Quincy. Soon were heard the metallic ring of hammers and chisels against hard rock, the percussion of blasting, the sound of carts and railroad cars straining under heavy loads of granite, and in time the roar of saws and polishing discs as rough granite was turned into smooth, beautiful building blocks. A new breed of people, with differing foreign backgrounds and contributions, entered the stage to work in the quarries and to stay and become part of a rising industrial scene.

Shipbuilding has been an important activity since the 1600s. In 1789 the ship, *Massachusetts*, was built, then the largest American merchant vessel. The year 1854 saw the arrival of shipbuilder Deacon George Thomas. The launching of his last vessel, the *Red Cloud*, brought to a close the square rig era in Quincy. The Fore River Engine Company, founded by Thomas Watson of telephone fame, moved to Quincy in 1900. As the Fore River Ship and Engine Company and as the Bethlehem Steel Company Yard, it was one of the foremost builders of naval and merchant vessels in the country for over sixty years. As the General Dynamics Yard today it is still the largest industry in the South Shore area.

Quincy, ever desirous of improving her people's lives has stressed the importance of education since Joanna Hoar, in-law to the first Quincy, began teaching youth in her home in Wollaston in 1638. In 1875 an enlightened school committee engaged Colonel Francis W. Parker as superintendent. He introduced the "Natural Method," or what would be called the "Quincy System" of education, adapted from his observations of German education. Old, dull methods were thrown out, and new, exciting, fun methods of individualized teaching were used. It became so effective and well-known that by 1878 so many were coming to observe that it became difficult to teach.

Today Quincy is a prosperous industrial city and busy suburb of Boston. Yet ghosts of earlier dramas still influence the life of this historic city, which continues to grow and to adapt to the changing needs of her citizens.

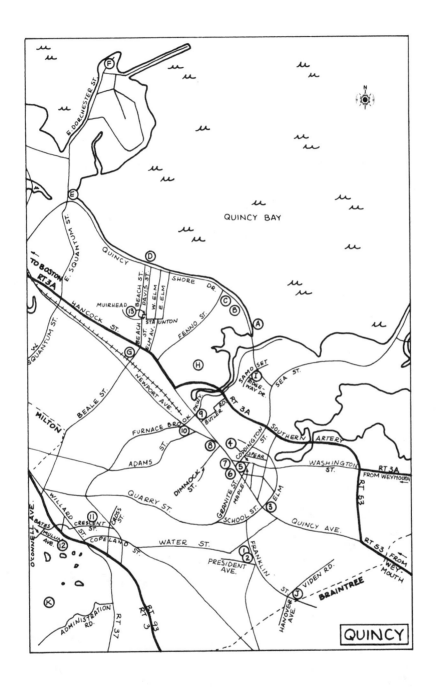

QUINCY

DIRECTIONS:
Enter Quincy from Weymouth on Route 53, Quincy Avenue, or enter Quincy from Boston on Route 3A, Hancock Street. If coming from Weymouth, after crossing town line it is 1.4 miles to where Route 53 turns right. Do not turn here, but go straight on Quincy Avenue another .8 mile to Water Street (sign "to" Route 128). Turn left on Water Street, go .3 mile to traffic light, turn left on Franklin Street.

#1
John Adams' Birthplace
133 Franklin Street
1681
Open seasonally, fee
charged
NHS HABS

The Adamses' birthplaces are a short distance down on the right side of Franklin Street.

From a background of men who planted seeds and tilled the earth came John Adams. He planted seeds of political and legal ideas which upon maturity became the foundation for the United States Constitution and democratic form of government.

Adams Birthplace

National Park Services

Adams National Historic Site Library

From this house John Adams left for Harvard College in 1750 where, with fear and trepidation, he presented himself before President Holyoke and the Harvard tutors for his admissions examination. In a day when Harvard students were treated according to family class rank, John Adams stood on his own merit. His family, while honest farmers and respected local deacons, had little in the way of social status. His graduation from Harvard proved to be the first step in a career that would take him from unknown circuit lawyer to president of the United States, from a small Colonial town to the capitals of the world. It began the Adams legacy that would continue for over three centuries.

John, the first son of Deacon John and Susanna Boylston Adams, was born on October 30, 1735, in this early saltbox farmhouse, probably built by Joseph Penniman in 1681, at the foot of Penn's Hill. His father instilled two vital forces in young Adams' life. First, he taught him a love and a respect for the land. To this his beloved Quincy, John would return time and again, tired in body and weary of mind and soul, to be refreshed as he worked in the fields, rode the lanes, or tramped the woods. Second, his father instilled in him a burning desire for knowledge. This encouraged him to develop one of the finest legal minds in Massachusetts. He would be called upon to defend the eight British

291

soldiers following the Boston Massacre* and to write many of the legal opinions used in Boston prior to the Revolution. He was instrumental in the writing of the Declaration of Independence, the Massachusetts Constitution, and his famous *Defense of the Constitutions of Government of the United States of America*, which greatly influenced the United States Constitution.

Upon the death of Deacon Adams, John's birthplace was willed to his brother, Peter Boylston Adams, along with 140 acres. John inherited the adjacent saltbox with nine acres, where he moved with his new wife, Abigail,* in 1764. These two Adams homes standing side by side, as in mutual support, are the only adjacent presidential birthplaces in the United States. In 1897 John's great grandson Charles Francis Adams, Jr., had the homes restored, allowing the Quincy Historical Society and the Daughters of the American Revolution to run them as historic shrines. The properties were given to Quincy in 1940 ending over 200 years of Adams ownership. In 1979 the City of Quincy deeded the two birthplaces to the United States. They are now run by the National Park Service.

#2
John Quincy Adams'
Birthplace
141 Franklin Street
1663
Open seasonally, fee
charged
NHS, HABS

The John Quincy Adams' Birthplace is adjacent to the John Adams' Birthplace.

In this unpretentious Colonial farmhouse lived the second and sixth presidents, the only father and son to serve in that office. Its warm hearth signified home to John* and Abigail* for over twenty years. Here they started their married life in 1764 and raised their children, Abigail, John Quincy,* Susanna (died in infancy), Charles, and Thomas.

As John Adams with his legal talents became embroiled in the defense of Colonial rights, this home became a political forum where all who gathered were tuned to the same fine pitch—that of combating British control and taxation without Colonial consent. Their thoughts soon went beyond Quincy and beyond their own colony of Massachusetts to a sense of brotherhood with the other colonies. As these early patriots linked symbolic arms in this common cause they grew in strength and their vision of independence became clearer.

John left this home and his family many times during those twenty years. But whether he was in Philadelphia with the Continental Congress or serving as minister to France or England, for him his home was always this farmhouse that held his "dearest friend" and children. In later years when Abigail joined him in England she would write, "My little cottage encompassed with my friends, has more Charms for me than the drawing-room of St. James. . . ."[26]

During the year 1779, in his study to the left of the front door, John, along with Samuel Adams and James Bowdoin, wrote the draft for the Massachusetts Constitution, which set forth John's ideas of three separate branches of government, checks and balances, and a bill of rights.

In this "Little Cottage" on July 11, 1767, John Quincy Adams, named for his maternal grandfather, was born. A precocious and serious child he spent his early childhood here, where he was tutored by his mother and John's law clerks. Yet before he was eleven, when most children today are entering fourth grade, young Johnny left the warmth and security of his home and sailed with his father in 1778 across storm-tossed, British-infested seas to France. There he attended the Passy Academy in Paris. From there he wrote his brother these adult thoughts, prophetic of what would be his own life-style. "We are Sent into this World for Some end, it is our duty to discover by Close study what this end is & when we once discover it to pursue it with unconquerable perseverance."[27] He later attended the University of Leyden in Holland. At fourteen he accompanied Francis Dana to Russia as private secretary and interpreter. From Russia Johnny returned to the colonies, where he received his degree from Harvard. By the time he was twenty John Quincy had been schooled formally and practically in the world of national and international affairs with a knowledge and an understanding that few others twice his age would ever have. As a senator, ambassador, representative, secretary of state, and sixth president of the United States, he brought honor to himself and to his country. He was instrumental in acquiring Florida, obtaining a treaty with Spain, extending United States lands to the Pacific, writing the Monroe Doctrine, abolishing the Gag Rules and preserving the right of petition, and setting down many of the ideas that were later proclaimed in Lincoln's Emancipation Proclamation.

As you visit this early saltbox, built by Samuel Belcher circa 1663, notice the central chimney with a fireplace in every room, the wide floorboards, and the period furniture—all which show life as it was when John Q. Adams lived here. The farmhouse is filled with historic ghosts of years past. For from here young Johnny and Abigail ran to the top of Penn's Hill during the Battle of Bunker Hill and later to see the British fleet evacuating Boston. (see site J) In the kitchen, Abigail melted down her pewter spoons to make bullets for neighboring soldiers. And in the parlor a lonely Abigail sat alone at night reading John's letters and writing many of her famous ones. Yes, history comes alive in every room, and you have a better understanding of those significant Colonial years and of the part the Adamses played in them.

#3	*Return on Franklin Street and drive to*
Christ Church	*School Street, second four-way intersec-*
12 Quincy Avenue	*tion. Turn right on School Street and go*
1728, 1875	*one block to corner of Quincy Avenue,*
Open for services	*traffic light. The church is on the far right*
	corner. Turn right to park at church.

The oldest Episcopal parish, not founded by government action, in Massachusetts is here in this staunch, stone building, their fourth edifice. Her grass-roots beginnings came from her people, not from edicts of ruling English governors or town authorities. The strong Victorian-Gothic structure, with stone walls two-and-one-half feet thick, houses a congregation whose forebears began meeting in homes to worship as the Church of England in the late 1600s. In 1703 their first minister was sent from England. The old Christ Church Cemetery, nearby on School Street, marks the site of their first church building of circa 1725.

By 1727 their first "Yankee-educated" rector, the Reverend Dr. Ebenezer Miller, began his thirty-six years of devoted service. Their second Yankee-educated rector, Edward Winslow, a reluctant Tory, departed in 1777. Through amazing lay leadership and occasional clergy the parish survived the Revolutionary War period, keeping its congregation, building, and glebe, a remarkable accomplishment.

Finally, in 1832, they built their second church on the present site. Tragically, fire removed it in 1859 and its stone replacement in 1873. Then in 1875 the present solid local granite house of worship, with beautiful, richly colored stained-glass windows and impressive sanctuary, arose.

A prized possession of Christ Church is a silver communion chalice presented by Caesar, a slave of Dr. Miller. The church also has its original pewter vessels. As a congregation of Jacobites, it received no royal gift of silver from Queen Anne.

The church has an even richer inheritance in her preserved ancient records and the amazing number of volumes of theology, Bible commentary, and prayer books dating as far back as the early 1600s. Many were brought in 1703, sent with their missionary by the "Society for the Propagation of the Gospel in Foreign Parts." Now solid Quincy granite protects the fine traditions of the pioneering Episcopal church.

#4
Thomas Crane Public Library
40 Washington Street
1882
Open as library
NRHP

Turn right when exiting from parking area; at immediate traffic light turn right on Elm Street. Continue on Elm, bearing left to Washington Street, traffic light, and turn left. The library will be on the right in about two blocks. Park here for #4–7.

A magnificent edifice dominates the main square of Quincy. It is considered architect Henry Hobson Richardson's* "most perfect" Romanesque creation, and its photo in the *Encyclopaedia Britannica* is present to illustrate the finest work of the outstanding American architect. Intentionally not symmetrical, the arrangement of the mass still creates a pleasant balance of rugged strength. The foundation is of Quincy granite, rough-hewn North Easton pink granite forms the walls, and Longmeadow brownstone provides horizontal bands in rich accent. The warm red roof contrasts with expanses of blue sky and green grass to provide further Richardsonian highlighting through variations in materials and colors.

The interior is even more wealthy in fantastic detail. You enter through the newer wing on the right, and follow the connecting hall on the left to the reference area, the original Richardsonian section. Study the carvings around the powerfully elegant fireplace, worthy of any castle along the Rhine. The whole room is rich in ornately carved North Carolina white pine of varying hues provided by nature, warm yet sophisticated. From the fireplace allow your eyes to gaze to the right to the small stained-glass windows, particularly the "Old Philosopher" in the center, created by John LaFarge* and considered his best work.

This outstanding work of American architecture was given to the town by the Crane family in honor of Thomas Crane, a Quincy boy who learned the granite cutters' trade and later gained a fortune in stone in New York. His wife, Clarissa Starkey Crane, was a prime mover of this enterprise as was son Albert, who purchased and removed the buildings near it, completing the pleasant open green effect.

#5
United First Parish Church
(Unitarian) in Quincy;
Church of the Presidents
Hancock and Washington
Streets
1636, 1828
Open all year, donations
NHL, HABS

Walk to intersection of Washington and Hancock Streets at library corner. The back of the church is diagonally across the street.

The United First Parish Church known as the "Stone Temple" was designed by Alexander Parris,* noted Greek Revival architect. (He was paid $500, which included supervising the construction.) The Doric portico features huge twenty-five-foot Tuscan columns supporting the massive front gable. Plain-cut blocks of Quincy granite form the facade and clock tower, topped by the gold-capped open belfry.

The "Stone Temple" was created of granite from John Adams's* lands, helped by funds he designated for it in his will. The austere simplicity of mass of the exterior is matched by the magnificent interior. As you enter you feel that this is truly a church worthy of the presidents, as indeed John Quincy Adams* was president when it was built. The royal height of the sanctuary's domed ceiling is distinguished by plaster bas-relief. John Quincy Adams owned pew number fifty-four of these lovely enclosed pews facing the Santo Domingo mahogany pulpit.

Downstairs, there is a small museum containing models of earlier churches, the weathervane of the Hancock Meeting House, and very early photos and paintings of Wheelwrights, Adamses, and Quincys.

In the Adams crypt under the portico a black iron gate leads to the all-white room and simple stone tombs of John and Abigail Adams* and John Quincy and Louisa Catherine Adams.* Wreathes are given each year by the president of the United States, delivered by a naval officer, as John Adams was president when the Navy was established. A visit provides moving insight into the importance and interrelationship of church, town, and federal government, duties and loyalties so beautifully expressed for all by the Adamses.

The church's history goes back even further than the Adamses to the beginning of the town. It was established as the "Chappel of Ease" in 1636 when Quincy was part of Boston with the Reverend John Wheelwright* delegated to preach. Wheelwright was soon banished by the colony in 1638, as was his sister-in-law Anne Hutchinson,* for daring to voice beliefs not those of the dominating Puritans.

The congregation thus began with a heritage of religious freedom. It has had many names, four buildings, and many fine ministers, among them the Reverend John Hancock,* father of the first signer of the Declaration of Independence. Historically and architecturally recognized and valued, the church continues its long devoted service to the past, the present, and the future.

#6
Hancock Cemetery
Hancock Street
c.1640
Open as cemetery

The Hancock Cemetery is across Hancock Street from the front of First Parish Church.

This well-cared-for old burying ground is one of the most fascinating in the country. It seems too small to contain all the history, mystery, and artistry found within its simple arched entry and protective wrought-iron fencing.

History, yes, the earliest pioneering settlers were buried here. The oldest identified grave dates from 1646. It is the grave of Henry Adams, the great-, great-grandfather of President John Adams,* who placed here the solid monuments to all four generations of Adamses who preceded him. More members of the Adams dynasty followed, and both Presidents Adams were buried here before being interred in the special crypt in the church across the street.

Another great Quincy family well represented are the Quincys themselves. Colonel John Quincy,* for whom the city was named, was a Massachusetts provincial leader and grandfather of Abigail Adams. Buried here is Josiah Quincy,* called "the Patriot" and "Boston Cicero," one of the six Josiah Quincys to earn recognition.

The oldest surviving gravestone is the Reverend William Tompson's dated 1666. Tompson was the first minister of the town, after Wheelwright's* removal. The Reverend John Hancock,* a later minister and father of the patriot, is buried in the Ministers' Tomb. The poetic inscription for this tomb was created in 1708 by the first native American poet, Benjamin Tompson, son of the first minister.

Mystery, yes, some of the stones hint at stories not completely revealed even today. The tomb of the family of the Reverend Leonard Hoar, third president of Harvard, bears a three-hundred-year-old weighted message. Recently the General Court proclaimed the Reverend Hoar exonerated of the implied misdeeds of this liberal thinker. And some facts are still unknown about the tragedy surrounding the grave marked for John R. Grieve. John at twenty-two and his fifteen-year-old beloved were found dead, their deaths attributed to an overdose of Spiritualism.

And artistry, yes, much philosophy and beauty are revealed through studying the designs and epitaphs found here. Stonecutters' arts are evident, with photos of stones frequently selected for illustrations.

#7
City (Town) Hall, 1844
Constitution Common, 1980
Hancock Street
Open all year, no fee

The City Hall is next to the Hancock Cemetery and Constitution Common is next to the City Hall on Hancock Street.

Quincy Square's wealthy display of American monumental architecture continues—from Richardsonian Romanesque library, to Greek Revival church, and now to Neoclassical *City Hall*. Solomon Willard,* father of the granite industry, designed the (then) Town Hall whose Quincy granite front facade is considered one of the finest of the classical style in this country. The 1979 reflective glass addition provides fascinating contrast. Another interesting comparison is the cost factor: $280 to Williard for the design and supervising the construction of the 1844 building, which cost $19,115.93. The 1979 addition cost was 1.9 milion dollars.

The facade is formed of Quincy granite blocks with full-height balanced Ionic pilasters and decorative stone carvings between window stories. Within, the second-floor great hall provided a fitting background for town moderator John Quincy Adams II and town leader Charles Francis Adams, Jr.

The welcome green oasis of *Constitution Common* is next to the City Hall. The Common with its modern granite sculpture is dedicated to the privileges and responsibilities of democratic government and to John Adams as chief author of the Massachusetts Constitution. Quincy thus recognizes the vast significance of Adams' contributions to democratic government. For the principles of the Massachusetts Constitution were later incorporated within the federal Constitution and many other state constitutions.

#8
Adams Academy
8 Adams Street
1872
Open all year, no fee
NRHP

Return to your car. Continue on Washington Street, driving to right of church to Hancock Street. Turn right on Hancock, go to first traffic light, turn left on Dimmock Street. Academy is on the right.

Adams Academy represents many of Quincy's outstanding contributions to humanity at large and to the United States in particular. It was built of staunch Quincy granite and brick, with funds and materials provided by John Adams,* who specified in detail his desires for his school.

John Adams left funds to accrue to build a stone schoolhouse in which would be provided the old-style classical education. He directed also that it be on the site of John Hancock's* birthplace to honor that patriot and the Josiah Quincys,* father and son, who lived there. In 1872, in this high Victorian Gothic stone schoolhouse, Adams Academy opened. A fine, classical school, it was noted for its high quality masters, most important in this tutoring-type system. In other fields, Adams Academy won the first known interscholastic football game in New England against Phillips Academy at Andover in 1875.

Now the Academy is home to Quincy's active historical society. Inside, bright white walls contrast sharply with dark, heavy timbers rising to the cathedral ceiling in the two large main rooms. They have historic memorabilia of the railway, granite, shipping, and glass industries as well as Indian artifacts, early furnishings, textiles, photographs, prints, paintings, and sculpture, plus a 5,000 volume research library. Some displays are rotated to allow in-depth studies. This history-steeped building and collections are well worth a visit.

#9
The Quincy Homestead
34 Butler Road
1685, 1706
Open seasonally, fee
charged
NRHP

Turn left as exit from Academy, then turn left at traffic light and take the right fork of the road which is Hancock Street. Go three blocks to Butler Road and turn right. The Homestead is on the left corner. Limited parking.

Edmund Quincy II, a man revered by his fellow townspeople, was town moderator, a member of the General Court, and later a member of the Council of Safety, which governed the colony following Governor Andros's removal in 1689. It was this influencial leader who built a "New House" here in 1685 on land acquired by his father, the first Edmund, about 1635.

The early house was filled with Quincy children, one of whom was Edmund III, who married Dorothy Flynt and became the respected Judge Edmund Quincy and royal councillor. It was Judge Edmund who inherited the family domicile which he renovated and enlarged in 1706.

In the old kitchen notice the open beams, low ceiling, wide floorboards, spacious fireplace with built-in oven and hanging caldron and kettle. The room's furnishings are of the seventeenth and eighteenth centuries. Herbs hang from the beams, and Dorothy Quincy Hancock's spinning wheel stands in one corner.

Duck your head and step into the hall and the part of the house which was redone by Judge Edmund. The dining room speaks of gracious living with its enclosed beams, paneled walls, smaller Delft-tile fireplace, and oriental wallpaper. A beautiful portrait of Dorothy, daughter of Edmund IV and wife of John Hancock, hangs next to the bay window.

Across the hall is the parlor where, were you a guest in the 1700s, you would be greeted by the charming Mrs. Quincy and her dignified husband. Behind the fireplace paneling you can see the earliest fireplace in the house. Observe the lintel beam and herringbone-brick backing. Beautiful period furniture completes the room and its feeling of hospitality.

Adjoining the parlor is Tutor Flynt's study and bedroom above. Henry Flynt, Judge Edmund's bachelor brother-in-law, taught Harvard students for fifty-five years and spent many of his summers here. Up the winding stairway was his small bedroom. The bed is conveniently placed in a closetlike area which backs on the chimney, thus providing greater warmth for the occupant.

Next is the guest or best bedroom. Notice the elaborate fireplace, the four-poster with a George III trunk at its foot, and the beautiful blockfront chest. Across the hall is another spacious bedroom and behind that is the older section of the house, at one time the servants' quarters. Again you see the exposed beams and lower ceiling.

The last room on the tour boasts the famous windowpane on which John Hancock is said to have scratched with Dorothy's engagement ring, "You I love and you alone." These romantic words can still be seen as you end your tour of the Quincy Homestead and your brief glimpse into the lives of the Quincys during the late 1600s and 1700s.

The two Quincy homes, Josiah's (see #13) and Edmund's overflowed with youthful enthusiasm and social festivities as well as the higher pursuits of intellectual and political exchange. The colonies were moving away from Puritanism and awakening to a new feeling of freedom which swept the colonies into the growing pains of independence. Dorothy, the youngest child of the last Edmund to live here, married one of the leaders of that impending Revolution. She and John Hancock, President of the Continental Congress, put their fortunes and their lives on the line for the freedom they believed in.

#10
Adams National Historic
Site
135 Adams Street
1731
Open seasonally, fee
charged
NHS

Return to Hancock Street and turn left. Drive back to traffic light at Adams Street; make a sharp almost 300° turn to right. Follow Adams Street a few blocks. The Adams Mansion is on the right, at the corner of Adams and Newport Avenue just after going over railroad overpass.

John Adams* wrote from the Netherlands in 1782, "My dear blue Hills [of Quincy], ye are the most sublime object in my Imagination. At your reverent Foot, will I spend my old Age, if any."[28] The fulfilling of this dream began five years later when John was serving as the first United States minister to the Court of St. James in England. John's and Abigail's thoughts turned more and more to their beloved Quincy. Realizing their familiar saltbox would no longer hold all the possessions they had acquired abroad, they purchased in 1787 this lovely old country home built by Leonard Vassall in 1731.

Upon returning to the United States, before assuming the office of vice-president, John supervised the revitalization of his new lands. He returned permanently to this home in 1801 to spend his final twenty-five years surrounded by his family in the Quincy he loved so well. Here he learned of his son's election as sixth president of the United States. Here, fittingly, on July 4, 1826, just a few hours after Thomas Jefferson's death, John Adams left this world he had spent his life serving.

The estate was willed to John Q. Adams.* Though he rarely lived here more than a few months at a time it was for him an oasis, a place for mental and physical rejuvenation and his only "real home." It served as the "summer White House" for both presidents.

Following John Quincy's death in 1848, the "Old House," as it was then lovingly called, continued as home to two generations of Adamses. John Quincy's son, Charles Francis, famous ambassador during the Civil War, lived here. While it was General Grant who won the Civil War on the battlefields, it was Charles Francis Adams who, with open, direct, honest negotiations won the war of diplomacy in England. Single-handedly he kept England from openly supporting the South and prevented the delivery of ironclad ships made by British sympathizers for Southern use. The slightest error of diplomacy could have changed or ended the history of the United States. Two of his sons, Henry and Brooks, lived on here after their father's death. Both had served as private secretaries to Charles Francis during different, but equally vital, diplomatic assignments, and both became prolific, meaningful writers.

The Old House was last lived in by Brooks Adams, who died here in 1927. In a time when preservation was hardly thought of, the Adams heirs preserved this historic house with their own money, outside private donations, and by opening it to the public for a fee. The property was given as an Adams memorial to the federal government in 1946 and is now supervised by the National Park Service.

The historic mansion is set amidst well-landscaped grounds with beautiful formal gardens laid out by Mrs. Charles Francis Adams so that they are colorful every season of the year. In many cases the gardens are outlined with dwarf boxwood planted by the Vassall family. A York Rose planted by Abigail Adams* still survives. Dormers pierce the slate gambrel roof of this Georgian Colonial. The home is fronted by a granite and brick wall, which appears to protect this sacred piece of history from the modern day turmoil, while the softness of its wooden gates offers a warm welcome.

Upon entering the mansion you have the feeling that the Adams family has just stepped out and will return for dinner. This feeling of immediacy is what makes the mansion and the people who lived in it seem so real. For the house is just as it was when Brooks Adams died. The well-informed guides lead you through the rooms, and thus through the lives of the four Adams generations, pointing out each family member's furnishings, and illustrating their particular historic significance. All the furnishings are authentic and belonged to the Adams family.

You first step into the original seven-room home bought by John and Abigail in 1787. In the parlor at the left, Abigail shelled peas, folded laundry, and greeted guests all in the same gracious, efficient manner. Here she entertained thirty-six guests on the occasion of John's eightieth birthday.

The dining room holds silver and furniture belonging to each generation as well as a Gilbert Stuart portrait of John Adams in his eighty-eighth year. The two portraits of Martha and George Washington were painted by Edward Savage at John's request for the unheard of sum of $46.66.

Leaving the dining area you cross the hall into the 1800 section added by Abigail while John was serving as president. She added six rooms which included the long, gracious formal parlor for entertaining and a large, spacious study above for John. The parlor, where many dignitaries such as Lafayette and Monroe were entertained, displays several family portraits and furnishings brought back from the first American Embassy in Holland.

The study above contains John and Abigail's desk given them as a wedding present from the Boylstons; Henry Adams' desk from which many of his books were written; John Q. Adams' globes; and the historic wing-back chair in which John Adams died.

A book-lined hall, built by John Q. Adams, connects the study with the bedroom area. The guest bedroom boasts a Napoleon sleeping bed which belonged to Daniel Webster.* The presidential or master bedroom holds Abigail's writing desk, their four-poster, and a special short-legged chair used by Charles Francis who had a bad back. John Quincy's bed is found in Brooks Adams' bedroom as well as an unusual Biblical tile-edged fireplace done by Sadler. Brooks' photographic works adorn the walls.

Next to the house in a separate building is the magnificent water- and fireproof library, requested in John Q. Adams' will, which houses the Adames' 14,000-volume library. The slate-roofed Quincy-granite building, with hand-laid Italian tile floor and oak bookshelves and paneling, has a special air circulating system which preserves the books. The scholarly atmosphere is sharpened by books on every subject, fiction and nonfiction, in eleven different languages. Here is John Adams's writing desk in which he said he had a pigeonhole for each department of government. You can also see the famous desk which John Q. Adams used in the House of Representatives, and at which he suffered a fatal stroke while still actively serving his country.

The historic estate has responded to the heartbeat of Adamses from 1787 until 1927. It has known the wonder of birth, the anguish of death, the elation of political victory, the agony of defeat, the unity of generations, and the tensions of family problems. Through the good and the bad years the Old House has stood for solidarity and home to a family who played a major role in the growth of thirteen independent colonies which developed into a unified world power.

#11
John Winthrop, Jr., Blast
Furnace Remains
Crescent Street
1644
Open all year, no fee

Continue on Adams Street to Furnace Brook Parkway, traffic light, and turn left. Follow Furnace Brook Parkway .7 mile to Cross Street and turn right. Take first right on Crescent Street, and the Blast Furnace will be on the right just before the cemetery. Parking available on street.

The hardy colonists of Massachusetts Bay quickly became self-sufficient in filling their most basic needs with the exception of necessary iron for nails, pots, and tools. They aimed to fill this gap in 1644 with the construction of an iron furnace in the colonies. Purportedly the Virginia Colony did have an earlier iron furnace but unfortunately it came to an abrupt and tragic end. It blew up with the initial firing, and fear-crazed Indians slaughtered all colonists connected with this unknown monster.

By comparison, Quincy's blast furnace fared better. The governor's son, John Winthrop, Jr., became agent of an English "Company of Undertakers" which raised 1,000 pounds for building an ironworks in America. They were granted 3,000 acres for a wood supply, a twenty-one year monopoly, and militia exemption for their workers. The result was this furnace in which was produced the first commercial iron in this country. Unfortunately, the bog iron ore did not meet expectations and waterpower was not adequate, so operations ceased by 1653. From here went ironworkers to found ironworks in Saugus,* Taunton, and other places.

Over three centuries later, Roland Wells Robbins* supervised the excavation here in Quincy that revealed the 1644 remains of the John Winthrop, Jr., iron furnace. These excavated remains are to be seen today. Nearby, a sketch shows how the furnace appeared and operated in 1644.

#12
Granite Railway Incline
Mullin Avenue
1826
Open all year, no fee
NRHP

Follow Crescent Street straight through at traffic light where it becomes Bates Avenue. Continue over expressway and turn left on O'Connell Avenue and then left again on Mullin Avenue. The Incline is at the end of Mullin after going through what looks like a factory area. Parking is available.

The story of granite is layered throughout Quincy's history. Before 1666 the second meetinghouse was created of granite fieldstone. In the 1700s more buildings arose from Quincy granite, such as the 1754 King's Chapel* of Boston.

Architect Solomon Willard selected Quincy granite for the Bunker Hill Monument* in 1826, and a new facet of American architecture featuring huge blocks of Qunicy granite was born. Willard, called "Father of the Granite Industry," was the responsible genius. Blocks of the size he specified were unknown. He left architecture to create the methods, tools, and equipment used to obtain and fashion the huge blocks. As each question or obstacle arose, he invented a solution, making massive granite blocks available for building, and Quincy famous.

Quincy's success resulted from the combination of the advantages of Quincy granite and the availability of saltwater transportation. Transportation to the water was provided by the Granite Railway. Railway machinery-inventor Gridley Bryant built this Granite Railway and Granite Incline of Quincy in 1826. Transporting Quincy granite from quarry to water for the Bunker Hill Monument was the first freight contract of this first commercial railway in the United States.

The remaining Granite Railway Incline can still be seen—a monument to Quincy's granite industry and brilliant people. Between two obelisks rise the remains of Bryant's historic, unique Incline, down which came massive granite blocks on railcars to link with the railway. You can climb the rough granite, lined with traces of rails, to the quarry beyond.

#13
Colonel Josiah Quincy
House
18 Muirhead Street
1770
Open seasonally, fee
charged
SPNEA, NRHP

Return on Crescent Street to Furnace Brook Parkway, turn left on the parkway, and follow it back 1.7 miles to Hancock Street. Turn left on Hancock and go .7 miles to Elm Avenue, traffic light, and turn right on Elm. Drive to where Elm splits and turn left on Staunton, go one block to end, turn right and immediately left on Muirhead. The Quincy House is on the right. Parking is available on street.

Here stands the ancestral home of six Josiah Quincys* who as patriots, mayors of Boston, president of Harvard, and authors brought continuing honor to the "Quincys of Quincy."

The first Josiah, with brother Edmund IV,* and brother-in-law Edward Jackson, owned a shipping firm in Boston. In 1748 one of their ships, the *Bethel*, had an unusual and lucrative encounter with a Spanish treasure ship. Caught by surprise the weaker Colonial merchant ship rigged her portholes with logs and spars to look like guns and ran lanterns and odd clothing and equipment up the rigging to present a ghostlike man-of-war. The masquerade worked. They outbluffed the Spaniards who gave up without a fight. The loot from the captured ship was enough to make each of the three partners financially secure.

In 1753 Josiah returned to his native town and moved into the old Hancock Parsonage (see #8), which soon became a social and civic center of the town. Sadly the historic home burned in 1759. Eleven years later Josiah built this Georgian mansion, with its gracefully balanced facade crowned with a monitor, here on ancestral land, part of the first Quincy grant in 1635.

The strategic location on the shore of the bay proved invaluable during the Revolutionary War. Here Josiah, Sr., kept a close eye on British movements and reported directly to General Washington. On October 10, 1775, he watched General Gage sail for England, and recorded the event for posterity by scratching it on a pane of glass in the upstairs window. Then in March of 1776 he watched the British evacuation of Boston. As the last sail disappeared over the horizon he was filled with relief and hope for his beloved colonies. Yet he was greatly saddened, for aboard one of the ships was his son, Samuel, leaving Boston as a loyal Tory.

Josiah, Jr., supported his father's patriotic fervor and was known as "the Patriot" and the "Boston Cicero" for his strong and eloquent speeches against British control and for colonial liberty. Unfortunately, his health was not equal to his spirit, and he died at age thirty-one in 1775 before seeing the independence he so avidly sought.

Josiah III continued to bring honor to the name of Quincy. He served as president of Harvard College and "Great Mayor" of Boston, at which time he was the prime mover behind the Quincy Markets.* In later years he authored several books including a memoir of John Quincy Adams,* a lifelong friend. His son, Josiah IV, was also a distinguished mayor of Boston and prominent businessman. His grandson, Josiah (6th), completed the succession by being the third Quincy to be mayor of Boston.

As you walk through this historic home, imagine it aglow with the Quincy life-style, which would have been an interesting potpourri of social elegance, patriotic fervor, political maneuvering, literary endeavors, and educational achievements. The furnishings are of the appropriate period, many of which, along with the wall and decorative pieces, belonged to the Quincy families. Visiting Adamses or John Hancock* probably sat on the Chippendale settee in the best parlor. The third Josiah added the ell and enlarged the dining room in 1806 so that he might better entertain his political friends before the open fireplace edged with English Sadler tiles.

Climb the stairs, which interestingly lead from the rear or bay side of the house. The rear bedroom was named the Franklin Room for its famous guest. On the dresser are the comb and brush sets used by the third and fourth Josiahs. A rare picture of Lafayette,* made when he visited the United States in 1824, hangs on the wall. An interesting quilt, made from 5000 pieces of British fabric, each the size of a shilling, adorns the bed.

Throughout the large open house you can sense the wealth, prestige, and political power of the Josiah Quincys. Once a quietly elegant mansion on 250 acres overlooking the bay, it is now a beautifully preserved home amid neighboring houses.

This ends the guided tour section of the Quincy tour. To continue tour follow Muirhead Street to Beach Street and turn right on Beach Street. Take Beach to Quincy Shore Drive and turn left. Enjoy the scenic beauty of Quincy Bay as you follow the Shore Drive along the water's edge. Then, bearing left, return to Route 3A. At Route 3A turn right and follow it into Boston for the continuation of the tour.

Quincy Beaches and Parks and Additional Points of Interest

Quincy Shore Drive	Interesting, scenic coastline drive along Quincy Bay with fascinating views of islands and skylines, bay and industry; open all year, no fee
Caddy Memorial Park Quincy Shore Drive near Fenno Street	Named for World War Two Congressional Medal of Honor winner, a nice playground with bike path and trails; parking; open all year, no fee
Grossman's Park Quincy Shore Drive and Fenno Street	Named for Quincy's Grossmans of building supplies industry; peaceful edge of the marsh park with benches and paths; parking; open all year, no fee

(D) Wollaston Beach
Quincy Shore Drive

Long expanse of gravelly sand, gradual beach, not too crowded in summer; views of Boston, Squantum peninsula, Houghs Neck; parking; open all year, no fee

(E) Moswetuset Hummock
East Squantum Street
near Quincy Shore Drive
NRHP

On this small, tree-covered, arrowhead-shaped peninsula in the early 1600s was the seat of Massachusetts Indians. Called "Mos" (arrowhead) "wetuset" (hummock) from which original name Massachusetts evolved, it is still bounded by old Indian fishing grounds, the sea, defense-serving marshes, and ancient planting grounds. You can easily walk the paths of this small elevated natural park to enjoy a wide view of the harbor; parking; open all year, no fee

(F) Myles Standish Cairn
Squaw Rock Park
Squantum Peninsula, end
of Dorchester Street

Cairn near site of landing of Captain Myles Standish, Squanto, and others on September 30, 1621; in natural birch-covered park with paths to beautiful, varied views of Dorchester, Boston skyline and harbor, and Long Island; rest rooms; parking; open all year, no fee

(G) Site of beginning of Howard
Johnson Chain
Beale Street near
Newport Avenue

Where Quincy boy "Buster" Johnson had variety and newspaper store in 1925 and began making ice cream; stone marker and benches; parking nearby; open all year, no fee

(H) Merrymount Park
Hancock Street, Route 3A
Southern Artery

Extensive park given by the Adams family to Quincy; parts remain virtually unchanged since days of earliest settlement; added recreational facilities include ball fields, playground equipment, trails; parking; open all year, no fee

(I) Maypole Park
Samoset Avenue

A tiny park, a steep hill, a lone marker for the site of the magnificent cedar depicted on Quincy's seal; with the unmarked site nearby which once held the antler-topped maypole of early Quincy history; parking on street; open all year, no fee

(J) Abigail Adams Cairn
Franklin Street at Viden
Road

Site from which Abigail Adams and son John Quincy watched smoke from the burning of Charleston and heard guns of Bunker Hill on

June 17, 1775; Cairn erected 1896; cairn rises above open rock in tiny park, easy climb to views; on street parking; open all year, no fee

K **Blue Hills Reservation Milton, just west of Quincy Access Route 138 Route 28**

Huge refuge, largest recreational area in state, just south of Boston and west of Quincy; with 1885 weather observatory, two other observation towers, stables, bridges, ruins of old Turning Mill, an old farm and barn, Trailside Museum, refreshment stand, rest rooms; activities include golf, hiking, horseback riding, nature study, picnicking, skating, skiing (Nordic and Alpine), swimming; parking; open all year, no fee usually

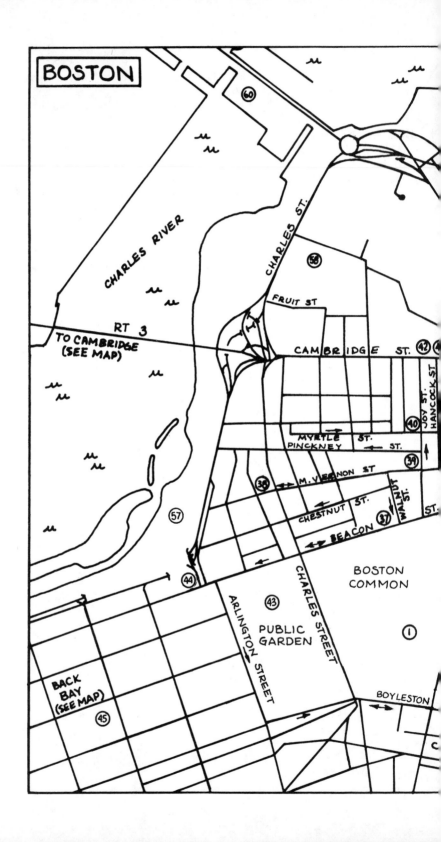

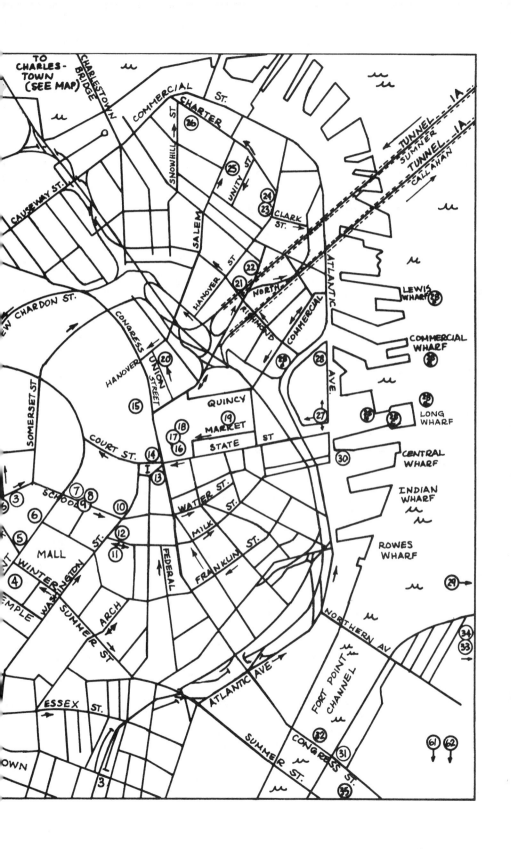

BOSTON

Walk Boston's neighborhoods for the true, rich flavor and character of this fascinating city. Driving can be a frantic blur except where suggested to outlying points of interest.

DOWNTOWN—Where in 1630 first settlers founded Boston; now still-Colonial-patterned wandering streets include shopping mall, government center, theaters, Chinatown, and Faneuil Hall; here begins Boston's Freedom Trail, *America's first urban historic trail; follow red brick line through the city to historic sites along three-mile roundtrip walk; points on trail marked by "FT" in following text*

Visitor Information Centers, staffed by helpful, knowledgeable guides and much printed information:

Boston Common Visitor Information Booth, Tremont Street at Bostom Common, open daily, all year; marked I on map

Boston National Historical Park Visitors Center, 15 State Street, opposite State House, National Park Service (see #13) open daily, all year

Bostix Ticket Booth, Faneuil Hall; entertainment information and tickets; open daily, all year

Special Tours

Art Boston 227-6901

Art New England 277-3686

Boston by Foot 367-2345

Horse Drawn Sightseeing Tours 583-5651

1. FT—***Boston Common,*** NRHP, 1634, Tremont, Park, Beacon, Charles, Boylston Streets; open daily, all year, no fee; large park, remains common land well over three centuries after purchase as common grazing land and militia training ground; small burial ground near Boylston Street; Shaw Memorial to first Black regiment has National Park interpreter-guide at Beacon and Park Streets, no fee; beginning of "Emerald Necklace," chain of parks and green space designed by Frederick Law Olmsted* extending from Common, to Boston Public Garden,* along Commonwealth Avenue, Fenway, Riverway, Jamaicaway and pond, to Arboretum* and Franklin Park and Zoo,* NRHP

2. FT—***Massachusetts State House,*** NRHP, NHL, HABS, 1795, Beacon Street across from Common* (727-3676); open all year, no fee; guided tours focus on architecture, history, and

legislature; land belonged to John Hancock family; boldly impressive building designed by Charles Bulfinch,* Boston's Federal architect and the country's first native-born architect; archives museum goes back to Pilgrims

3. *Boston Athenaeum,* NRHP, NHL, 1847, 10½ Beacon Street (227-0270); open limited times all year, no fee; guided tours of elegant historic private library-arts club, library access available to researchers

4. *St. Paul's Cathedral,* NRHP, NHL, 1819, Tremont Street and Common; open all year, no fee; massive Greek Revival by Parris* and Willard* built by Boston's first families

5. FT—*Park Street Church,* 1809, Park at Tremont Street; open all year, no fee; here William Lloyd Garrison gave first public abolitionist speech in 1829

6. FT—*Granary Burying Ground,* 1660, Tremont Street; open daily, all year, no fee; graves of Paul Revere, John Hancock, Sam Adams, victims of Boston Massacre,* traditional model of Mother Goose, Mary Goose

7. FT—*King's Chapel and Burial Ground,* NRHP, NHL, 1754, corner Tremont and School Streets (523-1749); open all year, no fee; America's first Church of England established 1686, now Unitarian; Boston's first burial ground next, c.1630, graves of *Mayflower* Pilgrim Mary Chilton and Massachusetts Bay Colony leaders including Governor John Winthrop*

8. FT—*Franklin Statue,* 1856, Old City Hall grounds, School Street; open all year, no fee; first Boston portrait statue, of native son, with tablet of Ben Franklin highlights; the bold French Second Empire period *Old City Hall* is beautifully restored for adaptive use as restaurant and offices, NRHP, NHL, HABS

9. FT—*Site of First Public School,* School Street, plaque outside Old City Hall grounds; here was country's first public school in 1635, original site of Boston Public Latin School

10. FT—*The Globe Corner Bookstore,* NRHP, *Boston Globe* office and bookstore now, 1712, corner School and Washington Streets (523-6658); open weekdays all year, no fee; here gathered literary heroes, among them, Ralph Waldo Emerson, Nathaniel Hawthorne,* Oliver Wendell Holmes; small memorabilia and book collection, as well as bookstore

11. FT—*Birthplace of Benjamin Franklin,* 17 Milk Street; not open to public; bust of Franklin and commemorative plaque mark birthplace

12. FT—*Old South Meeting House,* 1729, NRHP, NHL, HABS, Washington and Milk Streets (482-6439); open daily, all year, fee; explores role of the Old South Meeting House in Revolutionary history of Boston; with exhibits; here a 1773 meet-

ing's anger burst into Boston Tea Party; here worshipped
black poetess Phyllis Wheatley

13. ***Boston National Historical Park Visitors Center,*** National Park
Service, 15 State Street, across from Old State House (242-
5642); open daily, all year, no fee; excellent starting point
from which to explore Boston; slide show orientation on
Freedom Trail; rotating exhibits; information services include
helpful, knowledgeable guides, much printed information,
and computer answer machines; check here for current calen-
dars of events; rest rooms available

14. FT—***Old State House,*** 1713, NRHP, NHL, 206 Washington Street
(242-5655); open daily, all year, fee; museum of Boston history
in Boston's oldest public building; was first British then
Massachusetts State House; here Declaration of Independence first read in Boston

15. ***City Hall Plaza,*** Government Center, once Scollay Square area,
finished 1975; open all year, no fee; guided tours through
massive concrete City Hall; open gathering spaces surrounding, host concerts, rotating exhibits, informal attractions;
architecturally interesting and contrasting 1841 Sears Crescent Federal commercial building across from plaza.

16. ***Where's Boston?*** 60 State Street; open daily, all year, fee; multimedia show and exhibit of contemporary Boston

17. FT—***Boston Massacre Site,*** 1770, near Old State House; open
daily, all year, no fee; here on March 5, 1770, violence
erupted after a year of British occupation of the city; former
slave Crispus Attucks was killed as he led a mob assaulting
British soldiers; patriots fanned the propaganda flames

18. FT—***Faneuil Hall,*** 1742, NRHP, NHL, enlarged 1805 by
Bulfinch,* Congress Street at head of Quincy Market (223-
6098); open all year, no fee; "Cradle of Liberty" held fiery
Revolutionary meetings; now first floor shops, meeting hall
above, and third floor museum of the 1638 Ancient and
Honorable Artillery Company of Massachusetts; topped by
famed pre-Revolutionary grasshopper weathervane

19. FT—***Quincy Market,*** NRHP, NHL; open daily, all year, no fee;
now popular pedestrian mall, intriguing shops and eateries
abound in these preserved markets-warehouses designed by
Greek Revival architect Alexander Parris*

NORTH END—*Boston's oldest, Italian-American flavor, busy and
noisy with life, open air market*

20. ***Capen House,*** c.1713, Union Street; open all year as Union Oyster
House since 1826, Boston's oldest restaurant; peopled with
history: first paymaster of Continental Army Ebenezer Hancock, America's first newspaper entrepreneur Isaiah
Thomas, Duc de Chartres later King Louis Phillipe, and
visitors Daniel Webster,* Adamses, Hancocks, Quincys

Paul Revere Mall and Old North Church

21. *Moses Pierce-Hichborn House,* NRHP, NHL, HABS, 1711, 29 North Square; open all year, (winter by appointment through Paul Revere House 523-1676) guided tours through restored and furnished three-story brick house

22. FT—*Paul Revere House,* NRHP, NHL, c.1680, 19 North Square (523-1676); open daily, all year, fee; Boston's oldest house, where Revere lived before and after Revolution; focus on people, architecture, and furnishings

23. *St. Stephen's Church,* NRHP, 1804, 401 Hanover Street at Clark Street; open daily, all year, no fee; only Charles Bulfinch designed church remaining; impressive Federal with brick facade, white pilasters, ornate-cornices, finials, bell tower, and domed cupola

24. *Paul Revere Mall,* 1933; open daily, all year, no fee; known as Prado, includes famous Paul Revere statue by Cyrus Dallin, sidewalls laid with bronze plaques detailing Boston's history

25. FT—*Old North Church,* 1723, NRHP, NHL, HABS, Corner Salem and Hull Streets (523-6676); open daily, all year, no fee;

this oldest-standing historic Boston church beautifully retains many original features; traditionally here on April 18, 1775, signal lanterns sent Paul Revere on ride

26. FT—*Copp's Burying Ground,* NRHP, 1660, Charter Street; open daily, all year, no fee; originally North Burying Ground, Boston's second; here buried Cotton Mather, many old Boston names, and over 1,000 blacks since 1638; site also of British fortifications during Battle of Bunker Hill

WATERFRONT—*once home of Boston Tea Party and later industry; now revitalized wharves and warehouses have become restaurants, shops, apartments, museums, and parks*

27. *Harborwalk,* begins at Old State House (#14), blue Harborwalk sidewalk symbols lead along State Street, past Custom House Tower (with open-to-public observation platform), Quincy Market,* to Waterfront Park,* wharves along Atlantic Avenue, Aquarium,* Children's Museum,* and Boston Tea Party Ship;* self-guiding pamphlet available at National Historical Park Visitors Center across from Old State House; walk about one mile long

28. *Waterfront Park,* Atlantic Avenue; open daily, all year, no fee; peaceful vantage from which to view harbor, amazing restoration and adaptive uses, and whole waterfront scene including

    a 1710 Long Wharf

    b c.1830 Gardner Building once warehouse now Chart House Restaurant

    c 1845 Custom House where Nathaniel Hawthorne worked

    d 1858 Gridley Bryant*-designed Mercantile Wharf

    e 1833 Commercial Wharf

    f 1836 Lewis Wharf with restored and reused granite building

29. *Boston Harbor Islands,* each island has own personality—historic sites, rocky or sandy shore, wilderness and wildlife—in dramatic contrast with Boston skyline so near; sixteen of the over thirty harbor islands are part of *Boston Harbor Island State Park,* some others are city-controlled, thus most are open to public, no fee; reach by ferry to Georges Island, from there free water taxi in summer to Lovells, Gallops, Grape, Bumpkin Islands; facilities vary from island to island and include: boat piers, camping with permit, fishing, guided walks, hiking, historic fortifications, picnicking, rest rooms, swimming; Georges Island has information desk, refreshment stand, and Fort Warren* NRHP, NHL (see Hull #4);

glaciers ground bedrock leaving drumlins and rock ridge which became the harbor islands; over 6,000 years ago Indians camped here; in 1614 Captain John Smith explored; Colonial farms by 1630, continent's first lighthouse by 1713; important defense fortifications from Colonial times through World War Two; Harbor ferry and other cruises:

Bay State, Long Wharf, 723-7800

Boston Harbor Cruises, Long Wharf, 227-4321

Massachusetts Bay Lines, Rowes Wharf, 749-4500

A. C. Cruise Lines, Northern Avenue Bridge

30. *New England Aquarium,* Central Wharf; open daily, all year, fee; over 7,000 exotic fish, world's largest circular glass tank, separate float and pool with dolphin show; benches, harbor view

31. *Children's Museum,* Museum Wharf, 300 Congress Street (426-8855); open all year, fee; truly a museum for children with all "hands-on" creative activities to see, touch, do and think about

32. *Boston Tea Party Ship and Museum,* Congress Street Bridge (338-1773); open daily, all year, fee; "hands-on" museum and replica ship with presentations and costumed tour guides

33. *Fish Pier,* Northern Avenue, pier before "no-name" restaurant; scene of Boston's active fishing industry; fish markets, harbor industry color

34. *Commonwealth Pier Exhibition Hall,* Northern Avenue; open all year, Boston Computer Communications Market Center; Boston's international high technology hardware exhibit center

35. *Fort Point Channel Area,* Summer, Congress, A Streets; just across Fort Point Channel, behind Children's Museum;* open all year, no fee; "Soho of Boston"; walk area of artists and studios; scheduled open houses and festivals; information 423-4299

BEACON HILL—*residential area of hills, fashionable since late 1700s, delightful study of historic architecture particularly when highlighted dawn or dusk; Louisburg Square a fascinating example; bisected by Charles Street and its interesting small shops; designated historic district, NRHP, NHL, HABS*

Black Heritage Trail, Boston Afro-American National Historic Site, Beacon Hill; black and silver signs trace history of black community; tours given by appointment only through Museum of Afro-American History, Inc., 455-7400, Box 5, Roxbury, Ma. 02119; fee charged

36. *Chester Harding House,* 1808, NRHP, NHL, 16 Beacon Street (742-0615); open all year, no fee; once home of artist now Boston Bar Association; ring bell at entry to see Federal reception room

37. *Appleton-Parker Houses,* c.1818, 39–40 Beacon Street, Women's City Club (227-3550); open limited times all year, fee; elegant double house of Beacon Street; here Longfellow married Fanny Appleton

38. *Charles Street Meeting House,* 1807, corner Charles and Mt. Vernon Streets; open by appointment through Museum of Afro-American History, Inc. (455-7400); fee; antislavery headquarters, here spoke Garrison, Harriet Tubman, Frederick Douglass; outside retains Federal elegance dominated by clock tower and belfry

39. *Nichols House Museum,* 55 Mt. Vernon Street (227-6993); open all year, fee; see life on Beacon Hill as you tour private home designed by Bulfinch and admire furnishings and art

40. *African Meeting House,* NRHP, 1806, 8 Smith Court, Joy Street, African American National Historic Site; first Black church in New England; Garrison founded New England Anti-Slavery Society here in 1832; restored simple Federal brick; now oldest surviving black church building in country; not yet open to public

41. *Old West Church,* NRHP, NHL, HABS, 1806, 131 Cambridge Street (227-5088); open all year, no fee; handsome Federal; first building destroyed by British; time nearly destroyed this one; later used as library; now Methodist church

42. *First Harrison Gray Otis House,* NRHP, NHL, HABS, 1796, SPNEA Headquarters, 141 Cambridge Street (227-3956); open all year, fee; well-informed guides give tours through Charles Bulfinch's classic Federal; once home to Boston Mayor and Congressman Otis; focus on history, people, antiques

BACK BAY—*Filled marsh in the mid-1800s, with streets named alphabetically, provides interesting museum of nineteenth-*

Boston Public Garden

century American architecture and living study; Boston Public Gardens, shops, galleries, cafes, residences, and churches with Tiffany stained-glass windows; designated historic district, NRHP; see Back Bay map insert

43. **Boston Public Garden,** NRHP, Arlington, Boylston, Beacon, Charles Streets; across from Common;* open daily all year, no fee; paths through beautifully landscaped grounds featuring flowers, shrubs, trees, and the famous Swan Boats, fee

44. **Gibson House Museum,** 1859, 137 Beacon Street, between Arlington and Berkeley, Victorian Society, New England chapter (267-6338); open all year, fee; only Victorian house open in Boston's Back Bay, furnishings of 1890s; Society also offers walking tours and other special events

45. **First Baptist Church,** NRHP, 1872, Commonwealth at Clarendon Street; open daily all year, no fee; first church designed by Richardson;* frieze by Frederick Auguste Bartholdi, creator of Statue of Liberty; huge stained-glass rose windows by Louis Tiffany

46. **(New) Old South Church,** NRHP, 1877, Newbury, Dartmouth, and Boylston Streets; open daily, no fee; North Italian Gothic built when Third Church of Boston left Old South Meeting House

47. **Boston Public Library,** 1895, NRHP, Boylston Street, Copley
    Square; open all year, no fee; designed by Charles Follen
    McKim, the magnificent Renaissance structure harmonizes
    with the varied architecture dominating Copley Square,
    notably the Richardsonian Trinity Church* and powerfully
    elegant modern Hancock Building;* library has low profile in
    granite with arched windows, bronze figures by Bela Pratt;
    with huge equally impressive interior highlighted by murals
    by Abbey and Sargent

48. **Trinity Church,** 1872–1877, NRHP, NHL, Copley Square; open
    daily, all year, no fee; guided tours of Henry Hobson Richard-
    son's* masterpiece of Richardsonian Romanesque set in Cop-
    ley Square amid other grand high Victorians and modern
    Hancock Building; towers, turrets, and pinnacles seem
    countless; the rich interior is warmed by paintings and
    stained glass by John La Farge;* water levels below are
    regulated to saturate the 4,500 wooden piles supporting
    foundations; first minister, the Reverend Phillips Brooks,
    wrote "O Little Town of Bethlehem"

49. **John Hancock Observatory,** Copley Square, 200 Clarendon
    Street at St. James Street (247-1977); open daily, all year,
    fee; magnificently modern Hancock Building, tallest in New
    England; sixtieth floor view plus four multimedia exhibits
    featuring Boston at different times and moods, including
    "Skyline Boston" and "Boston 1775"

50. **Museum of the First Corps of Cadets,** 227 Commonwealth Avenue
    between Exeter and Fairfield Streets; open by appointment
    (267-1726); fee; military history museum of one of nation's
    oldest military organizations from 1726; once at Corps Ar-
    mory at Arlington and Columbus, NRHP; now four stories of
    arms, uniforms, flags, paintings recreate sounds and sights of
    nation's important military history

51. **Institute of Contemporary Art,** 955 Boylston Street (266-5152);
    open all year, fee; collection presents most significant modern
    art; presents development of present-day art, modern mas-
    ters plus innovative new talent; French Romanesque build-
    ing was police station in 1886

52. **Skywalk Observation Deck, Prudential Tower,** Huntington Ave-
    nue, Boylston Street (236-3318); open daily, all year, fee;

fiftieth floor has full 360 degree view from New Hampshire to Cape Cod

53. *Christian Science Center,* Huntington and Massachusetts Avenues (262-2300); open all year, no fee; several programs and tours offered: "A Light Unto My Path" a nondenominational multimedia Bible exhibit; tours of publishing house of *Christian Science Monitor* include Mapparium, a glass globe of the earth in which you walk, plus glass bridge and reflecting pool; tour of the 1894 Mother Church focuses on its Romanesque architecture

54. *Symphony Hall,* NRHP Massachusetts at Huntington Avenue; open all year, fee; magnificent hall has noted acoustics amid elegant surroundings; home of the Boston Symphony Orchestra, Boston Pops; hosts other classical music performances; for program and ticket information dial "concerts"

55. *Museum of Fine Arts,* 465 Huntington Avenue; open all year, fee; one of world's finest collections of fine and decorative arts from ancient to modern; particularly notable are Asiatic art collection (world's largest), paintings from eleventh to twentieth century (especially French Impressionists), Egyptian old kingdom objects; for calendar of special exhibits and events dial "answers"

56. *Isabella Stewart Gardner Museum,* 1900, 280 The Fenway; open all year, voluntary donation; Italian palace of Boston's most unusual, lavish hostess; priceless treasures and art; colorful gardens within; classical music performed in Old World concert hall, regularly throughout year, no fee

POINTS OF INTEREST BEYOND CENTRAL BOSTON; see central Boston map

57. *Esplanade,* a park on Charles River; open daily, all year, no fee; performances at Hatch Shell by Boston Pops Orchestra, Boston Symphony Orchestra, Boston Opera Company, Boston Ballet; seasonal, no fee

58. *Massachusetts General Hospital Bulfinch Pavilion,* NRHP, NHL, c.1818, Fruit Street off Charles Street (726-2000); open limited hours all year, no fee; guided tour of Bulfinch*-

designed building with black and green cupola of Ether Dome where ether first used in major surgery; slide presentation of hospital history

59. **Charles River Dam,** Charles River, tours by appointment only (727-0059); all year, no fee; explore and ride locks of Charles River Dam; exhibits and excellent audio-visual history of dam and harbor; access: from Charlestown to City Square to Warren Avenue, red brick building beyond fence at end of Warren Avenue

60. **Museum of Science and Hayden Planetarium,** Science Park, Charles River Dam (723-2500); open daily, all year, fee; extensive and varied displays, programs, demonstrations, some "hands-on," all aspects and fields of science, fascinating to all ages

61. **Dorchester Heights National Historic Site,** NRHP, NHS, Thomas Park, South Boston; open daily, all year, no fee; monument to George Washington's victory when Henry Knox and men placed Ticonderoga cannons on heights and forced British to evacuate Boston on March 17, 1776

62. **John F. Kennedy Library,** University of Massachusetts, Boston Campus, off Morrissey Boulevard, specially marked exit off Route 3, Dorchester (929-4500); open daily, all year, fee; exhibits warmly relive career of JFK and politics, plus extensive archives available for research

63. **Arnold Arboretum,** NRHP, NHL, Arborway, Route 1 and Center Street, Jamaica Plain (524-1718); open daily, all year, no fee; over 6,000 trees, shrubs, vines—many labeled; 300-acre park designed by Frederic Law Olmsted,* funded by Harvard, established in 1880 by New Bedford merchant James Arnold*

64. **Franklin Park Zoo,** Blue Hills Avenue and Seaver Street, Route 1 to Route 28, Dorchester; zoo and bird world open daily, all year, no fee; Chidren's Zoo open extended season, fee; exhibits indoors and outdoors; children's petting and feeding zoo; educational programs

CHARLESTOWN—*Where Puritans came in 1629 before settling Boston; long a shipbuilding center; town burned after Battle of Bunker Hill; now restoration progresses; across Charles River via Charlestown or Fitzgerald bridges; see Charlestown map insert*

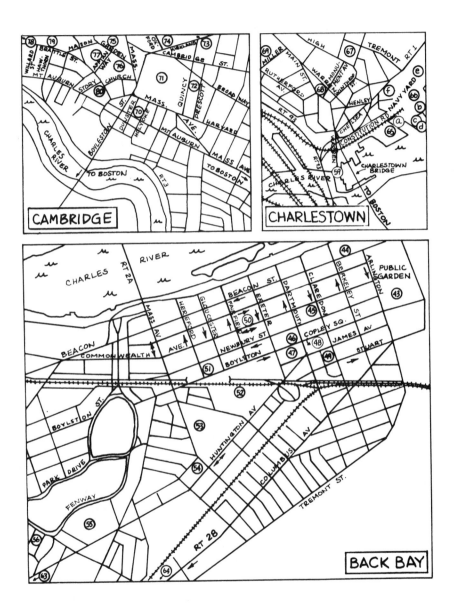

CAMBRIDGE

CHARLESTOWN

BACK BAY

USS *Constitution* and Boston Skyline, July 4th turn about cruise

65. FT—*Bunker Hill Pavilion,* "Whites of Their Eyes," next to USS *Constitution* (241-7575); open daily, all year, fee; three dimensional, multimedia re-creation of first Revolutionary battle Bunker Hill

66. FT—*Charlestown Navy Yard,* NRHP, NHL, 1800, (242-5601); open daily, all year, no fee, parking available right outside yard; includes:

    a. *USS Constitution,* NRHP, NHL, 1797, open daily, all year, no fee; *Old Ironsides* oldest ship afloat; in late 1700s blockaded pirates of North African Barbary states; defeated British Navy in War of 1812; now takes "turnaround" cruise in harbor every July 4th; tour historic ship with expert Navy guides

    b. *Constitution Museum,* near *Old Ironsides,* (426-1812), open daily, all year, fee; history, construction, and life on board, with multimedia presentation; building was 1832 Engine House

    c. *Dry Dock,* America's first, 1830

    d. *USS Cassin Young,* tour World War Two destroyer

    e. *Ropewalk,* one of fourteen buildings here designed by Alexander Parris,* here most of Navy cordage made, only complete ropewalk remaining in country

    f. *Commandant's House,* 1805

67. FT—**Bunker Hill Monument,** 1826, NRHP, NHL, 43 Monument
Square (241-7505); open daily, all year, no fee; obelisk de-
signed by Solomon Willard* at redoubt site of fortification of
Revolution's first battle; once called Breed's Hill, now Bunker
Hill; climb stairs to great view; living history programs on
weekends weather permitting; Square also features array of
Victorian period houses

68. **Old Warren Tavern,** pre-1780, 2 Pleasant Street, corner Main
(241-8500); open all year as restaurant; probably Charlestown's oldest building, structure and upper windows original,
rest carefully restored; named for beloved prime mover of
Revolution, patriot leader Joseph Warren who died at age
thirty-four in the Battle of Bunker Hill; note other historic
houses in triangle: *Timothy Thompson House,* c.1794, 119
Main Street, a classic Federal; and *Timothy Thompson, Jr.
House,* 1805, on Pleasant Street; with other Georgian and
Federals on Warren Street

69. **Phipps Street Burying Ground,** NRHP, 1631, between Main and
Rutherford Streets, enter at Phipps Street; open daily, all
year, no fee; one of three oldest in Boston, 1642 oldest marker

CAMBRIDGE—*Founded 1630, home of first college, Harvard, also
MIT, Radcliffe; academic, residential, commercial center;
across Charles River from Boston; suggest drive to Harvard
Square area via Massachusetts Avenue, park, walk; see
Cambridge map insert*

Brattle Street and Cambridge Walking Tour, follow blue oval
markers along "Tory Row" (Brattle Street), where even the
theater has exhibits to wander through, and beyond to other
Cambridge historical houses and sites; pamphlet through
Cambridge Historical Commission

70. **Holyoke Information Center, Harvard University,** between Massachusetts Avenue and Mt. Auburn Street (495-1573); open
daily, all year, no fee; offers guided tours of Harvard, maps,
information; parking lot suggested on Mt. Auburn Street at
Brattle Street

71. **Harvard Yard,** NRHP, between Cambridge Street and Massachusetts Avenue; open daily, all year (Yard only), no fee; original
campus, America's first college; historic buildings frame the
Yard, enclosed since 1636; buildings include: ivy-clad Massachusetts Hall, NRHP, NHL, 1718; bell tower and cupola-

capped Harvard Hall, 1764; Hollis Hall, 1762; Bulfinch-designed Stoughton Hall, 1804; Holden Chapel; Holworthy Hall, 1812; and most imposing Bulfinch-designed University Hall, NRHP, NHL, 1813

72. *Fogg Art Museum,* 32 Quincy Street (495-2387); open daily, all year; no fee; fine arts collection spanning civilization, largest of any university

73. *Busch-Reisinger Museum,* 29 Kirkland Street (495-2338); open all year, no fee; significant collection of Central and Northern European art

74. *Harvard University Museum,* 24 Oxford Street at Divinity Avenue (495-2248); open daily, all year, fee; four museums, including archeology and ethnology, zoology, botany, and mineralogy; special glass flowers exhibit

75. *Cambridge Common,* 1631, Garden Street; open daily, all year, no fee; common grazing land where militia trained, elections were held, and people listened to speakers such as fiery revivalist George Whitefield*; see trees named for memories "Election Oak," "Whitefield Elm," "Washington Elm," and captured British cannon

76. *Christ Church,* NRHP, NHL, HABS, 1761, Garden Street; open daily, all year, no fee; classic New England architecture, beautifully restored; began as Anglican church; when Tories fled became patriots' barracks; on December 31, 1775, General and Mrs. George Washington worshipped here in pew ninety-three; next is *Old Burying Ground,* 1635, where early settlers and first eight Harvard presidents buried

77. *Radcliffe Yard,* Garden Street; open daily (Yard Only), all year, no fee; Georgian-style administrative center of college includes 1806 Fay House, possibly Bulfinch-designed

78. *Lee Nichols House,* 159 Brattle Street; open all year, limited hours, fee; built 1657, now Cambridge Historical Society

79. *Longfellow National Historic Site,* NHS, HABS, 1759, 105 Brattle Street (876-4491); open daily, all year, fee; striking Georgian mansion with regal projected and pedimented pavilion; built for Loyalist Major John Vassall, became Washington's headquarters in 1775; later, Harvard Professor Henry Wadsworth Longfellow and wife Fanny Appleton created mecca for worldly greats including Charles Dickens here; Longfellow lived forty-five years here, wrote most of his

Longfellow Home

famous works; books and furnishings remain much as left by Longfellows in 1882; National Park Service offers regular guided tours
80. *Brattle House,* NRHP, HABS, 42 Brattle Street, 1727, Loyalist owner left, Major Thomas Mifflin occupied, was Washington's aide-de-camp, commissary-general; now Cambridge Center for Adult Education

HISTORY OF LYNN, NAHANT AND SWAMPSCOTT

Early Lynn included Swampscott, Nahant, Saugus, Lynnfield, and Reading. Within these boundaries was found a wealth of natural beauty—from silvery beaches to high coastal cliffs, from protected river banks to the unguarded peninsula of Nahant. Here natural beauty and ruggedness balanced between wild winter storms and calm, idyllic summer days.

This well-endowed land was included in a land grant sold by the Council of England in 1628 to six English patentees. One of the six patentees, John Humphrey,* was a man of prestige and wealth, who, while still in England, was chosen the first deputy governor of Massachusetts Bay Colony in 1629. From England he did much to obtain money and supplies for the Massachusetts Bay Colony. In 1634 Humphrey sailed for the New World and settled on an extensive farm in Lynn, where he ably served his settlement and colony for seven years before returning to England.

The infant settlement grew as groups of colonists arrived and began tilling the lands in this predominantly farming community. In 1635 two shoemakers, Philip Kertland and Edmund Bridges introduced an industry that would govern the economy of Lynn for nearly three centuries. In the early 1640s Thomas Dexter and Robert Bridges set the groundwork for the first complete ironworks in the country, which would be known in 1643 as Hammersmith on the banks of the Saugus River. Thus as early as the 1600s the lifestyle of Lynn was determined by working men who took pride in their craftsmanship.

Lynn was established as Saugus in 1630. Two years later, her first meetinghouse was built on the corner of Shepard and Summer Streets, and her congregation gathered under the often-questionable leadership of the Reverend Stephen Bachiler, whose lifestyle and beliefs were a little too liberal for early Lynn. He was soon asked to leave.

Their second minister, the Reverend Samuel Whiting, was loved and respected by his church and community for forty-three years. In honor of this beloved pastor's hometown in England the town was named Lynn in 1637.

The 1700s brought growth and change to Lynn. In 1726 shipyards were built at Liberty Square. The year 1750 witnessed the arrival of Welshman John Adams Dagyr, who raised the quality and efficiency of making ladies' shoes to the level of Europe's craftsmanship. About 1793 Ebenezer Breed introduced the use of morocco leather, which added a new industry in itself and a new dimension to shoemaking. He was also instrumental in having Congress impose a duty on foreign shoes, which greatly protected the local shoe industry.

The 1800s saw the shoe industry flourishing with the introduction of the sewing machine, the move from small shoemakers' shops to large brick manufacturing centers and the invention of the lasting machine by Jan Matzeliger. Resort hotels were built in Lynn, Swampscott, and Nahant, where inland neighbors and visitors could enjoy the beauty of the seacoast. Other industries such as textiles, brick, chocolate, tools, hardware, and electric works took their place in industrial-oriented Lynn. Fishing and lobstering added to the economy. By 1850 Lynn's industries had grown to the point where she became a city. Today's largest industry in Lynn was first founded in 1883 as the Thomson-Houston Electric Company. It merged in 1892 with the Edison General Electric Company and is now known as the General Electric Company, the largest manufacturer of electrical products in the United States.

In 1889 a great holocaust destroyed 334 buildings with a reported loss of $4,959,989, as fire spread from Almond Street through the center of Lynn. Thanks to a dynamic mayor, the Honorable Asa T. Newhall, and a determined citizenry, within two years 465 new buildings were erected. Her industrial community revived, building nearer the railroads which had come to the city in the mid-1800s. Sadly, in November of 1981, less than one hundred years after the Great Fire of 1889, many of Lynn's restored buildings were lost in another tragic fire. But like the great Phoenix, she will rebuild.

Three interesting women take their places in the history of Lynn. Though certainly not of equal importance, each had her own special contribution to make. Chronologically, the first, Moll Pitcher, affected only the lives she touched. During the late 1700s people from all walks of life made their way to her small, unadorned cottage on Essex Street, seeking her mystical powers as a fortune-teller and possible clairvoyant. Her words swayed many a business venture and delayed or hastened many a ship's departure. The second, Lydia E. Pinkham, started in 1873 the production of a patent medicine that became as familiar in households as today's aspirin. Her Lydia Pinkham Elixir was advertised to cure female ailments and was produced at 271 Western Avenue until 1973. It is still being made in Puerto Rico, thus keeping her name and herbal medicine alive. The third lady, Mary Baker Eddy,* had the most lasting and far-reaching influence of all. She founded the Church of Christ, Scientist in 1879, which has brought comfort, strength, and healing to people throughout the world.

Swampscott, Lynn's early fishing village, incorporated as a town in 1852, has always retained her loyalty to the sea and still boasts an active fishing and lobstering fleet. Here Theophilus Brackett invented the very seaworthy Swampscott Dory in 1841 and Ebenezer Thorndike adapted the lobster pot in 1808 to a rectangular design which proved easier to stack. The 1800s saw gracious hotels with unparalleled views built along her beautiful coast. According to historian James R. Newhall, Swampscott had become so famed a "watering place" that during 1872 ten to eleven thousand visitors enjoyed the elegant facilities and congenial company of this fashionable resort. Here Elihu Thomson* built in 1889 his home with its magnificent interior paneling and carved woodwork. In his home laboratory he developed some of his electrical patents, which ultimately formed the basis for much of General Electric's work. Frederick Law Olmsted* laid out many of the streets, gardens, and park area along Monument Avenue. Swampscott continues to draw summer residents and visitors to her ever-changing, ever-beautiful coastal world.

Nahant, incorporated in 1853 as the smallest town in Massachusetts, first served as common wood lots and pastureland for the people of Lynn. Prior to 1803 there were only three permanent homes on her rugged peninsula. By the 1820s, even before the road was built from Lynn in 1848, summer hotels were welcoming Boston's aristocracy. They came by steamboat to enjoy silvery beaches and beautiful ocean vistas. Cornelius Coolidge* laid out roads and built substantial homes at East Point, where in later years Henry Cabot Lodge* and his brother-in-law, George Abbot James lived. Frederick Tudor* came to Nahant in 1824 and spent much of his time beautifying the peninsula. He built a hotel, Maolis Gardens, and Town Wharf, where steamboats once docked and which is now home to Nahant's active fishing and lobstering fleet and her summer flotillas of yachts, sailboats, and small craft.

Lynn, Swampscott, and Nahant continue to offer the hospitality of their beaches and seacoast to tourists and residents alike. These three follow their tradition of combining natural beauty with prideful work.

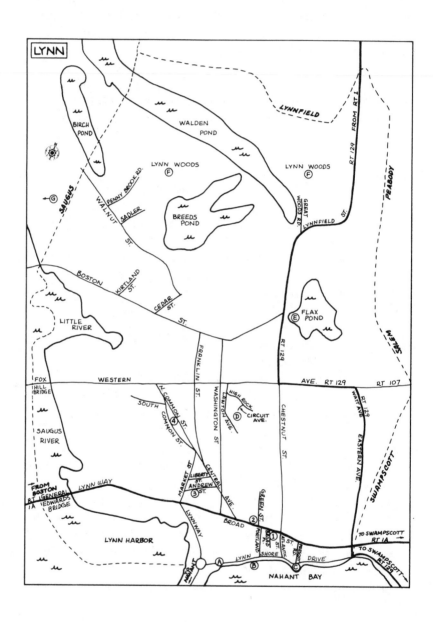

LYNN

DIRECTIONS:
From Route 1 follow Route 129 going east. Follow Route 129 in Lynn. From Boston enter Lynn by Route 1A over the General Edwards Bridge onto the Lynnway, which runs into Broad Street.

#1
Mary Baker Eddy House
12 Broad Street
c.1870s
Open seasonally and by
appointment, no fee

From Route 1 take Route 129, Lynnfield Street, 4.2 miles to where Route 129 turns a sharp left on Western Avenue. Do not turn, but continue straight on Chestnut Street 1.3 miles to Route 1A, Broad Street. Turn right on Broad Street. The Eddy House is immediately on the left. Park behind, just past house on Broad Street Place (Dead End).

In a rocking chair in an attic room of this home, Mary Baker Eddy completed the final fourteen pages of her book *Science and Health* in 1875. It was the culmination of nine years of prayer, searching the Scriptures, and teaching and practicing metaphysical healing. In that small room, undoubtedly cold in winter and hot in summer, with its skylight open to the stars and the eternity of the sky, she found a sanctuary from worldly hostilities and distractions. In 1866 Mary had been miraculously healed, after a severe fall, through reading and sudden insight into the scriptures. (see Swampscott #3) Since that time she had searched relentlessly for a true understanding of Christian healing, and for how she could impart that great knowledge to others. Thus the completion of her book, which set down her basic beliefs, proved to be the first concrete step in the stairway to Christian Science faith, which now serves and helps thousands of people throughout the world.

As you visit the home, envision a delicate, dedicated, and devoted lady teaching her students and guiding her followers. In the front parlor Mrs. Eddy was ordained as a minister of her faith. In this home she was married to Asa Gilbert Eddy in 1877. And from here she preached in Boston and in 1879 received the charter for the Church of Christ, Scientist.

Rocking Chair where Mary Baker Eddy finished her book
Science and Health

The Mary Baker Eddy House is owned, and has been restored, by the Christian Science Church. A few of the furnishings belonged to Mrs. Eddy, but in most cases the rose colors and furnishings were of the type and period that she would have used. Let the well-informed guides, who have an obvious love for the home, bring its history alive for you.

#2	*Exit from Eddy House parking area.*
Lynn Historical Society	*Turn left on Broad Street and at the first*
Hyde-Mills House	*traffic light turn right on Green Street.*
125 Green Street	*The Lynn Historical House is the first on*
1836	*the left.*
Open all year, no fee	

Lynn history unfolds as you walk through the museum within the Hyde-Mills House. You realize the importance of Lynn's early developing shoe industry as you study displays of tools, methods, materials, and a unique medallion of 234 different shoe soles, one for each manufacturer in Lynn in 1892.

A separate 1830 early shoe-factory building, a "ten footer," is in the backyard. You see the four benches set up, tools ready, smell the air full of the aroma of shoemaking, take in the apparent clutter just waiting for the cordwainers to appear. Here was very early division of labor. Women worked at home on the uppers; men attached these to the soles, in the "ten footers," amid lively discussions of politics and religion. In 1832 women started organizing trade unions as the home cottage industry moved to small factories and drew problem-causing lines between owners and workers.

Lynn achievements are evident in other displays within the museum. Some of General Electric cofounder Elihu Thomson's* pioneering experimental work with electricity can be seen. There are many paintings by Lynn artists or featuring Lynn subjects. The "Singing Hutchinson"* family, like an early Trapp Family, is represented, as are the main characters of a Lynn Woods* legend, a pirate and his two ladies.

The museum house was built in 1836 by two carpenters, Hyde and Mills, as a two-family home with the early speculative potential of renting a small upstairs apartment above each half. The rooms are carefully preserved and furnished from Lynn houses. Halls, basement, and an addition expand the museum to include displays of a Colonial room taken from a home begun in 1775, a fire exhibit, and a hands-on industrial room. You will see the Samuel McIntire* eagle from the 1804 Lynn Academy, as well as a Simon Willard clock and many other arrays of treasures and memorabilia reflecting Lynn life.

#3
GAR Building and Museum
58 Andrew Street
1885
Open all year by
appointment, donations

Return to Broad Street and turn right. At "V" in road bear left following Route 1A signs. At second traffic light turn right on Market Street, go through railroad underpass to third traffic light and turn right on Liberty Street. Go one block, turn right; go one block, turn right on Andrew; park in that block either on street or in parking lot. GAR Building is on left in middle of block.

The Grand Army of the Republic building stands as a lasting memorial to the Lynn men and women who served in the Civil War. The following quote from 1861 demonstrates their patriotism. "In five hours after the requisition arrived, two full [Lynn] companies were armed and ready for duty. . . . These two companies . . . became celebrated in the early part of the war, for discipline, promptness and heroism."[29]

With over two thousand members, Post 5 in Lynn was the largest

Civil War Veterans' post in the country. In 1922 the building was turned over to the city with a board of seven unpaid trustees to maintain it as a permanent Civil War memorial. Meetings continued here until 1934, with the last member dying in 1944. For the next forty years the building was used for a variety of activities, saw days of vandalism, and parts were rented out for small businesses as they are today.

Then in 1974 Joe Shanahan, appreciating the historic value of the building, began to organize and create a military museum. Today, thanks to his efforts and those of the board of trustees and the city of Lynn, several rooms are retained as museum rooms with the perfectly preserved Grand Hall on the third floor, the pièce de résistance.

Starting on the ground floor, visit the banquet hall where World War One veterans still meet. The walls are covered with framed pictures of their comrades-in-arms who died during that first world conflict. A picture of the final review of the Massachusetts 26th at Camp Devens on April 22, 1919, adds to the emotion of the room. Climb the stairs past the huge painting of three local brothers killed in the Civil War. Then enter the display rooms where you will see regimental and divisional histories, swords, guns, pictures, badges, flags, and uniforms. Climb a second flight to see additional relics from the Civil War as well as pictures and diagrams of the hated Andersonville Prison.

Then, step into the Grand Hall where you can almost see veterans filling the galleries and their commanders at appropriate podiums. The walls of this superbly preserved hall are covered with 1,148 pictures of Civil War veterans, all of whom belonged here. This Grand Army Memorial Building and Museum is truly a living memorial to its founders.

#4
Lynn Common
Lynn Public Library, 1900, NRHP
Old West Burying Ground
Open all year, no fee

Continue on Andrew Street; take first right on Market Street. Turn left at second traffic light, City Hall Square. Go one-half block and stay to left on North Common Street, where the Lynn Common begins.

Lynn's impressive *Common* is appropriately shaped like the sole of a shoe, symbolic of Lynn's way of life for two centuries. It was once the active hub of the town, with the Old Tunnel Meeting House standing in the center. The Common is bounded on the east by an 1873 Civil War

Monument cast in Munich and on the west by the Old West Burying Ground.

The magnificent *Lynn Public Library* at North Common and Franklin Streets is a study of classic Greek-Roman Revival architecture built in 1900. Full-height Corinthian columns mark the entrance to this dominating stone structure. Within, stone, marble, and tile floors lead to walls of ornate carvings, columns, pilasters, and a huge historic mural. Ceilings are most elaborate with rosettes and patterns repeated in the rotunda, reading room, and balcony areas.

You can drive for blocks along the central open green, lined with paved paths and benches. Many interesting varieties of architecture—representing different eras of history, wealth, and values—can be found in the homes and other buildings surrounding the Common. They mingle with practical twentieth-century three deckers as well as the turreted Armory and the Classical High School.

At the far end of the Common is the *Old West Burying Ground* at the corner of Elm Street. The neatly kept, well-fenced ground is the final resting place of Lynn's earliest settlers, including the Reverend Samuel Whiting* of the first meetinghouse, poet-historian-engineer Alonzo Lewis, and Moll Pitcher,* noted Revolutionary-times fortune-teller. Across South Street is the oldest remaining church building, now the Gregg Neighborhood House. Greek Revival, it was built in 1830 with the steeple added in 1851. Nearby are early homes with historical date markers.

This ends the guided tour section of Lynn. Return on the other side of the Common taking South Common Street back to Market Street (traffic light and City Hall Square); bear right on Market and follow it back across Route 1A. Follow signs to Nahant. You are now on Lynnway; follow it to rotary. First right off rotary leads over causeway to Nahant.

Lynn Beaches and Parks and Additional Points of Interest

 **Lynn Shore Drive**   Scenic drive from Nahant causeway to Swampscott with unobstructed open-ocean views; can be heavily trafficked; limited parking; open all year, no fee

(B) **Lynn Beach**
    Lynn Shore Drive

Continuing expanse of open sandy crescent; benches, bicycling, jogging, lifeguards, paved paths along beach, picnicking, swimming, walking; limited on street parking; open all year, no fee

(C) **Red Rock**
    Lynn Shore Dirve, foot of
    Prescott Street

Small grassy promotory extending beyond Lynn Beach into Nahant Bay; opposite Christian Science Church, symbolic as Red Rock was a favorite meditation site of Mary Baker Eddy;* benches, picnicking, walking; no parking; open all year, no fee

(D) **High Rock Park**
    end of Circuit Avenue

Once Indian land, scene of bonfires and celebrations; highest point in Lynn; rugged rock-topped summit capped by crenolated, castle-like tower; magnificent fifty-mile panoramic views of Lynn and Harbor, Nahant, Swampscott, and onward to Boston skyline and western hills; stone cottage and land owned in 1800s by "Singing Hutchinson"* family, who traveled Europe giving concerts for social causes; they gave land to city; overexultant 1865 celebration of Civil War victory burned original wooden observatory; playground; limited parking; open all year, no fee

(E) **Flax Pond**
    Chestnut Street, Route
    129

Pretty pond seen from Chestnut Street, with houses all around; once scene of colonial times flax-soaking where women washed and prepared flax along the shores; bathhouse, benches, lifeguards, picnicking, playground, swimming; limited on street parking; open all year, no fee

(F) **Lynn Woods**
    Access:
    Great Woods Road
    Pennybrook Road

Over 2,000 acres of woods, streams, ponds, hills, boulders, caves reachable by many trails; from Great Woods Road an access road to left leads to interesting old stone municipal golf club, in winter a cross-country ski center with trails and lessons; Pirates' Glen and Dungeon Rock are site of fascinating legend involving pirates and reference to a grand Spanish lady, an Indian princess, and a Colonial American beauty; details vary, though there are paintings of pirate Thomas Veal, Spanish Clorinda, and American Arabel at

Lynn Historical Society Museum;* presence of pirates was explained by furtive arrangements to purchase chains and other hardware from Saugus Ironworks; silver hidden in woods for purchases; story expands with pirate Thomas Veal living in Lynn Woods with (or without) one or more of legendary ladies until earthquake closed cave and created Pirates' Dungeon in 1688; later twelve-year attempt to discover alleged treasure resulted in many blastings producing nothing but rubble and deep trench; area marked by Dungeon Rock, in which you can see outline of sleeping pirate guarding treasure; facilities: hiking, jogging, nature classes in summer, picnicking, skiing; parking; open all year, no fee

Saugus Ironworks
National Historic Site
244 Central Street
Saugus
NHS

Nearby Saugus has National Historic Site, reconstructed c.1650, Saugus Ironworks, first complete ironworks in country; fine restoration guided by architects of Williamsburg; demonstrates beginning of vital American industry; can watch process demonstrated; includes Ironmakers House (an interesting seventeenth-century historic house, restored by Wallace Nutting in 1915); iron furnace, forge, slitting mill; self-guided touring; parking; open all year, no fee

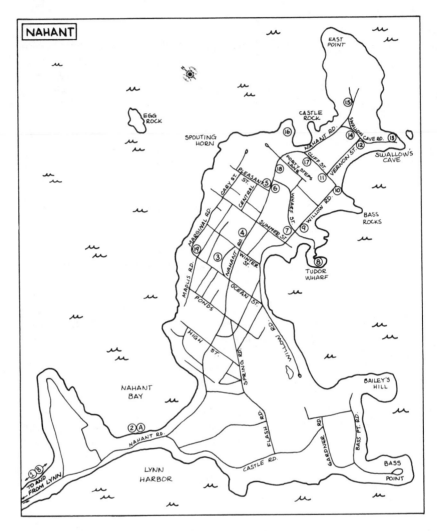

NAHANT

DIRECTIONS:
Enter Nahant from Lynn by taking either the Lynnway or Lynn Shore Drive to Nahant Road, which leads over causeway to Nahant. A drive is suggested as there is no public parking for nonresidents beyond Nahant Beach. Off season, pausing to appreciate a historic building or fantastic view is allowed, as well as ten-minute parking at stores or other public buildings.

A drive will allow you to relive Nahant's interesting past—from days of Indian summer camps to Colonial cattle grazing, a leap to Boston Brahmin summer cottages, then to elaborate (now gone) hotels—

including introductions to Nahant's distinguished citizens. Here among the people who have enjoyed Nahant's ocean advantages are such as the Cabots and Lodges, poets and governors, judges, ambassadors, congressmen, cabinet members, and United States Presidents Taft and both Roosevelts, as well as Harvard presidents, tennis greats, American cup contenders, and people for whom cities were named, the Lowells and Lawrences.

As you leave the traffic circle in Lynn and enter the causeway, now Nahant Road, #1 *Nahant Beach** is on the left. Nahant Beach is the beginning of the beautiful crescent of sandy beach reaching from Nahant along Lynn's coast to Swampscott. The beach is lined with benches and has bathhouse and parking with entrance at the Nahant end. (parking fee)

Continue on Nahant Road which was a sandbar until the mid-1800s, past the former #2 *Coast Guard Station* now a recreation center for members of the armed forces with "walk on" beach privileges for all.

Continue on Nahant Road; take the fourth left on Ocean Street; and immediately turn right onto a curving road that leads up to the Nahant Country Club. Here #3 the *Nahant Historical Society* has its headquarters and museum. Intriguing special exhibits vary, such as one featuring wedding gowns of three generations of Lowell brides. (open seasonally, limited hours, no fee)

The Club's old stone walls of Nahant granite were raised about 1824 for the summer home of Nahant's unusual benefactor, Ice King Frederick Tudor.* Tudor perservered through scoffing, bankruptcy, and debtor's imprisonment to create and capture the ice market for such as Havana and Charleston, as well as icing English drinks as far away as Canton and Calcutta. He devised insulated boats for refrigeration and overcame every obstacle to accomplish the arrival of New England ice in tropical lands in the 1830s, timed beautifully to provide a much-needed crutch for Boston's East India trade. He is also credited with planting trees on Nahant, no mean feat for early settlers had cut trees on woodlots and opened pasture land to ocean winds. He planted Balm of Gilead trees as windblocks, then many successful fruit trees and vegetable crops within their protection. His home was purchased in 1889 by renowned Nahant summer people to become the exclusive summer club which hosted much early lawn tennis. It was the General Electric Thomson Club from 1940 to 1965 and is now the Nahant Country Club.

Follow the country-club drive to Winter Street and turn right. Take the first left back onto Nahant Road. On the left in the middle of the first block is #4 at 298 Nahant Road. Here, in this pre-1841 Georgian-appearing house, summered *Harriet Beecher Stowe*.

Continue on Nahant Road to the corner of Pleasant Street where #5 the *Nahant Public Library* is on the left, home of Massachusetts's third public library. It began in 1819 in one of Nahant's first schools, the Old Stone Schoolhouse. In 1895 this Neo-Gothic structure of Weymouth seam-faced granite, Ohio sandstone trim, and green slate roof was built to house the library and town hall. In 1912 the Town Hall was built, separating the two. Within, the dark cypress woodwork of the main room is complemented by the quartered oak of the impressive reading room, both with intricately carved molding, panels, and fireplaces. Museum displays are found throughout.

Across Nahant Road from the library is #6 at 339 Nahant Road, a part of the original 1829 "Gentlemen's Residence," a country estate with outbuildings now separate houses. It was built by a Codman, owned by a Paige whom Daniel Webster* frequently visited, then owned by textile magnate Abbott Lawrence.

From Nahant Road, take next right on Wharf Street and follow it around three blocks to Willow Street. On the right, at the corner of Willow and Wharf Streets is #7 162 Willow. Part of the home was once the boardinghouse where guest *Henry Wadsworth Longfellow* wrote the "Golden Fleece" and part of "Hiawatha." Across the street is Marjoram Park with benches, walks, and magnificent views of the Boston skyline.

Continue on Wharf Street out to #8 *Tudor Wharf*, historic landing place of Boston steamboats and pilot boats. From here harbor pilots were summoned to guide ships coming into Boston Harbor. The wharf is now picturesquely decorated with working lobster and fishing gear as well as being home port for recreational sailors. You can see nearby Bailey's Hill and the sites of old forts with World War Two gun emplacements still visible.

After leaving the Town Wharf turn right on Willow, and #9 the *Fremont House* will be the second driveway on the right at 171 Willow. Marked by a gatepost and lamp, the weathered shingle house is off the road, toward the water. Here summered General and Mrs. John C. Fremont before Civil War times. The fierce abolitionist and persistent explorer who conquored the west was called the "Pathfinder" and was also the first Republican candidate for president. His wife, Jessie Benton Fremont, was the daughter of a powerful senator and herself an expressive writer, noted for her beauty, brains, and abilities.

Continue on Willow Road to the sharp left turn where it becomes Cliff Street, and #10, 211 Willow Road, is on the right. *Cornelius Coolidge*, architect and builder of some of Boston's Beacon Hill mansions, became the first summer real estate developer of the North Shore when he laid out streets and started to build houses here. Some remain today, such as this much-modified home at 211 Willow Road. Nearby at the cove, the old wharf once landed steamboats full of summer visitors to the Nahant Hotel, when Nahant was called "Cold Roast Boston." Around the corner, at 44 Cliff Street on the right, Oliver Wendell Holmes summered.

Following Cliff Street you see #11 the *Nahant Village Church* on the left at the head of Vernon Street. The stone, wood, and slate Gothic Cottage–style building houses a happy combination of congregations, forming an ecumenical protestant church. The chapel has beautiful stained-glass windows.

Turn right onto Vernon Street and drive to the end. Turn right; the first house on the right is #12 another Cornelius Coolidge house at 20 Swallow Cave Road. The rambling stone and wood structure, with its many porches, gables, and chimneys, was the scene of a film on the Brinks Robbery.

Drive to 3 Swallow Cave Road #13 where the Franklin Delano Roosevelts gathered when their son John married the daughter of the house, *Ann Clark*, in 1938. The wedding ceremony was in the church with the reception at the country club in Nahant. The adjacent white pillar marks the walk-on access to Swallow Cave.

Turn around and drive to 36 Swallow Cave Road #14, first house past Vernon Road. Also built by Coolidge, it was formerly the Appleton estate where the *first lawn tennis* was played in this country in 1874. Here and at the country club, tennis pioneers, F. R. and Richard Sears and Jim Dwight, were early "sticky" players. Dwight became the first Yank to play at Wimbledon, organized the United States National Lawn Tennis Association, and was named father of American tennis.

Across from the former Appleton estate is the entrance to #15 *East Point*, the site of the 1823 Nahant Hotel, the first grand hotel of America's first established summer colony. It was builty by Colonel Thomas Perkins, China-trade merchant and Boston-based entrepreneur, whose own summer cottage was Nahant's first. The elite of Boston were drawn here by excursion boats promising possible glimpses of an often-sighted sea serpent as well as the healthy air and elegance. All combined to "drain every drawing room in Boston worth draining"[30] to the extent that some even made do with quarters over the chicken house. One Perkins granddaughter was Elizabeth Agassiz, founder and president of Radcliffe College. Her husband, Louis Agassiz, was a Swiss naturalist and had a marine lab and aquarium at Nahant.

After the hotel era ended, Nahant remained a select Boston Society. East Point became home to the Lodges, typical of Nahant's aristocrats. The land later became a Nike site and now is the Marine Science Institute of Northeastern University.

Continue on the road, which becomes Nahant Road at curve opposite East Point, past Forty Steps Beach; and pause just before Cliff Street. From here you can see #16 the strikingly Greek Revival 1829 house which looks like a *Greek Temple* on the right. It was designed by Samuel Eliot and was home to the Mifflin family of publishers. The observation tower is now the office of the naval architect owner.

To the left, a short way down Cliff Street on the right, you see #17 the *Lodge Villa*, at 5 Cliff Street. It was given to Senator Henry Cabot Lodge's mother by her father in 1850 and was to have been developer Coolidge's own showplace before creditors intervened. Uniquely painted, it has remained structurally unchanged since those early days of summer grandeur and is on the National Register.

Bear right on Nahant Road. On the left, the second house after Forty Steps Lane is #18 the *Whitney Homestead*, at 369 Nahant. Possibly as early as 1717 part of this structure was the home of Samuel Breed, designated innkeeper. After the last Breed left in 1817 new owner Jesse Rice added a wing and the "Rice House" became the ancient hotel mentioned by Nathaniel Hawthorne.* Another wing was added in 1859 by new owner Albert Whitney, who continued the hotel enterprise which survived into the twentieth century. It is now a long, clapboarded Colonial-style double house, with portions being the oldest in town.

Turn right on Pleasant Street; take second left on Cary Street; and continue on road staying close to water. Where the road turns away from ocean vista, on the left is #19, the *Rock Temple*, on a ledge with magnificent views of Nahant Bay and Egg Rock on your right. This interesting native-stone structure is all that remains of what was claimed to be America's first full-scale amusement park. Maolis Gardens were created by Ice King, then Fun King Frederick Tudor (see #3) at age seventy-six as Nahant's hotel era died. Picture, if you can, this area fenced, treed, with restaurant, pool, dance hall, hotel, pavillions, ice cream parlor, swings, and carnival games. The remaining Rock Temple is also called the "Witch House," from the story of a cave under it said to have been used during Salem witchcraft times to hide a woman and her two daughters.

This ends the guided tour section of Nahant. Follow Ocean Street back to Nahant Road. Drive back over causeway; turn right on Lynn Shore Drive staying next to the water; and continue to Swampscott.

Nahant Beaches

A) **Short Beach or Coast Guard Beach Nahant Road**

Sandy beach at former Coast Guard station, which is now recreation center for members of the armed forces; "walk on" privileges only; open all year, no fee

B) **Nahant Beach Causeway to Nahant off Lynn Shore Drive**

Beautiful, long, open sandy beach, links with Lynn's beach to form inviting crescent to walk, bike, jog along; facilities: bathhouse, benches, concession stand, lifeguards, path, picnicking; parking; open all year, parking fee in season

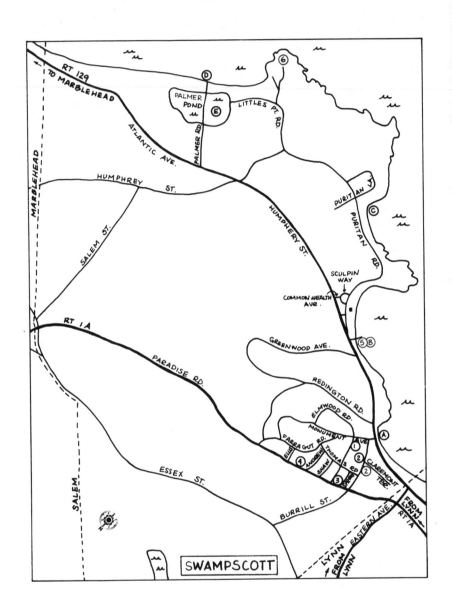

RT 129
TO MARBLEHEAD
MARBLEHEAD
ATLANTIC AVE.
PALMER POND
PALMER RD.
LITTLES PT. RD.
HUMPHREY ST.
SALEM ST.
HUMPHERY ST.
PURITAN V.
PURITAN RD.
SCULPIN WAY
COMMON WEALTH AVE.
GREENWOOD AVE.
RT 1A
PARADISE RD.
REDINGTON RD.
ELMWOOD RD.
MONUMENT AVE.
FARRAGUT RD.
ELLIOTT ST.
ANDREW RD.
THOMAS RD.
SHAW RD.
CLAREMONT TER.
ESSEX ST.
SALEM
BURRILL ST.
FROM LYNN RT 1A
LYNN
FROM EASTERN AVE.
FROM LYNN

SWAMPSCOTT

346

Swampscott

DIRECTIONS:
From Route 95 drive east on Route 129 through Lynn all the way to
the water; cross Route 1A; and turn left on Humphrey Street, Route
129. Follow Humphrey Street along the water into Swampscott.
From Lynn take Route 1A, Broad Street, or Lynn Shore Drive.
Keep to water's edge and enter Swampscott on Humphrey Street.

#1
Elihu Thomson House
Town Administration
Building
Monument Avenue and
Elmwood Road
1889
Open all year as town
offices, no fee
NHL

*From Humphrey Street take first left on
Monument Avenue, which is a divided
road; keep to right of monument and continue up right side of divided road one
block and turn left on Elmwood Road.
The Thomson Building is on the left at
corner of Elmwood and Monument. Park
behind Thomson Building off of Elmwood
Road for #1-2.*

Swampscott may well be unique in the grandeur of its town administrative offices, housed within the sedate manor house of General
Electric cofounder Elihu Thomson. Visitors are encouraged to ask
questions as knowledgeable town employees are proud of their lavish
surroundings.

The red brick Georgian Revival mansion rose in 1889. The front
facade features a Corinthian Palladian-style front portico, quoined
corners, broken scroll pediments, and pink Vermont slate hip roof
capped by balustrades repeated over the portico and crowned by urn
finials. But the greatest pleasure awaits within—probably the finest
wood carvings found in New England today. Enjoy each unique
molding, fireplace wall, window, and panel to appreciate the magnificently hand-carved hard oak.

Now town offices occupy the preserved elegance of the first floor's
sitting, dining, breakfast, music, library, and billiard rooms. The
central hall's unexpectedly delicate carvings include the impressive
stairway with detailed balustrades. The town seal above was designed
by a Civil War medal-of-honor winner and features a member of the
fishing-oriented Phillips family at the helm.

347

Elihu Thomson House Town Administration Building, Swampscott

Upstairs, the study dominates, with deep mahogany paneling and carved oak in definite Moorish flavor carried even to fireplace tiles. In the hall you see the grill through which Professor Thomson's visitors could hear the pipe organ which he built at the age of seventeen, creating and inventing as he constructed it. Speaking-tube outlets can still be seen in this unique home which was illuminated by electricity long before the public knew of such a possibility. Down the hall was the entrance to the once open, arched passage way which allowed Thomson private access to his laboratory above the attached carriage house.

Electrical engineer, inventor, teacher, and holder of over seven hundred patents, Elihu Thomson shared his innovative intellect with the people of Swampscott, Lynn, and ultimately the world. Six years after graduating from high school in Philadelphia, he was teaching chemistry as a full professor at that same school. With Edwin J. Houston, he designed an arc lighting system which resulted in the formation of the American Electric Company in New Britain, Connecticut in 1880. A group of Lynn businessmen bought the New Britain Company and brought the ingenious Thomson and company to Lynn. In 1886 it became the Thomson-Houston Company. In nine years, with final backing from J. P. Morgan, the Thomson-Houston Company merged with the Edison General Electric Company to form the General Electric Company. Thomson, who invented the first high-frequency generator and transformer, three-coil generator, electric welding by the incandescent method, and watt-hour meter to name only a few, served as consultant to GE for forty-five years until his death in 1937.

#2
Swampscott Public
Library, c.1915
Atlantic One, 1845
Burrill Street
Open all year, no fee,
access for Atlantic One
through fire station

The back entrance to the Library is at the rear of the parking lot. Atlantic One is across Burrill Street from the front of the Library, at the corner of Claremont Terrace.

The *town library* was built about 1915 with the same architectural feeling as the Elihu Thomson House, which is not surprising as the Thomsons gave the land and much of the building. Within the library is the Baldwin Room, a comfortable, sunlighted setting inviting research and appreciation of the Swampscott memorabilia collected here.

Across from the library is the proud *Atlantic One*, the oldest active fire kit in the United States. The hand tub was built by an apprentice of Paul Revere in 1845 and was once the only fire protection for Swampscott. After a long career of direct fire fighting, it now competes successfully in musters throughout New England, with its dedicated crew of volunteers.

#3
Mary Baker Eddy House
23 Paradise Road
c.1855
Open seasonally and by
appointment, fee charged

Exit from parking lot, and turn left on Elmwood Road. Follow Elmwood two blocks to Paradise Road; turn left; the Mary Baker Eddy House will be immediately on the left. Parking is just before house.

Paradise Road was aptly named, for this house on Paradise Road is where Mary Baker Eddy's* miraculous healing took place.

In 1865, seeking the peace and renewal of the seashore, Mary Baker Eddy (then Mrs. Patterson) rented rooms in this bright cheery home. It then had lovely gardens and lawns, willow-shaded pond, and meandering stream called the Jordan by its owners. At this time Mary Patterson was an established writer with deep interest in church and temperance work.

On February 1, 1866, an event occurred that would change her life and ultimately bring comfort and healing to thousands. On her way to a temperance meeting in Lynn, she slipped and fell, severely injuring herself to the extent that the doctor felt she might not live and certainly would never walk again. The following day she was brought back to her rooms in Swampscott. On Sunday, February 4, she asked the Reverend Jonas B. Clark, who had been called to attend her, for her Bible. While reading Matthew 9:1–8 a revelation of a deep eternal truth came to her. As a result she was able to leave her bed and walk into the parlor where friends were waiting in great sadness, fearing for her life. The joy of her miraculous healing started her on a nine-year search for an understanding of that healing and insight into how she might impart this healing knowledge to others. (see Lynn #1)

Mary Beecher Longyear, a devoted follower of Mrs. Eddy, bought this house in 1921 to have it restored and maintained as a memorial to Mary Baker Eddy and to the special part it had played in her life. The house was purchased from George Newhall, the milkman who had been sent on February 3, 1866, to tell the Reverend Clark of Mrs. Patterson's severe fall. Today the house is done in the same period furnishings that would have been used in 1866. Several pieces belonged to Mrs. Patterson. A certain sense of expectation is felt as you enter her bright sunny bedroom with its appropriate quote on the wall, "Do Right and Fear Not." For here Mary overcame fear and began a crusade that culminated in the establishment of the Church of Christ, Scientist.

#4
John Humphrey House
99 Paradise Road
c.1637
Open seasonally and by
appointment, no fee

Exit from parking lot and turn right. The Humphrey House is .2 mile on the right just past Andrew Road; before traffic light. But continue to traffic light, turn right and park on Ellis Street. Walk back to house.

A gem of a house, with parts which could well date to the 1630s, the John Humphrey House is the oldest in this and many other towns. It is further distinguished by the people for whom it was named and probably built, Massachusetts Bay Colony's first deputy governor, John Humphrey,* and his wife, Lady Susan. It has since had many additions and alterations and was moved to this site in 1891.

You are immediately in the 1600s when entering the small front hall with well-seasoned banister and narrow, steep stairway. The parlor leaps to Victorian times with furnishings and other treasures from Swampscott's summer hotel era, including appropriate costumes. The back of the house shows its age beautifully, especially in the deep patina of unusual "king's boards," two-feet-wide boards which line the

John Humphrey House

stair wall. The king's mark is visible, showing lumber meant for the Royal Navy only. That Humphrey dared to use this wood openly was a sign of royal favor.

Even in its most rustic state, this house was grand for its period. Some original Delft fireplace tiles remain and were probably brought here by the Humphreys in 1634. The upstairs was finished, an unusual feature that early. In the oldest room a cut in the wall lets you see the hand hewn beams, handmade bricks, and mortar mixed with seaweed. Records show the Humphreys brought timber and bricks with them to build their home.

As you study Swampscott memorabilia you feel the history of the town. Swampscott was noted for the many desperate lifesaving rescues her people made, and photos tell that story. You can see mementos of fire-fighting, shoemaking, early lighting, drugstores, and guns. Here is reference to Swampscott's boast of the oldest highway in the country. From King's Beach in Lynn through Humphrey Street and Puritan Road this ancient Indian path was used by white settlers as early as 1628 and legally declared a public highway on July 5, 1669.

This steeply pitched garrison house is clapboarded and has Georgian-type dormers, balanced windows, and central front door. It is beautifully maintained by the Swampscott Historical Society and its resident caretakers.

#5
Fisherman's Beach
Fish House, 1896
Chaisson Park
Swampscott Club, 1789
Humphrey Street, Route 129
Open all year, no fee for beach and park; rest restricted use

Turn around on Ellis Street and go back to Paradise Road; turn left and drive .3 mile to Burrill Street at traffic light. Turn left on Burrill and follow it into Humphrey Street. In .4 mile on far corner of Ingalls Street is the Swampscott Club at 360 Humphrey on the left. Chaisson Park and Fisherman's Beach are on the right, and the Fish House is at the fork of Route 129 and Puritan Road. Facilities: benches, jogging, lifeguards, walking; on-street parking only.

A beautiful crescent of fine sand facing the open sea is *Fisherman's Beach*, where the town pier stretches out to meet the tide. Here also is the *Fish House* built in 1896 by the town for its fishermen. And so it remains today, now the only town-owned fish house in New England.

Chaisson Park borders Fisherman's Beach and is named for Swampscott-born General John C. Chaisson, former chief of staff of the United States Marine Corps. The anchor memorial is believed to be all that remains of the bark *Tedesco* which sunk with all aboard off Swampscott in 1857. The English cannon was cast in 1798, captured by Salem privateer *Grand Turk* in the War of 1812, and later used as a fog signal by Swampscott fishermen.

Across is the *Swampscott Club* at 360 Humphrey Street. The house was built in 1789 on land purchased with a cow and is now one of the oldest social clubs, remaining adamantly for men only. Its guest book has been signed by United States presidents.

#6
Marian Court Junior College of Business
35 Littles Point Road
1890s
Open as school, tour by appointment, no fee

Bear right at fork onto Puritan Road; Route 129 goes left. At 53 is boathouse, where first monoplane purchased by U.S. government was built, on right .1 mile just before Sculpin Way. Continue on Puritan Road .9 mile to Littles Point Road. (All along Puritan Road are scenic roads providing beautiful coastal views amid fine old estates. The first road after Littles Point Road is Phillips Beach Avenue with

*the Oliver Wendell Holmes, Jr., estate on
the left. Public access is allowed on these
roads though marked private.) Turn right
on Littles Point Road; drive .2 mile to
Marian Court Junior College. Parking is
available.*

Marian Court, now home to a school in this envy-inspiring setting, was called White Court when it was the summer White House of President Calvin Coolidge* in 1925. The Coolidges enjoyed a quiet and relaxed life in these peaceful, impressive surroundings while Swampscott bustled with the activity of secret servicemen and many others drawn to the national figures.

The thirty-room mansion was built in the late 1890s by Frederick Smith, and much of the lavish, ornate detail of the interior was added after the Coolidge era by the last private owner, the Timothy Falveys. Now students enjoy use of the estate from formal dining and drawing rooms to converted classrooms with ocean views and the expansive, geranium-surrounded porch facing the sea. The opulent surroundings can be enjoyed as you relive this elegant era while walking from one grand room to another. Floors of marble, pegged wood, or inlaid parquet complement hand-painted murals on canvas-covered walls and ceilings. The original library is paneled in teakwood from Peru, and now serves as a beautiful chapel for the Sisters of Mercy who operate the college. The impressive stairway leads to more classrooms and offices, once bedroom suites with fireplaces even in dressing rooms.

Outside, the well-maintained grounds provide a fitting setting for the soft-yellow stucco walls and Ionic columns forming the court. Balanced wings of many and varied windows are designed to allow most rooms abundant visual access to the magnificent ocean vista of Marian Court.

This ends the guided tour section of Swampscott. Return on Littles Point Road to Puritan Road; turn right; and follow Puritan Road around to Atlantic Avenue. Turn right on Atlantic Avenue, Route 129, and follow it into Marblehead to continue tour.

Swampscott Beaches and Parks

All open all year with limited or private parking only, no fees.

(A) **King's Beach**
Humphrey Street at
Monument Avenue

Steps lead down to this beautiful, open, wide, sandy crescent beach, also accessible by ramp near the Lynn line; behind neighboring restaurants is a cliff written about by Henry W. Longfellow who stayed here; on street parking only.

(B) **Fisherman's Beach***
(Blaney's)
Chaisson Park
Puritan Road as it leaves
Humphrey Street

Open, sandy beach, with pier, Fish House, and Chaisson Park with memorials, benches, and fine ocean views; on street parking only. Just beyond, on Puritan Road, rear of 53, is boathouse (with marker) where in 1917 G. Norman Albree designed and constructed the first monoplane purchased by the U.S. government called the Albree Scout #116.

(C) **Whales Beach (Eisemanns**
Beach)
Puritan Road

Entrance off Puritan Road is marked by rocks for access to beach; further on is an exedra, a semicircular stone seat; parking lot on Humphrey Street has footpath to beach.

(D) **Phillips Beach**
off Palmer Road

A "walk on" beach with private parking only.

(E) **Palmer Pond**
Palmer Road, Ocean
Avenue or Shepard
Avenue

Acres of pond and marsh, a wetland bird sanctuary for nature study and hiking.

HISTORY OF MARBLEHEAD

From island to peninsula, from a background of political independence, farming, and familiarity with the sea came some of the early settlers of Marblehead. Leaving their temperate islands of Guernsey and Jersey in the British Channel, they sailed for the New World, settling in 1629 near Peach's Point in what would later become Marblehead.

These islanders, though loyal to the British Crown and church, had had little contact with faraway Parliament or the Church of England. It was this independent, self-sufficient way of life which gave them the ability to survive and ultimately prosper on the rocky, sea-pounded, yet beautiful peninsula of Marblehead.

Also to the plantation of Marble-Harbor, as it was first called, came Isaac Allerton of Plymouth and his son-in-law Moses Maverick in 1631. They set up a fishing station, launching Marble-Harbor on what would be its basic way of life for centuries. Allerton soon moved on, but Maverick remained to become one of the first selectmen, when Marblehead was incorporated in 1649.

True to their independent ways, there was no organized church and thus no colony-recognized governing power in early Marblehead. For, according to Puritan law, one had to be a church member to be a freeman, and only freemen were allowed to vote or hold office. Their main guiding influence was missionary William Walton from 1638 until 1668. Though he never was ordained and never formally organized a church, he was a faithful friend and counselor to this hardy group of people. Finally in 1684 the Reverend Samuel Cheever was called to officially organize their church. Their independent side had realized the wisdom of mutual support and the need for limited organization.

The treacherous ideology of witchcraft came like a dark cloud which descended on one Wilmot Redd of Marblehead. Sadly two emotional girls from Salem Village accused her of witchcraft. She was tried, sentenced, and executed in 1692. Compassion and acceptance had been exchanged for fear and superstition. Fortunately this tragic era in Marblehead was short lived.

In 1715 the Reverend John Barnard* was called to assist the

Reverend Cheever at the First Congregational Church.* Though his call caused a split in the congregation, his economic insight encouraged local fishermen to send their catches to markets in the West Indies and Europe. Trade increased, men took pride in their work, isolation decreased, and Marblehead joined the outside world.

By the mid-1700s Marblehead was a flourishing port with sixty merchants engaged in foreign trade and over eighty schooners plying the fishing banks off Newfoundland. This period until the Revolutionary War proved to be Marblehead's most prosperous. Such merchant greats as Colonel Jeremiah Lee* and "King" Robert Hooper* built beautiful mansions in town to which they invited famous people of the day. Marblehead's spirits soared.

The Revolutionary War put a halt to commercial enterprises, allowing time for merchant patriots Colonel Jeremiah Lee, Colonel William R. Lee,* Robert Hooper, Sr.,* Azor Orne,* John Glover,* and Elbridge Gerry* to lead these independent Colonials. Colonel John Glover was ordered by General Washington to equip and man vessels for military use. The first such naval vessel commissioned was his *Hannah*, which sailed from Beverly Harbor September 5, 1775. Marblehead's own Captain John Manly captained one of the first privateers. On November 29, 1775, Manly, in the schooner *Lee*, captured the British brig *Nancy* and claimed the "first naval victory in which the British flag was struck to American colors."[31]

Throughout the war, Marblehead privateersmen played havoc with British ships, capturing desperately-needed supplies. Her militia, under Colonel Glover, served from Cambridge to Long Island, across the Delaware to victory at Trenton, to Saratoga, and to final victory at Yorktown. Few towns in New England gave as much proportionately of men, money, and livelihoods as did Marblehead.

Following the war, merchants such as John Hooper, Jr. and Sr., and Colonel William R. Lee reestablished their fortunes and Marblehead's prestige in the world of trade. Fishing vessels returned to the Grand Banks, and Marblehead's ships could be found in every port of call.

During the War of 1812, in spite of personal loss, Marbleheaders supported the war and the government. Once again they offered their services as privateersmen with roughly one-fifth of their population involved in the unpopular conflict.

After the War fishermen returned to the sea and prospered until 1846 when the elements struck a devastating blow. Sixty-five seamen were lost on the Grand Banks during a brutal storm—a mortal blow from which the fishing industry never fully recovered.

The ever-resourceful Marbleheaders turned their attention to another industry which had begun in 1825—one not dependent on the whims of weather and sea—the manufacturing of women's and children's shoes. Another breath of fresh air appeared in the presence of shoe-manufacturer Joseph Bassett. He not only ran a successful shoe factory, but bought land on which he built small houses. He guaranteed occupants employment and allowed them the opportunity to purchase homes through monthly salary deductions. He introduced the sewing machine and invented a "binding" attachment, which dramatically increased shoe production. During the depression of 1873 his company not only stayed open, but offered employment to those laid off from other shoe factories, thus stabilizing the economy.

Another blow lay waiting to strike Marblehead. In 1877 a devastating fire reduced the business section to smoking embers, losing seventy-six buildings, and leaving ninety families homeless and fifteen hundred people out of work. Marbleheaders rebuilt in two years only to be struck again in 1888 by another disastrous fire, this time taking its toll and ending for all practical purposes Marblehead's shoe industry.

Yet a new industry was taking hold. The beauties of Marblehead Neck, and the magnificent, protected harbor it creates, were discovered in the 1860s. The first summer residents purchased land where they pitched tents to enjoy the summer months. Later the tents were replaced by seasonal cottages, gracious hotels, and more recently by luxurious summer and year-round residences, which have brought wealth, beauty, and stability to Marblehead. The summer residents were quickly captured by the thrill of salt spray and taut sails and the joy of racing on Marblehead's blue waters. Understandably the picturesque harbor became known as the "Yachting Capital of the World".

During the summer her docks are a pleasant mixture of working seamen and day sailors—all with eyes reflecting the deep blue of the ocean and their hearts lost to its beauty and power.

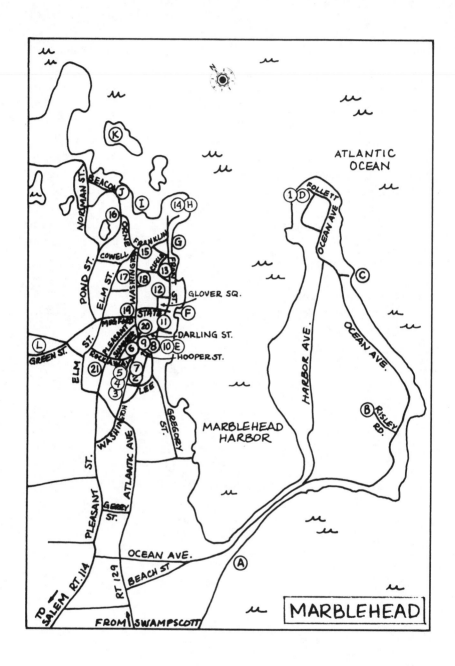

MARBLEHEAD

DIRECTIONS:
Enter Marblehead either on Route 114 from Salem or on Route 129 from Swampscott. Follow the route chosen to Ocean Avenue in Marblehead, where you turn right, following Ocean Avenue to the causeway leading out to Marblehead Neck and #1.

#1
Chandler Hovey Park, 1948,
Marble Light, 1835,
end of Follett Street on
Marblehead Neck
Open all year, no fee

Drive over the causeway to the Neck; bear right on Ocean Avenue. Follow Ocean Avenue around the Neck 1.6 miles. Just before Ocean Avenue makes a sharp left turn, there is a sign on the right for Castle Rock. Park, walk the short path, and climb Castle Rock for an inspiring view of the coast. The beautiful vista runs from Tinker Island on the south to Cape Ann on the north. Continue on Ocean Avenue, bearing right which becomes Follett Street. Chandler Hovey Park is at the end of Follett Street. Facilities: picnicking, rest rooms; parking.

This picturesque park, given by Chandler Hovey in 1948, is for artists, sailing enthusiasts, picnickers, and ocean lovers. On a clear summer's day, as you watch the many scheduled boat races with sails silhouetted against the blue sky, you understand why Marblehead is called the "Yachting Capital of the World." From here you can see the coast of Beverly, Cat Island, and overlook beautifully protected Marblehead harbor and town, with its towers of Abbot Hall and Old North Church standing against the skyline like benevolent big brothers. In Colonial days Cat Island was home to the much-dreaded and controversial hospital for smallpox inoculations, finally burned by fearful opponents. The island has since boasted a summer hotel called Island House, a children's sanitarium, and is now used as a camp by the Marblehead YMCA.

A white stone tower lighthouse was built on this point in 1835 to protect Marblehead's homecoming seamen. It was first manned by Ezekiel Darling, who had been a gunner aboard the famed *Constitu-*

tion. Keepers lived in an attached keeper's house, climbing the 134 steps twice daily to tend the oil lamp. In 1895, for practicality rather than beauty, the picturesque white tower was replaced by today's strong steel tower. In 1920 the light, which is one of the few to show a steady green light, was electrified and today is automated. This point of land, watched over by the tall green light, is one of the prettiest spots in Marblehead.

#2
Abbot Hall
Washington Square
1876
Open as Town Hall all year,
no fee
NRHP

Exit from Hovey Park and turn right; follow road returning on Harbor Avenue or Ocean Avenue to causeway. Drive over causeway to Atlantic Avenue, traffic light, Route 129, and turn right. Follow Atlantic Avenue .5 mile to Washington Street; turn right and follow Washington Street to top of hill and Abbot Hall, which will be on the right. Park here to enjoy #2–7.

From nearly every point in this intriguing town you see this tall, massive building, which becomes more impressive as you get closer. Mostly brick capped with slate, the Romanesque masterpiece is severely geometric, with a variety of stone and brick patterns, windows, and colors. Abbot Hall's dominating clock and bell tower commands the town.

Inside you begin to understand Marblehead. The Selectmen's Office is the place to begin, for here lives "The Spirit of '76." The warm centennial celebration painting of fifer, drummer, and drummer boy was created by Archibald M. Willard. It was given by General John H. Devereux, Marblehead patriot and father of the model of the drummer boy. It symbolizes the spirit of the War for Independence—how it felt, at all ages and intents, to care so strongly for liberty, to leave the known to fight for freedom and a new nation.

Other walls display the original 1684 town land deed, mementos of ships and fishermen both modern and historic, and art featuring national figures connected with the town. In the halls sailing ships, famous sons, and maps are depicted above displays of Marblehead relics.

The Romanesque interior features rich wood paneling, high ceilings, and an ornate double stairway leading to the restored frescoed auditorium above. Representative of Marblehead achievement and Victorian strength, Abbot Hall proudly tops the picturesque modern-day profile of the town.

Massachusetts Department of Commerce and Development, Division of Tourism

"The Spirit of '76" in Abbot Hall

#3
John Hooper Mansion
187 Washington Street
c.1803
Private

The John Hooper Mansion is across Washington Street from Abbot Hall.

As you leave Abbot Hall notice the row of elegant mansions across Washington Street, all once occupied by members of the prestigious Hooper family, who for many years were leading merchants in the town's commercial trade.

John Hooper lived in this grand three-story Federal from 1803–1855.

From the unusual enclosed widow's walk above, John could observe the return of his ships laden with cargo from Europe, the West Indies, China, and the Far East. His home spoke of wealth, position, and influence. The rear section was built first and the front, with its side to the street, a few years later. Notice the gracious, curved portico at the entrance, inside shuttered windows, and the inviting grounds.

In addition to his mercantile trade John Hooper held the office of president of the Marblehead Bank, which he guided to a position of influence and stability in New England. His son, Samuel, born here in 1808, served as a representative and state senator. From 1861 until his death in 1875 he was in the United States House of Representatives, where he was instrumental in establishing the National Banking System. Thus the Hooper influence went beyond Marblehead all the way to the United States government.

#4
Colonel William R. Lee Mansion
185 Washington Street
1743
Private

The Colonel William R. Lee Mansion is next door to the John Hooper Mansion.

Colonel William Raymond Lee, nephew of Jeremiah Lee,* lived here following his gallant service in the Revolutionary War. During the war he served under General Glover.* Congress thought so highly of his services that its members recommended him for the office of adjutant-general of the army, though he declined it. Colonel Lee treated the captured General Burgoyne and his troops, who were under his guard, with humanity and fairness. When the grateful Burgoyne returned to England he arranged for the secret escape of Colonel Lee's brother, Captain John Lee, who had been imprisoned in England. Following the war Colonel Lee graciously entertained General Washington here in his home.

The rear section of the home was built in 1743 in Georgian-style architecture for "King" Robert Hooper.* The later addition of its Federal features is credited to architect Charles Bulfinch.* Three stories tall, the house is rusticated, with wood beveled to resemble stone ashlar, and has quoined corners. It features a columned portico and glassed-in belvedere atop the roof.

#5
Robert Hooper, Sr.
Mansion
181 Washington Street
1769
Private

The Robert Hooper, Sr. Mansion is two doors down from the Colonel William R. Lee House.

Patriot Robert Hooper, Sr.,* built this two and one-half story late Georgian home in 1769. Robert, Sr., was one of the town's leading merchants prior to the Revolution, carrying on a prosperous trade with the West Indies, Spain, Portugal, and Russia. As the clouds of rebellion covered the sky, he committed his wealth and his influence to the Revolutionary cause along with patriots Azor Orne, Jeremiah Lee,* Elbridge Gerry,* and John Glover. Their combined efforts did much to bring about final victory.

In later years the mansion was home to son Robert, Jr., who became one of the leading merchants following the Revolution. Robert, Jr., lived here with his wife, Mary Glover, daughter of the Revolutionary hero, General John Glover.* Their son, John, (see #21) was born in this family home in 1794. He in turn married Lydia Blackler, daughter of Captain William Blackler.* Thus son and grandson, through their marriages, united patriotic families of Marblehead.

In 1824 the widow Mary Glover Hooper received the Marquis de Lafayette at the door of this Georgian home. In earlier years she had danced with the Marquis at the Jeremiah Lee Mansion during his triumphant visit in 1784—old patriotic loyalties were reaffirmed.

#6
Jeremiah Lee Mansion
161 Washington Street
1768
Open extended season, fee
charged
NHL, HABS

Walk down the hill across Rockaway Street to the Jeremiah Lee Mansion, which is on the corner. Parking is available.

The splendid Jeremiah Lee* Mansion is a fitting monument to a merchant prince of historic Marblehead. Lee was a "codfish aristocrat" whose fleet of ships took cured Marblehead-caught fish to the West Indies and Europe and returned with salt, wine, iron, molasses, and sugar. Profits from this lucrative trade were lavishly dispensed to

Jeremiah Lee Mansion

produce one of the finest mansions in Colonial America for Jeremiah and Martha Swett Lee and their six surviving children.

Sadly, Lee did not live long in his fine home, finished in 1768. An ardent patriot and active member of the Committee of Safety he met with Elbridge Gerry,* Azor Orne,* John Hancock,* and John Adams* on April 18, 1775, near Concord. That night, when hiding from British patrols in a cornfield, clad only in night clothes, he caught an illness fatal within a month.

The unique magnificence of the pure Georgian, three-story mansion is evident everywhere you look. The massive regal facade is carefully rusticated, using sand in limestone-gray paint over thick beveled boarding, to resemble stone. The deep sides are as detailed as the front, which features a central pavillion with fanlight in the pediment. Quoined corners, prominent dentils, Ionic-columned portico, and cupola-capped hip roof further distinguish the outer appearance.

As you enter through the ten-panel Georgian door, you are struck by the regal formality of pre-Revolutionary elegance. The spacious entry hall spans the entire depth to the majestic broad staircase beyond. The Great Room or Banquet Hall is on the left, the formal reception room where Washington, Lafayette, Monroe, and Jackson were received.

Featured are full native-pine panels, beautiful, hand-carved woodwork, and elaborate Grinling Gibbons–style fireplace wall. Painted a mustard color during the Lees' residency, the woodwork was later hand-grained to resemble English oak by portrait painter William Bartoll.

In the hall the broad, sweeping Santo Domingo–mahogany boxed staircase is a true box case, one stair on top of the other, with no other support. Notice stair end carvings of rosette-and-leaf motif as well as the intricate balusters of three alternate rope-twist patterns. The landing is the size of a small room, beautifully lighted by the great arch window, flanked by nineteenth-century copies of John Singleton Copley portraits of Jeremiah and Martha Lee.

The original spectacular handmade landscape wallpapers of the halls and two front rooms on the second floor have been traced to the London manufactory of paper-stainer William Squire. One other set is in New York's Metropolitan Museum of Art from the Van Rensselaer house, but the Lee Mansion's are the only known papers of this time surviving in the place for which they were designed. Their decorative schemes divide walls into framed pictures of classical themes and elegant rococo curves symbolic of the English and European splendor desired by prosperous Colonials. The works of Italian artist Giovanni Paolo Pannini are the model for the landscape scenes of the halls, while the classical ruins scenes of the second floor drawing room are based on engravings by Pierre Antoine de Machy. The second floor family parlor's less formal scenes are based on French painter Joseph Vernet's work. These more personal Marblehead themes of fishermen and Neptune are appropriate for this merchant-prince family.

Another rare feature is the fireplace tile work of John Sadler and Guy Green of Liverpool. These rare, transfer-printed, signed fireplace tiles are found in three rooms, the polychrome tiles of the second floor southeast room being particularly notable.

Furnishings are lavishly appropriate to the period and social level of the Lees, and include rare Queen Anne, Chippendale, and Hepplewhite pieces, plus American side chairs from John Hancock's Beacon Hill house and two treasured Lee side chairs of Massachusetts Chippendale. Extensive collections of other furniture, china, silver, pottery, Marblehead artifacts, and paintings are displayed.

Martha Lee carried on the Lee hospitality after her husband's death, though she was forced to sell much of their ornate furnishings. Later the mansion housed a sedate bank before the Marblehead Historical

Society purchased it in 1909. The society, led by Mrs. Francis Crowninshield and her brother Henry du Pont, "transformed the Lee house
into one of the most beautifully restored and furnished house museums
in the country."[32]

#7
Washington Square
Houses private

Walk back up Washington Street to Wash-
ington Square, which includes Abbot Hall
and the houses around the square. Start
on far side of Abbot Hall.

Washington Square is a sturdy elevation from which to unravel
Marblehead's circuitous streets and winding paths to explore the
fascinating town. In the 1600s it was called Windmill Hill when
colonists came to the common land to draw their water. Some of the
Common remains outlined by stone pillars.

Now the Square is a beautiful, formal reminder of periods of
Marblehead history very much alive today. Just below and across from
the Hall, at *198 Washington Street* is a house which was built in the
1600s and retains some of its early Colonial features with the far side
and third floor added in later centuries.

Across Washington Street is a group of stately Georgian and Federal
mansions. (see #3-5) Turning the corner of the Common changes the
architectural style to later Greek Revival at number *4 Washington*
Square dated c.1850. Next, at *number 8*, time moves back to classic
Federal. Diagonally across at *number 10* this house from the 1700s was
once known as "Little Jug Inn" and has an unusual bow to the front
lines, slightly suggesting the prow of a ship. Further on, *number 16*
jumps to the late 1800s and Queen Anne style.

Return to number 10. Go a short distance on Tucker Street, away
from the Square, and turn right on Lookout Court. Not only does
Marblehead have fascinating examples of many architectural periods,
but how they adapt and cling to their challenging rocky promotory
sites is equally intriquing. Lookout Court is a good example of this and
offers an excellent view as well. *Number 5* is "Lookout" house, built in
the 1700s for customs officer–pilot Captain Dixey. It is a neat, tiny
three-storied Georgian with notable doorway pilasters and fanlight.
From the top, Captain Dixey watched the harbor and signaled ships'
arrivals. Just beyond the house a narrow path leads to the road below
and the brick house where pilots waited for the signaled call to pilot an
incoming ship.

#8
Lafayette House
2 Union Street
1731
Private

Return to your car; go around square so as to make a left on Lee Street. Follow Lee Street down the hill and turn left. At the end of the street, where it meets Union Street, is the Lafayette House.

This quaint Georgian Colonial house, with its missing corner, is the main character of a warmly remembered Marblehead legend. It begins when America's good friend Lafayette returned to visit with his son George Washington Lafayette in 1824. His grand coach had to negotiate Marblehead roads, which were no straighter or wider than they are today. When his coach was halted here, the ardent patriot homeowner was happy to chop away a corner of his home to make way for the general.

A more mundane explanation for the missing corner surmises it was to allow passage of rum wagons, whose drivers occasionally sampled their loads. The name of the house suggests which story is preferred.

#9
King Hooper Mansion
8 Hooper Street
1728
Open all year except
January and February as
Marblehead Arts
Association, fee charged
NRHP

Drive to the left of the Lafayette House. This will be Hooper Street. Follow it one-half block to the King Hooper Mansion, which is on the right. Also notice next door at 2 Hooper Street the granite bank building whose name plate reads "Grand Bank" 1831. Here stands the only bank named for fishing grounds and, appropriately, for the Grand Banks, which were the source of so much of Marblehead's wealth.

The King Robert Hooper* Mansion is a combination of two gracious homes. Robert's father, Greenleaf, built the gambrel-roofed, three-story rear section about 1728. In 1747 his son, Robert, added the front three-story Georgian mansion with its facade of quoined corners, wood grooved to resemble stone, and dentiled cornices. Here King Robert lived in gracious splendor, surrounded by beautiful furnishings, in a home where the prominent of the day were welcomed and entertained.

A man of convictions and great business acuity, Robert Hooper left his special mark on Marblehead. He was one of the leading merchants prior to the Revolution, and his ships took the name of Marblehead to nearly every port in Europe and the West Indies. Through his efforts and those of other merchants, Marblehead reached her time of greatest prosperity.

Robert Hooper was called "King," not for his power and influence, but for his benevolence and integrity. This was a rare compliment to a wealthy employer by hardworking, uneducated fishermen, who were dependent upon him. With the same fervor that made him loyal to his men and his ideals, so he was loyal to his king and mother country. Torn between two loyalties, not wishing to raise a hand against either, he left Marblehead for Nova Scotia at the time of the Revolution. Years later he returned but never regained the wealth or prestige he had once known.

Enter the front door and step into the world of eighteenth-century prosperity. To the left is the drawing room with unusual double-dentil moldings, hand-carved paneling, and portrait copies of Washington, Lafayette, and Mrs. Hooper. (There were four Mrs. Hoopers and eleven children.) Next move to the rear section built by Robert's father. The borning room shows the old stenciling and curved ceiling of earlier Colonial living. The rear pine room carries out the same era with bull's-eye window allowing light to a stairway leading to the cellar kitchen and old brick-arched wine cellar. The dining room, though part of the older house, was remodeled by Robert for more elaborate entertaining with fine moldings, fluted pilasters, and a Delft-tiled fireplace.

Climb the impressive stairway to the front bedrooms. The fine paneling of doors and fireplaces was made by ships' carpenters to create the illusion that the room was curved much as a ship's cabin might have been.

Above on the third floor is an unusual ballroom with its original chandelier set in an eight-sided dome. Once used as a gym when the house was owned by the YMCA, it is now used as an art gallery by the Marblehead Art Association. During King Hooper's day wealthy merchants, political leaders, and close friends were entertained here with the grand hospitality of the eighteenth century.

#10
Crocker Park
Front Street
1886
Open all year, no fee
Access off Front Street
opposite Union and Darling
Streets

From Hooper Street turn right on Washington. Follow Washington to middle of next block, where there is parking behind stores. There is limited parking behind Ice Cream Parlor or fee parking in rear of lot. Park here for #10 and part of 11. Walk through lot to Front Street and Crocker Park entrance, slightly to the right off

Front Street. Or from Washington Street take first right on Darling, turn left on Front and drive to Town Wharf, park there for #10-13. Walk back to Crocker Park.

Crocker Park, once covered with fish flakes drying cod for Colonial trade, is now a high prominence of land given by Uriel Crocker in 1886 and later added to by his sons so that all might forever enjoy the harbor and town they so loved. From here you overlook the beautiful harbor dotted with buoys in winter and in summer filled with a myriad of boats which appear to dance in the water, responding to wind and tide, waiting for the call to the open sea. Ever present are the fishing and lobstering boats which keep the harbor true to its earliest way of life. On the left is the entrance to the harbor guarded by Cat Island* and the lighthouse. Directly across is Marblehead Neck* with Corinthian, Eastern, and Pleon Yacht Clubs obvious on the waterfront. To the right is the causeway with Graves, Boston,* and Minot's* lights visible on a clear night. Behind you the skyline of Marblehead is pierced by such landmarks as Abbot Hall* and Old North Church,* which are intermingled with houses of varying shapes, colors, and architecture, all blending into the rocky, rugged peninsula.

Immediately behind the grass-covered park stands a replica of a Viking Castle, built in 1926 by artist Waldo Ballard to represent a smaller version of Eric the Red's castle. Though private it adds to the tradition of the sea and the early Viking explorers.

At Crocker Park the salt air fills your lungs and soul, the view refreshes your mind, and the swooping gulls and exuberant honking geese welcome you to Marblehead and a way of life that makes the New England coast unique.

#11
Front Street Tour
Boston Yacht Club
Town Wharf
Club and houses private, walk and wharf open all year, no fee

Wander Crocker Park end of Front Street. The Boston Yacht Club is to your right and the Town Wharf to the left. Parking is available at Town Wharf.

As you drive, preferably walk, around Marblehead's narrow, curving ways, you continually notice her amazingly adaptive architecture clinging to the headland's immovable ledges. Front Street provides the best opportunity to study this phenomenon. From here you can view a fascinating array of roofs at all angles and elevations. This skyline capped by Abbot Hall* is uniquely Marblehead.

Front Street begins with the *Boston Yacht Club*, New England's oldest, whose Marblehead branch was established in 1890, after its 1866 Boston beginnings. As in other parts of town, many houses have informative date plaques telling the first owner's name and occupation. Front Street was the home of fishermen, shoemakers, landsmen, and ships' carpenters, who built their comparatively modest Colonials, Georgians, and Federals close to the sea.

As you walk along Front Street drink in the color of everyday eighteenth century life, which can be appreciated today. At the foot of State Street is the *Town Wharf* with benches from which to observe the heart of Marblehead. The scene includes the boat-filled harbor, lobster-pot-stacked wharf with boats constantly arriving for services, nearby yacht dealers and marine-related shops, and the adjacent huge crane-topped yacht yard. The wharf is the window of the waterfront.

#12	*From Town Wharf walk up State Street*
General Glover Home	*one block to Glover Square; turn right.*
11 Glover Square	*The Glover House is at the head of the*
1762	*square. Notice the 1686 Captain Natha-*
Private	*niel Norden House at 15 Glover Square.*
NHL	

The first marine general, John Glover,* and his Marblehead regiment made a unique contribution to the successful outcome of the Revolution. It was his men who successfully evacuated Washington's troops from Long Island in almost total silence, under cover of dark, amid the ever-present British fleet. They also evacuated the sick, as well as munitions and supplies, from New York ahead of the occupying British. Later they were instrumental in the famous crossing of the Delaware and leading the advance attack on Trenton. Glover's regiment fought bravely on land and sea. They combined the talents of seamen and soldiers creating a new service which in time would be known as the United States Marines.

Prior to his promotion to General, Colonel Glover prepared and manned vessels for military use, with his own *Hannah* being the first vessel commissioned under Washington's orders. (see Marblehead history)

John Glover, born in Salem in 1732, was first a shoemaker, then a successful fisherman and merchant and builder of this Georgian gambrel house in 1762. During the war he became a close friend of General Washington and faithfully served his country to the detriment of his own business and family. Following the war he returned home where he again became a cobbler to make ends meet for his motherless family of eleven. He later remarried and moved to a farm near Salem, now known as the General Glover Restaurant.

#13
Circle Street Tour
Fisherman's Shack
John Homan House, c.1695
Skipper Benjamin Ireson
House,
Screeching Woman Cove
Homes all private, walk the
Circle

Continue around Glover Square to Front Street. Turn left, continue two blocks to Circle Street. Walk or drive its length, returning to Front Street. Screeching Cove is on the water side of Front Street opposite the end of Circle Street.

A tiny, natural-shingle *Fisherman's Shack* and Cordwainer's Shop at 116 Front Street marks the entrance to Circle Street. This appropriate reminder of days past and the importance of Marblehead fishing and home shoe industry is now a tidy home. As you enter Circle Street, you face another weathered shingled house, with a cod over the door indicating a fisherman's home, at 31 Circle Street. The left side was built about 1695 for cooper and mariner *John Homan.* The attached right side, now an art gallery, was built for sailmaker John Graves and fisherman John Curtis about a century later.

A tragic tale surrounds the home of *Skipper Benjamin Ireson* at 19 Circle Street. Accused of passing a sinking ship without going to her aid, he was tarred and feathered and dragged through town in a dory. A poem by John Greenleaf Whittier expanded the story to include Marblehead women doing the revenging and immortalized the unfortunate skipper. He died a broken old man, his innocence realized later.

More tragedy awaits at the end of Circle Street, at *Screeching Woman Cove.* This lovely cove was purportedly the scene of a brutal murder, some say involving pirates. The victim, a sea captain's daughter, is said to return on the anniversary of her death, when bloodcurdling screams pierce the calm of the cove.

#14
Fort Sewell
End of Front Street
1644, 1742
Open all year, no fee

From Circle and Front Streets drive NE to the end of Front Street and Fort Sewell; limited parking available on left side of Front Street just before fort. Facilities: benches, picnicking, rest rooms, views.

Here is the perfect location, whether for observing sailboat races; enjoying the peaceful view of harbor, Neck, and ocean beyond; or for defending the town against possible Indian, pirate, French, or British attack.

In defense of their settlement, Marbleheaders built earthworks here as early as 1644. A hundred years later in 1742 much of the present fort was built with a fund of 716 pounds allotted by the General Court. Sir Harry Frankland, collector of the Port of Boston, was retained to oversee the construction. Sir Harry brought both romance and protection to the town. When he first arrived at the Fountain Inn off Orne Street he saw a ragged yet beautiful sixteen-year-old girl named Agnes Surriage* scrubbing the stairs. She completely captured his attention and later his heart. With her parents' permission, his new ward was educated in Boston. The beautiful and graceful Agnes traveled everywhere with him much to the consternation of Massachusetts and London society, who ostracized her. It wasn't until 1755, when Agnes saved Sir Harry's life during a terrible earthquake in Lisbon, that Sir Harry married Agnes, thus ending their romance in a "happy ever after" state.

During the War of 1812 the fort, named for Chief Justice Sewell, was repaired and manned. At that time British prisoners were held here much to the concern of the townspeople. The fort was again manned during the Civil War. In 1892 it was officially dedicated as a public park and has been enjoyed as one ever since. From this rugged promontory a beautiful panoramic view reaches from Little Harbor and Gerry Island on the left, across Boston Bay and Cat Island to Marblehead Neck, and to the town itself.

#15
Franklin Street Houses
Hearth and Eagle House,
30, c.1715
Ambrose Gale House, 17,
c.1663
Devereux House, 16, c.1764

Return on Front Street, taking first right on Franklin Street to view the Franklin Street Houses.

Parson Barnard House, 7, c.1716
Mary A. Alley House, 6
Private

Franklin Street is one of the oldest byways in town and has many interesting Colonial and Georgian homes. Named for admired patriot Ben Franklin, it was home to many people important to Marblehead and beyond. At 30 Franklin Street the circa 1715 *Hearth and Eagle House* is the name and setting of Anya Seton's novel, and was home to Vice-President Elbridge Gerry's* father. The yellow-clapboarded early Georgian still proudly bears its eagle over the door.

Built about 1663 for fisherman *Ambrose Gale*, the house at 17 Franklin is probably the oldest in Marblehead. It seems little change has occurred through the centuries as the broad Colonial retains many valued features. Across the street, at 16 Franklin, is the later (circa 1764), more patrician, Georgian-style home of the *Devereux* family. Descendant General John Devereux gave the "Spirit of '76" to Marblehead.

At 7 Franklin Street, on left before Washington Street, is the *Parson Barnard* House*, the classic Georgian home of the very wise pastor. With early economic foresight, the Reverend John Barnard encouraged fishermen and sea-oriented Marbleheaders to establish international trade. This brought their depressed economy up to its golden age, reflected in the architecture throughout the town. The apartment building on the right at 6 Franklin was the *Mary A. Alley House*, given to the town by devoted teacher Alley and used as the emergency hospital for Marblehead until a larger one was built. How varied are the lives and houses along this one small byway of long ago.

#16	*Go to the end of Franklin Street and turn*
Old Burial Hill	*right on to Orne Street. Follow Orne*
Agnes Surriage Well	*around and up the hill. On the corner of*
Old Brig, 42 Orne Street	*Orne and Pond Streets is Old Burial Hill.*
House private	*Agnes Surriage Well is at end of Fountain*
	Inn Lane beyond historic marker.

On one of the highest points, commanding the harbor and land, Marblehead's first meetinghouse was raised. Now you see intriguing old gravestones of the churchyard amid Marblehead's rocky ledges, with benches from which to enjoy quiet peace and unmatched views and to contemplate the lives and history around you. The oldest stone dates to 1681, and many of these ancient markers bear delicate carvings and interesting inscriptions. Here are the graves of four early ministers, Parson Barnard* among them. From the Revolution are six hundred graves including General Glover's.*

Here is honored "Black Joe," a man who as a slave served in the Revolution and later hosted happy Election Day crowds at his tavern on Gingerbread Hill. His wife, Aunt Crese, baked still-popular "Joe Froggers," a ginger cookie named for Joe and the many frogs in the pond nearby. The 1691 tavern still stands, a red saltbox private home on Gingerbread Hill.

The tallest memorial is appropriately to James Mugford, Jr., who with power and courage led his men aboard his Continental Cruiser *Franklin* to Revolutionary victory. He had been impressed on a British gunboat and there learned of ammunition and stores due to arrive in Boston. He was rescued by his equally courageous wife when she faced the British captain and won her husband's release with weapons of words. Mugford went on to capture the armed British supply ship and with sheer personal will controlled her crew and brought in the most valuable catch of the war. Ironically, he was killed in a fierce battle as he left Boston Harbor after seeing his prize into port.

The obelisk is a memorial to the sixty-five Marblehead fishermen lost in the Gale of 1846, a tragedy which also tolled the death knell for large-scale commercial fishing here.

Below, the *Agnes Surriage Well* still can be found just within the fence of a house at the end of Fountain Inn Lane, a reminder of the romance of Marblehead fisherman's daughter Agnes and dashing, highborn Sir Harry Frankland. (see #14)

Across, at 42 Orne, *The Old Brig* was built about 1720 and was home to Edward Dimond and many stories of his powers as a wizard and those of his granddaughter Moll Pitcher.* (see Lynn history)

#17
The First Church of Christ in Marblehead
Old North Church
41 Washington Street
1684, building 1824
Open all year for services, seasonally and by appointment at office on Stacey Street

By cemetery turn left and follow Pond Street to Cowell Street; turn left, go to end; turn left; take next left and follow road down hill and around to right, coming out on Orne Street. Turn right onto Washington Street. The church is a short way down on the right.

From almost any point in town, the distinctive cupola-topped bell tower of Old North can be seen as a dominating part of Marblehead's skyline. As her steeple reaches skyward, so her congregation's roots reach back into the 1600s and Marblehead's first settlement.

Missionary William Walton serviced the first settlement from 1638 until 1668, with a meetinghouse built on Burial Hill* in 1648. However, it wasn't until 1684 that the church was formally organized under the Reverend Samuel Cheever,* a man deeply loved and revered by his followers. In 1715, to lessen his burdens, an assistant was sought. Two men, the Reverends Edward Holyoke (home standing at 119 Washington) and John Barnard* (home standing at 7 Franklin) were considered. Barnard won. Those strongly supporting Holyoke left to form the Second Church. The Reverend Barnard proved to be a dynamic leader not only of his church, which he served for fifty-five years, but of the community, doing much to help establish its early commercial prosperity.

Today's beautiful stone and wood edifice was erected in 1824 and substantially remodeled in 1886. The present fifty-two-inch, gilded copper codfish weathervane was first placed atop the second meetinghouse in 1696. Its silhouette against the sky remains as a combined symbol of Christianity and of the "sacred cod" which brought commercial prosperity to Marblehead.

The large open sanctuary, Colonial white with red carpeting, has unusual paneling at the front of the church, where the cross is done in relief flanked by Ionic pilasters. On a Communion Sunday, the Communion table is set with beautiful and rare sacramental silver dating from a 1672 English cup, a 1693 Dutch influenced beaker up through eighteenth-, nineteenth-, and twentieth-century pieces. The special silver combines the sacred and the historic of this first church in Marblehead.

#18
Elbridge Gerry Birthplace
44 Washington Street
1742
Private
NRHP

The Gerry Birthplace is across Washington Street from the church.

Across from Old North Church stands Captain Thomas Gerry's Homestead, where son, Elbridge Gerry, was born in 1744. Elbridge ably served his town and new country during the Revolution as a member of the Committees of Grievances, Safety, and Correspondence, a signer of the Declaration of Independence, as well as representative to the Continental Congress, Provincial Congress, and Constitutional Convention, and a member of the XYZ Affair in France. Even though he worked laboriously on the Federal Constitution he was unable to sign the final draft for he felt it did not adequately protect the liberties of America. In 1810 he was elected governor of Massachusetts. The term gerrymandering, which refers to the practice of maneuvering political districting, came from his administration. In 1813 he culminated a dedicated career of public service as vice-president under James Madison.

In later years this house became the home of Revolutionary Captain William Blackler, a member of General Glover's division, who captained the boat that carried General Washington across the Delaware River prior to the battle of Trenton. Though the house has been greatly altered over the years, it is reminiscent of historic events dear to Marblehead and the country.

#19
Town House
Market Square,
Washington and Mugford
Streets
1727
Open all year, no fee
NRHP

Continue on Washington Street .2 mile to the Town House at intersection of Washington, Mugford, and State Streets. Go to right around Town House and continue on Washington Street.

Marblehead's "Cradle of Liberty," the Town House, is possibly the oldest municipal building to continuously serve its town. Here Committee of Safety patriots Lee* and Orne* led Marbleheaders toward revolution; here Vice-President Gerry* began his political career; and here men gathered to answer their country's call to the wars of two centuries.

Built on the old jail site, it housed public markets, town meetings, school, and town offices. Later it hosted Civil War GAR meetings, stored Fire Department equipment, and was the Police Department headquarters. It still serves the town as offices and is used for special functions.

The stately Georgian structure appears almost Greek Revival since it was raised by its high granite foundation in 1832. With bright-yellow clapboards and white quoins and trim, the Town House dominates the Square.

#20
St. Michael's Church
11 Summer Street
1714
Open all year, no fee
NRHP

Continue on Washington Street around bend past Jeremiah Lee Mansion, and take first right on Rockaway Street. Take first right on Summer Street; St. Michael's Church is on the left. Limited parking.

St. Michael's Church is the result of a dream of early British and Marblehead sea captains who wanted to build a handsome church in which to worship as Anglicans. They were supported from the first by British Royal Governor Sir Francis Nicholson and later by open-minded Puritan Parson John Barnard.* This original St. Michael's was designed from the captains' memories of a Christopher Wren church in London and was constructed by American ship carpenters in 1714. It was one of the first Anglican churches to arise despite much strong Puritan disapproval. Her second minister, the Reverend David Mossom, married George and Martha Washington in Virginia where he moved after serving here.

"St. Michael's is founded upon a rock and the gates of Hell cannot prevail against it. . . ."[33] This strong statement comes from Ashley Bowen, seaman extraordinaire, historic diarist, and loyal Anglican, at the time of the Revolution when St. Michael's was forcibly closed. Its historic bell was too exuberantly rung, by patriots who broke into the church when Independence was declared, and had to be recast by another patriot, Paul Revere, whose name is clearly marked on it.

In 1888, rescued from fire damage, decay, and other renovations, St. Michael's again emerged as the handsome church dreamed of by her founders. The renovation achievement is credited to Samuel Roads, Jr., town historian, state representative, senator, and devoted parish clerk of St. Michael's. Roads was such a successful inspiration to contributors that his senate colleagues donated the Moses window later named in his honor.

The beautiful woods and stained-glass windows of the Victorian Gothic restored sanctuary still create feelings of warmth, dignity, serenity, and antiquity. St. Michael's continues to stand as a notable monument to its founders and members past and present.

#21
John Hooper House
69 Pleasant Street
1830
Private

Drive back to Washington Street; turn right and go back around to Rockaway Street again. This time go to top of hill and turn left on Pleasant Street. Go one-half block to the John Hooper House at 69 Pleasant Street, on the right.

In 1830 John and Lydia Hooper built this imposing Greek Revival mansion, with its touch of Federal influence in the balustrades, in what was then considered the new part of town. They brought to the home a combination of success, wealth, and family prestige. John was the grandson of General John Glover* and son and grandson of wealthy merchants Robert Hooper, Sr.,* and Robert Hooper, Jr.* He was a successful sea captain and merchant, carrying on the family shipping interests in Europe, Russia, China, the East Indies, and Africa. Lydia, daughter of Captain William Blackler,* Revolutionary hero and successful merchant, brought her own social influence to the mansion. Here they entertained the economic and social leaders of Marblehead.

Directly across the street, in a building now occupied by the Old Colony Bank, is the Greek Revival facade of what was once another beautiful Hooper mansion, belonging to John's brother, Robert. Robert handled the legal affairs for the Hooper overseas trade, preparing bills of lading and insuring cargoes. The loss of sixty-five Marblehead seamen and many vessels owned or insured by the Hoopers in the tragic storm of 1846 all but broke the financial and maritime spirit of Hooper interests as well as that of the town of Marblehead.

This ends the guided tour section of Marblehead. Continue on Pleasant Street, bearing right onto Lafayette Street, Route 114, and follow Route 114 into Salem to continue the tour.

Marblehead Beaches and Parks and Additional Points of Interest

(A) **Devereux Beach Ocean Avenue at causeway to Neck**

Open gravelly-sandy crescent beach, view of Marblehead Neck to north and to south coastline of Swampscott and Nahant and lighthouses of Boston's outer harbor; covered picnic and bench area, lifeguards, rest rooms, swimming; ample parking; open all year, parking fee in season.

(B) **Marblehead Neck Wildlife Sanctuary Massachusetts Audubon Society Risley Road off Ocean Avenue on Marblehead Neck**

Mortared stone gates lead from cul-de-sac to paths within sanctuary; bird-watching, picnicking, nature study; small parking lot; open all year, no fee.

C Castle Rock*
Ocean Avenue
Marblehead Neck

Just past castle built by a Lydia Pinkham* heir is a public path to spectacular open headland; climb its rocky ledges to breathtaking open ocean vista; limited on-street parking; open all year, no fee.

D Chandler-Hovey Park*
Marblehead Light*
end of Follett Street
Marblehead Neck
(See #1)

A small park with magnificent views of Marblehead's fascinating harbor, islands, and open sea, prime viewing for Marblehead Race Week; can walk rocky ledges to foot of light; picnic at tables; rest rooms; parking; open all year, no fee.

E Crocker Park*
Front Street
(See #10)

Open rocky ledges have benches, paths, and nooks from which to enjoy the most fantastic view of Marblehead Harbor, the Neck across, and causeway on right; turn around for inland view of Marblehead's unique roof-line collage capped by Abbot Hall;* picnicking, swimming and diving from floats; open all year, no fee

F Town Wharf*

Heart of Marblehead's great boating interests—pleasure yachts and practical boats; stone wharf well above sea; always a boat moving in for wharf services; picnicking, rest rooms, walking; parking; open all year, no fee.

G Screeching Woman Cove*
(See #13)
Fort Beach
Front Street at Circle and
Franklin Streets

Another Marblehead rocky beach; best at high tide; great views; limited on-street parking; open all year, no fee.

H Fort Sewell*
end of Front Street
(See #14)

Beautifully preserved fort on rugged promontory from which to enjoy views of Marblehead's shores and out to sea; benches, paths, picnicking, rest rooms, walking; limited parking; open all year, no fee.

I Gas House Beach
Access lane off Orne
Street
by sharp left hand curve
before Fountain Inn Lane

Below Fountain Park; small sandy beach; at low tide can walk to nearby island; walk-on beach; open all year, no fee.

(J) **Fountain Park**
Orne Street

Once a fortification, Fort Washington, manned by local Marbleheaders aided by Lafayette guards and Marblehead Light Infantry; nothing remains from the fort used during the Revolution and War of 1812; now old headland is open to all; with benches and covered area from which to enjoy one of the best views in scenic Marblehead: beautiful open sea and clear view of islands, and the Salem-Beverly shores, lighthouse to north; limited on-street parking; open all year, no fee.

(K) **Crowninshield Island or**
Brown Island
Near end of Beacon
Street
on right

Small neatly mortared stone wharf, access to Crowninshield Island directly across; at low tide can walk to this inviting island preserved by Trustees of Reservations.

(L) **Old Powder House**
37 Green Street

Built about 1755, where powder once was stored for French and Indian wars, the Revolution, and the War of 1812; round, carefully bricked structure in good shape; shingle roof appears thatched; mortared stone wall near street; not open but viewable all year, no fee.

HISTORY OF SALEM

Her founders came to establish a successful fishing and trading post. Her early settlers sought freedom to worship according to their own beliefs and the opportunity to govern their own lives. Their successes and their failures can be measured by their deeds.

A small group led by Roger Conant* founded Salem, known as Naumkeag, in 1626; receiving John Endicott* as governor in 1628. In the next year six ships laden with four hundred settlers and 140 cattle arrived; their church was gathered; and a successful settlement was established. A year later, in 1630, the Crown appointed John Winthrop* governor. He, along with fellow Puritans, arrived aboard the *Arbella*. Winthrop remained only a few weeks in Salem, quickly moving the seat of government to Charlestown. Though Endicott was replaced as governor, he, along with Roger Conant and others, continued to lead their settlement. It grew to be a successful trading and fishing village called Salem, a derivation of Shalom, meaning City of Peace.

The year 1692 placed the only real blight on Salem's history, one that neither she nor the world will ever forget. The mystical actions of several young girls in town caused people to believe evil spirits were at work. Fellow citizens, regardless of past contribution, obvious piety, or station in the community, were subject to sudden unreasonable attacks, examinations, and jail sentences. Hysteria hit, and reason flew. The first people were accused of witchcraft on February 29, 1692; by May 1693 the panic had basically subsided. During the interim, twenty were put to death, several hundred had been imprisoned, and all had lived in constant fear. Thus concluded fifteen months of infamy that have seared the pages of history for nearly three hundred years.

The year 1670 witnessed the arrival of the first of Salem's many great merchants, Philip English, who established a prosperous trade with the West Indies, Spain, France, and Holland. In the mid-1700s he was followed by wealthy merchant and shipowner Richard Derby,* who added to Salem's wealth and prestige as a seaport. Then the Revolutionary War brought Salem's commerce to a standstill. In true fighting spirit, she outfitted 158 vessels which as privateers preyed on, and did great financial damage to, the British fleet.

The long-term effect of building larger vessels for privateers ultimately caused Salem to embark on her greatest commercial ventures. Following the war it was those larger ships that were able to sail halfway around the world opening up new and lucrative trade routes. Backed by such prominent and daring merchants as Elias Hasket Derby,* William Gray, and Joseph Peabody, Salem's docks were once again alive with seamen and her harbor filled with vessels of every tonnage.

The captains and seamen of Salem, with their courage and intuitive knowledge of the sea, should be listed in maritime history among the greats of the world. It was those rugged Salem maritime pioneers who, between 1784 and 1800, first opened trade with the Cape of Good Hope, the Isle of France, Calcutta, Bombay, Canton, Java, Sumatra, Madagascar, Zanzibar, Manila, Mocha, St. Petersburg, and Sydney.

With modern navigational systems and instant communications, it is easy to forget the difficulties under which these men sailed. They went forth in sailing vessels completely dependent on the winds and at the mercy of the currents, with the ever-present danger of a calm sea suddenly turned into mountains of untamed waves pummeled by gale winds. With only a compass, they sailed uncharted waters, skillfully avoiding treacherous rocks and reefs. During long voyages they had to contend with sickness, death, lack of proper food, loneliness, possible mutiny, and pirates. And when they finally reached port, there was always the possibility of unfriendly natives and the ever-present ruthless competition of British and European merchants. But for the man of Salem the promises of new oceans to sail, new countries to discover, new trade routes to develop, and fortunes to be reaped made it all worthwhile.

This newfound prosperity, along with treasures brought back from foreign ports, began to show in the homes of successful sea captains and wealthy merchants. The very talented Federal architect and wood-carver, Samuel McIntire,* was engaged for many of the beautiful mansions. This special wealth can still be seen in Salem.

Following the Civil War, her maritime prosperity experienced a slow decline. While her ships still plied the seven seas, many entered through Boston and other larger, deeper ports. Railroads took over much of her coastal trade. Wisely she turned from sea-oriented industries to land enterprises which soon prospered. Salem was famous for her tanneries, which became her leading land industry during the 1800s. She also manufactured cotton, jute bagging, boots, shoes, and lead. The late 1800s saw her harbor again active with a coastal trade bringing in large quantities of coal used in her own mills and for distribution to the mills in Lawrence and Lowell.

Throughout her long history the citizens of this ideally oriented maritime city have always had a high percentage of saltwater pulsating through their veins. Here have lived famous sea captains, privateersmen, merchants, fishermen, and navigators. Her waterfront along with historic buildings and homes throughout the city has been lovingly preserved by citizens proud of their unique heritage.

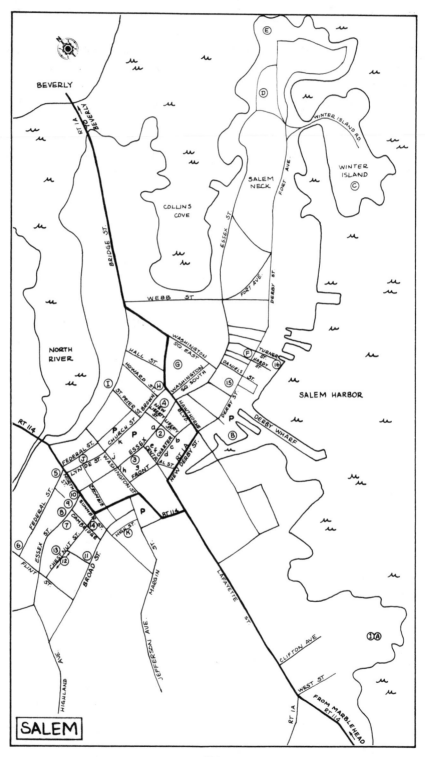

SALEM

SALEM

DIRECTIONS:
Enter Salem on Routes 1A or 114, both of which join at Lafayette Street

#1
Pioneer Village
West Street
Open seasonally, fee charged

Drive NE on Lafayette Street. Where Routes 1A and 114 meet, turn right on West Street. Pioneer Village is at the end of West Street.

As you approach through Forest River Park (see A), you see a tiny, First Period village barely visible beyond the peaceful duck pond. This is Pioneer Village, a carefully researched replica of circa 1630 Naumkeag (Salem), created in 1930. The tree-covered landscape appears much as it did, even to herb and flower gardens amid the wilderness. The Village clings to the harbor, its essential avenue of communication and supply. Early replica dwellings range from wigwams to darkly weathered thatched or shingled tiny cottages to the two-story replica of Governor John Endicott's* "Fayre House." These pioneering colonists' way of life comes alive as you see crude yet ingenious facilities for fish drying, black smithing, brick making, wood cutting, and evaportion of sea water to obtain salt.

#2
Peabody Museum of Salem
161 Essex Street
1799 Museum, 1824 Hall
Open all year, fee charged
NRHP

Return to Lafayette Street and turn right. Continue .7 mile into Salem to traffic light where Routes 114 and 1A divide. Bear left on Route 114 to central parking plaza. Pass parking plaza on left to end, going straight on Washington Street (marked to 1A). Turn right on Church Street to parking lot or garage. Park here for #2-4. Walk from far end of parking area by St. Peter's stone church; go to right of church one-half block to New Liberty Street. Turn right, walk one block to Peabody Museum on right at beginning of mall.

Peabody Museum of Science

You are a captive the moment you step inside and gaze at the first item to catch your eye, the large reenactment of Salem's early 1800s waterfront. The Peabody Museum continues to imprison your attention throughout its many rooms and buildings of permanent and changing displays. This oldest continuously operating museum in the country is a maritime museum with special focus on worldwide ethnology and Essex County natural history. It is a vibrant museum with treasures continuously arriving.

Maritime history comes alive, and you sail historic ships with amazing men to unbelievable ports. Comprehensive collections include log books, documents, navigational devices, tools, centuries of figureheads (including one carved by McIntire*), portraits of ships, merchants and captains of Salem and the Orient, and over seven hundred ship models. The Crowninshield* family mementos feature a full-scale reproduction of the saloon of their noted yacht *Cleopatra's Barge*. The China trade collections, ships furnishings, and scrimshaw round out the unequaled exhibits which faithfully retell Salem's remarkable marine history.

From early coasting ventures through more exotic trade with China, India, Sumatra, the West Indies, and the Pacific Islands, Salem ships returned; and her people were never the same again. The East India Marine Society was founded in 1799 for three bold, interesting purposes: to care for families should harm come to a seafaring member, to improve navigation for sailing trade adventures, and to form this museum of "natural and artificial curiosities."

A two-stemmed pipe from Sumatra in 1799 was the first item of ethnology in the museum. These farsighted sea captains were probably their country's first contact with the unusual and then unknown cultures revealed at this museum. You appreciate and understand life-styles of the Pacific Islands, India, Japan, China, and the American Indian as they were before the influence of other cultures. The Polynesian collection is the country's finest. You see the last surviving Marquesan outrigger canoe, the ancient Hawaiian war god Kukaili-moku, the oldest Penobscot Indian canoe in existence, and the best collection of Japanese household arts and crafts anywhere in the world, including a popular display of netsuke, belt toggle sculpture.

The natural-history section began in 1799 also, with an elephant's tooth. Other "natural curiosities" followed, such as the first ostrich, peacock, fireworks, and penguin. Now the natural-history department focuses on Essex County and coastal New England. Varied displays of specimens and sketches in appropriate settings include birds, fish, mammals, snakes, one hundred varieties of beans, many decoys, and a turtle still dripping oil one hundred years later.

The ancient Marine Society moved to its new quarters here in 1824 with President John Quincy Adams* giving the opening address. In later years, the name changed to honor a major donor, George Peabody.

Education programs are essential components of this excellent museum. You realize this as you watch excited children, whose guides fascinate them with living history, stop to listen, and hear a story which helps you appreciate these treasures further and carry their memory and meaning with you.

#3
Essex Street Mall

As you leave the Peabody Museum you are in East India Square and the attractive Essex Street Mall which includes many historical sites. (see map for locations)

Ⓐ *East India Square Fountain*, Essex Street, symbolizes Salem's historic relationship to ocean and Far East, sculptured shorelines of waterworn granite and cobblestone depict lines of colonial and modern times.

B *Goult-Pickman House,* Corner Liberty and Charter (NRHP) Streets, private, claimed c.1638 date makes it oldest house in Salem; home of Judge Benjamin Lynde,* Massachusetts chief justice, presided at Boston Massacre trial, son also chief justice.

C *Charter Street Burying Point,* 1637, oldest in Salem; only known original stone of *Mayflower passenger* (Richard More); Governor Simon Bradstreet's tomb at highest point; also buried here: Chief Justice Benjamin Lynde, Cotton Mather's brother Nathaniel, Samuel McIntire,* and witchcraft court members the Reverend John Higginson and Judge John Hathorne.*

D *Grimshawe House,* 53 Charter Street, private; Peabody home while Nathaniel Hawthorne* courted daughter Sophia; figured in his novella, *Doctor Grimshaw's Secret.*

E *Salem Fraternity,* 11 Central, 1811; beautiful Federal commercial building designed by Boston's Bulfinch* in McIntire's Salem; bank and insurance office where Nathaniel Bowditch* presided and was first insurance actuary; 1899 Salem Fraternity established America's oldest boys' club here, still active.

F *London Coffee House,* Central Street, c.1698; where patriots gathered, heatedly discussed hated British taxes.

G *Old Town Hall,* On *Derby Square* off Front Street, NRHP, 1816; neat brick Federal Period highlighted by delicately detailed windows, fan-arched heads, center Palladian; visit Chamber of Commerce within; upstairs formal hall with soft gold walls, graceful chandeliers; surrounding Derby Square was site of McIntire's most magnificent mansion, the Elias Hasket Derby* Mansion.

H *First Meetinghouse Site,* Corner Essex and Washington Streets (Daniel Low and Company now); this converted Victorian church building was fourth on site where First Meeting House stood 1634-1673.

I *Salem Springs Site,* Essex and Washington Streets, source of town pump, tradition immortalized by Hawthorne in *Twice Told Tales.*

J *City Hall,* 93 Washington Street, 1838, NRHP; Greek Revival highlighted by wreath-decorated frieze and gilded McIntire eagle; second-floor Council Chamber, beautifully solemn, remains as arranged in 1838, lined with portraits, royal blue wainscoting, ornamental gold.

K *Lyceum,* 43 Church Street, now open as restaurant; began in 1830 when hosted Webster, Lowell, Adams, Holmes, Thoreau, Mann; wooden building replaced by brick before 1894; 1877 hosted Alexander Graham Bell and first public demonstration of telephone when he spoke to assistant Thomas Watson in Boston.

#4
Essex Institute, 1848, and
museum houses
within Institute grounds
Plummer Hall (Museum)
1857
John Tucker Daland House
(library) 1851
Doll House (Quaker
Meetinghouse) c.1688
Lye-Tapley Shoe Shop 1830
John Ward House, 1684,
NHL
Crowninshield-Bentley
House, 1727, NRHP
Gardner-Pingree House,
1804, NRHP
Andrew-Safford House,
1818, NRHP
132 Essex Street
Open all year, some houses
open seasonally, fee
charged
NRHP

Walk back past where car is parked to right of St. Peter's Church again. This time walk straight on Brown Street to the Essex Institute on the right in the middle of the next block. Other institute house museums at different locations within Salem are #5 Peirce-Nichols, #6 Assembly House, #8 Ropes Mansion.

Here are the treasures of Salem. Here you can see seven nationally significant historic houses beautifully and authentically furnished, browse through a fascinating museum of history and art, or pursue detailed research in a unique library. The Institute began in 1848 with the merger of two earlier societies, one historical, one natural history, and remains one of the oldest, most recognized regional historical societies. It offers programs of education, publications, lectures, symposia, and other special events.

The central core of Essex Institute is beautifully housed in two joined Victorian mansions, Plummer Hall and John Tucker Daland House. *Plummer Hall*, built in 1857 for the Salem Athenaeum, provides a fitting background for museum displays. Priceless antiquity is found at every turn with the second-floor permanent galleries most interesting. Here outstanding collections of historical artifacts, decorative and fine arts, and architecture record the lives of a representative group of real people from 1630 on.

Rich experience and discovery await in this well-labeled and classified museum. In the main gallery are three period rooms, among the country's earliest, set up in 1907 by the Institute's pioneering preservationist, George Francis Dow.* Across are interpretive displays of the seventeenth and eighteenth centuries, and the special doll and toy world apart. You see the importance of Salem and Essex County in maritime trade, the resulting wealth, and how it was translated into artifacts and architecture.

The research half of the Institute's central core is the 1851 *John Tucker Daland House,* designed by architect Gridley J. F. Bryant. (See Quincy #12) The regal drawing room of wealthy merchant Daland is now the reading room. The extensive library contains an usually fine collection of regional documents, manuscript collections, and invaluable books. Shelves of books reach toward tall ceilings; twin ornate fireplaces wear priceless urns on mantels topped with huge gilt mirrors; and tables and chairs invite you to study.

The grounds of the Institute are inviting also. A doll collection and toy exhibit are presented in what was probably Salem's first *Quaker Meetinghouse.* The circa 1688 structure was moved here in 1865, one of the first buildings to be moved for preservation. Nearby, a "ten footer,"* The *Lye-Tapley Shoe Shop* from Lynn, is complete with all the paraphernalia necessary for the shoe workers of this early factory.

Museum Houses Located at the Institute

The circa 1684 *John Ward House,* NHL, as the oldest, is a good house museum with which to begin. It successfully creates the mood and appearance of the seventeenth century, with much framing and some floor sections from the original First Period house. To preserve it, the house was moved and restored by architectural-historian George Francis Dow and the Institute in 1910. Dow's front rooms and their furnishings interpret life and culture of the seventeenth century, and the lean-to section added by 1732 contains nineteenth-century cottage industries set up by him. There is a fascinating 1830s apothecary shop with myriads of tiny containers, some with original contents, plus archaic tools for pulling teeth or letting blood. Next, the complete weaving room is followed by a once-common-in-Salem Cent Shop and its curiosities.

To progress forward in time the next house is the *Crowninshield-Bentley* (106 Essex Street), a rare example of Salem's interesting eighteenth-century. Seafaring fish-merchant John Crowninshield began the house in 1727. It was added to and remodeled several times, thus creating a truly representative 1700s home, in which Crowninshields lived until 1832.

Crowninshields soon rivaled Derbys in their important contribution to Salem's maritime supremacy—a supremacy which strengthened as the families united in marriage. John Crowninshield's daughter, Elizabeth, married America's first millionaire Elias Hasket Derby.* And John's prominent son, George, married Derby's sister, Mary. Crowninshields succeeded as mariner-merchants and as wartime privateersmen. Their ship *America* alone captured twenty-six prize ships and realized over a million dollars. Benjamin W. Crowninshield, son of George and Mary, became secretary of the navy under President Madison. His brother, George, Jr., pioneered in pleasure yachting with his brig *Cleopatra's Barge** sold after his death to the Hawaiian monarch for his royal yacht. Their dashing cousin, sea captain Benjamin Crowninshield, lived in half this house and was responsible for its major remodeling in 1794.

Reverend Doctor William Bentley—pastor, historian, naturalist, politician—lived here nearly thirty years, a boarder of Widow Hannah Crowninshield's. This man of many talents is best known as the writer of important New England diaries. His great curiosity and ability to note details combined to create diaries which recounted spirit and feelings as well as facts. Everyday life at all levels is pictured from his Salem arrival as pastor in 1783 until his death in 1819.

The house restoration, furnishings, and artifacts are carefully authentic for the three generations of Crowninshields who lived here. Dr. Bentley's room looks as if he just stepped out, soon to return to his chair, a relic he collected. The Thomas Jefferson portrait and treasured Governor Endicott 1630 sundial represent some of his many interests. Half the house is restored to about 1762 and the remainder to the 1794 remodeling which created the "Beverly jog" and the front's cohesive Georgian appearance.

The next period house within the Institute grounds is the 1804-1805 *Gardner-Pingree House* at 128 Essex Street. It is everything a grand

Federal mansion should be. Considered by many to be Samuel McIntire's* finest surviving work, it beautifully expresses the success of its first owner during the glorious times of Salem's greatest prosperity.

The front facade quietly demonstrates impressive dignity and splendor. The highlighting rhythm and balance of windows and string courses across the warm brick structure are crowned by the balustraded hip roof. The portico, with beautifully carved Corinthian columns and pilasters, draws you toward the delicately fan and side-lighted door.

You enter through a classical McIntire doorway into a lavish interior. The entry hall demands time to study delicate carvings and applied molded ornaments which are McIntire's signature. Stairway balustrades and tread ends, detailed arch and door frames, and subtly elaborate cornices vie for your attention. The double parlors on the right are equally spectacular. The intricate yet warm detail of the fireplaces is unmatched. Sheaves of wheat, rosettes, garlands, baskets of fruit, sprays of laurel, dentils, and reeded areas are delicately carved or applied with artistic integration and balance.

The neoclassical perfection of the Federal style architecture is complemented throughout the house by the furnishings which together express Salem's vast wealth before the War of 1812. Some furnishings and decorative arts were brought by Salem captains from all over the world, reflecting her cosmopolitan interests. Notable wallpapers, preserved from other historic houses of Essex County, are found here. There are seven panels designed by Fragonard fils in 1808, printed by Dufour, and a hand-painted paper by Michael Felice Corné.

John Gardner's splendid mansion did not always bring its merchant-owners good luck. Gardner's business success ended too soon, with the War of 1812. Joseph White, the next prosperous merchant-owner, at age eighty-two was murdered in his bed here in 1830. Then owner David Pingree began to turn the tide, only to have his mercantile interests decline. However, his land purchases made his son David the largest individual landowner in New England and even in the mid-1930s depression worth twenty million dollars. The Pingree family crowned ninety-nine years of living here by giving their magnificent mansion to the Institute in 1933.

The last mansion to tour within the grounds is the *Andrew-Safford House*, crown jewel of the late Federal Period, built 1818–1819 at 13 Washington Square. Tall, monumental, vertical, this strong mansion features an elaborate Corinthian columned and balustraded portico capped by a Palladian window. The smooth Flemish bond-brick facade is quietly ornamented by delicate keystone window lintels and crowned by a balustrade around the whole house, with a smaller balustrade at the crest of the hip roof. On the imposing south side four full height, off-centered, Doric columns dramatically draw your attention and attest to the wealth of the first owner, John Andrew, shipowner and commission merchant in Russia. A stable wing is attached, partially sheltering the formal brick-walled garden of the estate.

The high Federal interior hints at the beginnings of Greek Revival in the formal double parlor with its elaborate ceiling of rosettes. The wallpaper is Dufour's masterpiece, original to the house. Across is the Victorian room, remodeled during that era by later owner James Safford, leather manufacturer and merchant. Home now to the Institute's director, the mansion is open on a limited basis.

#5
Peirce-Nichols House
80 Federal Street
c.1782
Open all year, fee charged
NRHP

Return to your car. Turn left, exiting on Church Street. Turn right on Washington Street; go one short block, and turn left on Federal Street. Go one block, cross North Street, and the Peirce-Nichols House will be on the right at the corner of North and Federal Streets. Essex Institute House.

The Peirce-Nichols House provides a magnificent opportunity to understand the architectural evolution and social history of seafaring Salem in her prime period. You get to know successful merchant-shipowner Jerathmiel Peirce, who had the great foresight to hire twenty-four-year-old Samuel McIntire* to design his grand home. Here you meet this great architect through his original work.

On the left you see McIntire's classic Georgian parlor with heavy, bold paneling and molding. Across the hall in perfect contrast is his remodeled 1801 Federal parlor with its lighter, more delicate woodwork. Here is a unique find: six McIntire carved and upholstered settees, with rosettes and acanthus leaves, designed for the Federal room and the recesses they still occupy. Other exciting pieces of the Peirce-Nichols family are found here, including the elaborately carved four-post canopy bed attributed also to McIntire, plus appropriate furnishings from other estates in the area.

The front facade features strong, full-height corner pilasters, balustrades at roof line and crown, and commanding fence with original delicate flame-topped urn finials carved by McIntire. Even the interesting outbuildings survive, including stable and countinghouse. The gilded McIntire eagle, which once crowned the storage area, now is safely displayed within the house.

The North River once reached the backyard where first owner Jerathmiel Peirce's ships docked and he carried on his successful mercantile enterprises. Peirce's financial success built this house and remodeled it for beloved daughter Sally's wedding in 1801. His financial collapse lost the house, which soon returned to the possession of son-in-law George Nichols, and remained in the family until it came under Essex Institute control in 1935. In the last two generations there were groups of spinster sisters who lived out their lives here where a sister said, "Cupid passed by . . . with drooping wings and averted eyes."[34]

The Peirce-Nichols House is the gateway to more fascinating historic houses along Federal, Essex, Chestnut, and Broad Streets. (see also #6-14) Neat brick sidewalks and interesting Georgian, Federal, Greek Revival, and Victorian houses stand close to the walks and draw you to this atmosphere of other eras. These neighborhoods are particularly pretty on a clear day with the sun highlighting mellow whites, yellows, grays, blues, and bricks of historic Salem. Accurate, informative date plaques add dimension to your appreciation.

#6
Assembly House
138 Federal Street
1782
Open all year, fee charged
NRHP

Continue NW on Federal Street to number 138, which will be on the right. The Assembly House is an Essex Institute house. A more elaborate McIntire can be seen just beyond at 142 Federal Street, the Cook-Oliver House. Gateposts and wood finishing touches are believed to be McIntire's from his grand Derby Mansion, once commanding Derby Square.* The house was built circa 1802 and the design is attributed to McIntire. The house is private.

It is easy to picture grand receptions for Lafayette in 1784 and Washington in 1789, gala balls, concerts, lectures, and other entertainments hosted here. For these were the purposes for the building of the Assembly House in 1782 by a small number of Salem's elite. When later replaced as a social and cultural center, the fine building was remodeled by McIntire* c.1798 to become a fashionable private home.

The graceful front facade was further adorned by McIntire's addition of window-placement symmetry, four pairs of second-story Ionic pilasters, the wide pediment with its delicate fanlight, and roof-crowning balustrade. His beautiful, elaborated doorway, with rosettes and bellflowers, is now shadowed by the porch with its massive grapevine frieze, carved leaves, and fruit, added after 1833.

Within, the Assembly House interprets Salem's rich and varied history in the furnishings of different generations through the nineteenth century. Trade with the Far East is evident in the east parlor with furnishings from China, Zanzibar, and India. The dining room of fine Salem Chippendale and the second-floor Victorian parlor provide interesting contrast and complement the McIntire woodwork. Many family pieces were donated by Mary Silver Smith who also gave this, her family home, to the Institute.

#7
Greymoor
329 Essex Street
1870
Open all year, fee charged.

Continue on Federal; turn left on Flint Street, go one block to Essex Street and turn left. On Essex notice the Library on the left at 370 and the Athenaeum on the right, in the next block, at 337.
The Salem Library, a brick mansion built in 1855, was given the city by Mary Ann Ropes Bertram, widow of admired Salem benefactor, Captain John Bertram. The private library, the Salem Athenaeum, began in 1810 and was frequented by Nathaniel Hawthorne. This impressively pillored porticoed structure was built in 1906. Greymoor is on the right at 329 Essex. Park here for #7-10.

Beautifully restored Greymoor was once the Legion Hall. Now it is a grand Victorian museum of furnishings and related collections in addition to an architecturally interesting home with impressive interior detail.

#8
Ropes Mansion
318 Essex Street
c.1727
Open seasonally, fee charged, no fee for garden
NRHP

The Ropes Mansion is at 318 Essex on the left. Essex Institute House.

The magnificent formal garden of the Ropes Mansion features countless annual blooms which provide continuing color and beauty. The large variety of plants includes rare shrubs from China, a gift of the Arnold Arboretum.* A fish pool and sundial add to this refreshing, peaceful spot.

The garden and mansion and all its furnishings are gifts to you from the Ropes sisters, Mary and Eliza, the last of four generations to live here. The mansion was purchased by Judge Nathaniel Ropes II in 1768 from the Barnard family, who built it after 1727. The esteemed judge tragically died of smallpox the night a mob attacked his home in 1774, questioning his allegiance to the Crown. Ropes family members continued here, some moving but retaining their loyalty, with two sisters of the Cincinnati branch returning as the last Ropes generation. They died in the early 1900s.

Each generation made architectural changes. The classic Georgian house, with balanced windows, dormers, and balustraded gambrel roof, has been moved back from the street and raised. The handsome period fence and commanding posts and urn finials were added in the 1894 renovations.

The Ropes sisters set up displays which remain where feasible. Most outstanding is the china and glass collection, which includes over three hundred pieces of Nanking-pattern Chinese export porcelain and possibly the largest single set in the world of Irish cut glass, which was purchased in 1817.

The mansion is furnished entirely with family pieces, including rare period furniture in Chippendale, Queen Anne, and Hepplewhite styles and oriental rugs brought by Salem ships. The double parlors on the left remain as remodeled in 1894 in the Colonial Revival style with mainly Empire furnishings. On the right, the 1835 renovation period dining room with all its original furnishings, features the straw-yellow color popular in those Greek Revival times. Upstairs Elizabeth's room was left by her mother just as it was when Elizabeth died at age twenty-four in 1842, the only child of the judge's granddaughter, Sally Ropes Orne. Next is Sally Orne's room, also remaining as she left it at her death in 1876. Her wedding portraits here are by Samuel F. B. Morse, better known in connection with the telegraph.

You feel as if you are visiting a prestigious Salem family and leave with the warm feeling of having shared their pleasant, gracious way of life.

#9
First Church in Salem
316 Essex Street
Organized 1629, building
1835
Open for services and by
appointment

On the east side of the Ropes Mansion is the First Church in Salem.

First Church is not only the first church organized in Salem, but the first Colonial Congregational Society to be formally organized in America, and still continue as an active religious society to the present day. The First Parish Church in Plymouth was organized earlier in 1606, but in Scrooby, England.

In 1629 the ship *Talbot* arrived in Salem with three ministers aboard. Two, the Reverends Samuel Skelton and Francis Higginson, remained in Salem organizing their church. The third, the Reverend Ralph Smith, traveled to Plymouth, where he became their first settled minister. The friendship between the two colonies had earlier caused Plymouth's Doctor Samuel Fuller to treat sick settlers in Salem. At that time he was instrumental in encouraging Salem colonists to accept Plymouth's Congregational form of religious meetings. As a result, on July 20, 1629, the settlers of Salem cast ballots to determine whether the Reverend Higginson or Skelton would be their minister or teacher. This was undoubtedly the first time ballots were used to choose ministers in the colonies. Following the balloting, the First Church organized August 6, 1629. Within the year Higginson died, but not before writing the church's covenant, which is still said at every Sunday worship service. It can be seen on a plaque in the sanctuary.

First Church has had many interesting historical milestones. The Reverend Roger Williams* served as third minister before being driven from the colony for his unorthodox views of true religious freedom. He went on to found the state of Rhode Island, where he instigated religious and political freedom. The Reverend Hugh Peters, fourth minister, did much to stimulate economic growth. He encouraged building of ships in Salem, fishing from Winter Island, planting and marketing hemp, and the building of a water-mill, glasshouse, and saltworks. He later returned to England, where he supported Cromwell's revolution and was charged with aiding in the demise of King Charles. He was hung, quartered, and his head placed atop a pole on London Bridge.

In 1692 two church members, Rebecca Nurse and Giles Cory, were accused of withcraft. They were harangued in church by the Reverend Nicholas Noyes before one was hung on Gallows Hill and the other crushed to death, the sad result of misguided religious zeal.

Seven groups left at different times to form sister churches, the last of which founded North Church in 1772 on the corner of Lynde and North Streets. It was from that church on February 26, 1775, that the Reverend Thomas Barnard left his pulpit to intervene at North Bridge,* where British Colonel Alexander Leslie was confronted by Colonial Colonel Timothy Pickering's* militia. The militia had raised the drawbridge, preventing the British from crossing and confiscating Colonial arms. Following a scuffle over the use of local boats, the first Colonial blood of the forthcoming Revolutionary War was drawn by a British sword. The Reverend Barnard suggested a compromise. The British troops were allowed to cross the bridge to save face, if they advanced only fifty paces, then withdrew to Marblehead Harbor. Thus the first confrontation with British troops ended in peaceful negotiation.

In 1923 First and North Churches again united with the combined congregations meeting in this, the North Church building, which is today renamed First Church. Step inside this bold, impressive, castle-like English Gothic church. It was built of Quincy granite in 1835 by architect Gridley J. F. Bryant, son of the inventor of the granite railway* in Quincy. Notice the exquisite stained-glass windows—two by Tiffany, one by LaFarge,* one by Reynolds—given by the Parker* games family, and two rear windows from the Children's Chapel of the Second Church. The rich wood tones of the rectangular doored pews, the altar, and the quatrefoiled ceiling symbolizing the cross, fill you with a sense of reverence and history. For this church has freely moved from the strict discipline of Puritanism through Calvanism to a liberal Christian Unitarian Universalist church.

#10
Witch House, 1674,
310 Essex Street
Benjamin Thompson
House, 314 Essex
Nathaniel Bowditch House,
North Street
Captain William Driver
Memorial, Essex and
Summer Streets

On the east side of First Church is the Thompson House; next is the Witch House; around the corner on North Street is the Bowditch House; and the Driver Memorial is across Essex Street.

**Only the Witch House is
open, seasonally, fee
charged**

This site has housed two historic men, both dedicated to justice, yet representing opposing views.

The first, the Reverend Roger Williams,* lived here circa 1634–1635 while he served as minister to the First Church, which at that time was located on the corner of Essex and Washington Streets. He was a man devoted to religious and political justice—believing "civil magistrates should have no authority over the conscience of people and that they had no power to punish for heresy."[35] For these beliefs and others of religious freedom, he was ostracized from Massachusetts. Forty years later Jonathan Corwin bought the site from Captain Nathaniel Davenport and rebuilt the home to create what is now called the *Witch House*. Not having drunk from the same fountain of compassion and freedom as Roger Williams, Corwin allowed "justice" to condemn innocent people.

Led by emotional children, people of Salem let superstition, fear, misguided religious fervor, and even jealousy overrule their common sense of compassion and justice. As reason fled, innocent neighbors, friends, and even wives were accused and charged with imagined events, which resulted in death to twenty people and imprisonment for hundreds.

It all began March 1, 1692, when the accused Tituba, Sarah Osborn, and Sarah Good were examined in Salem Village, now Danvers, by magistrates John Hathorne* and Jonathan Corwin. The three, accused of witchcraft, were sent to jail in Boston to be held for trial. In June the witch trials opened in Salem with Jonathan Corwin sitting as one of the judges. The actual trials were held at the courthouse on Washington Street, while meetings of judges and jurors—and it is believed some pretrial examinations—were held here at Judge Corwin's home.

By May of 1693 all executions were over and most of the prisoners released from jail—ending a tragic reign of terror. New Englanders awoke to what they had done; many requested public forgiveness; days of humiliation and prayer were held; and the ugly demon of superstition was slain.

Today Judge Corwin's home has been restored to his time. Its open-beam keeping room and kitchen illustrate life in the late seventeenth century. Notice the large fireplace with built-in oven, Colonial kitchen utensils, reversible 1690 table, pewter ware, and early one-hand Clark clock. Step across the hall to the best room, used Sundays and for special occasions. Here you will see a twenty-four-inch pine table, English slant-top desk, American banister chairs, and a cabinet with secret drawer.

Above the best room was Judge Corwin's bedroom and probably the room where frightened defendants were questioned. Outside, the dark gabled roof and overhanging second floor seem to add to the picture of fear and superstition that must have been felt in this upstairs room. Though these events took place roughly three hundred years ago that ominous feeling still seems to prevail. May its awareness be a reminder that common sense and mercy must always be in harmony with justice.

At 314 Essex is the boyhood home of *Benjamin Thompson*, later known as Count Rumford, inventor of the Rumford stoves and ovens. Behind the Witch House is the garden where Roger Williams prepared some of his sermons, and to the right, facing North Street, is the *Nathaniel Bowditch* House* (NHL), where the famed navigator and mathematician lived. Bowditch wrote the *Practical Navigator* in 1802. The revised book is still used by the navy. Across Essex Street is a memorial to *Captain William Driver*, who was the first to call the flag "Old Glory."

#11
Pickering House
18 Broad Street
1651
Open all year, limited hours and by appointment, fee charged

Return to your car, continue on Essex to Summer. Turn right on Summer Street; go two blocks to Broad Street; and turn right. The Pickering House is in the second block on the right, opposite Winthrop Street.

A unique experience awaits you—an opportunity to share and feel part of a ten-generation family tradition—as your gracious hostess, Mrs. John Pickering, welcomes you to their home. The Pickering House is the oldest house in this country continuously occupied by one family.

With New England charm, Mrs. Pickering invites you to enter, to sit in their living room, to talk about the Pickerings and their home, and to see some of the mementos they have treasured over the centuries. You browse through a family scrapbook and find letters from Presidents Washington, Adams, and Jefferson to an ancestor, Colonel Timothy Pickering.* Colonel Pickering was quarter master general of the Revolutionary Army, President Washington's Indian negotiator, post-

master general, secretary of war, then secretary of state. He became
President Adams' secretary of the navy and later secretary of state.
This amazing Pickering was a farmer also, first president of Essex
Agricultural Society, and winner of a plowing contest at age seventy-
five.

Near the scrapbook is an interesting desk made by the Reverend
Theophilus Pickering, uncle of Colonel Timothy, second minister of
Essex, whose home remains here today. Above is the portrait and
needlework of Mary Pickering Leavitt, whose thimble remains on the
frame where she left it prior to her death in 1805. It is surrounded now
by photos of modern grandchildren.

Warm family treasures continue as you are escorted from room to
room—a mirror from Portugal, a bonnet-topped highboy from Salem,
china from the world, a wine cooler from President Washington.
Elegant, formal family antiques blend pleasantly with the many periods of the house to provide an unequaled setting for today's gracious
yet practical living.

Carpenters and farmers, Pickerings came from England in 1630 and
settled here. The house began in 1651 when the first John Pickering
built a two-room half house on his farm, which included most of this
beautiful section of Salem. In 1671 the next John Pickering added the
other half to form a modest two-story, central-chimney Colonial. By
1722 gables were added, the roof line in back had become a saltbox, and
by 1842 the Gothic peaks, trim, and fence created today's appearance.

The house continued to be passed down, usually father to son, each
adding his personality. The ten generation result, a wonderful tradition
now protected by a foundation, is yours to enjoy while you visit.

#12
Chestnut Street
Viewable all year, all
houses private except the
Stephen Phillips House at
34 Chestnut Street (see
#13)
NHL

*Continue on Broad Street to Flint Street
traffic light. Turn right and go two blocks
to Chestnut. Turn right and enjoy Chestnut Street.*

Chestnut Street is considered by many to be "the finest, best
preserved and most aristocratic thoroughfare in America."[36] Whether
or not you agree, you will be suitably impressed by the row of elegant
Federals, with a sprinkling of Georgian and Greek Revival, on both

Chestnut Street Houses

sides of the dignified, wide "thoroughfare." Salem's mighty sea captains and merchants lived here in New England splendor during Salem's most prosperous years. Brick walks invite you to stroll along, slowly appreciating the ornate doorways and stately facades of elegant Salem in the early 1800s. One house is open to the public (see #13), a fine example of the grand homes of this avenue and their equally grand owners.

#13
Stephen Phillips Trust
House
34 Chestnut Street
early 1800s
Open seasonally, fee
charged

The fifth house on the left, at 34 Chestnut Street, is the Stephen Phillips Trust House.

A beautiful fence with often-photographed, delicately elaborate urn finials encloses this stately Federal mansion. So impressive and staunch here, it is hard to believe it was brought to this site from Danvers in the mid-1800s. Moved in two sections, it was linked by a central portion after its arrival. The Stephen Phillips House was actually a portion of a grand estate called Oak Hill built for Nathaniel West. Believed to have been designed by McIntire,* the West mansion

402

and its story are a featured exhibit at Boston's Museum of Fine Arts,*
with several rooms reconstructed there. West was married to Elizabeth Derby, and their notorious divorce exploded their world.

Sea Captain Stephen Phillips, who was in the China trade and other
ventures during Salem's prime, built the Phillips' ancestral home at 17
Chestnut Street. His son, the Honorable Stephen C. Phillips, expanded their mercantile efforts, served in Congress, and as Mayor of
Salem donated his salary to education. His son, Stephen H. Phillips,
was Massachusetts attorney general. His son is the Stephen Phillips
who bought this house in 1914.

Unique family heirlooms and furnishings of five generations of
Stephen Phillipses are here for you to see in this elegant mansion. For
your brief stay, you feel part of this fine family as you see china,
oriental rugs, rare furniture, and all the treasures you expect of a
prosperous Salem sea captain and his worthy descendants.

#14   *Farther along on the right on the corner of*
Hamilton Hall   *Chestnut and Cambridge Streets is Ham-*
9 Chestnut Street   *ilton Hall.*
1805
Open when not being used
for social functions, no fee
NRHP

Hamilton Hall was designed by Samuel McIntire,* built in 1805, and
named for admired Federalist and frequent Salem visitor, Alexander
Hamilton. Here Lafayette was honored in 1824 at the gala occasion
attended by three hundred. Its grand ballroom is pleasantly lighted by
large Palladian windows with fluted columns, simple entablatures, and
ropelike dentils. Gilded Russian mirrors top twin fireplaces.

#15   *At the end of Chestnut Street, cross Sum-*
Salem Maritime National   *mer Street and continue two blocks to*
Historic Site   *central parking plaza and turn right.*
Derby Wharf, 1764   *Drive three-fourths of the way around the*
Custom House, 1819   *central parking plaza. Turn right on New*
Bonded Warehouse, 1819   *Derby Street and follow it to the Salem*
Scale House, 1829   *Maritime National Historic Site. The*
Narbonne House, 1670   *Custom House and historic houses will be*
Derby House, 1762   *on the left and the wharves on the right.*
Hawkes House, 1774   *There is parking on the right just before*
West India Goods Store,   *the wharves.*
1800

Derby Street
Open all year, no fee
NRHP, HABS

The heartbeat of Salem can be felt in the nine-acre historic maritime site which has been restored, preserved, and maintained by the National Park Service since 1937. Let your imagination superimpose late eighteenth-century and early nineteenth-century life on the scene before you. Tied up at Derby Wharf might have been Elias Hasket Derby's* 300-ton *Grand Turk* just back from China with a cargo of teas and nankeens or the *Mount Vernon* back from the Mediterranean full of silks and wines, reaping a profit of $100,000. Or it could have been the *Revenge,* one of the fastest and most profitable privateers, unloading her captured prize. This was a time of adventure, great risks, and rich rewards for the bold and the daring. Between 1785 and 1799 Elias Derby sent his ninety-one vessels on 180 voyages to every port of call from China to the West Indies.

The building of *Derby Wharf* was begun by Richard Derby* about 1764. In 1806 it was lengthened to service more and larger vessels, and in 1871 the range lighthouse was added. Along Derby Wharf were

Massachusetts Department of Commerce and Development, Division of Tourism

Salem Maritime National Historic Site

warehouses holding everything from tea, fish, and lumber to exotic birds, rare wines, and imported porcelain. During the years of privateers, the warehouses held captured cargoes waiting to be auctioned, and in later years cotton for use in adjacent factories.

Now enter the *Custom House*, just as the captains of old would have done to register their cargoes, obtain bills of lading, or pay import taxes. The Custom House collected over twenty-five million dollars between 1789 and 1879, listing 14,000 foreign entries. This dignified Federal-style building with granite steps, fanlight-topped doorway, classical pillars, and cupola-topped hip roof is all carefully watched over by a golden eagle holding the United States shield. Inside is the surveyor's office made famous by Nathaniel Hawthorne in his book *The Scarlet Letter.* Here Hawthorne served as surveyor from 1846 until 1849. The main business offices are set up as they were last used for active maritime business. In the old vault room, where the ships' records were kept (now at Essex Institute*), is an interesting ten-minute slide presentation.

Attached to the rear of the building, entered from the outside, is the *Bonded Warehouse,* which held goods waiting to be reshipped or to have duties paid. Here you can see sample shipments of yesteryear, such as pepper from Sumatra, sugar from the West Indies, annatto dye from the East Indies, and coffee beans from Arabia. Upstairs is the old hoisting winch and a large model of the brig *Leander,* a vessel built in 1821 at the shipyard across the street for Joseph Peabody and used in the China and opium trade.

Behind the Custom House is the 1829 *Scale House* where the measuring and weighing devices used for the port's surveyor were stored. These articles were portable and used over the years to measure incoming cargos on fifty different wharves in Salem.

On the Essex Street side of the Maritime Site is the *Narbonne House,* built in 1670. This house shows the architectural progression of a documented seventeenth-century house through its natural additions made by subsequent owners. It was originally a 1670 half house, and the gambrel roof section was added about 1720. Further nineteenth-century changes have been found on the interior.

As you leave the Narbonne House, moving toward the Derby House, observe the buildings before you. Here is a cross-section of Salem. The seventeenth-century Narbonne House, the eighteenth-century Georgian Derby House, the late eighteenth–early ninteenth century Federal Hawkes House and nineteenth-century Custom House are all set against the backdrop of historic Derby Wharf and the ever vital harbor.

Tour the *Derby House* built by Captain Richard Derby* for son Elias Hasket Derby in 1762. Here Elias, his wife, Elizabeth Crowninshield Derby,* and family of three sons and four daughters lived until the end of the Revolutionary War. From here Elias oversaw his early shipping business, shared in the excitement of his returning prize-laden privateers, and after the war sent forth his ships to open new trade routes throughout the world. Walk through the rooms and see where America's first millionaire lived. Notice the paneled wainscoting and fireplaces, inside shutters, window seats, wide floorboards, and period furniture. The back room, which might have been used as a study by Elias, has the most ornate of the fireplaces and a secretary similar to what he would have used. From this small, unassuming room, his influence reached around the world, through his ships, their captains, and their cargoes.

His three sons were ships' captains. A brother, Captain John Derby, carried the news of the Lexington and Concord encounter to England, and eight years later it was his ship that sailed into Salem Harbor with word of the Peace Treaty.

Adjacent to the Derby House is the *Hawkes House*, initially built by Derby and used by him to store goods brought back by his privateers. In 1801 the building was bought by Benjamin Hawkes, who finished it as the lovely Federal home you see today.

On the far side of the Derby House, at the corner of Derby Street and Palfrey Court, is the *West India Goods Store* built by Captain Prince and set up today to illustrate such a store during the 1800s. Here would have been sold goods brought back by the Prince ships. As you enter the door, the intriguing aromas of imported teas, coffees, and spices remind you of those earlier trade routes and life in the nineteenth century, which was Salem in the days of sail.

#16
House of the Seven Gables
Historic Site
House of the Seven Gables, 1668
Hawthorne's Birthplace, c.1750
Hooper-Hathaway House, 1682

Continue east on Derby Street .2 mile to entrance, which is on right off Derby Street by way of either Hardy Street or Turner Street.

The Counting House, 1840
Retire Becket House, 1665
54 Turner Street
Open all year, fee charged
NRHP

If you have read Hawthorne's *House of the Seven Gables*, a visit here is a must, and if you have yet to enjoy his prose, this complex sets the stage for Hawthorne and his book. Here you can see the House of the Seven Gables, Hawthorne's Birthplace, and two homes built in the 1600s which give you a glimpse into Salem life in three centuries.

Nathaniel Hawthorne, brought up in Salem and deeply influenced by his Puritan ancestry, incorporated much of Salem life in his writings. Well-read, intellectually curious, he often visited the home of his cousin, Susannah Ingersoll, which is now called the House of the Seven Gables. She filled his mind and imagination with stories of their ancestors and life in early Salem. He learned of the first Hathorne (then spelled without the w) who settled in 1630 and was a persecutor of Quakers; of Colonel John Hathorne* who became a judge at the infamous witch trials; and of the legendary curse issued by a convicted witch, "God will give you blood to drink."[37] He also knew that the house had been built on the site of an earlier home; that his cousin lived almost as a recluse in her later years; and that a cent shop had been part of the house. All of these ideas as well as names and places from Salem played in Hawthorne's mind, ultimately appearing interwoven in the book *The House of the Seven Gables*.

The exterior of the house, now restored to its earlier seven gables, appears dark and foreboding, as if it had untold dark secrets. The interior quickly dispels that sentiment with a sunny, warm feeling of the home of a prosperous Salem merchant. For that is exactly what it was.

The initial four-gabled house was built in 1668 by Captain John Turner, a young, ambitious man who attained a respectable fortune in trade with Barbados before he died in 1680. His son John II carried on the family business and added three gables to the house in the 1690s. He had the hand-hewn beams and painted walls of the formal parlor covered and hung with paper, and replaced small diamond-shaped windows with larger double-hung sash. Thus he created the present bright cheery room with its own special view of Salem Harbor, where his ships might well have lain at anchor.

House of the Seven Gables

John III, lacking his ancestors' business shrewdness, finally sold the house in 1782. New owner Captain Samuel Ingersoll had several of the gables removed, modernizing the roof line. It was his only daughter, Susannah, who lived in the house with her adopted son, Horace, during Hawthorne's time.

In 1908 Caroline O. Emmerton, a woman of extraordinary vision and purpose, realizing the historic significance of the house, bought and restored it. Miss Emmerton was at the same time deeply committed to Settlement House work. She wisely combined her two interests. She opened the House of the Seven Gables to the public for a fee and used the income to support the historic house and her Settlement House work. This creative and practical idea is still operating. Today two settlement houses, Emmerton Hall and Phippen House, are serving the neighborhood.

Upon admission to the complex, there is an interesting video presentation which sets the background for your tour. As you enter the House of the Seven Gables notice the old kitchen fireplace which served as the heart and warmth of the household. On its hearth is an old crusie lamp and nearby a 1600s wine chest. Through the half-doorway can be seen a replica of an old-fashioned cent shop, once owned by many a merchant's or captain's wife. Here she sold things brought back by her husband or useful items made by, or collected by, herself; thus taking in a little extra cash for household needs.

The dining room, which in Hawthorne's story was Hepzibah's parlor, begins to bring alive both the story and gracious living of the nineteenth century. Here is a chair reminiscent of where the judge died in the story. On the wall is a portrait of Susannah Ingersoll and a Simon Willard banjo clock. A Martha Washington chair, a Hepplewhite sideboard, and Hawthorne's checkerboard add to the interest of the pleasant dining room. Beside the fireplace is the secret passageway to Horace's small gabled bedroom above. Inside the fireplace is hidden the lever that opens the special panel where one might escape in a hurry. Adjacent to the bedroom is the attic with its original wide floorboards, wooden pegged beams, and fascinating model of the house. From here move to the bright, cheery master bedroom with portraits of Hawthorne and his wife, Sophia Peabody. Now descend to the gracious formal parlor with paneled fireplace wall, set-in, hand-carved shell-shaped cupboards, and portraits of Hawthorne at fifty-four, John Turner III, and his daughter Mary. An 1830 piano and a desk and chair used by Hawthorne complete the perfect ending to a beautifully restored historic home.

After leaving the House of the Seven Gables enjoy the beautiful gardens, watched over by horticulturalist Daniel Foley, on your way to the *Hooper-Hathaway House* built in 1682. In the old kitchen you will see three carefully finished upright beams, which are believed to have been part of Governor John Endicott's* circa 1630s home. The exposed beams, unfinished walls, and large fireplace of the kitchen speak of the seventeenth century while the finished walls, moldings, smaller fireplace, and inside shutters of the parlor speak of the eighteenth century.

Next door is the 1840 *Counting House* which is set up as a captain's office might have been in the 1830s and 1840s. On the desk are signed documents by Nathaniel Hawthorne. A tape explains the room and its earlier uses.

The gabled roof, central chimney, red clapboard *Birthplace of Nathaniel Hawthorne* proudly joins this complex, moved here from Union Street in 1958. The house was probably built around 1750. The parlor is done in furniture of the 1700s with an unusual 1610 English lantern clock on the wall. The study honors Nathaniel Bowditch,* famed navigator and mathematician. There is a painting of the ship

America on which Nathaniel Hawthorne's father sailed as first mate. This ship had the honor of bringing the first elephant to America. Upstairs is the bedchamber where Nathaniel was born July 4, 1804. From this beginning, he would become one of America's loved and respected literary giants.

Brick walks, carefully planted gardens with varying colors and textures, flowering shrubbery, and large guardian trees unify this historic complex. The red of Hawthorne's Birthplace stands out against the dark brown of the other historic homes, and the varying roof lines are interestingly silhouetted against the sky.

This ends the guided tour section of Salem. Exit from House of Seven Gables, turn right on Derby Street. Take fourth left on Webb Street. Follow Webb to end, turn right on Route 1A, Bridge Street, for Beverly.

Salem Beaches and Parks and Other Points of Interest

Ⓐ Forest River Park*
end of West Street

Pleasant peninsula in Salem Harbor; contains Pioneer Village;* paths along fields, knolls, trees, ledges, and natural beaches; facilities: ball fields, bathhouse, benches, lifeguards, picnicking, playground, swimming pool, walking; parking; open all year, seasonal parking fee

Ⓑ Pickering Wharf and "The Voyage of the India Star"
Derby Street

Popular, successful adaptive reuse of waterfront with many shops, restaurants; wharf and boat rental; information center, small museum of Salem's maritime history with diorama, maps, charts; theater for "Voyage of the India Star," a modern multimedia presentation—see and understand role of owner, insurer, captain, wife, family, and sailors to cabin boy, with ever-present thrill of high-stake gamble of Salem's maritime splendor; parking; open all year, no entrance fee for Pickering Wharf or museum, fee charged for "Voyage"

C Fort Pickering
Derby Street to Fort
Avenue, right on Winter
Island Road
NRHP

End of Winter Island Road; fortified since century before Revolution; Civil War last major use, ruins remain from that era; nearby abandoned lighthouse; later Coast Guard, now Salem owned; great views of harbors, islands, open sea; use not planned yet; permitted to walk in, explore; no parking, no fee

D Fort Lee
Fort Avenue
above first parking lot of
Salem Willows, on left
after Winter Island Road

Possibly Naumkeag Indian vantage point; fortified 1742; at top see points of star where cannon stood; great view, paths; parking; open all year, no fee

E Salem Willows
end of Fort Avenue

Extensive amusement park at water's edge, food concessions; boat rides at pier, tidal beach; acres of walks, willows, views; facilities: benches, picnicking, playground, rest rooms, swimming, walking; parking; open all year, amusements seasonal, no entrance fee

F Ye Olde Pepper Companie
122 Derby Street

Since 1806 "America's oldest candy company"; home of famous Salem "Gibralters," a sweet which would not spoil on long sea voyages, jar of some 148 years old, still edible; open all year, no entrance fee

G Salem Common
Washington Square
Hawthorne Boulevard

Most impressive Common, octagonal bandstand, paths; size appropriate for the surrounding dignified grand homes of Salem's most prosperous period; Common land since 1685, then training field; McIntire designed gateways when fenced in as Washington Square in 1802, carvings on triumphal arch are reproduction, his originals are at Essex Institute; he designed 74 Washington Square East with beautiful, classical entry, and others; Joseph Story House, NHL, corner Winter Street, home of speaker of Massachusetts House, Chief Justice US Supreme Court, here hosted President Monroe 1819 and General Lafayette 1824; statue of Salem founder Roger Conant across at Brown Street; on-street parking; open all year, no fee

(H) Salem Witch Museum
Brown Street
Across from Common

Formidable, stone Romanesque church; now Witch Museum, gift shop, theater; thirty minute multimedia; scenes reenact story of witchcraft terror; mood setting; open all year, fee charged

(I) Parker Brothers
190 Bridge Street
Parking Lot #2
Building #1

Forty-five minute tour of three floors of game-making factory; follow manufacturing process; must make reservations many months in advance; parking; open all year, no fee

(J) Witch Dungeon
16 Lynde Street

Reenact witch trials, tour re-created dungeon, village, Gallows Hill; spooky setting; open seasonally, fee charged

(K) Gedney House c.1650s
21 High Street
SPNEA
NRHP

Architecturally valuable house begun 1650s; unusual with two rooms down, one up, and lean-to on side; early 1700s roof line changed, added second chamber above; later added lean-to in rear; can see to bare beams inside to follow architectural changes; Cox House, c.1775, NRHP, next door at 19 High Street; Gedney House open by appointment only through SPNEA

Harbor Tours
North Shore and Boston
Cruises
Whale watching, charter,
fishing

Pier Transit Co. 744-6311; Salem Willows Pier, Central Wharf (Derby Waterfront). Barnegat Transportation Co. 745-6070, Pickering Wharf

HISTORY OF BEVERLY

Beverly evolved from Salem into her own right as a productive agricultural and seafaring town. In 1636 Roger Conant,* John Balch,* and three others each received two hundred acres at the head of Bass River, which became known as Bass-riverside settlement. This little settlement grew, and in 1667 they established their first church under the Reverend John Hale.* A year later they were incorporated as the town of Beverly. By 1683, with her fine protected harbor, she became a lawful port of entry, thus setting the basic life-style for the next two hundred years.

The witchcraft panic of 1692 hit Beverly with the same fanaticism that was felt in Salem. Only here, while many were accused, none were executed. When the Reverend Hale's wife was accused, that was too much for the good minister. He well knew what a kind and gentle woman she was. Re-evaluating his own thinking, he discarded earlier prejudices, took a strong, positive stand, and almost single-handedly broke the spell in Beverly.

From the mid-1700s through the Revolutionary War leading merchants and patriots such as George, Andrew, and John Cabot,* Moses Brown,* and Isreal Thorndike, guided the town through commercial prosperity and then through the rigors of a war for independence. Twenty-one days before the Declaration of Independence was signed Beverly agreed to stand for independence if the Continental Congress voted for it. On September 5, 1775, the *Hannah,* owned by John Glover* of Marblehead, sailed from his wharf in Beverly commissioned as the first naval ship by General George Washington.

Following the war, the Essex bridge was built connecting Beverly with Salem; America's first power-driven cotton mill was erected in Beverly; and fishermen and merchant ships reawakened the harbor commercially. Beverly grew and prospered. The mid-1800s saw Beverly ships in Spanish, South American, and West Indies ports.

The 1800s also witnessed the rise of the shoe industry—first as a home industry, then later consolidating in large brick factories. The United Shoe Machinery Company opened its doors in 1904 and has had

413

a strong positive economic influence on Beverly ever since. The huge factory produces shoemaking and other special machinery.

The nineteenth and twentieth centuries saw lovely fashionable homes built in Beverly, especially along the waterfront, in Beverly Farms, and Pride's Crossing, where many of the wealthy of the day spent their summers or lived year-round. Proud of her past, mindful of her future, Beverly continues as a pleasant place to live and work.

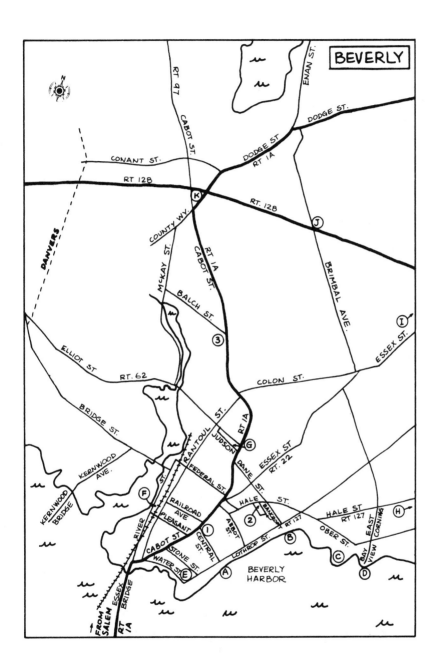

BEVERLY

BEVERLY

DIRECTIONS:
From Salem, drive north and enter Beverly on Route 1A over the Essex bridge onto Cabot Street, following signs for Route 22. Or, from Route 128, take Exit 20, Route 1A, onto Cabot Street, approaching from the opposite direction.

#1
Cabot House
117 Cabot Street
1781-1782
Open all year, fee charged
NRHP

The Cabot House is at 117 Cabot Street, .3 mile north of the Essex Bridge, on the corner of Central and Cabot Streets. Park along Central Street. Beverly Historical Society Headquarters is located here.

You are invited to visit the Cabots, " . . . by far the most wealthy in New England"[38] according to a 1780 source. The Revolution was just ending as John Cabot built this grand three-story mansion, the first brick dwelling in Beverly. During the Revolution, he and his brothers became the most active privateering family in Beverly, reaping rewards which established the Cabot fortune still enjoyed by that family two hundred years later. Their homes were showplaces. John's is here on Cabot Street, brother Andrew's mansion became the now-modified City Hall; their mother's home on Central is now adapted for many apartments; and brother George's grand mansion unfortunately did not survive.

In the Cabot House beautiful early Federal features remain in paneled walls, simple dentils at ceiling and fireplaces, Dutch tiles, and the box enclosure staircase. The parlor contains many possessions of Captain Moses Brown, a contemporary and friend of the Cabots and, like them, a merchant prince and patriot. Furnishings throughout date to the 1830s and are mostly from Beverly's historic families.

Pewter crafted by Israel Trask and Ebenezer Smith is appropriately displayed as Beverly was known for this important home industry. Portraits of pepper trade captains and merchants, primitives by Luke Prince, a military collection, a children's room, and a maritime room are some of the special features found in the Cabot House. The notable

Massachusetts Department of Commerce and Development, Division of Tourism

Cabot House

textile collection is particularly strong in nineteenth-century treasures.

In the hall are portraits of Lucy Larcom, an early writer who focused on the concerns of Lowell textile working girls, and Hannah Hill, who began what is believed to be America's first Sunday school.

The room across from the parlor was the home of the Beverly Bank in 1802, tenth oldest bank in the country. Beverly Savings Bank was also formed here. The room is reminiscent of its banking days with its dominating vault.

Period rooms mix intriguingly with special interest exhibits and changing displays. Together they provide a fascinating tour through this fine Revolutionary period mansion and a glimpse into the lives of the legendary Cabots.

#2
Hale House
39 Hale Street
1694
Open seasonally, fee
charged
NRHP

Continue north on Cabot Street to Hale
Street, the fourth right just before the
church, and turn right. Follow Hale
which bears left, house is on right just
after Bancroft Avenue.

John Hale, freshly graduated from Harvard College, came to Beverly in 1664 as a religious teacher. Three years later the small settlement was granted permission to establish its own church, calling John Hale as first minister. Here he served with unusual courage and wisdom for forty years, leaving only briefly in 1690 as chaplain to the expedition to Canada.

In 1692 he became embroiled in the witchcraft trials, first as a minister and then more importantly as husband of an accused. The Reverend Hale,* knowing his wife Sarah's gentle nature and the impossibility of the accusation, did some deep soul searching. He threw off earlier prejudices, stepped out from under the blanket of fanaticism, and took a strong stand in support of his wife and other accused witches. His stand swayed the community and brought to an end the horrors of witchcraft trials in Beverly. To further explain his thinking he wrote a most enlightening book. *A Modest Inquiry Into the Nature of Witchcraft*, a copy of which can be seen in his home today.

In visiting the Hale House you see a home lived in by Hale descendents since 1694. The earliest part still bears the high peaked roof and original timbers and construction. The dining room section added by grandson Dr. Robert Hale in 1745 shows Georgian influence, with recessed window shutters, a decorative corner cupboard, white walls, and English hand-blocked wallpaper. Numerous additions were made in the nineteenth and twentieth centuries as family size and fortune grew. Furnishings throughout the house came from Beverly families and represent the different furniture periods of nine progressive generations. A clock and chest were left from the Hale-family descendants.

In the rear of the house, beyond the rose garden, stand three magnificent beech trees, which could well represent at least three of the more famous Hales. One, of course, for John who established the first church in Beverly and later took a vital stand against witchcraft. One for his grandson, Nathan Hale, who as a Revolutionary hero left the immortal words, "I only regret that I have but one life to lose for my country."[39] And the third for Unitarian minister and writer Edward Everett Hale, author of *A Man Without a Country.*

#3
Balch House
448 Cabot Street
c.1636
Open seasonally and by
appointment, fee charged
NRHP

Return to Cabot Street, turn right, and continue 1.1 miles through town; over railroad track, past the huge United Shoe Machinery building to the Balch House on the left, at the corner of Cabot and Balch Streets.

The ancient Balch House still quietly stands on one remaining acre above the traffic of Cabot Street, once the area of the Bass River, when this historic house was built.

"Old Planter" John Balch built the two rooms of the right-front gabled section about 1636 on his 200-acre grant. This early structure remarkably remains, now one of the two oldest wood-frame houses in the country. The original beams are even older, English oak cut in England and shipped as ballast.

The Balch House has been restored to its classic First Period, based accurately upon clues found in the structural elements. The 1600s furnishings reenact the 1648 inventory recorded at John Balch's death.

The left side was added about 1650 by John's son Benjamin, whose birth after the charter was received made him the first male born in the Massachusetts Bay Colony. Benjamin Balch lived here until the early 1700s with his three successive wives and thirteen children. When son David died mysteriously at age nineteen, witchcraft entered the scene. Though his 1690 death became part of the trials and testimonies, these were not substantiated by the Balch family.

In the left-front room, the dominating loom and weaving art represent the trade of many later Balches. The Balch family has owned the house for three centuries and continues to aid in its support. Now the historic Balch House is owned by the Beverly Historical Society. Their three fine houses span history and architecture. The First Period circa 1636 Balch House, the 1694 early Georgian Hale House, and the 1782 early Federal Cabot House make an impressive array to visit.

This ends the tour.

Beverly Beaches and Parks and Additional Points of Interest

(A) Independence Park
Lothrop Street, Route
127, foot of central Street

Flags snap proudly in sea breezes above a pleasant historic park; green expanse dotted with benches and cannons; views of islands and sea; breakwater marks sandy/rocky beach; General Glover's* fourteenth regiment was based at this Continental Army post; here Glover read the Declaration of Independence to his troops; limited on-street parking; open all year, no fee

(B) Dane Street Beach
Lothrop Street, Route
127, foot of Ocean
through Hale Streets

Grassy fields lead to open beach, views of harbor islands; facilities: bathhouse, benches, playground, swimming; limited on-street parking; open all year, no fee

(C) Lynch Park
Ober Street, lined by
Waldemar Avenue and
Evergreen Drive;
entrance opposite
Oceanside Drive

Whole point of land, once grand estate, is now beautiful ocean park; extensive beach, lawns, tree-lined paths, formal brick-walled gardens; former stable houses snack bar; facilities: bandshell, benches, paths, picnicking, playground, snack bar, swimming, walking; sticker parking only; open all year, no fee

(D) Hospital Point Light
End of Bay View Avenue

Point fortified in Revolution; had 1801 smallpox hospital; 1871 lighthouse now part of private residence; view of Salem and Beverly Harbors; DAR monument; limited, temporary parking; open all year, no fee

(E) Fish Flake Hill
Water, Front, Davis,
Stone,
South Bartlett Streets
NRHS

Historic District, overlooked harbor, where fish dried on flakes and houses led right to wharves; here General John Glover's wharf extended from Front Street to harbor, where he launched the *Hannah*, his Marblehead ship outfitted in Beverly and commissioned by Washington; District listed on National Register of Historic Sites as "a unique cluster of Revolutionary War homes"; Captain Hugh Hill's at 50 Front Street is most elaborate, a fitting Federal for merchant privateer Hill; on-street parking; drive through all year, no fee

F Beverly Depot
River Street and Pleasant
Street; West of tracks
NRHP

Modest brick and stone Richardsonian-style depot, now adaptive reuse as restaurant; still active rail service; parking; open all year, restaurant fees

G Cabot Street Cinema
Theatre
286 Cabot Street at
Judson

Noted for regularly featured stage magic spectaculars; also special films, oldies or modern; street parking; open all year, fee charged

H Pride's Crossing;
Beverly Farms
Hale Street, Route 127,
drive along

Drive east on Hale Street along road of interesting houses, including Henry Cabot Lodge's restored 1734 Widow Patch House at 269 Hale, to Pride's Crossing; 1879 Railroad Depot, now charming general store; Pride's Crossing was Newport-level Boston and New York summer colony; see $100,000 circa 1900 fencing of Henry J. Frick estate (house gone); on to Beverly Farms, another restored depot, and more elaborate estates along Hale and West Streets; drive all year, no fee

I Long Hill
Essex Street near
Wenham line
Trustees of Reservations
headquarters

Peaceful 114 acre estate of fields, orchards, forests, and wetlands; 400 varities flowers, shrubs, trees; 1918 house reproduction of 1800s Charleston, South Carolina, home; summer home of Ellery Sedgewick, author, editor of *Atlantic Monthly;* perennial garden 1916 by Mabel Cabot Sedgewick; facilities: cross-country skiing, formal gardens to view, nature study, paths, walking; parking; open all year, fee charged

J North Shore Music Theater
Dunham Road off
Brimbal Road, off Route
128

Popular summer theater with name stars, year-round special offerings, and school programs; parking; open all year, fee charged

K Site of First Powered
Cotton Mill
Route 1A Dodge Street,
next to fire station

First cotton mill in country, 1778 site marked by tall sign on busy corner; John Cabot* one of founders; clear, detailed historical description made by President Washington when he visited mill and Cabots in 1789, his practice to note great early accomplishments in his new country

NOTES

1. Mark Twain letter, Millicent Library, Fairhaven, Mass.
2. Federal Writers' Project, *Fairhaven, Massachusetts*, American Guide Series, Board of Selectmen of Fairhaven, 1939, p. 52.
3. Knipe, Mabel Hoyle, "Thee Will Fill It Up!" Fairhaven, 1979, p. 9.
4. Letter dated October 10, 1833, from Bird Island Light keeper; owner Marion Channing.
5. Bible. Matthew 7:25.
6. Briggs, Rose T., "Spooner House" booklet.
7. From plaque on wall of First Parish Church in Plymouth.
8. Declaration of Independence.
9. Bacon, Edwin M., *Historic Pilgrimages in New England*, New York, Silver, Burdett & Co., 1898, p. 109.
10. Deane, Samuel, *History of Scituate, Massachusetts*, Boston, James Loring, 132 Washington St., 1831, p. 151.
11. Scituate Historical Society pamphlet.
12. Deane, Samuel, *History of Scituate, Massachusetts*, Boston, James Loring, 132 Washington St., 1831, p. 246.
13. Scituate Historical Society pamphlet.
14. Bigelow, E. Victor, *Narrative History of the Town of Cohasset Massachusetts*, Boston, Press of S. Usher, 1898, p. 189.
15. Trueblood, Rev. Roscoe E., *Historical Sketch of the First Parish and Its Meeting House*, Discourse delivered Dec. 14, 1947 on the 200th anniversary of the meetinghouse, p. 11.
16. Ibid., p. 13.
17. Arber, Edward, editor, *Captain John Smith Works*, 1608-1631, Whatman Papers, The English Scholars Library, p. 205.
18. Ibid., p. 204.
19. Snow, Edward Rowe, "Minot's Light", Quincy, Mass., brochure by Quincy Cooperative Bank, 1981, p. 13.
20. Field Enterprises Educational Corporation, *World Book Encyclopedia*, Volume 12, p. 126.
21. Justine, Mildred L., Hingham Historical Society booklet, p. 2.
22. *History of Hingham*, Vol. 1, Part II, published by the town, Cambridge, University Press, 1893, p. 27.

23. Old Colony Chapter Daughters of the American Revolution, *Hingham*, 1911, p. 100.
24. *History of Hingham*, Vol. 1, Part II, published by the town, Cambridge, University Press, 1893, p. 42.
25. *History of Weymouth Massachusetts*, Vol. 1, published by Weymouth Historical Society, 1923, p. 99.
26. Russell, Francis, *Adams: An American Dynasty*, New York, American Heritage Publishing Company, Inc., 1976, p. 110.
27. Ibid., p. 143.
28. Ibid., p. 94.
29. Lewis, Alonzo and James R. Newhall, *History of Lynn, Lynnfield, Saugus, Swampscott, and Nahant* 1629-1864, Lynn, 1865, p. 464.
30. Garland, Joseph E., *Boston's North Shore*, Boston, Little, Brown and Company, 1978, p. 33.
31. Roads, Samuel, Jr., *History and Traditions of Marblehead*, Boston, Houghton, Osgood and Company, 1880, p. 119.
32. *Antiques Magazine*, Dec. 1977, p. 1172.
33. Miles, Dorothy F., *O How We Have Loved Thee, The Story of Old St. Michael's Church*, 1976, p. 8.
34. Pulsifer, Susan, *Witch's Breed; The Peirce-Nichols Family of Salem*, Cambridge, 1967, p. 398.
35. *Visitor's Guide to Salem*, Essex Institute, Salem, 1953, p. 7.
36. Chamberlain, Samuel, *A Stroll Through Historic Salem*, New York, Hastings House, 1969, p. 7.
37. *Visitor's Guide to Salem*, Essex Institute, Salem, 1953, p. 7.
38. Beverly Historical Society booklet.
39. Field Enterprises Educational Corporation, *World Book Encyclopedia*, Vol. 9, p. 19.

INDEX